Advanced Programming

DESIGN AND STRUCTURE USING PASCAL

ADDISON-WESLEY PUBLISHING COMPANY

Reading, Massachusetts • Menlo Park, California • Don Mills, Ontario
Wokingham, England • Amsterdam • Sydney • Singapore
Tokyo • Mexico City • Bogotá • Santiago • San Juan

Lawrence H. Miller

University of California, Los Angeles

Advanced Programming

DESIGN AND STRUCTURE USING PASCAL

To Olivia, and to Rita

This book is in the
Addison-Wesley Series in Computer Science
Michael H. Harrison, Consulting Editor

James T. DeWolf • Sponsoring Editor

Bette J. Aaronson • Production Supervisor
Margaret Hill • Copy Editor
Melinda Grosser • Text Designer
Intergraphics • Illustrators
Kris Belanger, Belanger Associates • Art Consultant
Ezra C. Holston • Production Coordinator
Hugh Crawford • Manufacturing Supervisor
Dick Hannus, Hannus Design Associates • Cover Designer
Vanessa Piñeiro • Cover Illustrator

Library of Congress Cataloging in Publication Data

Miller, Lawrence H.
    Advanced programming.

    Includes index.
    1. PASCAL (Computer program language)   2. Electronic
digital computers — Programming.   I. Title.
QA76.73.P2M55   1986   001.64′24   84-28297
ISBN 0-201-05531-7

ABCDEFGHIJ-DO-89876

PREFACE

Writing large programs and solving interesting programming problems are disciplines that require a combination of many skills and experiences. A student must be familiar and at ease, obviously, with the particular programming language. He or she must have a sense of organization, along with the experience of breaking apart complex problems into smaller, manageable pieces, the strength to be able to avoid some of the temptations of "design by coding," and the patience to learn and to build from the insights of others.

Working on large programs means that the student views his or her work as part of a whole that communicates with other parts and has a life span greater than his or her own involvement with the program. And it certainly means having the knowledge of good program development skills, useful data structures, and algorithms and algorithmic analysis techniques to know intuitively that his or her program pieces are reasonably done.

These are the topics this book sets out to cover. Students are highly motivated by the programs and capabilities that they *see* in personal machines today. But how can they write an interactive spreadsheet program such as

VisiCalc® (developed in Chapter 14) without expression evaluation techniques, and without ideas about graphs of dependencies? How can they understand and use their code and be concerned about its efficiency, when they traditionally are concerned about shaving an instruction here or there, but have no guidance about efficient *classes* of algorithms? And how can they learn, quickly and effectively, about writing large programs, good coding style, modularity, extensibility, and other important topics, unless they see large, well-written programs, and model their own code on them?

Advanced Programming: Design and Structure Using Pascal has been used as the text for the advanced programming/problem-solving course at UCLA (the CS2 course), and has evolved from this experience. The book's emphasis is on data abstraction, selection and analysis of algorithms, and efficient program construction. There are two substantial case studies and several smaller ones. The first case study is an interactive function plotter, which is built over several chapters, beginning with its specification and design in Part II and extending throughout the rest of the book, as the data structures and algorithms to implement it most efficiently are acquired. The second case study is a mini spreadsheet program that combines both expression evaluation and topological sorting of the graph of cell dependencies.

Organization

The book is divided into four parts. It follows closely the outline of ACM curriculum '85 for the CS2 course. Some of the topics have been extended to take advantage of the interactive computing environments most students are likely to experience today.

Part I: Programming Style and Language

Part I is a reintroduction to good programming style and habits. Chapter 1 discusses the thought patterns needed to write programs — high-level thinking and planning, along with low-level planning because of the limitations in many languages and environments. Chapter 2 reviews the Pascal programming language.

Part II: Program Design and Development

Part II is a progression of topics on program specification, design, development, coding, testing and debugging. It culminates with the first implementation of the first case study, an interactive function plotter. A high level (and informal) functional specification and the high level design is developed in Chapter 3. Chapter 4 is about coding programs: Program structure, modularity, user interface design issues, and all the low-level coding details that one must adhere to in producing good code; Chapter 5 looks at the run-time behavior of programs, run-time errors, where error handling ought to occur, and run-time efficiency. And Chapter 7 combines all of these and develops the code for the first case study, an interactive function plotter. Because students are not yet familiar with the necessary techniques of expression evaluation, the plotter is built in layers. This chapter also develops the code that takes an external file of x,y pairs and plots them to the output.

Part III: Data Structures and Algorithms

Part III is the next step in the process that a good, active student goes through: Now the student knows about putting programs together, it's time to look at the internals and learn to program elegantly (data structures) and efficiently (algorithms). The development in Part III is motivated by program and programmer needs, but develops the material as reusable packages of structures and techniques: Abstract data types. Chapter 8 covers list structures and introduces linked lists. Chapter 9 introduces the notion of abstract data type, and packages together routines for manipulating stacks and queues. A post-fix expression evaluator is added as a front end to the plotter of Chapter 7. The importance of abstract data types is reinforced and the advantages of good program design and structure are demonstrated by the ease with which the new routines are added to the plotter.

Chapter 10 extends the linked structures of Chapter 8 through multi-linked structures: Trees and graphs. Chapters 11 and 12 present a collection of important algorithms designed to illustrate the notions of algorithmic efficiency. Chapter 11 covers sorting methods, Chapter 12 searching. Some useful, practical techniques fall cleanly and naturally out of algorithm design. The end of Chapter 11 looks back at just how it was possible to go from n^2 sorting techniques, for example, to $n\log_2 n$ techniques, and discover a method for converting a notoriously poor technique, bubble sort, into an efficient one. Students are excited about this chapter because it appeals to the tinkerer in all programmers, and offers them a method for tinkering that ought to lead to better, faster programs.

Because Part III contains a substantial body of material, we have included an additional applications oriented section at the end of each chapter: PROGRAMMING NOTES. Programming notes give additional insight into the use of the techniques developed in the chapter. Each chapter, of course, also includes a collection of exercises, motivated by specific algorithms or examples in the text.

Part IV: Application Case Studies

Part IV presents the second case study — the mini spreadsheet program. This program brings together many of the topics covered in the book, and is particularly interesting because it is built from "spare parts" from the other case studies: The display is represented as a two dimensional array of expressions. The expressions are acquired interactively using the parser developed for the function plotter. And the order of evaluation of the display is determined using graph structures developed in Part III. All in all, though the program is nearly 1,000 lines, it is highly modularized, and easy to understand. It shows the power of the data structures and the recursive expression parsing techniques. Besides, it is a useful interactive program that can be easily extended to include additional capabilities.

Acknowledgments

This book is the reflection of ideas and insights of several people: Buz Uzgalis, who first thought it was important to let students struggle with complexity; David G. Kay and Dave Smallberg, who have provided valuable in-class use; and the many teaching assistants who have used the material as notes or have contributed to the overall tone — Mike Campbell, Scott Spetka, Dave Booth, Tony Noe, Dennis Finn, Uri Zernick, Russ Schmallenberger, Yehuda Afek. I am most indebted to Alex Quilici for his outstanding and unbelievably energetic work on programs, exercises, content critique, and all around enthusiasm.

I owe a debt of gratitude to the UCLA Computer Science Department for their support of this work and the use of their valuable resources.

I am grateful, too, for the time and thoughtful critiques of many people outside UCLA who have read early drafts of this manuscript. Their suggestions have contributed in no small measure to its final (and, I hope, successful) form: Sara Baase, University of California, Berkeley; Douglas Comer, Purdue University; Barry Donahue, Central Washington University; John D. Gannon, University of Maryland; Peter B. Henderson, State University of New York at Stony Brook; Henry F. Ledgard, Amherst, Mass.; and Sharon Salveter, Boston University.

The people at Addison-Wesley, and my editor, Jim DeWolf deserve the thanks of the entire computer science community for their support of new directions, and their courage and encouragement. Finally, I am thankful to my wife Rita, who has managed to stay with me through all of this and, of course, to the person who made it all possible, Col. Anton Vigorish.

Los Angeles   *LHM*

CONTENTS

PART II

Program Design and Development

3 **PROGRAM SPECIFICATION AND DESIGN**   95

4   **PROGRAM CODING**   **125**

5   **THE RUN-TIME BEHAVIOR OF PROGRAMS**   **171**

6

TESTING AND DEBUGGING   **193**

7

**IMPLEMENTING THE FUNCTION PLOTTER —
THE FIRST LAYER**   **225**

PART III

Data Structures and Algorithms

8

LINKED LISTS   **245**

9 DATA STRUCTURES USING LISTS: QUEUES AND STACKS   271

10 MULTI-LINKED STRUCTURES — TREES AND GRAPHS   325

11 ALGORITHMS: SORTING   375

12 ALGORITHMS: SEARCHING   415

PART IV

Applications Case Studies

13 PARSING EXPRESSIONS — THE FINAL LAYER OF THE FUNCTION PLOTTER   445

14   MINICALC — A MINIATURE SPREADSHEET   483

APPENDIX 1   MACHINE REPRESENTATION   533

APPENDIX 2   PASCAL SYNTAX   551

PROGRAMMING STYLE
AND LANGUAGE

PROGRAMMING STYLE

1.1   Good Programs and Bad Programs

Take a look at the Pascal programs in Figs. 1.1 and 1.2. They both are designed to read a file containing integers and to compute the average and median. These programs should be understandable even if you do not know Pascal. Figure 1.1 looks like programs you were probably told to write in earlier programming courses; it contains nicely specified data types, well-named and commented functions, and a cleanly written main program. Figure 1.2 looks like an example of what everyone has been telling you to avoid.

Why is one really better than the other? After all, both programs correctly compute the average and median of the numbers in the file. Each produces identical output for identical input. By the end of this text, if not substantially sooner, you will understand why Fig. 1.1 is "better" than Fig. 1.2. Curiously, however, we cannot really begin to understand this concept of subjective goodness until we have attempted to write, debug, run, and modify programs of significant size.

Looking over these programs, you might be tempted to say that the program in Fig. 1.1 really is not so "good" after all. It appears to use sorting solely for the purpose of finding the median, and there are techniques for finding the median that do not require sorting (as we will see in Chapter 11). Furthermore, you might point out, this is a particularly poor sorting algorithm. You would be right, of course, on both accounts! We *can* find the median without sorting, but if we must resort to sorting, because we need the array sorted for other reasons, we certainly should be able to find a more efficient algorithm. But we would be making a mistake to take that point of view at this time. After all, the "purpose" of this program is to find the mean and the median of a data file of integers. Our first concern ought to be: does it correctly (and with reasonable efficiency) find these values?

We will develop (and find techniques for handling) a number of other concerns in this book. For this program, we are concerned with questions of *extensibility*: Could the program be easily extended to find the averages of a file of reals? Could it be *modified* to take input from the terminal rather than from a file? How *flexible* is it in terms of the size of the array that it can handle? We will also look at questions of *efficiency*, programmer as well as machine: If we take the *entire* time it takes to design, write, run, test, and debug this program, what percentage of that time is spent sorting the array? Obviously, probably not very much! We will look at questions of *maintenance* and *modifiability*: If it turns out that we really do not like the sorting algorithm, how easily may it be changed to a sorting routine we do like? Since the sorting has been encapsulated as a separate procedure, changing to a more efficient algorithm ought to be fairly straightforward —

just replace this procedure with another we believe sorts faster. In fact, in Part III we will examine other sorting techniques encapsulated in procedures that can be simply "plugged in" to programs (such as the mean/median one) without changing anything else. In some cases, however, a change in our ideas about how to perform a particular task may require changes that

Figure 1.1. A "good" example of a program to find the average and median of a set of integers.

```
program GOOD (input, output, DataFile);
{
Compute the mean and median of a data file of integers. The data resides on file DataFile.
Only the first MAX entries are used.
INPUT:    Data file of integers.
OUTPUT: Mean and median of the input values. If the file contained no values, mean and
          median are set to 0.0.
}
const
  MAX       = 1000;                      {maximum number of values allowed in input}
type
  intarray   = array [1..MAX] of integer;
var
  Ave        : real;                     {the average}
  DataFile   : text;                     {input file}
  Med        : real;                     {the median}
  n          : integer;                  {the actual number of values read}
  numbers    : intarray;                 {array of values from input file}

  procedure GetInput (var numbers : intarray; var count : integer );
  {
  Reads input and stops on end of input file, or if the number of elements is greater than
  MAX. Upon exiting, count is the actual number of values read from the input.
  }
  begin
    reset (DataFile );
    count := 0;                          {actual number of values read}
    while not eof (DataFile ) and (count < MAX ) do begin
      count := count + 1;
      readln (DataFile, numbers [n] )
    end
  end;  { GetInput }
```

(continued)

Figure 1.1. (continued)

```
function Average (numbers : intarray; n : integer ) : real;
{
Computes the mean of the array of n integers. If n is ≤ 0, then Average returns 0.0.
Averages first MAX values if n > MAX.
}
var
    i           : integer;
    sum         : real;
begin
    sum := 0.0;
    if n > MAX   then
        n := MAX;                        {error checking on n}
for i := 1 to n do
 sum := sum + numbers [i];
if   n <= 0   then
 Average := 0.0
else
 Average := sum / n
  end; { Average }


function Median (numbers : intarray; n : integer ) : real;
{
Computes the median of the array of n integers. If n is ≤ 0, then the median is set to 0.0. If
n is greater than MAX, only the first MAX values are used. Sorts the array internally before
finding the median.
}

  procedure Sort (var   numbers : intarray; n : integer );
  {
  Sorts the array in place. Algorithm: exchange sort.
  INPUT:     numbers – The original array of values
             n –The actual number of values in array numbers
  OUTPUT:   numbers is sorted in place, from low to high
  }
  var
     i, j       : integer;                {loop counters}
     temp       : integer;                {temporary for exchanging two values}

  begin
    for i := 1 to n − 1 do
      for j := i + 1 to n do
        if numbers [i] < numbers [j]   then begin     {exchange them}
          temp := numbers [i];
          numbers [i] := numbers [j];
          numbers [j] := temp
        end
    end; {Sort}
```

```
begin  {Median}
  if n <= 0 then
    Median := 0.0
  else begin
    if n > MAX then
      n := MAX;
    Sort (numbers, n );                              {first sort the array}
    if odd (n) then
      Median := numbers [n div 2 + 1]
    else
      Median := (numbers [n div 2] + numbers [n div 2 + 1])/ 2.0
  end
end; {Median}

begin {main}
  GetInput (numbers, n );                            {get input; number read returned in n}
  Ave := Average (numbers, n );
  Med := Median (numbers, n );
  writeln;
  writeln ('Average and Median of ', n : 1, ' values');
  writeln;
  writeln ('Average : ', Ave : 7 : 2 );
  writeln ('Median : ', Med : 7 : 2 )
end.
```

affect the entire program, for example, changes in data structures that use linked structures (Chapter 8), but that cannot be isolated in just a single procedure. And, of course, we are concerned about the *reliability* (or *correctness*) of the program: Does it really find the median and average of a file of integers?

We can ask the same questions of the second program (Fig. 1.2), the "bad" one, as we asked of the "good" one. But we should note that it is not clear that we are sorting, or doing anything that we can reasonably describe, in this program. All we can tell (as a result of the *writeln* statements) is that we appear to be calculating the average and the median of the values in the data file.

In fact, we are sorting in Fig. 1.2. The sorting technique appears quite reasonable. We start at the beginning of the array and compare the new number with each element in the array in turn. When we finally reach a point where the new number is larger than the array element, we insert the new value into the array by *shifting* all the remaining elements over

```
program BAD (input, output, DataFile);
var
i, j, k : integer;
found : boolean;
DataFile : text;
s, m, number : real;
a : array [1..1000] of real;

begin
reset(DataFile);
s := 0.0;
i := 0;
while not eof(DataFile) do begin
  i := i + 1;
  readln(DataFile, number);
  s := s + number;
  found := false;
  j := 1;
  while (j < i) and not found do begin
    if number > a[j] then begin
      found := true;
      for k := i downto j + 1 do
        a[k] := a[k - 1]
    end else
      j := j + 1
  end;
  a[j] := number
end;
s := s / i;
if i div 2 = 0 then
  m := (a[i div 2] + a[i div 2 + 1]) / 2.0
else
  m := a[i div 2 + 1];
writeln ('Average and Median of ', i : 1, 'values'); writeln;
writeln ('Average : ', s : 7 : 2);
writeln ('Median : ', m : 7 : 2)
end.
```

Figure 1.2. A "bad" example of a program to compute the average and median of a set of integers.

one place (see Fig. 1.3). This technique is called *insertion sort*. Interestingly enough, it is not really less efficient than the technique used in Fig. 1.1, the "good" program. Both have the property that computing time goes up as the *square* of the number of elements to be sorted. That is, if we double the number of elements in the array, we require about four times the computing time; if we triple the number, about nine times the computing time will

Figure 1.3. Example of insertion sort: 6 is to be inserted just before 10, so all the values to the right must be shifted one place to make room.

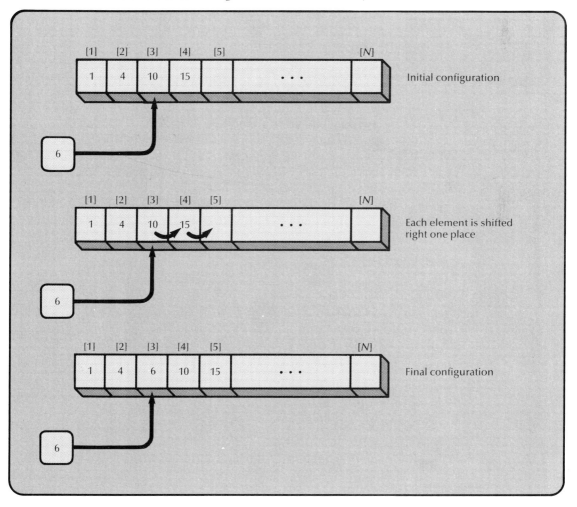

be required. The sorting technique used in Fig. 1.2 is poor for reasons other than just efficiency; the code does not make the technique clear; it is difficult to verify in any rigorous way that the various loops actually end up with the array sorted (it seems difficult to verify even intuitively); and there appears to be no clean way of changing the algorithm if we decide at a later time to try for a more efficient one.

There are a number of problems, of course, with the second program (as there are, in fact, with the first). It reminds us of a child's book where you had to find all the weird things hidden in a drawing. The "weird" things in this program fall into a number of areas, all of which we will discuss in depth in this book. The techniques that we will apply to make the "good" program good are necessary in order to make the programming effort a better, more efficient one for us (as programmers) and a more reliable one for those who depend on the correctness and the modifiability of our programs.

We don't intentionally set out to write poor programs. If we're very careful about examining the programs we write, we may learn what it is that makes some poor and others good. A better method of learning about good programs, and what makes them good, is to study other good programs. For that reason, this book contains a number of programs and two large case studies that are designed for study: one of the case studies is developed over a number of chapters. By the time you're done with this book, you will have a set of useful techniques that will improve the quality of the programs you write, make the program writing task easier and more manageable, and will allow more attention to be paid to efficiency considerations and selection of the most appropriate data structures and algorithms.

1.2   Characteristics of Programs

Programs pass through a number of distinct phases before they are finished gems, worthy of our trust. Some of the phases and the behavior we must be concerned with include:

- Behavior at program writing time
- Behavior at compile time
- Behavior at run-time

It would be most desirable if we could find errors and get a strong understanding of the properties of the program during writing time. That is, we would like to use languages and techniques that make it less likely to introduce errors into our programs, and to make it easier for us to spot errors as they occur. The least desirable time to find errors is during run-time. A number of characteristics of the Pascal programming language (which we review in Chapter 2) help reduce errors at the time we write a program:

■ Pascal has a highly specified program structure
■ Pascal has a limited statement syntax: syntax errors are less likely to
  be made
■ Many Pascal environments provide program writing tools: syntax directed editors, program formatters, style analyzers, etc.

Errors that are not detected at the time a program is written may be
caught at *compile* time. Generally compile-time errors are related to incorrect
Pascal statement structure (syntax), using variables without properly declaring
them (scoping or declaration), or assigning values to variables that are not
compatible with the way they were declared (type clash). A good compiler
can also assist in finding some semantic errors; for example, some compilers
flag variables or procedures that are not used or set. These "warnings" can
be a key to mistakes in coding and in our understanding of the use of
variables and procedures in our code.

At *run-time*, Pascal generally abandons us! In the case of a run-time
error, most Pascal systems will crash. The standard Pascal environment
provides no ability to catch (trap) run-time errors. These run-time errors
include arithmetic overflow, illegal (out of range) array indexing, illegal
pointer references, etc. The problem of unrecoverable run-time errors is a
particular problem on input. Take, for example, a simple program designed
to draw straight lines on a graphics display terminal. Graphics terminals
provide in hardware the ability to draw straight lines between end points
given in screen coordinates. So we'll assume that a procedure *LINE*
(x1,y1,x2,y2) has already been provided which draws on the screen the
straight line between (x1,y1) and (x2,y2) (see Fig. 1.4, where *LINE*
(180,380,750,750) has been performed). In this figure, we are assuming the
existence of a high resolution graphics terminal of size 1024 by 1024, with
the origin in the lower left corner.

Typically we might provide a program fragment such as the following
one to request and read values of x and y, draw the straight-line segment
between the two points (x1, y1) and (x2, y2) by calling *LINE*, and loop until
end of file:

```
            . . .
while not eof do
  begin
    write ('Type end points for next segment: ');
    readln(x1,y1,x2,y2);
    LINE(x1,y1,x2,y2)
  end;
            . . .
```

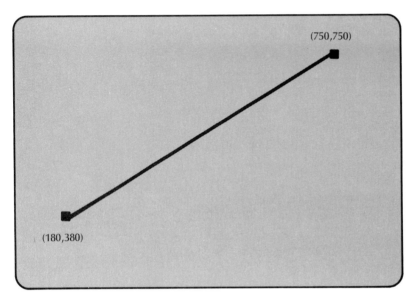

(750,750)

(180,380)

Figure 1.4. A high-resolution graphics display, showing a straight line from (180, 380) to (750, 750). (The *x* and *y* coordinates run from 0 to 1023, with their origin at lower left.)

With slight modification to the *readln* statement, and with the proper hardware, values of x1, y1, x2, and y2 could be input via a tablet or mouse, as in Fig. 1.5. Surprisingly sophisticated picture editors can be created using Pascal and relatively inexpensive graphics terminals. The only requirement is that we be able to generate the correct instructions to actually draw lines on the screen (that is, to implement procedure *LINE*).

There is at least one serious flaw in the preceding piece of code: if the user were to accidentally type a value for x1, y1, x2, or y2 of the wrong type, the program would crash. If this piece of code were in fact part of a picture creation and editing system, the user (an artist, a writer, or another programmer) would be justifiably upset to find that potentially large amounts of work may have been destroyed.

"But," you say, "the Pascal *readln* statement requires that the value being read matches the type of the variable. I'll just have to print out a warning — 'TYPE INTEGERS ONLY' — and let the user be careful."

This solution is unsatisfactory for a number of reasons. First of all, it assumes the user knows what an integer is! But it also assumes that the hardware generating the input (for example, a joystick) is producing integers. "Well," you counter, "I'll just change the type of x1, y1, x2, and y2 to real. Then the users, or the hardware, can produce whatever kind of numbers they want." Not an unreasonable correction, but then someone types a ',' for the decimal point, or an alphabetic character (a letter), perhaps by accident. Again, most Pascal run-time environments will crash with a message such as "Illegal input." At this point we might try to handle this contingency by providing a simple instruction and an example or two.

Now we face up to the true problem of the integer (or the real) read: *people make mistakes*. Consequently it is our responsibility as programmers to reduce the negative effects of user errors. We will come back to this topic of interactive programming and the design of user interfaces in later chapters. For now, let us explore an alternative, and fairly simple, means of handling input errors: all input will be in character format. Number conversions will occur only after the input string is considered correct.

What an unfortunate state of affairs. We have been taught that we write programs by looking first at the big picture, then at successively smaller

Figure 1.5. Typical graphics system I/O.

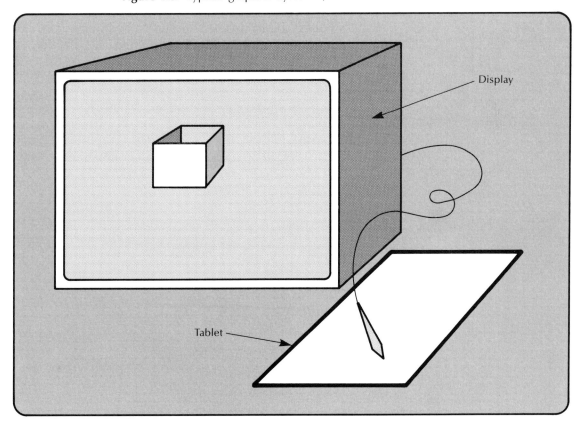

pieces, and now we find that we must be concerned with very low-level implementation details. But this is exactly what makes programming such a fascinating discipline. We are constantly pulled in two opposing directions: high-level thinking, top-down design, and solution generality versus implementation detail, poorly written compilers, insufficient run-time support, and hardware limitations. To the extent that we develop, write, and implement programs satisfying the needs of the former while successfully overcoming the limitations of the latter, we may consider ourselves on the path of becoming good programmers. Throughout this text we concern ourselves with the people who will be using our programs, along with those of us who write the programs or who may have to modify the programs after they are written.

We finish this section by examining a code fragment that simulates the Pascal *readln* of a single real value. We write it as a procedure (called *NEWREADLN*) which returns *two* values, one real (the number entered) and the second a boolean: *true* if the input is legal, *false* if not. (It might seem more appropriate to write this as a Pascal function instead, since we are specifically returning a boolean variable that we will always want to test. However, writing it as a procedure is closer to the actual Pascal *readln* procedure. After reviewing Chapter 2, you should be able to modify the procedure to a function, as necessary). Since programmer-defined Pascal procedures may not use a variable number of parameters, we cannot directly simulate the system-defined *readln* (which may have zero or more parameters; the first one may be a file, the others of scalar type). Our *NEWREADLN* procedure reads a single real value.

As a first-level description of the procedure, correct input must be as shown in Fig. 1.6. This is an elaboration of the Pascal syntax diagram for a real number.

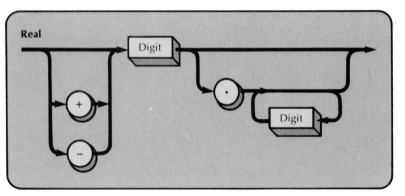

Figure 1.6. Syntax of a real number.

The use of syntax diagrams is not just for clarity of presentation. We can write code more or less directly from the diagram. We just have to remember that the diagram does not tell us what to do about errors. However, our definition of the NEWREADLN procedure already tells us what to do: set the boolean parameter to *false*, and exit. Then the *calling* program is responsible for providing reasonable feedback to the user or for replacing an incorrect value with a suitable default value.

In examining the syntax diagram, we note three major loops:

1. Scan over leading blanks.
2. Process the integer part of the number, including the sign (that is, all digits before the decimal point).
3. Process the fractional part.

Fig. 1.7 illustrates the algorithm with the number 257.31. To process the integer part, first the 2 is evaluated and added to an accumulating sum. Then when the 5 is read, we multiply the previous sum (2) by 10, then add the 5; now the sum is 25. Finally the 7 is read. Again, first multiply the previous sum (25) by 10, giving 250, then add the 7, giving 257. The next character is the decimal point '.' That completes the integer part of the number.

Finally, we must process the fractional part correctly. Each digit must be multiplied by the appropriate power of 10 before adding: the first digit by 0.1, the second by 0.01, the third by 0.001, and so on. When a blank or end of line is encountered we must recheck the sign and multiply the result by -1 if the sign is ' $-$ '. We trace this in Fig. 1.7(b).

We must be certain that we handle errors, since that is the purpose of writing our own version of *readln* in the first place. We do this by keeping the second parameter as an indication of whether any illegal input is entered. The only valid characters are ' $+$ ' or ' $-$ ', the digits '0' through '9', and a decimal point, '.'. The first character of the number may be a sign. Subsequent characters must be a digit, a blank, or a decimal point. When the decimal point is read, all subsequent characters must be digits until a blank or end of line is encountered. At any time that we are expecting a certain character or digit, and an illegal one is entered, we set the boolean parameter *ok* to *false* and exit the current loop. Fig. 1.8 shows the code for the finished procedure. The comments in the code relate to the syntax diagram (Fig. 1.6).

The only aspect of the program that will not be clear to anyone without Pascal programming experience is the process by which individual characters are converted to integers. This is done at the line with the comment '{convert to integer here}'. The conversion is accomplished through the Pascal *ord* function. *ord* is a built-in function which takes a single character and returns

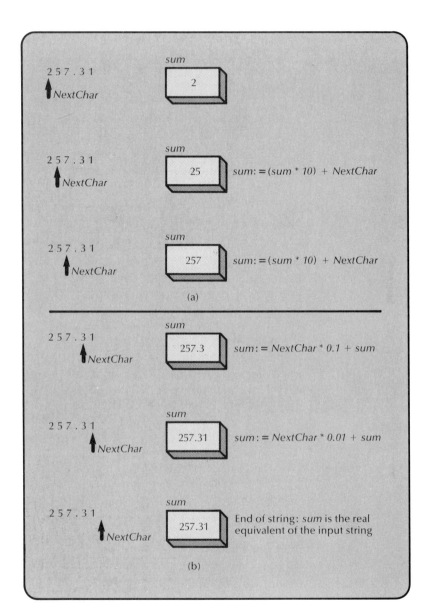

Figure 1.7. (a) Trace of conversion of 257.31 from character to real — showing integer part. (b) Trace of conversion of 257.31 from character to real — showing fractional part.

Figure 1.8. *NEWREADLN* — ▶ An expanded Pascal *readln* procedure.

```
procedure NEWREADLN (var value : real; var ok : boolean);
{
Converts typed (character) input into a real number, returned in variable value. ok is set to
true if the number contains no illegal characters, false, otherwise.
}
var
   ch            : char;            {the current character}
   factor        : real;           {inverse power of 10}
   minusflag     : real;           {+1.0 or −1.0 for negative numbers}
begin
  ok := true;
  value := 0.0;
  {FIRST PHASE — SCAN OVER BLANKS}
  repeat
    read(ch)
  until ch <> ' ';
  {SECOND PHASE — PROCESS INTEGER PART}
  minusflag := 1.0;
  if ch = '−' then begin                        {test for neg. value}
    minusflag := −1.0;
    read(ch)
  end else if ch = '+' then
    read(ch);                                   {just ignore the '+'}
  {Not '+' or '−', so just process the digits}
  while ok and (ch <> '.') and (ch <> ' ') do   {convert the integer part}
    if not (ch in ['0' .. '9']) then
      ok := false
    else begin
      value := value * 10.0 + (ord(ch) − ord ('0'));   {convert to integer here}
      read(ch)
    end;
  {At this point, ch = '.' or ' '}
  {PHASE THREE — PROCESS FRACTIONAL PART}
  if ok and (ch = '.') then begin
    factor := 0.1;
    read(ch);
    while (ch <> ' ') and ok do                 {scan until blank or illegal char}
      if ch in [ '0'..'9'] then begin
      value := value + (ord(ch) − ord ('0')) * factor;
      factor := factor * 0.1;
      read(ch)
    end else
      ok := false
  end;
  if ok then
    value := minusflag * value                  {mult by −1.0 if necessary}
  else
    readln
end; {NEWREADLN}
```

its "collating sequence." The collating sequence for characters is machine dependent, but in general, a numerical character ('0' through '9') does not map into the corresponding digit 0 through 9. However, the Pascal collating sequence is defined in such a way that the following relationships hold:

$$ord(`0`) < ord(`1`) < ord(`2`) < ... < ord(`9`), \text{ and}$$

$$ord(i + 1) = ord(i) + 1$$

Consequently the following also holds:

$$ord(`i`) - ord(`0`) = i,$$

where i is a single character for a digit in the range 0 through 9. This material is reviewed in Chapter 2, along with the related functions $succ$, $pred$, and chr.

1.3   The Rest of the Book

In this chapter we have set the tone, and some groundwork, for the rest of the book. We have done this in a somewhat unorthodox manner: we have looked at what ought to be straightforward programming situations and discovered within them the seeds of difficulty. We have also seen that there are some very definite differences between "good" and "bad" programs, even quite small ones. Writing good programs requires discipline and a rigorous following of systematic guidelines for data structuring, control structuring, parameter passing, commenting, user interface design, and error handling. This book assumes that you want and need to write good programs. The only thing lacking is a set of tools and techniques for doing so. Writing good programs need not be a particularly difficult task, but it will require that you organize, design, and write a number of substantial (that is, large) programs. And surprisingly enough, following rigidly constrained stylistic guidelines, rather than stifling imagination and creativity, liberates the programmer to spend his or her time looking at the interesting parts of programming: exploring alternative algorithms, computing an interesting result (with confidence in its correctness), getting an interesting application or system up quickly and efficiently.

In the rest of this book we explore a number of topics in some detail, all leading to more efficient problem solving and better programs, developing useful data structures and algorithms and introducing important theoretical topics. Chapter 2 is a short review of the Pascal language, with emphasis on the data and control structures needed for later chapters.

In Part II we take up in more detail the material begun in this chapter: solving large problems and writing correct, complete, and efficient programs. Part II supports a layered development and implementation of a substantial case study that we continue through the rest of the book: an interactive function plotter. The plotter forms the core of a programming discipline that you are encouraged to follow. We view the structure as a pipeline of transformations that takes data of one form and evaluates it or transforms it to a form suitable for the next piece of the pipeline. At the end of Part II, we code the first layer of the plotter: we take a table of x-y values from an external file and plot them to the display. Later, as our knowledge of data structures and abstract objects increases, we add layers that allow a user to enter a function directly, and the program generates the table. In Part IV, we extend the development of the plotter to more elaborate functions.

Part III presents the programming techniques of data structuring which makes use of constructed (user-defined) data types in Pascal. We will see that when we construct new types, we will also want to construct new operations that can be performed on them. This packaging together of a data type and its allowable operations will enhance our ability to write correct programs and to be assured of their correctness.

In Part IV we look at application areas. We finish the function plotter and introduce the concepts of representing and evaluating functions that form the heart of the notion of reuseable code that we carry over into the last chapter. We develop a powerful scheme, called recursive parsing, that allows for fully parenthesized functions in the plotter. Finally, the last chapter combines many of the topics of the text into a fascinating (and popular) case study, an interactive spreadsheet program. It's an important chapter because it ends up with a quite useful and sophisticated program. And we get there by looking carefully at what we've done before (in data structures and algorithms, and in program design and development strategies) in order to find the ideas, and even the code, that we use to implement the program.

Exercises

1. We claim that Fig. 1.1 is a "good" program and Fig. 1.2 is a "bad" one. However, a number of changes can be made to the "good" program to make it even better. This exercise involves finding and fixing these problems. Be sure that when a change is made to the "good" program, it works as intended,

before going on to make the next change. (By the way, if you do not already know Pascal, try rewriting Fig. 1.1 in the language of your choice.)

a) Often more data is supplied to a program than the program was designed to accept. The program should write out an informative message before it terminates. When the file that the "good" program reads contains more than MAX entries, the user should be informed of how many entries were actually in the file, as well as how many entries can be processed. Additionally, the "good" program should not compute the median. If no entries are read (the file was empty), the user should also be informed, and no median should be computed. To test the program without having to provide a file of 1000 values (the initial value of MAX), change MAX to 10, and recompile the program. Test the program with files containing differing numbers of entries, making sure some test cases have more than MAX entries.

b) Besides the mean and the median, some other statistical measures of importance are the *range*, the *standard deviation*, and the *variance*. The range is defined as the difference between the largest and smallest value. To determine the variance of a set of numbers, find the mean, the difference between each number in the set and the mean, and the squares of these differences. Computationally the variance v is defined as:

$$v = \frac{\sum (x_i - \bar{x})^2}{n - 1}$$

The standard deviation is the square root of the variance. Modify the "good" program to print out the range, the standard deviation, and the variance of its input.

c) The sorting method used in the "good" program would be improved slightly by sorting the numbers as they are read in. Use the insertion sort method described in this chapter (actually, the method used in the "bad" program) and sort the numbers as they are read in. If you are familiar with any other sorting method, feel free to use it instead.

d) Besides statistics on a group of data as a whole, users want to see the data broken down into subgroups. One way to see information about subgroups is a histogram. (Histograms are bar charts representing the number of values in a particular range, over a set of ranges; we do a histogram program in Chapter 2.) Another less commonly used method is to break the data up into fixed size groups and print the ranges for each of these groups. Modify the "good" program so that it prints out the ranges for groups of size n/10, where n is the number of entries read in.

2. Changes to a poorly written program are often difficult to make. Repeat the preceding exercise for the "bad" program. If it seems easier to rewrite parts of the program rather than changing them, go right ahead and rewrite.

3. Assume you were paid a fixed price to make the preceding changes to the "bad" and "good" programs.
    a) Which program would you prefer to make the changes to?
    b) Why might the "good" program be easier to change?
    c) What changes might be easier to make in the "bad" program?
    d) What specific programming techniques make one program *easier* to change than the other? (For example, use of appropriate identifier names.)
    e) What specific programming techniques make one program *harder* to understand than the other?

4. Our version of the *readln* procedure (*NEWREADLN*) is a good simulation of the Pascal *readln* statement. To make our *readln* an improvement over the standard *readln*, we could make a number of changes.
    a) Certain errors causing a run-time error using the standard Pascal *readln* procedure also cause our routine to stop with a run-time error. Modify *NEWREADLN* to be a *function* that returns *true* if no errors occur and *false*, otherwise. In addition, the function should write an appropriate error message if an error occurs. Errors to check for include: reading end of file when a number is expected, no number on the line, and funny characters as part of the number.
    b) Perhaps defining a number to end on the first nondigit as opposed to the first blank would be better. Why? Modify *NEWREADLN* to define a number this way. Also, make it note an error if there is a sign not directly followed by a number.
    c) Many programs need to be able to deal with scientific notation. Modify *NEWREADLN* to read numbers in scientific notation. (A syntax diagram for a number in scientific notation is available in Appendix 2.) If you read a number that ends on a nondigit that is also an 'e', look at the next character to determine if the number is in scientific notation.
    d) Some routines may wish to print their own error message depending on the error. Some routines may also need to know if the number was an integer, real, or in scientific notation. Modify *NEWREADLN* so that it no longer prints error messages. Instead, it should return an enumerated type of (*REALNUM, INTNUM, SCINUM, ENDFILE, NONUM, BADNUM*). Also write a calling routine that uses this type and writes an appropriate error message.

THE PASCAL LANGUAGE

2.1   Programming In Pascal

The language we use to express algorithms and programs in this book is the programming language Pascal, which was developed by Niklaus Wirth in the early 1970s. This chapter assumes that the reader has had an introductory programming course, not necessarily in Pascal, and that it will take only a small amount of work to learn the syntax and semantics of Pascal. Such an assumption about learnability is not unwarranted because Pascal (named after the sixteenth century French mathematician Blaise Pascal) was designed intentionally to be compact, concise, and with a well-specified statement semantics. By semantics, we mean the action a statement performs — in Pascal, the action of all statements is clearly defined and predictable, regardless of the particular computer on which the program runs. Consequently there is very little to learn in Pascal that you have not already seen in almost any other programming language.

In this chapter we present the language in abbreviated form, describing the syntax of the various statement and data types, and the semantics of the statement types. Pascal is a formally defined language. By this we mean that the semantics (the meaning) of each statement type is contained in the language definition. Prior to this, many programming languages (FORTRAN, for example) tended to grow up piecemeal, with little attempt at formal definition. Our description of Pascal will follow "Standard Pascal," as defined by the International Standards Organization (ISO).

Pascal has several aspects that make it particularly easy to learn and to use to write programs. Further, its properties make it possible to write *correct, modifiable, efficient* code in an efficient, top-down manner. These features include:

1. *Compact, highly constrained program format.* All programs have a similar format: constants are declared first, then user-defined data types and variable declarations, then any procedures and functions, and finally the main program. As a result, programs are easier to read and to modify since important declaratory information is in the same place in every program.

2. *Limited but complete numbers of statements.* All of the control structures necessary for writing well-structured code are present, but there are not so many, nor are there so many variations, that the language becomes overly complex.

3. *A useful collection of predefined data types.* Pascal supports the predefined types integer, real, character, and boolean. In addition, arrays of any of the predefined or user-defined types may be used, and the indexing may be any scalar type.

4. *Rich set of data types.* User-definable data types, including arrays, records, and pointers. In addition, Pascal supports data types not often found in other languages, which again assists in writing *readable* code. These data types include sets and enumerated types.
5. *Variable names of unlimited length.* As a result, in combination with the rich user-defined data structures, code may become self-documenting.
6. *Very general subroutine mechanism.* Procedures and functions, including recursion, with multiple parameter-passing mechanisms are all supported.

Regrettably Pascal is missing some aspects that would help make it more powerful and useful as a general programming language for a broad range of applications. Specifically, Pascal I/O is very limited. It has no predefined string data type, nor predefined string operations. By providing a limited set of statements, certain Pascal program constructs can become unnecessarily complex. Also, Pascal has no mechanism for separate compilation nor a mechanism to reach operating system–level constructs, and consequently, standard Pascal cannot be used to write system-level programs. Pascal arrays must be declared at compile time, which means we must estimate in advance the maximum size of arrays. In addition, procedures or functions that take arrays as input parameters are defined to work on arrays of one size only, the size at which the array is declared at compile time.

None of these shortcomings is serious in any real sense (except perhaps for the inability to access system-level resources). The inability to write system-level code in Pascal has caused a number of manufacturers to define extensions to Pascal, including the ability to link together modules written in other programming languages.

From our point of view in developing fail-safe, user-responsive interactive programs, the major problem is not with the language itself, but in its run-time environment. Standard Pascal does not provide mechanisms for trapping illegal input, arithmetic overflow, system interrupts, and so on. We already saw in Chapter 1 that the consequence of this required us to rewrite the Pascal *read* procedure for reals in order to protect us from incorrect input. We could easily conclude on the basis of these shortcomings that perhaps Pascal is not a good choice as a general-purpose programming language. Pascal is no different, however, from any other language in having shortcomings that we must code around. The solution, it might seem, is simply to design the "perfect" language, the union, perhaps, of all the best features of a number of languages. But this only provides relief for a short time. In some sense, Pascal was designed to be an improvement over a number of languages of the late 1960s and early 1970s. But advances in hardware and programming needs are so rapid today that any design will have aspects that are soon outdated. The rapid rise of interactive programming, graphics, real time environments, and so on has led to difficulties with Pascal. The next change in languages may reflect the movement to nonprocedural forms, back-tracking, functional languages, object-oriented programming, and so on. So, in this book, we think of Pascal as a tool, one that allows us to communicate programming and problem solving ideas, and to explore important, interesting algorithms and applications.

2.2   Pascal Program Structure

Pascal program structure follows a rigid format as shown in Fig. 2.1, a program template. We show this structure more compactly using a syntax, or racetrack diagram in Fig. 2.2. In these diagrams, the rounded-corner boxes represent "terminal" symbols, that is, words or symbols that are not defined

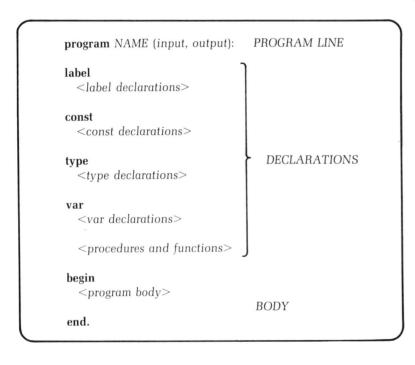

Figure 2.1. Template for a Pascal program.

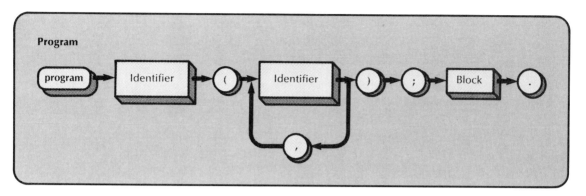

Figure 2.2. Syntax diagram for a Pascal program.

further in the language. The rectangular boxes are "nonterminals." They are further defined in other racetrack diagrams. All of the syntax diagrams for Pascal are contained in Appendix 2.

Within the declarations section, labels, constants, user-defined data types, variables, and procedures are defined in that order. Each of these is optional, as shown in the syntax diagram, Fig. 2.3.

2.2.1 Constant Declaration

Constants are named identifiers with values that may not change during program execution. They are defined by giving the name, an equal sign, and the value. A constant can be of any scalar type, that is, integer, real, character boolean, or a character string. The type of a constant is determined from its context: a signed or unsigned "whole" number is an integer; a number conforming to the syntax for a real, is a real, and so on. Examples of constant declarations include:

```
const
    MAXARRAY     = 100;                    {'integer'}
    N            = 15;                     {'integer'}
    X            = 15.17;                  {'real'}
    A            = 'Z';                    {'character'}
    ALWAYSTRUE   = true;                   {'boolean'}
    MESSAGE      = 'Please type your name';  {array of characters}
```

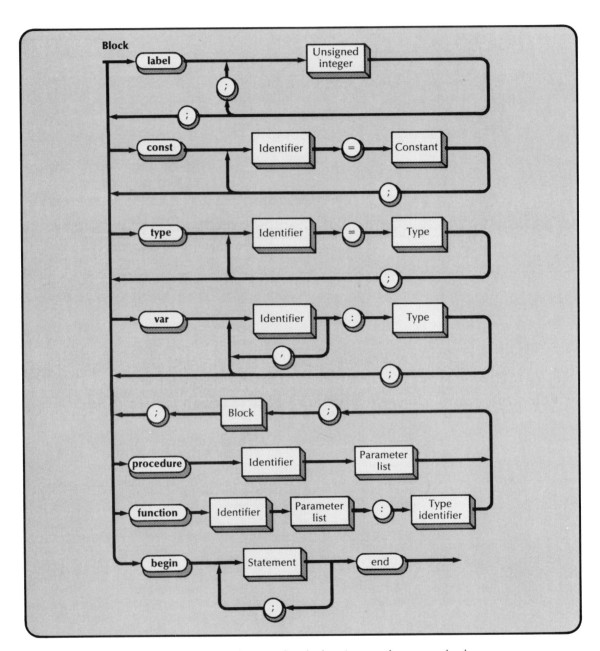

Figure 2.3. Syntax diagram for declarations and program body.

2.2.2 Type Declaration

Type declarations are used for defining user-defined types, including enumerated types, subrange types, arrays, sets, and records. The syntax is quite
simple. Type declarations may refer to constants defined in the **const** declarations. Examples of type declarations include:

type

ARRAYINDEX	= 1..MAXARRAY;	{subrange}
INTARRAY	= **array** [ARRAYINDEX] **of** integer;	{array}
POSINTEGER	= 1..maxint;	{subrange}
NEGINTEGER	= − maxint..− 1;	{subrange}
OPERATORS	= **set of** char;	{set}
CLASS	= (freshman, sophomore, junior, senior,	{enumerated}
	graduate, unknown);	{...type}

2.2.3 Variable Declaration

Variable declarations associate a symbolic name with a variable of a specified
type. Pascal is strongly typed — variables must be declared before being
used. As we will see in Section 2.3, operations are performable only on
variables of the specified type. There are a number of reasons for strongly
typed languages: it is necessary to distinguish between integers and reals
because of different storage representations between them (see Appendix
A); strong typing contributes to predictable program behavior and facilitates
program verification and debugging. Figure 2.4 is a simple program to find
the maximum and minimum values in a file of integers, reading from the
standard input. Note that each variable used in the program is declared to
be an integer. It is a type violation if a real is entered when an integer is
expected; for clarity, we use the standard readln procedure, rather than
Chapter 1's NEWREADLN.

2.2.4 Functions and Procedures Declarations

Pascal has two subprogram types: functions and procedures. In addition,
there are two parameter passing mechanisms: call by value (or simply,
"value" parameters), and call by reference, (**var** parameters).

   Procedures in Pascal are like subroutines in most other languages. The
syntax is shown in the racetrack diagram in Fig. 2.5.

   The calling syntax for procedures is straightforward. The name of the
procedure is given with the actual parameters in parentheses. In Chapter 1
we saw procedures to compute the mean and median of an array of integers.
The parameters in the procedure declaration are called "formal parameters."
The actual values for these parameters are determined at the time the procedure
is invoked, and the formal parameters are replaced with actual parameters.

```
program MAX (input, output);
{Find the maximum and minimum values.}
var
  max                : integer;                    {maximum value in input}
  min                : integer;                    {minimum value in input}
  NextValue          : integer;                    {next input value}
begin
  max := −maxint;
  min := maxint;
  while not eof do begin
    readln(NextValue);
    if NextValue > max then
      max := NextValue
    else if NextValue < min then
      min := NextValue
  end;
  writeln;
  writeln('Max :   ', max : 1);
  writeln('Min :   ', min : 1)
end.
```

Figure 2.4. Program to find the minimum and maximum of a file of integers.

Figure 2.5. Syntax diagram for procedures and functions.

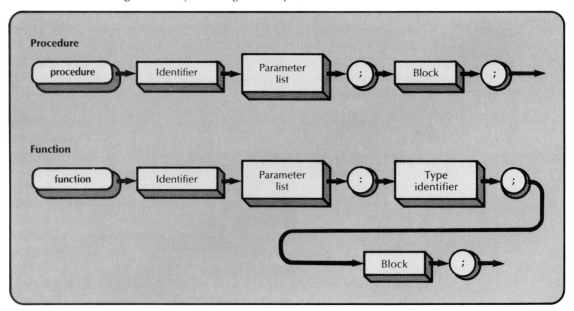

Functions are analogous to mathematical functions, in that they are defined to return a single value of their parameters. Mathematically we define a function as a mapping $f : (d_1, d_2, ..., d_n) \rightarrow r$, a mapping from a domain to a range. Pascal functions capture this single-valued notion, though they are more powerful than this. An example is a function *POWER* which takes a value A to an exponent $B : POWER(A,B)$ is defined as A^B. Pascal does not define an exponentiation operator. Consequently we make use of the identity:

$$A^B = e^{B \ln A}$$

where e is the natural base 2.71828..., and ln is the natural (base e) logarithm. Pascal does provide both a natural log function (*ln*) and exponentiation to base e (*exp*). Since exponentiation does not necessarily return a real ($-1^{1/2}$ returns an imaginary number, for example), we will define this function for integer powers only; the base will be a real, and the function will return a real. Unfortunately, as Fig. 2.6 shows, $ln(A)$ is undefined for $A \leq 0$, so

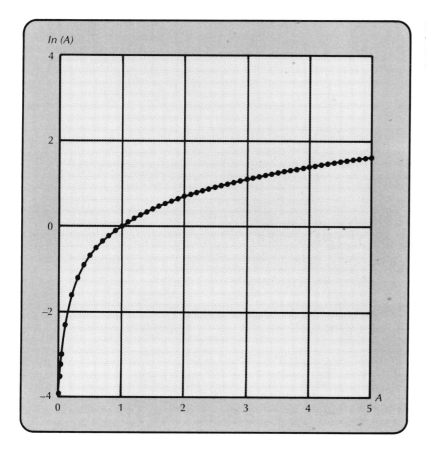

Figure 2.6. Plot of *ln* (A) versus *A* for *A* from 0 to 5. Note that *ln* (A) is undefined for $A \leq 0$.

we cannot use the formula for something as simple as -1^2. Consequently we define 0^X to be 0 for any integer X, and when A is < 0, A^B to be $|A|^B$ when B is even, and $-|A|^B$ when B is odd.

Since *POWER* is a function returning a real, it can be used wherever a value of type real may be used (see Fig. 2.7). Note that the value is returned by assigning to the *name* of the function. To set a variable C to be A^B, we write the statement

$$C := POWER(A, B);$$

Procedures are routines that do not return a value. Other than that distinction, they are identical to functions. In general, we use a function if we are returning a single value that is related to its inputs, but that does not change any of the inputs. A procedure is appropriate when more than one value is being returned. On occasion we will use a function to return more than one type of value; the function value itself can be used to indicate whether processing was normal or not (that is, we explicitly define a boolean function, whose value is *true* if there were not any errors and *false* otherwise).

Parameter types

In both procedures and functions, parameters may be either variable or value parameters. Generally, value parameters are used as input parameters, variable parameters are used as output. More formally, value parameters are local to the procedure; their values are copied to the named parameters when the procedure is invoked. When a **var** parameter occurs in a procedure, the value of that parameter is not passed to the procedure. Rather a pointer to the parameter is passed. Any changes to the parameter within the procedure

Figure 2.7. *POWER,* a function that returns *A* raised to an integer power *B*.

```
function POWER (A : real; B : integer) : real;
{Returns A to the (integer) B power.}
begin
   if A = 0.0 then
      POWER := 0.0
   else if A < 0.0 then
      if odd(B) then
         POWER := -exp(B * ln(-A))
      else
         POWER := exp(B * ln(-A))
   else
      POWER := exp(B * ln(A))
end; {POWER}
```

```
function GrossPay (hours, rate : real; var gross : real) : boolean;
{
MaxHours : Global indicating max hours allowed/wk
MaxRate  : Global indicating max rate of pay/hour
}
begin
  GrossPay := true;
  gross := 0.0;
  if (hours < 0.0) or (rate < 0.0) or (hours > MaxHours) or (rate > MaxRate) then
    GrossPay := false
  else
    gross := hours * rate
end; { GrossPay }
```

Figure 2.8. Sample function showing use of both **var** parameters, and function value.

are reflected in changes to the actual parameter outside the procedure. Variable parameters are indicated by prepending the reserved word **var** to their name in the parameter list. Both of these mechanisms are illustrated in the following examples.

procedure A (x : integer);
  Any changes to x inside A will not be seen outside the procedure.

procedure B (**var** x : integer);
  Any changes to x will be seen outside the procedure.

function C (x, y : real; **var** z : real) : boolean;
  Changes to x and y are not seen outside the procedure. Changes to z are seen. In addition, the function is of type boolean.

A simple example of function C might be used in a payroll application, Fig. 2.8. The input parameters are the hours worked and rate of pay. The value returned is the gross pay (rate*hours). The boolean is used as a flag to indicate that hours and rate are positive, but less than some maximum.

A typical calling sequence for GrossPay might be:

```
                    . . .
        begin
          if GrossPay (h, r, g) then begin
            {normal processing}
          end else begin
            {error handling routine}
          end
        end;
                    . . .
```

2.2.5 Recursion

Functions and procedures in Pascal may be *recursive*. That is, a function or procedure may call itself. Recursion is discussed in detail in Part III. However, at this point, we will illustrate the technique of writing a recursive subroutine in Pascal to show the syntax and semantics of recursive function/ procedure calls. Examples of recursive functions involve certain simple mathematical functions, as well as the more elaborate data structures and algorithms developed in Part III. We illustrate recursion with a function to compute N! (N factorial). First we note that N! is defined mathematically as follows:

$$N! = \begin{cases} N \times (N - 1)! & \text{if } N > 0 \\ 1 & \text{if } N \leq 0 \end{cases}$$

For any integer N, then N! is defined as the product of N and $(N - 1)!$. We stop the multiplication when N is less than or equal to 0. The function calls itself:

```
function factorial (N : integer) : integer;    {1}
begin                                           {2}
   if N <= 0 then
       factorial := 1                           {3}
   else
       factorial := N * factorial (N - 1)       {4}
end;                                            {5}
```

When N is less than or equal to 0, factorial is set to 1 at line 3. Otherwise, factorial is set to N times *factorial*(N − 1) at line 4. It is at line 4 that the function calls itself. Note that on line 4, we use the name of the function on the left side of the assignment statement (as is required within the function body). Additionally, on the right of the assignment statement, the function *factorial* is called again. The number and type of parameters (one integer parameter) in the call agree with the number and type in the function definition header.

2.2.6 Forward References

Functions and procedures may call other routines and may define other routines within them. However, to simplify the compilation process, Pascal requires that all functions or procedures be defined before they are used (called) in another procedure. This is not always possible, however, in the case of mutually recursive routines. Mutually recursive routines are ones that call each other. Suppose procedure A calls B, and procedure B calls A:

procedure A (x : $integer$);
begin

    $B(...)$;   {A calls B}

end; {A}

procedure B (y : $integer$);
begin

    $A(...)$;   {B calls A}

end; {B}

A is defined before B, but A calls B. If we were to define B before A we would still have a problem, since B calls A. To surmount this difficulty, we use the **forward** reference option for procedures and functions. Forward declarations are abbreviated procedure or function headers that let the compiler know that a name is a function or a procedure of a certain type, but that its actual definition will come later. The two procedures A and B should be defined as follows:

procedure $A(x$: $integer)$; **forward;**   {forward reference; body appears later}

procedure $B(y$: $integer)$;
begin

    $A(...)$;   {B still calls A}

end; {B}

procedure A;   {abbreviated declaration}
begin

    $B(...)$;   {Body of A: B is called}

end; {A}

Note that in the first declaration of A the usual header is given, with all of the parameters, but with the word **forward** included, as shown. When procedure A is actually defined after the definition of B, only an abbreviated header is used; no parameter list is given in the actual definition of A.

2.3 Data Types

Pascal has four predefined data types: integer, real, character, and boolean. We will briefly discuss each in turn, along with the operations defined on them. Appendix 1 presents the machine representation for these data types.

2.3.1 Integer

An integer is a signed or unsigned "whole number" requiring one word of internal storage. Its syntax diagram is shown in Fig. 2.9. Since the word size of machines differs, the largest integer is not predefined in Pascal. Rather, each compiler defines the built-in constant *maxint*. This is the largest integer available in that implementation. For 32-bit machines (such as IBM mainframes and DEC VAX), *maxint* has the value $2^{31} - 1$. This is 2,147,483,647, and the smallest integer is $-maxint$, $-2,147,483,647$. Any arithmetic operation that yields an integer outside the range $-maxint..maxint$

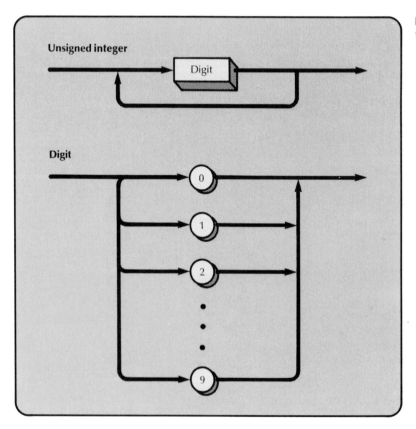

Figure 2.9. Syntax diagram for integer.

$$5 \textbf{ mod } 7 \;=\; 5 \qquad\qquad 5 \textbf{ div } 7 \;=\; 0$$
$$7 \textbf{ mod } 5 \;=\; 2 \qquad\qquad 7 \textbf{ div } 5 \;=\; 1$$
$$15 \textbf{ mod } 3 \;=\; 0 \qquad\qquad 15 \textbf{ div } 3 \;=\; 5$$
$$-23 \textbf{ mod } 5 \;=\; -3 \qquad\qquad -23 \textbf{ div } 5 \;=\; -4$$
$$-23 \textbf{ mod } -5 \;=\; -3 \qquad\qquad -23 \textbf{ div } -5 \;=\; 4$$

Figure 2.10. Examples of **mod** and **div**.

produces an arithmetic overflow error, and the program terminates with a run-time error.

The usual arithmetic operations are defined on integers and return an integer: addition, subtraction, multiplication, and division. Division is unique since arbitrary integer division can return a real. Consequently Pascal provides three division operators:

- ■ / is defined as real division; that is, A/B always returns a real, regardless of the type of A and B. The / operator always returns a real. An error results when an attempt is made to assign the result of a real division (/) to an integer variable.
- ■ **div** is defined as integer division; that is, it returns the integer part of A divided by B (A and B must both be integers).
- ■ **mod** returns the integer remainder when A is divided by B. Formally this is just A modulo B.

Examples of **div** and **mod** are shown in Fig. 2.10.

Variables may be defined as a subrange of the integers, as in the following declarations:

```
type
    POSINTEGER        = 1..maxint;
    NONNEGINTEGER     = 0..maxint;
    NEGINTEGER        = -maxint..-1;
var
    M                 : NONNEGINTEGER;
    N                 : POSINTEGER;
    Z                 : NEGINTEGER;
```

All assignments to M must be an integer in the range 0..*maxint*; assignments to N, a value in the range 1..*maxint*; and assignments to Z, only a negative value.

2.3.2 Real

Reals are defined as values containing a decimal point (Fig. 2.11). According to the syntax diagram, a real must have a leading digit, a decimal point,

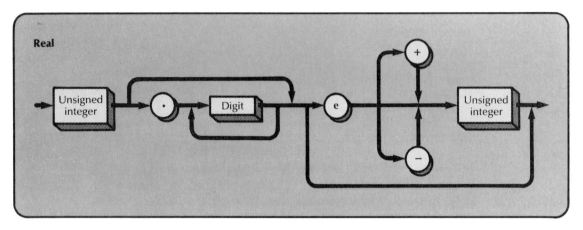

Figure 2.11. Syntax diagram for reals.

and a trailing digit, or it may be written in scientific notation. Some examples of legal and illegal reals are shown in Table 2.1.

The **div** and **mod** division operators are not defined on reals. Real division (/) returns a real and may be assigned to a real variable.

The largest real is machine dependent. Exact conversions in general are not possible because of rounding in the binary representation. Exact 0.0 can be stored, but values quite close to 0.0 may lead to a condition known as *underflow*. Values between 0.0 and 1.0 require negative exponents. The largest negative exponent on a DEC VAX is -38, for example. More information on typical real representations is presented in Appendix 1.

2.3.3 Character

Single letters or digits surrounded by single quotes are character data. The characters are the alphabetic characters 'A', 'B', ..., 'Z' and 'a', 'b', ..., 'z', the numeric digits '0', '1', ..., '9', punctuation, and any special or control characters defined in the local character set. Pascal also defines an ordering

Table 2.1. Examples of legal and illegal reals.		
Legal	**Illegal**	**Reason**
0.123	.123	no leading digit
123.0	123.	no trailing digit
$-0.003\text{e}00$	-0.003e	no power of 10

relation on these characters, so that 'A' < 'B' < ⋯ < 'Z' and 'a' < 'b' < ⋯
< 'z'. Similarly, '0' < '1' < ⋯ < '9'. However, the ordering between the
upper- and lower-case characters or between alphabetic and numeric characters is implementation dependent. The ordering is accessible through the
built-in functions *succ* and *pred*. *succ* returns the next character following
its argument, in the local character set. This is not defined, however, at 'Z'
and 'z'. That is, the successor of 'Z' and 'z' will be different on different
machines. In a similar way, *pred* returns the preceding character in sequence.
Again this is not defined for 'A' and 'a'. In this case and for the punctuation,
control, and special characters, *succ* and *pred* will be defined by the local
character set and thus are machine dependent. (*succ* and *pred* are more
general than this; see Section 2.3.6.)

For nonprinting characters such as the control characters, it is necessary
to know the local numerical equivalent. For example, if we wish to ring
the terminal bell on a terminal using the ASCII character codes, we note
that the ASCII bell character is given by the decimal value 7. We must
convert this value to its character equivalent using the *chr* function, and
then use this to ring the bell:

```
const
  BELLCODE      = 7;        {ASCII bell control code}
var
  bell            : char;
            . . .
{we assign the appropriate character to bell}
  bell := chr(BELLCODE);
            . . .
{now ring the bell}
  write(bell);

            . . .
```

Another way to perform this is to note that the bell code is actually control g:
Figure 2.12 is a more general function that returns the appropriate character
for a given control code.

As we saw in Chapter 1 (*NEWREADLN*) and also in Fig. 2.12, Pascal
provides a mechanism for type conversion between integer and character.
The built-in function *ord* takes a character value or expression and returns
its (machine-dependent) integer representation. This is one mechanism for
discovering the character set on your particular machine. Run the program
in Fig. 2.13 and examine the output. Table 2.2 gives the output for the
ASCII character set on the DEC VAX.

The *chr* function is the inverse of the *ord* function; it takes an integer
and returns the corresponding character. If the argument to *chr* is out of

```
function control(C : char) : char;
{
Takes a single character and returns the control character equivalent. For example, if the input
is 'g', the output is the character equivalent of control g (bell in this case).

If C is not an alphabetic character ('A'..'Z', 'a'..'z'), the null character (chr(0)) is returned.
Assumes ASCII character sequencing.
}
var
  null : char;                              {null char — chr(0)}
begin
  null := chr(0);
  {error checking}
  if not (C in ['a'..'z', 'A'..'Z']) then
    control := null                         {return null}
  else if C in ['A'..'Z'] then             {test for upper-case}
    control := chr(ord(C) − ord('A') + 1)   {upper-case}
  else
    control := chr(ord(C) − ord('a') + 1)   {lower case}
end; {control}
```

Figure 2.12. Control code function, returns control code for given character.

Figure 2.13. Program to print decimal equivalents of alphabetic characters.

```
program CODE (input, output);
{Print the decimal values of the characters 'A' .. 'Z' and 'a' .. 'z' in the local character set.}
var
  UC1, UC2        : char;
  LC1, LC2        : char;
begin
  UC1 := 'A';      UC2 := 'N';
  LC1 := 'a';      LC2 := 'n';

  repeat
    writeln (UC1, '    ', ord (UC1), '        ' UC2,'    ', ord (UC2),
      (LC1,'    ', ord (LC1), '              ' LC2,'    ', ord (LC2)   );

    UC1 := succ (UC1);    UC2 := succ (UC2);
    LC1 := succ (LC1);    LC2 := succ (LC2);
  until UC1 > 'M'
end.
```

Table 2.2. Output from Fig. 2.13 — numeric values of alphabetic characters.							
A	65	N	78	a	97	n	110
B	66	O	79	b	98	o	111
C	67	P	80	c	99	p	112
D	68	Q	81	d	100	q	113
E	69	R	82	e	101	r	114
F	70	S	83	f	102	s	115
G	71	T	84	g	103	t	116
H	72	U	85	h	104	u	117
I	73	V	86	i	105	v	118
J	74	W	87	j	106	w	119
K	75	X	88	k	107	x	120
L	76	Y	89	l	108	y	121
M	77	Z	90	m	109	z	122

range for the local character set (for ASCII, outside the range 0 to 127), the call to the function will fail with an "argument out of range" error. In general, calls to *chr* must be protected from this possibility.

2.3.4 Boolean

Boolean is a predefined type that can take on only two values, *true* and *false*. The predefined functions *succ* and *pred* are defined in such a way that each of these values is the successor and predecessor of the other, though this is rarely of much use. Note that the two values *true* and *false* are defined without surrounding quotes.

We define a set of "logical operations" on booleans: the operators **and**, **or**, and **not**. They are defined in Table 2.3; **not** has the highest precedence, then **and**, and finally **or**.

Using comparisons between numerical values and the boolean operators, we may perform multiple tests within conditional statements, as in the

Table 2.3. Results of boolean operators and, or, and not: T means *true*, F means *false*.				
A	*B*	*A* and *B*	*A* or *B*	not *A*
T	T	T	T	F
T	F	F	T	F
F	T	F	T	T
F	F	F	F	T

payroll function example in Section 2.2, Fig. 2.8. Since comparisons return a boolean, they may be used as the right-hand side of an assignment to a boolean variable.

Suppose we wish to set a boolean variable *errorflag* to be *true* if a real variable *hours* is outside a proper range, and to be *false*, otherwise. We could do this with a test such as:

> **if** (*hours* < 0.0) **or** (*hours* > *MaxHours*) **then**
>   *errorflag* := *true*
> **else**
>   *errorflag* := *false*

Or we may simply assign *errorflag* as the result of the test:

> *errorflag* := (*hours* < 0.0) **or** (*hours* > *MaxHours*);

This is correct, since the two comparisons (*hours* < *0.0*) and (*hours* > *MaxHours*) each return a boolean, and the logical operator **or** between two booleans also returns a boolean.

2.3.5 Arrays

Arrays in Pascal are sequences of values, each of the same type. Arrays may be one dimensional (vectors), two dimensional (matrices), or higher dimensioned. In addition, the underlying type may be any predefined scalar type (integer, real, character, or boolean) or user-defined type, including records, which we define in Section 2.3.7. Arrays are indicated by the syntax diagram (Fig. 2.14).

Figure 2.14. Syntax diagram for array declaration.

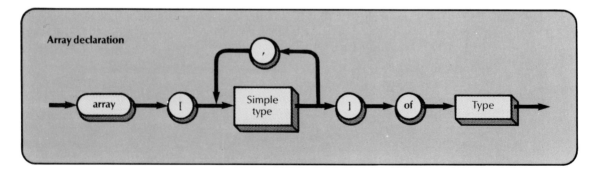

The indexing variable need not be an integer, but it must be a type that can be put into one-to-one correspondence with the integers, that is, an integer (or subrange of the integers), character, boolean, or user-defined enumerated type (discussed in Section 2.3.6). In particular, a real may not be used as an array index.

As an example of using a boolean index, we might wish to define two message types, one for a *true* index and one for a *false* index. We will use the following declarations:

```
const
  MAXSTRING    = 30;
type
  SHORTSTRING = array [1..MAXSTRING] of char;
var
  Message      : array [boolean] of SHORTSTRING;
```

In the program we assign the messages to *Message[true]* and *Message[false]*:

```
Message[true] := 'Value Within Range            ';

Message[false] := 'Value Out of Range            ';
```

Multi-dimensional arrays are described by giving the lower and upper bounds of each index. The type of each index or dimension must be the same. Here is a two dimensional array, representing a matrix of *N* rows by *M* columns:

```
type
  MATRIX        = array [1..N, 1..M] of real;
```

The upper and lower limits of each index need not be the same, however. The following declares an array of messages:

```
var
  MESSAGE : array [1..N] of SHORTSTRING;
```

Defining *MESSAGE* as an array of a named type makes the declaration clearer, more readable. We could have declared it in a single statement as in the following:

```
var
  MESSAGE : array [1..N] of array [1..30] of char;
```

A particular *MESSAGE* is accessed by indicating its index value. A particular character in a particular message requires two indices:

```
MESSAGE [5] := 'Illegal value on input   '; {pad to MAXSTRING chars}
```

To change 'input' to 'output' in *MESSAGE* [5]:

$$MESSAGE \: [5, 18] := \: 'o';$$
$$MESSAGE \: [5, 19] := \: 'u';$$
$$MESSAGE \: [5, 20] := \: 't';$$
$$MESSAGE \: [5, 21] := \: 'p';$$
$$MESSAGE \: [5, 22] := \: 'u';$$
$$MESSAGE \: [5, 23] := \: 't'$$

Higher dimensioned arrays are built up similarly.

2.3.6 Enumerated Types

An important aspect of Pascal data types that greatly enhances program readability (and consequently modifiability and verifiability) is *enumerated types*. This allows the programmer to define a new data type and to specify exactly the values that the type contains. The values must conform to the Pascal identifier syntax; that is, they must be names beginning with a letter. They cannot be specific values from the integers or reals. Note that in the following declarations, the values are enumerated without quotes:

var
   YearInSchool : (*freshman, sophomore, junior, senior, graduate, unknown*);

Assignments are made, again, without using quotes:

YearInSchool := *junior*;

The functions *succ* and *pred* are defined in terms of the order in which the values are enumerated: *succ* (*freshman*) is *sophomore*, and so on. As with characters, the predecessor of the first and the successor of the last are not defined.

We will give a code fragment in Fig. 2.15 that can be used to process student information based on year in school. The program is extremely simple, designed to give the total number of freshmen, sophomores, juniors, seniors, graduate students, and unknowns. Assume that the data is in the following format:

NAME AGE YEAR-CODE

Where NAME is a string of *MAXSTRING* (30) characters; AGE is an integer separated by at least one blank from NAME; YEAR-CODE is an integer; 1 for freshman, 2 for sophomore, 3 for junior, 4 for senior, and 5 for graduate. The data types used are declared in the declaration section of the program, Fig. 2.15(a). The procedure is shown in Fig. 2.15(b). For clarity we use the built-in *read*, rather than the *NEWREADLN* of Chapter 1.

```
const
  MAXSTRING      = 30;
type
  STRING         = array [1..MAXSTRING] of char;
  CLASS          = (freshman, sophomore, junior, senior, graduate, unknown);
```

(a)

```
procedure GetData (var Name : STRING; var Age : integer; var YearInSchool : CLASS);
{
Reads a data item and returns the enumerated type corresponding to the input value.
FORMAT:       Name—character string
              Age—integer
              YearCode—integer char.
RETURNS:      Name, Age and YearInSchool
}
var
  i              : integer;
  YearCode       : integer;
begin
  for i := 1 to MAXSTRING do                 {read the name}
    read(Name[i]);
  read(Age, YearCode);                       {read the age and the year}
  if not (YearCode in [1..5]) then           {check for illegal value}
    YearInSchool := unknown
  else
    case YearCode of
      1 : YearInSchool := freshman;
      2 : YearInSchool := sophomore;
      3 : YearInSchool := junior;
      4 : YearInSchool := senior;
      5 : YearInSchool := graduate
    end;
  readln
end; { GetData }
```

(b)

Figure 2.15. (a) Declarations for enumerated type example. (b) Reading values and returning an enumerated type.

2.3.7 Records

In an array, each element must be the same type. Records allow for the packaging under a common name of related values of *different* types. They are of particular value in linked structures, discussed in Part III. We continue

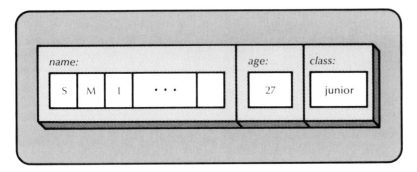

Figure 2.16. Record for student data.

the previous example in such a way that we package together the information on each student as a **record**. We want each student's data to look like Fig. 2.16.

We define this record using the type declaration of Fig. 2.17. The fields are selected by using the dot or selection operator (.).

```
student.age := 27;
student.class := junior;
student.name := 'SMITH, JOE    ';    {pad to MAXSTRING characters}
```

To assign individual characters of the *name* field, we must use both the dot operator to select the field of the record and the appropriate array index to select the individual character within the name field. Thus to change 'SMITH' to 'SMYTH':

```
student.name[3] := 'Y';
```

Figure 2.17. Declarations for student data example.

```
type
   StudentData    =
      record
         name     : STRING;
         age      : integer;
         class    : (freshman, sophomore, junior, senior,
                     graduate, unknown)
      end;
var
   student         : StudentData;
   next            : StudentData;
```

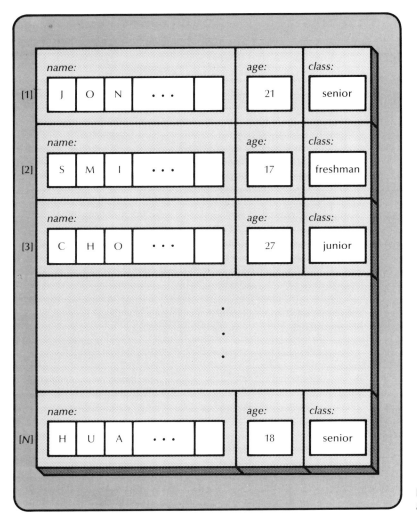

Figure 2.18. Diagram of an array of records.

An entire record can be assigned in a single statement, for example:

$$next := student;$$

We may also declare an array of records. The declaration:

```
const
  MAXARRAY        = 100;
var
  StudentDataBase : array [1..N] of StudentData;
```

is shown in diagram form in Fig. 2.18.

To set the *age* field of the third student to 17, we select the appropriate element of the array and use the dot operator to select the *age* field from that element, as follows:

$$StudentDataBase[3].age := 17;$$

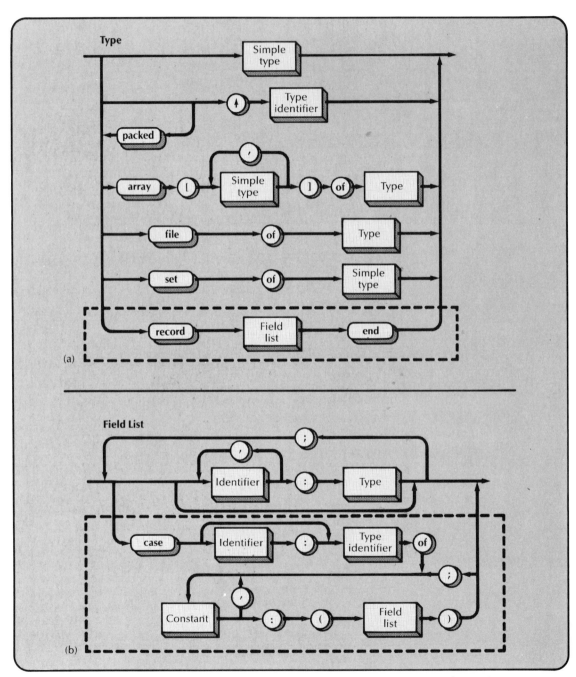

Figure 2.19. Syntax diagram for a variant record: (a) A **record** is a data type. (b) A dashed line outlines the variant record syntax.

Finally, since there is both indexing on the element of the *StudentDataBase* array (1..*N*) and on the *name* field (1..*MAXSTRING*) for each student, we indicate array indexing by associating the array index with the field that is physically closest to the identifier it indexes. To set the fourth character to 'J' in the first name, we use:

$$StudentDataBase[1].name[4] := `J';$$

Variant records

We may want to have records with fields that contain more than one type of value. Normally in a record the type of each individual field is fixed, though each field may be a different type. Variant records are used when a single field may contain more than one type of data. The syntax for a variant record is somewhat different from that of a normal record and shown in its syntax diagram (Fig. 2.19).

An example is a simple personnel record. Here the information in each record is the person's identification number (*id*), name, and sex (an enumerated type, *male* or *female*). If the sex is *male*, no additional information is kept in the record. If the sex is *female*, we would also like to keep the person's maiden name. The record is shown in diagram form in Fig. 2.20.

Figure 2.20. Diagram showing variant record.

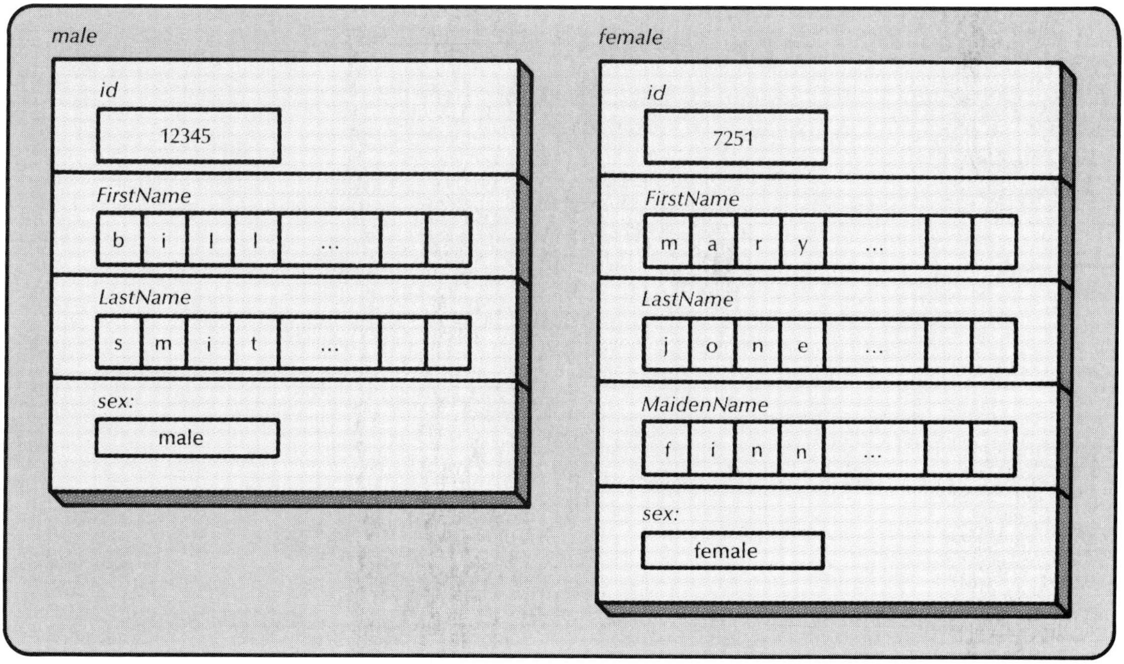

```
const
  MAXPEOPLE              = 5000;                      {or whatever is appropriate}
type
  sextype               = (male, female);            {enumerated type}
  PersonnelRecord       =                            {variant record}
    record
      id                : integer;
      FirstName         : STRING;
      LastName          : STRING;
      case sex          : sextype of
        male            : ();                         {nothing extra}
        female          : ( MaidenName : STRING)
    end;  {PersonnelRecord}
var
  PersonnelList                    : array [1..MAXPEOPLE] of PersonnelRecord;
```

Figure 2.21. Example variant record declaration.

Note that the data for a male has four fields; *id*, *FirstName*, *LastName*, and *sex*. The data for a female has five fields, *id*, *FirstName*, *LastName*, *sex*, and *MaidenName*. We declare this record with the type declaration of Fig. 2.21. (Note that STRING is not a predefined type; we first saw it in Fig. 2.15.)

Assignment to the various fields is performed in a similar manner as for regular records. An example for a *male* is:

```
PersonnelList [1].id := 4542344;
{pad names to MAXSTRING characters}
PersonnelList [1].FirstName := 'William         ';
PersonnelList [1].LastName := 'Smith           ';
PersonnelList [1].sex := male;
```

And an example for a *female* is:

```
PersonnelList [2].id := 1234567;
{pad names to MAXSTRING characters}
PersonnelList [2].FirstName := 'Shirley        ';
PersonnelList [2].LastName := 'Jones          ';
PersonnelList [2].sex := female;
PersonnelList [2].MaidenName := 'Grant          ';
```

Assignment to the *MaidenName* field of *PersonnelList* [1], when *PersonnelList*[1].*sex* is *male*, is an error, but it is not necessarily caught at run time. We must be careful when using variant records because the actual implementation may make possible what appear to be illegal assignments. There are a few syntactic rules dealing with variant records. Specifically, the variant part (after the **case** statement) must be the last field of the record. The field named in the **case** statement is also called the *tag* field. It is considered to be a part of the record (as we just saw where an assignment to *PersonnelList*[1].*sex* was made), and so its type must be indicated as seen in the example.

2.3.8 Sets

Sets are unordered collections of values, all of which must be from the same underlying type, called the *base type*. The base type of a set must be integer, character, or boolean (or a subrange of these) or a user-defined enumerated type. In particular, the base type of a set may not be the reals. There may be local implementation differences involving the maximum size of the base type: some installations allow the entire character set or entire range of integers, whereas others restrict the maximum number of elements. As a result, as useful as sets are in many applications, they are a potential source of local machine dependency.

We will run through a number of examples with sets, using the declarations of Fig. 2.22.

Set assignments are made using square brackets ([]) as in the following examples:

```
operators := [ ];                                          {empty set}
uppercase := ['A', 'E', 'I', 'O', 'U'];
undergrad := [freshman, sophomore, junior, senior];
lowerdiv := [freshman, sophomore];
upperdiv := [junior, senior];
operators := ['+', '-', '*', '/']
```

Figure 2.22. Type and variable declarations for examples using sets.

```
type
    CLASS            = (freshman, sophomore, junior, senior, graduate, unknown);
var
    A,B,C,D,E        : set of char;
    lowerdiv         : set of CLASS;
    operators        : set of char;
    uppercase        : set of 'A'..'Z';
    upperdiv         : set of CLASS;
    undergrad        : set of CLASS;
```

INITIAL ASSIGNMENTS

A := ['1', '+', 'b', '*'];
B := ['+', 'a', '*', 'b'];
C := ['1', '+', 'b', '*', 'c', 'd'];
D := [ ];   {empty set}
E := [ ];   {empty set}

DIFFERENCE

A-B	= ['1']
B-A	= ['a']
C-A	= ['c', 'd']
A-C	= [ ]

SUBSET

A<=B *is true*
A<B   *is false*   {not a PROPER subset}
D<=A *is true*   {empty set is a subset of
B< C   *is false*   all sets}

EQUALITY

(A=B) *is false*
(B=C) *is false*
(D=E) *is true*

INEQUALITY

(A<>B) *is true*
(B<>C) *is true*
(D<>E) *is false*

UNION

A+B	= ['1', '+', 'b', '*', 'a']
B+C	= ['+', 'a', '*', 'b', '1', 'c', 'd']
A+D	= ['1', '+', 'b', '*']
D+E	= [ ]

INTERSECTION

A*B	= ['+', 'b', '*']
A*C	= ['1', '+', 'b', '*']
C*D	= [ ]

MEMBERSHIP

'1' **in** A   *is true*
'1' **in** B   *is false*
'1' **in** D   *is false*

Figure 2.23. Examples of set operations. *A* through *E* as declared in
Fig. 2.13.

A number of operations can be performed on set data and relations
defined on sets. Figure 2.23 illustrates a number of these operations, using
the declarations of Fig. 2.22. The operations defined on sets are:

SET DIFFERENCE (−):   The difference between two sets is returned.
The result is a set.

SET INTERSECTION (*): The elements that are found in both sets are returned. The result is a set.

SET UNION (+): Elements that are in either, or both, of the two sets are returned. The result is a set.

SET EQUALITY (=): Equality of sets is tested. The result is a boolean. Two sets are equal when they contain the same elements. Since sets are unordered collections of objects, ordering is not used in determining equality.

SET INEQUALITY (<>): Set inequality is the opposite of set equality. The result is a boolean.

SUBSET (< =): The subset operator returns a boolean. For example, in *A*< = *B*, the two sets are compared. If *A* is equal to *B*, or a proper subset of *B*, the result is *true*. Otherwise, the result is *false*. A similar operator, proper subset (<), tests that *B* is a proper subset of *A* (that is, it is a subset of *A*, but not equal to *A*).

MEMBERSHIP (**in**): Membership using the operator **in** returns a boolean indicating whether a given scalar value (from the base type of the set) is an element of the set.

Figure 2.24 ties together some of the ideas in the use of sets. It is a program that reads and processes scores. The program defines two constants, *MINSCORE* and *MAXSCORE*, and performs error checking on each value as it is read. Scores are kept counted in one of two sets: *UniqScores* and *DupScores*. If a score is not in the range *MINSCORE..MAXSCORE*, the count of bad scores is incremented (we use the **in** operator for this test). Otherwise, if the score already exists in *UniqScores*, it is a duplicate and is unioned with *DupScores* (using the union operator, ' + '). At the end of the input, the number of elements (cardinality) of the sets is written out. Note the use of the set operators **in** (test for membership), + (union), and the **for** loop used to test if a value is in the set, in the function *cardinality*. We have not used *NEWREADLN* from Chapter 1 in order to keep the basic set functions clearer; however, we encourage the use of error checking procedures such as *NEWREADLN* whenever we can.

Figure 2.25 gives sample input data and the output generated with this input by the program of Fig. 2.24.

2.3.9 Pointers

Pointers are addresses. That is, a pointer type variable contains the *address* of the location of another variable. Addresses may not be read or written directly in Pascal. Pointer type variables are declared using the pointer (↑) declaration. Let *J* be a pointer variable that we would like to contain the address of an integer. *J* is declared as follows:

var
$J : \uparrow integer;$

Since Pascal is strongly typed, *J* can contain only the address of an integer. It may not contain the address of a real, boolean, etc. Pointers are particularly useful in linked data structures (to be discussed thoroughly in

Figure 2.24. Example of **set** operations.

```
program SETS (input, output);
{Demonstrates the use of the more common set functions.}
const
  MAXSCORE      = 100;                    { maximum score }
  MINSCORE      = 0;                      { minimum score }
type
  COUNTER       = 0..maxint;
  SCORETYPE     = MINSCORE..MAXSCORE;
  SETOFSCORES   = set of SCORETYPE;
var
  BadScores      : COUNTER;               { count of scores not in range }
  DupScores      : SETOFSCORES;           { set of multiply occuring scores }
  NextScore      : integer;               { next score }
  UniqScores     : SETOFSCORES;           { set of different scores }

  function cardinality(x : SETOFSCORES) : integer;
  {Returns the number of elements in set x. Makes initial check to see if the set is empty.}
    var
      count      : integer;               { element counter }
      next       : integer;               { position holder }
    begin
      if x = [ ] then
        cardinality := 0
      else begin
        count := 0;
        for next := MINSCORE to MAXSCORE do
          if next in x then
            count := count + 1;
        cardinality := count
      end
    end; {cardinality}
```

```
begin {main}
  UniqScores := [ ];      {initialize to empty set}
  DupScores := [ ];       {initialize to empty set}
  BadScores := 0;
  while not eof do begin
    read(NextScore);
    if eoln then
      readln;
    if NextScore in [MINSCORE..MAXSCORE] then
      if NextScore in UniqScores then              {count duplicates}
        DupScores := DupScores + [NextScore]
      else
        UniqScores := UniqScores + [NextScore]      {count unique scores}
    else
      BadScores := BadScores + 1
  end;
  writeln;
  writeln('Number of different (unique) scores : ', cardinality(UniqScores) : 4);
  writeln('Number of repeated scores : ', cardinality(DupScores) : 4);
  writeln('Number of out of range scores : ', BadScores : 4)
end.
```

Figure 2.25. Input and output from the sets example program.

```
INPUT:

   3     20     12     18     23
  20     32     89     99     24
  23     -5     78     97     45
  20     18    123     99     45
  20     99     20     23     12
  32     97     23     24     89
  -5     99     20     45     78

OUTPUT:

Number of different (unique) scores:     12
Number of repeated scores:               11
Number of out of range scores:            3
```

```
program PTRTEST (input, output);
{
Sample program illustrating the use of pointer variables, pointer assignments, and writing out
the values that pointer variables point to.
}
type
   INTPTR              = ↑integer;              {pointer to an integer}
var
   i                   : INTPTR;
   j                   : INTPTR;
   n                   : integer;
begin
   new (i );                                    {i points to empty new cell}
   new (j );                                    {j points to empty new cell}
   n := 5;
   i↑ := n;                                     {cell that i points to contains same value as n}
   writeln (i↑);
   j := i;                                      {i, j both point to same cell}
   j↑ := −7;                                    {changing j↑ also changes i↑}
   writeln (i↑)
end.
```

Figure 2.26. Program illustrating a use of pointer variables.

Part III). Figure 2.26 shows examples of the declarations and use of pointer variables. In this example the pointer variables may contain only the address of an integer. In Fig. 2.27 we trace the action of the program on i, $i\uparrow$ and j and $j\uparrow$.

With pointers, we need a special value indicating that the value points to an invalid address. Pascal provides the special value **nil**, which is used to indicate that a pointer is not pointing to any storage location. A thorough discussion of pointers and the use of **nil** is presented in Part III.

2.3.10 Files

A file is a sequential collection of values generally residing on external storage. Pascal predefines two files, the standard input (given the predeclared name *input*) and the standard output (the predeclared name *output*). The standard input and output are defined in the local environment. For batch systems, the standard input is generally the card reader or the input stream defined for the batch system and the standard output is generally the line printer or a system file which collects output for the line printer. In interactive systems, the standard input is the keyboard and the standard output is the display screen. *input* and *output* are predeclared as type text and text is a predeclared type, **file of** *char.*

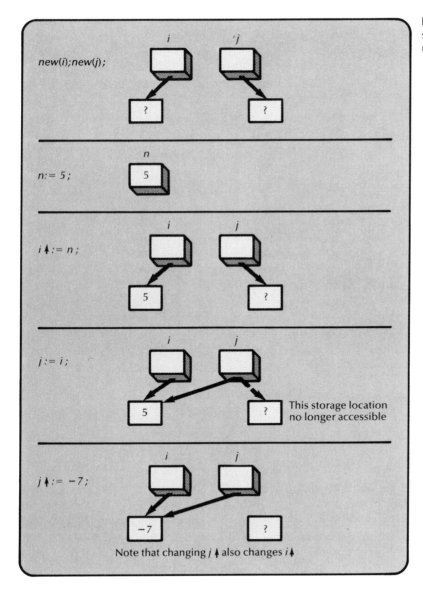

Figure 2.27. Examples showing the use of pointers, using pointers to integers.

A program may have an arbitrary number of additional files open for reading and writing. The only restriction is that a file may be used for only one operation; it may be opened for writing (output) or for reading (input). Consequently, when we want to read values from an input file, process them, and update them, two files must be used: one containing the original values, open for reading, and the other with the updated values, open for writing. All files are sequential files: data must be read or written in order.

In general, we use files for communicating with the outside world. Four statements are affected when file I/O is needed. These are:

- The **program** header, where the files must be named
- An appropriate **var** declaration for the file, indicating its type
- The *reset* or *rewrite* procedure, which opens the file for reading or writing, respectively
- The *read* or *write* statements, which contain the file name as an additional parameter

All files that are to have a lifetime beyond the current execution of the program (including *input* and *output*) must be declared in the program header:

> **program** *NAME* (*input, output, file1, file2, ..., fileN*);

The names should be the same as the external name of the file in the computer's file system (though virtually all systems provide a means of associating an external file with a different internal name). If a file is used only within a program, but does not need to be retained after the program's execution, a temporary file, then it does not need to be declared in the program header.

Files are sequential arrays of virtually any scalar or user-defined type, including records. Consequently we must define the type of the file in the declaration section.

We saw that the standard input and standard output are predeclared as type *text*. For *file1* and *file2* named in the program statement, we might declare them as:

> **var**
> *file1*   : *text*;
> *file2*   : **file of** *integer*;

A file must be specifically opened for either input or output (except the standard input and output). This is accomplished through the built-in procedures *reset* and *rewrite*, respectively. Near the beginning of a program, files used for input (reading) should be opened for reading using the procedure call *reset* (*file*). This procedure positions the file pointer to the first data item in the file and prepares the file for reading. It is an error if the file doesn't exist and unfortunately, Pascal does not have a mechanism to determine in advance whether a file exists.

Files used for output (writing) are indicated by the procedure *rewrite* (*file*). A *rewrite* opens the file for writing by positioning the file pointer at the beginning of the file. The previous contents of the file, if any, are erased. If the file does not exist, it will be created. A *reset* or *rewrite* must be performed on any file (except for standard input and output files) used for reading or writing, respectively.

Finally, when I/O involves a file other than standard input or output, the file name must be given as an additional parameter to the *read* or *write* statement. Figure 2.28 simply reads values from a file named *DataFile* and

Figure 2.28. Sample program illustrating the use of reading and writing external files.

```
program FileExample (input, output, DataFile, GoodData);
const
  MAXHOURS        = 100;                                  {maximum hours/week}
var
  BadCount        : integer;
  DataFile        : text;
  GoodData        : file of integer;
  hours           : integer;
  line            : integer;
begin
  reset(DataFile);                                        {open DataFile for reading}
  rewrite(GoodData);                                      {open GoodData for writing}
  BadCount := 0;
  line := 0;
  writeln;
  while not eof(DataFile) do begin                        {file argument to eof}
    line := line + 1;
    readln(DataFile, hours);                              {file argument in readln}
    if (hours <= MAXHOURS) and (hours > 0) then
      write(GoodData, hours)                              {file argument to write}
    else begin
      BadCount := BadCount + 1;
      writeln('Bad data value : ', hours : 5, ' at Line : ', line : 1)  {write to std. output}
    end
  end;
  writeln;
  writeln('There were ', BadCount : 1, ' bad values')
end.
```

writes them to a file named *GoodData*. Illegal values are presented to the standard output to notify the user. The program is not very interesting, of course, but it illustrates the correct use of file I/O.

Note that in Fig. 2.28 *GoodData* is *not* a text file. To read from this file in another program, we must declare it as the same type, **file of** *integer*.

2.4   Statement Syntax

There are ten executable statement types in Pascal:

Assignment
Procedure Call
if
case
while
repeat
for
with
goto
Compound (**begin..end**)

Breaking these down into simpler types, in fact only five are used regularly in most programs:

Assignment
Procedure Call
Conditional (**if** and **case**)
Loop (**while, repeat,** and **for**)
Compound (**begin..end**)

The syntax for each of the executable statement types is shown in the syntax diagrams in Appendix 2. Note that input and output (*read, readln, write,* and *writeln*) are not included as separate statement types: they are procedure calls, and are discussed in Section 2.5. Since the syntax of each statement type is quite straightforward, we will emphasize the semantics of each statement and illustrate each with a simple example.

2.4.1 Assignment Statement

The expression on the right of the assignment operator (:=) is evaluated. This value is then assigned to the identifier on the left side. The type of the expression and the identifier must be the same. No automatic type conversion is allowed, with two exceptions: an integer expression may be

Table 2.4. Examples of specific rounding and truncating a real.	
Statement	**Value assigned to *A, an integer***
$A := round\ (5.9)$;	6
$A := trunc\ (5.9)$;	5
$A := 5.9$;	illegal
$A := round\ (-5.9)$;	-6
$A := trunc\ (-5.9)$;	-5

"widened" to a real and the type of an identifier on the right side may be a subrange of the identifier on the left. No other implicit conversions are allowed.

Specifically, if we want to assign a real expression to an integer variable, we must explicitly state the conversion of the real, either by rounding or truncating using built-in functions *round* and *trunc*. This conversion is not decided by the compiler writer. Thus, for the integer variable *A*, Table 2.4 shows the effect of specifically rounding or truncating.

2.4.2 Conditionals

Conditionals allow the program to test the value or range of variables and to decide on alternative processing based on the result of the test. There are two conditional statements in Pascal: **if** and **case**.

If statement

The syntax of the **if** statement is shown in Fig. 2.29.

Figure 2.29. Syntax diagram for **if** statement.

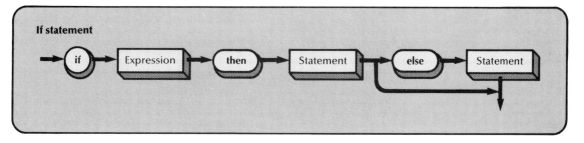

```
        if A then begin                      if A then begin
          if B then                            if B then
             S1                                    S1
        end else                               else
           S2;                                    S2
          S3                                   end;
                                                S3
```

A	B	Execute Next		A	B	Execute Next
true	true	S1		true	true	S1
true	false	S3		true	false	S2
false	?	S2		false	?	S3
	(a)				(b)	

Figure 2.30. Possible bracketing of the nested **if**: (a) the last **else** belongs to the first **if**; (b) the last **else** belongs to the second **if** — this is the default association of **else** with **if** in Pascal.

The semantics of the **if** statement are quite straightforward. The boolean expression is evaluated; it returns either *true* or *false*. If the expression returns *true*, the statement following the **then** clause is executed. The **else** clause is optional. If the boolean expression evaluates to *false*, the **else** clause, if present, is executed. Otherwise, control passes to the next statement in sequence. Either statement following the **then** or **else** clause may be another **if** statement. This leads to the "dangling **else**" problem: in a compound **if** statement, there is no a priori decision as to which **then** the last **else** belongs to. Figure 2.30 looks at two ways of parsing the nested **if** statement. In part (a), we would consider the **else** clause to go with the first **if**. In part (b), the **else** clause goes with the last. If we want to change the a priori connection of the last **else** with the last **if** we must use **begin-end**, as in Fig. 2.30(a).

As an example, in the following

```
if hours < MaxHours then
   if hours > 40.0 then
      rate := OverTimeRate
   else
      rate := NormalRate;
```

the **else** is considered to go with the last **then**, and corresponds to Fig. 2.30(b).

```
if year = 1 then                    if not (year in [1..4]) then
  S1                                  S5
  else if year = 2 then             else
    S2                                case year of
    else if year = 3 then              1 : S1;
      S3                               2 : S2;
      else if year = 4 then            3 : S3;
        S4                             4 : S4
        else                        end;
          S5;

              (a)                                  (b)
```

Figure 2.31. Comparison of nested **if** (a) vs. **case** statement. (b) Each S_i is an executable Pascal statement.

Case statement

Often we must do processing based on the value or range of a variable. For example, suppose we wish to process student data based on year in school. In Fig. 2.31(a), we see a typical statement construct: the nested **if** statement (where *year* is an integer variable). Such a statement structure is quite difficult to read and to modify because it can be difficult to trace which statement (S_i) belongs to which value of *year*. In Fig. 2.31(b), we show a clearer way to represent this nested **if** statement structure with the **case** statement. The syntax for the **case** statement is shown in Fig. 2.32.

Figure 2.32. Syntax diagram for **case** statement.

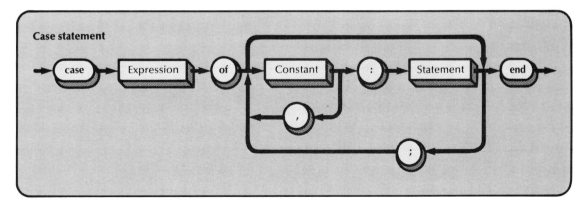

The semantics of the **case** are that the expression (**case** variable) is evaluated. The expression must return a single scalar value. This value is compared with each of the ordinal constant labels in the **case** statement. When one is found having the same value as the case variable, its corresponding statement is executed. Control then passes to the statement following the **case end**. It is a compile-time error if there are duplicate label values, and a run-time error if the case variable does not equal any of the label values. Consequently we must almost always guard the case statement with an **if** statement that tests the range of the case variable in order to protect the program from a run-time error. The labels may be any scalar type (but not real), but they all must be of the same type and agree in type with the case variable. The labels may also contain a list of values, but not a range (see the exercises for a suggested extension to the **case** statement). In the following, *NextChar* is a character. If *NextChar* is an 'A' or a 'B', S1 is executed; if it is '2', '4', '6' or '8', S2 is executed.

```
case NextChar of
    'A', 'B'              : S1;
    '2', '4', '6', '8'    : S2
end;
```

2.4.3 Loop Constructs

Looping is defined as the repetitive execution of one or more statements. The looping may be done unconditionally (via a **goto** statement) or conditionally, based on the value of one or more variables (**while, repeat, for**). The **while** and **repeat** are quite similar syntactically and semantically, and they are discussed together. The **for** statement repeats a statement (single or compound) a fixed number of times, based on the value of the loop index.

While/Repeat statement

The syntax for the **while** and the **repeat** statements is shown in Fig. 2.33.

The **while** statement is repeated as long as the boolean expression evaluates to *true*. This may be zero or more times. One important use is to control reading until reaching the end of file:

```
while not eof do begin
    readln(value);
    process(value)
end;
```

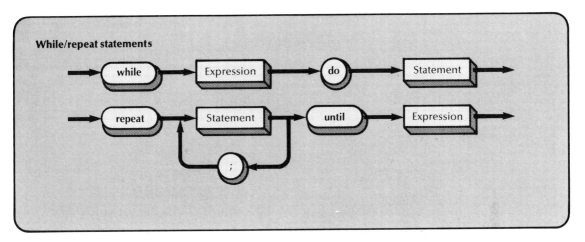

Figure 2.33. Syntax diagram for **while** and **repeat** statement.

It is also used when multiple conditions control the execution of a statement. In the sample program at the end of the chapter, we print out a line of asterisks (*), the length being equal to an integer value *values*[i]. However, we do not wish to print out more than the maximum number of asterisks that can fit on one line (*MAXCOLS*). One way to do this is by the series of statements:

```
k := 1;
while (k <= values[i]) and (k <= MAXCOLS) do begin
  write('*');
  k := k + 1
end;
```

k, *values*[i], and *MAXCOLS* are all of type integer. The loop will be executed as long as both conditions ($k <=$ *values*[i] and $k <=$ *MAXCOLS*) evaluate to *true*.

The **repeat** statement is similar to the **while** statement. In this case, however, the loop body will always be executed *at least* once. That is, the loop body is first executed, and then the boolean expression is evaluated. If the expression evaluates to *true*, the body is not executed again. If it evaluates to *false*, the body is executed again. The loop body is executed until the boolean expression evaluates to *true*. We rarely need to ensure that a loop is executed at least once. But this is occasionally needed in processing input from a terminal, where we want to continue reading until some special character is typed. The first phase of the *NEWREADLN* procedure, which reads characters until a nonblank is found, uses a **repeat** statement:

```
{FIRST PHASE — SCAN OVER BLANKS}
repeat
    read(ch)
until ch <> ' ';
```

For statement

When we must repeat a statement (or compound statement) a fixed number of times, we can use the **for** statement. The variable that controls the number of times the loop is executed is called the loop counter or loop index. As the syntax diagram (Fig. 2.34) shows, it must be an ordinal *variable* (not a constant). The initial and final values may be any integer or integer function, as long as the loop index is properly declared. The loop index may also be an enumerated type or a character variable, as long as an ordering is associated with it. The loop counter may not be a set variable because no ordering is implied on the elements of a set. The loop index is always incremented by either $+1$ or -1. That is, the next value of the loop index is always either the successor or the predecessor of its current value.

Figure 2.34. Syntax diagram for a **for** statement.

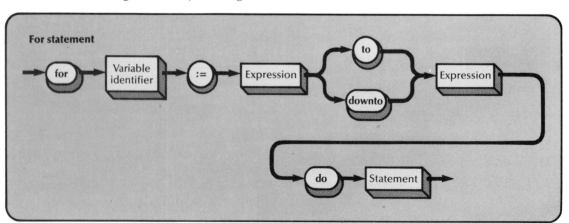

for *letter* := 'A' **to** 'Z' **do**   {*letter* of type char}
  counter[*letter*] := 0;

for *i* := *max* **downto** *min* **do begin**   {*i* of type integer}
  readln(x);
  process(x)   {do something with x}
end;

for *class* := *freshman* **to** *senior* **do**   {*class* is enumerated type}
  readln(*students*[*class*])

Figure 2.35. Examples of indexing in a **for** statement.

As a simple example we will set a matrix *I* to be the identity matrix. It is assumed that *I* has been declared as:

var
  I : **array** [1..N, 1..N] **of** *real*;

Then the following code fragment sets all elements of *I* to 0.0, and the main diagonal elements to 1.0:

for *j* := 1 **to** N **do**
  for *k* := 1 **to** N **do**
    I[*j*,*k*] := 0.0;
  for *j* := 1 **to** N **do**
    I[*j*,*j*] := 1.0;

The loop index of the **for** statement is incremented by +1 if the control word (**to**, **downto**) is **to**. It is incremented by −1 (that is, decremented by 1) if the control word is **downto**. No other increment is allowed. Even though the loop counter is a variable, its value may not be altered within the loop body. These restrictions tend to reduce the utility of the **for** statement; in general, the **while** statement may always replace a **for** loop. Figure 2.35 illustrates different possibilities for the loop index.

Goto and label statements

An unconditional jump or branching is performed via the **goto** statement. The statement executed after the **goto** is the one with the label given in the **goto** statement. A label is an unsigned integer of one to four digits and must be declared in a **label** declaration. A given label may appear on only one statement. As an example, suppose we wish to process positive input values differently from negative ones. This code fragment would be useful in this processing:

```
                      . . .
        label
            100, 200;
                      . . .
        begin {main}
                      . . .
            readln(value);
            if value < 0 then
                goto 100           {process negative values}
            else
                goto 200;          {process positive values}
                      . . .
        100 :                      {negative processing}
                      . . .
        200 :                      {positive processing}
                      . . .
```

As can be seen, the integer labels and the spreading around of the code make the **goto** a difficult structure to use and interpret correctly. This is not unexpected, since the use of **goto**'s tends to produce this type of "spaghetti code." In Pascal programs, **goto** structures can always be replaced with an **if**, **while**, or **repeat**, and they will generally yield more readable (and thus more easily modifiable) code. The previous example could be recoded more cleanly as follows:

```
        readln(value);
        if value <= 0 then
                . . .    {negative processing}
        else
                . . .    {positive processing}
```

2.5   Input/Output

Input and output are both rather limited in Pascal. Input is accomplished through the *read* and *readln* procedures. Output uses the two built-in procedures, *write* and *writeln*. Normally input comes from a predefined file, the standard input, known as file *input*. Similarly, all output goes to the standard output, called file *output*. The standard input is normally the card reader for batch (card) jobs and the terminal keyboard for interactive environments. The standard output is the printer or terminal screen. Even though almost all programs require input or output, these two files, *input* and *output*, must be declared in the **program** statement:

```
        program NAME (input,output);
```

2.5.1 Input

Input is via the *read* and *readln* procedures. In addition, file input can be accomplished via the *get* procedure. We will discuss *read* and *readln* in some detail. The *get* procedure will be discussed briefly since its use is more limited. *read* and *readln* are unusual because they take a variable number of parameters, as we see in the syntax diagram in Fig. 2.36.

When reading from *input* (as opposed to a file parameter specified in the *read* procedure), only real, integer, and character data may be read. No input is allowed to boolean variables, to an enumerated type, or to other user-defined types (though many environments have extended Pascal to allow this). Specifically the standard input is predeclared as type text. Pascal graciously translates strings of digits that represent legal integers or reals for us. If we wish to read an integer, we use a statement such as:

$$read(value);$$

where *value* is an integer. The *read* procedure for an integer or real variable begins at the current location in the input and scans over white space

Figure 2.36. Syntax diagram for *read* and *readln*.

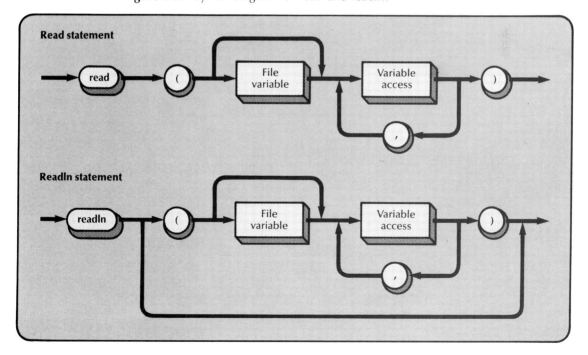

(blanks, tabs, etc.) until nonwhite space is found. This scanning will take place over cards or lines, if necessary. Finally, when a character of the appropriate type is found ('+', '−', digit), reading of the integer continues until any character that cannot be part of an integer is found. However, it is an error to attempt to read a value that cannot be an integer.

When multiple values are read via the same read procedure, the process continues. Scanning continues after the first value, skipping blanks until the next integer in the input is found. For example, suppose the standard input contains:

Line 1:	− 123	42
Line 2:	51	+ 87

Then:

$$read(value1, value2, value3, value4);$$

sets *value1* to − 123, *value2* to 42, *value3* to 51, and *value4* to 87. Note that *read* has continued across line boundaries. *readln* is similar to *read*, except that after the input occurs, the file pointer is automatically incremented to the beginning of the next line or card. Using the preceding data: *read(a,b)* sets *a* to − 123 and *b* to 42, whereas *readln(a); readln(b)* sets *a* to − 123 and *b* to 51. After the first *readln* a jump to the beginning of the next line occurs. The 42 will not be read.

The reading of real values works similarly. No scanning over blanks is performed for character data, however. Suppose *symbol* and *blank* have been declared as a character type, and all others as integers. Then with the following input (where _ is a blank):

Line 1: 1465 _ + ___ 23

Line 2:   − 27 _ * _ 41

Line 3: − 18 _ / ____ − 9

The following statements set values as follows:

readln(a, blank, symbol, b);	a = 1465	blank = ' '	symbol = '+'	b = 23
readln(a, blank, symbol, b);	a = − 27	blank = ' '	symbol = '*'	b = 41
readln(a, blank, symbol, b);	a = − 18	blank = ' '	symbol = '/'	b = − 9

It was necessary to read the blank separating the value of *a* from *symbol* because character read does not skip over blanks, as integer or real read does.

Two predefined boolean functions, *eof* and *eoln*, are useful in processing input data. *eof* is a boolean that is *true* whenever the current character being read is the last one in the file. More formally, *eof* is defined as *true* when the *next character* is the end-of-file marker defined in the local operating system. The use of *eof* allows us to read and process a variable amount of input data without knowing in advance how many values to process. Suppose we wish to read a file of integers and compute the average, and we do not know how many there are. The file consists of positive and negative integers, one per card or line. The following code fragment reads the file as long as there are more values to be read, and then it computes the average. Assume that *sum*, *count*, *average*, and *NextValue* have been declared as reals. For clarity, no error checking is performed on the input data.

```
          . . .
sum := 0.0;
count := 0.0;
while not eof do begin
  readln(NextValue);
  sum := sum + NextValue;
  count := count + 1
end;
{Compute the average. Careful about division by 0}
if count = 0.0 then
  average := 0.0
else
  average := sum / count
          . . .
```

The boolean *eoln* is *true* when the next character is the end-of-line marker defined in the local operating system; *false*, otherwise. We may use this to process characters until we reach the end of the line (*eoln* is *true*). The end-of-line character is converted to a blank before being handed to our program. The only way to test for the end of the line is through the *eoln* function. We follow the loop with a single *readln* so that input will begin with the first character of the next line or card.

```
while not eoln do begin
  read(NextChar);
  process(NextChar)
end;
readln;
```

Both *read* and *readln* may take an optional file variable, so that reading occurs from the file; *read(File, V)* or *readln(File, V)* will read from *File* if the file has been properly declared. For *readln*, *File* must be type text.

2.5.2 Output

Output is performed using the built-in procedures *write* and *writeln*. As with input, the procedures take an arbitrary number of parameters. The first may be a file; the rest are variables, constants, or expressions. *writeln* (but not *write*), may have zero parameters in which case it places an end-of-line character into the output. As with *readln*, *writeln* must have a file parameter of type text. The *write* and *writeln* procedures put onto the standard output the values of all expressions in the parameter list. A default field width is used for each different type. For integers, this is usually 10 columns, including the sign, which is always blank for positive integers and '−' for negative integers. Reals are printed in a normalized scientific notation. Again the number of significant digits and the number of columns (field width) depend on the implementation. Printing characters are printed using a single column width. Nonprinting characters (for example, *control* ('g'), which we saw is the ASCII bell character) do not take any space on the display or page. Figure 2.37 illustrates examples of *write* and *writeln*.

The array of characters is extended to the right with blanks, so that the entire 20 characters is written for the string s. The spacing is more clearly seen when more than one value is written on the same line. The statement would yield the output:

writeln(i,r,c,s,i);   15_1.23456000000000e + 02ZNow *is the time*_____15

Figure 2.37. Examples of *write* and *writeln*.

```
var
    i        : integer;
    r        : real;
    c        : char;
    s        : array [1..20] of char;
```

Assume the following assignments have been made:

```
    i := 15;
    r := 123.456;
    c := 'Z';
    s := 'Now is the time      '          {pad on the right to 20 characters}
```

Then the result of the following *writeln* statements (_ is a blank):

```
writeln('I =', i);              I_ = _____15
writeln('r =', r);              r_ = _ 1.23456000000000e + 02
writeln('c =', c);              c_ = Z
writeln('s =', s);              s_ = Now is the time
```

```
writeln(i:5, r:7:2);                    ___15__123.46
writeln(i:9, r:8:1);                    _____15___123.5
writeln('Value of i', i:1);             Value of i15              {Note: no space after i}
```

Figure 2.38. Output width field specifiers.

Constants and strings may be written so that output appears neater. In addition, field widths can be overridden to produce neater output and to produce reals that are not in scientific notation. To override the default, a field width specification is used. This consists of the expression followed by a colon (:), and then an integer variable or constant (specifying the size of the field). Then, for reals, a second colon and a second integer (specifying the number of digits to the *right* of the decimal point) must follow. The entire field width should be large enough to contain the number of digits to the left of the decimal point, the decimal point itself, and one extra space for the sign (which is always blank for positive numbers and ' − ' for negative value). If the field is not large enough, sufficient width will be used to print the entire number. Figure 2.38 gives further examples, using the same values of *i* and *r* as in Fig. 2.37.

Note that rounding automatically takes place on real output. Field width specifications for reals can be used to produce neat columns of data. Strings may be used to produce labeled output.

The *write* statement is similar to the *writeln*, except that with the *writeln* statement, an end-of-line character is automatically added at the end of the output. With the *write* statement, output continues on the same line. A *write* is useful when input is desired from the terminal, and a prompt is used to indicate to the user that input is needed. Here is a small code fragment that asks the user to type a value so that the program can compute its square root. For clarity, no error checking is performed on the input data.

```
        . . .
    writeln('Please type a value. Program will calculate its square root');
    write('> ');
  while not eof do begin
     readln(value);
     writeln('Value:', value : 10 : 2, 'Square root :', sqrt(value) : 10 : 2);
     write('> ')
  end;
        . . .
```

2.5.3 Get and Put

Reading and writing files does not occur directly in Pascal. Rather these routines call on lower level routines (though available to the programmer), *get* and *put*.

A file in Pascal is a sequential array of some data type (in the case of text files, the underlying data type is char; in the case of a file of some constructed (record) type, each file element is a record). Associated with the file is a file buffer, and its pointer. The file buffer is indicated by the name of the file followed by an up arrow (↑). The file buffer pointer points to the *next* component in the input file (see Fig. 2.39). Since the file name is associated with its buffer, the procedure *get(File)*, where *File* is of some file type, has the effect of causing the next component of *File* to be read into its buffer. The component is then available through *File* ↑ . The standard

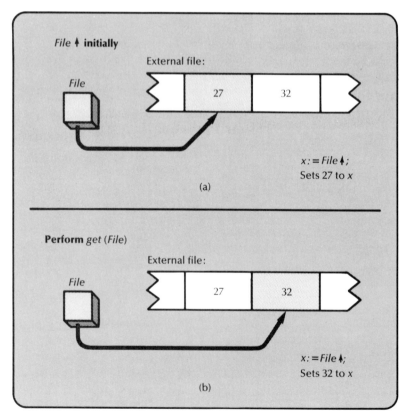

Figure 2.39. Diagram of file buffer pointer. (a) Configuration at some time *T*. (b) Configuration after performing *get(File)*.

procedure *read* is implemented in terms of *get*:

read(File, value);

is equivalent to the two statements

value := File ↑ ;
get(File);

First, the current value of the file (available through its buffer pointer, *File* ↑) is assigned to *value*. Then the file pointer is incremented to the next item in the file.

The call *get(File)* is illegal if *File* is not open for reading or does not exist. It is also an error to attempt a *get(File)* if *eof(File)* is *true*. Unfortunately this makes the proper handling of simple line scanning schemes tedious at best. In a number of programs in this book we are interested in scanning over blanks until a nonblank is found, first seen in the *NEWREADLN* procedure of Chapter 1. That procedure tacitly assumes, however, that there is a nonblank in the file. If we wish to scan over blanks until we find a nonblank, or until *eof* is *true*, we might write a routine similar to the following:

while (**not** *eof*) **and** (*input* ↑ <> ' ') **do**
get(input);

However, we have a problem because we cannot guarantee the order of evaluation of clauses of the **while** statement. Consequently we may have the condition that *eof* is *true*, and while attempting to compare *input* ↑ with ' ' (a blank). Such an inspection of *input* ↑ is illegal because *eof* is *true*. A solution involves breaking the **while** loop into two tests, by using an auxiliary boolean variable *done*.

```
done := false;
repeat
  if eof then
    done := true
  else if input ↑  = ' ' then
    get(input)
  else
    done := true
until done
```

We can conclude that, in general, to really "bulletproof" our code, we must tediously protect ourselves, as in the preceding code fragment.

A call to the procedure *put(File)* adds the current component of *File* ↑ to the end of *File*. It is an error if there is nothing to put there or if *File* does not exist or is not open for writing (via a call to *rewrite(File)*). The

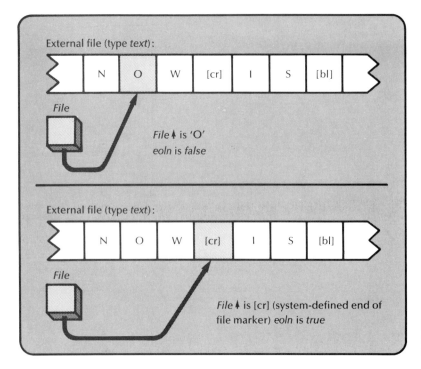

Figure 2.40. Examples of status of *eoln* for various states of *File*↑.

standard procedures *write* and *writeln* are implemented in terms of calls to *put*.

write(File, value);

is equivalent to

> *File*↑ := *value*;   {assign value to *File*'s buffer}
> *put(File)*;   {actually appends the value to the file}

After the call to *put(File)*, *File*↑ is undefined. Another *put(File)* without first assigning to *File*↑ is an error (see Fig. 2.40).

2.6 Example Program — A Histogram Generator

We tie many of the ideas of this chapter together into a program that produces histograms (bar charts) of numerical data. The program as currently written can be used to produce histograms of percentage score data. It will draw a histogram for integer values in the range of 0 to 99, producing one bar for each group of scores, where the grouping is by 10s. That is, it will produce a bar for the count of all values in the range 0 to 9, another for values in the range 10 to 19, another for values in the range 20 to 29, and so on, up to all the values in the range 90 to 99. Though these assumptions are somewhat restrictive, they are controlled through program constants, so that different ranges and groupings are possible simply by recompiling the program with changes to these values.

2.6.1 Program Input

The input to the program is a list of values, one per line or card. The values must be in the proper range, 0 to *MAXVALUE* (in this version, *MAXVALUE* is the constant 99). The input values are read in function *GetValue*. *GetValue* is a function that returns a boolean: *true* if the data is in the valid range (0 to *MAXVALUE*), and *false*, otherwise. Note that this function performs an integer read. As we noted in Chapter 1, this can be dangerous since the program terminates if an illegal character is entered. We have included the original version of *NEWREADLN* within *GetValue* even though it returns a real. Within *GetValue*, we round the real to an integer. We use the compiler directive #*include* "*NEWREADLN.i*" which accesses the file *NEWREADLN.i* containing the code for the procedure. The compiler then processes the lines as if they were found at that point in the program.

2.6.2 Program Design and Internal Operation

As each valid data item is read, it is counted into an appropriate data bucket. The data buckets are just counters for the range within which the current value is included. For example, if the input value is 27, the data bucket is 2 (found by doing an integer division of the value by the maximum number of groups: *value* **div** *MAXGROUPS*; in this case, 27 **div** 10, or 2). Since this value goes into group two, this is used as an index into the *valuebuckets* array. Figure 2.41 shows how the data buckets work.

When all the data have been read, each data bucket is a counter for the number of values in the appropriate range. Here the 0 bucket counts the number of values that were in the range 0 to 9, the 1 bucket counts the number of values that were in the range 10 to 19, the 2 bucket counts the number of values that were in the range 20 to 29, and so on. We then use this bucket array for the *DrawHisto* procedure.

The program is structured hierarchically so that the main program calls upon the routines it needs to get the data, count the current value into the appropriate bucket, and then, when out of data, print the histogram. The three functions that the program must perform are reading and validating the input, counting the current value into an appropriate bucket, and printing the histogram after all the input has been processed. We define three routines to accomplish these tasks: *GetValue* to read and validate the input, *Count* for counting the value, and *DrawHisto* for printing the histogram.

GetValue

Gets the next input value. Then we process the value based on its properties:

- Not an integer: Count this value as *ILLEGAL*
- Out of range: Count this value as *OUTOFRANGE*
- Otherwise: Count this value as *INRANGE*

The counts are kept in an array called *valuecount*. We can use Pascal's enumerated type mechanism to get mnemonic indexes:

```
type
    VALUETYPE          = (INRANGE, OUTOFRANGE, ILLEGAL);
                       = 0..maxint;
    COUNTER            = array [VALUETYPE] of COUNTER;
    COUNTERARRAY
var
    valuecount         :  COUNTERARRAY;   {Count errors of each type}
```

Figure 2.41. Current value as an index into data buckets. In the program, we only count the values — we don't actually move them into a bucket.

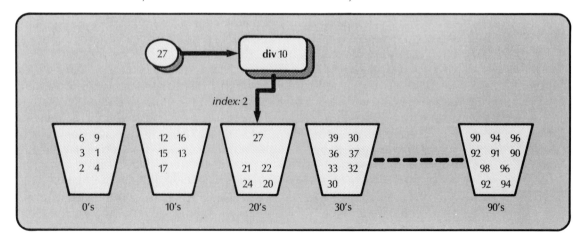

```
program HISTOGRAM (input, output);

   function GetValue;

   procedure Count;

   procedure DrawHisto;

begin {main}
   {initialize various counters}
   while not eof do
     if GetValue then
       Count;
   DrawHisto(valuebuckets);
   {output various information about the histogram}
end.
```

Figure 2.42. Skeletal program form for the histogram drawing program.

Count

In this routine we count the value into the appropriate bucket. Since error checking is performed in *GetValue*, we can be assured that the value will index a legal bucket.

DrawHisto

Finally, we draw the histogram, by placing a symbol *VALUEMARK* ('*' initially), one for each count in the bucket. If bucket *i* equals *n*, we need to print *n* symbols:

```
for j := 1 to valuebuckets[i] do
   write(VALUEMARK);
writeln(' ', valuebuckets[i] : 1)
```

If *valuebuckets*[*i*] is four, we get something like:

$$**** \quad 4$$

Unfortunately a bucket's value could be greater than the width of the output line. In this case, we must scale the value in the bucket so that it is between zero and the maximum number of available columns in the output. We use a program constant to indicate the maximum number of columns available (*MAXCOLS*). Then in *DrawHisto*, we make an initial pass over all the buckets to determine the maximum count. If this maximum is greater than *MAXCOLS*, we compute a scale factor, *MAXCOLS* divided by the maximum count. Before printing, we multiply the count of each bucket by the scale factor and print that many symbols. (Of course, we still print the actual count in the bucket; only the number of asterisks is scaled.)

In skeletal form, the program looks as shown in Fig. 2.42.

2.6.3 Output

The printing of the histogram occurs in procedure *DrawHisto* as we have just noted. This procedure produces a horizontal bar chart or histogram, with the lowest numbered bucket first. The bars are drawn using rectangles, one or more lines wide, with asterisks ('*') defining them. The actual width and the character used to draw the rectangles are defined as the constants *BARLINES* and *VALUEMARK*. The bar length is the number of entries in a given bucket, truncated to the maximum width of the output device (55 columns is appropriate for terminal output; up to 100 or more for printer paper output). The actual width is defined in constant *MAXCOLS* in *DrawHisto*. Each bar is labeled with its bucket number, which is the actual number of values in the bucket, even if the histogram had to be scaled.

Table 2.5. Sample data for histogram program.

78	71	75	91	10	70	83	87	15	85
72	38	61	9	56	6	13	24	23	14
23	58	65	81	16	66	53	46	99	100
52	93	90	72	43	94	33	42	3	80
46	28	14	13	37	65	4	2	20	89
90	65	16	45	6	36	10	46	63	26
29	51	14	96	31	12	62	9	65	26
57	65	73	67	99	71	47	87	85	59
16	69	96	39	29	4	86	96	5	78
68	31	76	63	85	71	96	13	79	69
67	72	45	100	26	19	54	10	92	94
4	2	91	93	51	28	81	34	46	44
10	58	70	73	43	8	54	76	46	100
84	28	62	23	34	65	94	98	24	18
35	59	34	70	75	84	33	89	88	84
93	63	94	44	60	22	88	78	61	11
89	40	48	39	25	2	75	45	83	53
20	8	59	46	60	32	51	82	3	97
56	54	7	53	91	91	14	87	47	37
90	27	11	21	56	79	64	100	64	23
63	56	87	45	66	67	68	69	45	55
58	234	65	34	−123	abc	243	56	76	23
98	12	63	−234	65	87	78	79	80	81
81	80	82	82	83	84				

```
  0  |***************  16
 10  |*********************  21
 20  |*********************  21
 30  |***************  16
 40  |******************  20
 50  |*********************  23
 60  |******************************  31
 70  |************************  24
 80  |******************************  31
 90  |************************  24

Number of out of range values:    11
Number of invalid values:          1
Number of valid values:          227
```

Figure 2.43. Sample output of histogram program using sample data.

Table 2.5 is a sample set of input data for the program. Normally one value is given on each card or line, but Table 2.5 shows the data in a more compact form. The program expects the file to contain one data item per line.

Note that there are some out-of-range items in the data and an illegal character string *abc*. These are counted as invalid data in procedure *GetValue*. Thus only valid data items are used in accumulating the bucket totals. The output of the program, using the data of Table 2.5, is shown in Fig. 2.43. The complete program is shown in Fig. 2.44.

Figure 2.44. Histogram drawing program.

```
program HISTOGRAM (input, output);
{
DESCRIPTION:   Histogram drawing program. Produces a horizontal bar chart of the counts
               of legal values, grouped into equal interval ranges.
INPUT:         A number of values (from the standard input) entered one per line.
OUTPUT:        Histogram of values, grouped into number of groups specified in the
               program constant MAXGROUPS.
AUTHOR:        L. Miller
VERSION:       3.0
}
```

(continued)

Figure 2.44 (continued)

```
const
  GROUPRANGE      = 10;                {range of values in each group}
  MAXCOLS         = 55;                {histogram output width}
  MAXGROUPS       = 10;                {number of value groupings}
  MAXVALUE        = 99;                {largest legal value}
  MINVALUE        = 0;                 {smallest legal value}
type
  GROUPINDEX      = 0..MAXGROUPS;
  BUCKETARRAY     = array [GROUPINDEX] of integer;
  VALUETYPE       = (INRANGE, OUTOFRANGE, ILLEGAL);
  LEGALVALUE      = MINVALUE..MAXVALUE; {legal value range}
  COUNTER         = 0..maxint;
  COUNTERARRAY    = array [VALUETYPE] of COUNTER;
var
  valuecount      : COUNTERARRAY;      {grouped values counter}
  value           : LEGALVALUE;        {current input value}
  valuebuckets    : BUCKETARRAY;       {count errors of each type}


function GetValue (var value : LEGALVALUE; var valuecount : COUNTERARRAY) : boolean;
{
Reads in the next value from the user. Returns true if the value is legal and in range, false
otherwise. Updates the value-type counter for the type of value read in. The value read in is
returned in the parameter value. Uses the procedure NEWREADLN, which returns a real; it is
rounded to an integer before processing.
}
var
  inputvalue      : real;              {actual user input from NEWREADLN}
  legalvalue      : boolean;           {errors noted here from NEWREADLN}
  nextvalue       : integer;           {converted to integer}

# include "NEWREADLN.i";

begin
  GetValue := false;                   {assume failure}
  NEWREADLN (inputvalue, legalvalue);
  if not legalvalue then
    valuecount [ILLEGAL] := valuecount[ILLEGAL] + 1
  else begin
    if inputvalue > maxint then
      inputvalue := maxint;            {careful about integer overflow}
    nextvalue := round (inputvalue);
    if not (nextvalue in [MINVALUE..MAXVALUE]) then       {value is out of range}
      valuecount [OUTOFRANGE] := valuecount[OUTOFRANGE] + 1
    else begin                         {value from user is ok}
      value := nextvalue;
      valuecount [INRANGE] := valuecount[INRANGE] + 1;
```

```
        GetValue := true
      end
    end
end;  {GetValue}


procedure Count (value : LEGALVALUE; var valuebuckets : BUCKETARRAY);
{Updates the count of values for the bucket that value belongs in.}
var
  bucket : GROUPINDEX;
begin
  bucket := value div GROUPRANGE;
  valuebuckets [bucket] := valuebuckets[bucket] + 1
end;  {Count}


procedure DrawHisto (valuebuckets : BUCKETARRAY);
{
Draws the histogram, formatting it according to the constants defined for screen width, and
scaling if there are too many values to fit appropriately on the screen.
}
const
  AXISMARK       = '|';              {marks the next axis}
  BARLINES       = 1;               {lines per histogram bar}
  LABELLINE      = 1;               {bar line where label should go}
  LABELWIDTH     = 5;               {width of the label field}
  VALUEMARK      = '*';             {marks the next value}
var
  nextbarline    : COUNTER;
  nextbucket     : GROUPINDEX;
  nextcolumn     : COUNTER;
  mostvalues     : COUNTER;
  scale          : real;


  function FindMax (valuebuckets : BUCKETARRAY) : COUNTER;
  {Determine which bucket has the most values, and returns the number of values in the bucket.}
  var
    mostvalues     : COUNTER;
    nextbucket     : GROUPINDEX;
  begin
    mostvalues := 0;
    for nextbucket := 0 to MAXGROUPS do
      if mostvalues < valuebuckets [nextbucket] then
        mostvalues := valuebuckets [nextbucket];
    FindMax := mostvalues
  end; { FindMax }
```

(continued)

Figure 2.44 (continued)

```
begin {DrawHisto}
   mostvalues := FindMax (valuebuckets);
   if mostvalues > MAXCOLS then                    {all values won't fit on a single line}
     scale := MAXCOLS / mostvalues                 {so we need to scale them}
   else
     scale := 1;
   for nextbucket := 0 to MAXGROUPS do
     for nextbarline := 1 to BARLINES do begin
       if nextbarline = LABELLINE then
         write (MINVALUE + nextbucket * GROUPRANGE : LABELWIDTH)
       else
         write (' ' : LABELWIDTH);
       write (AXISMARK);
       nextcolumn := 1;
       while nextcolumn <= round (valuebuckets [nextbucket] * scale) do begin
         write (VALUEMARK);
         nextcolumn := nextcolumn + 1
       end;
       if(nextbarline = LABELLINE) and (valuebuckets [nextbucket] <> 0) then
         write (valuebuckets [nextbucket] : 6);
       writeln
     end
   end; { DrawHisto }

begin {main}
   valuecount [INRANGE] := 0;                       {initialize error counts}
   valuecount [ILLEGAL] := 0;
   valuecount [OUTOFRANGE] := 0;
   while not eof do
     if GetValue (value, valuecount) then
       Count (value, valuebuckets);
   if valuecount [INRANGE] = 0 then
     writeln ('No histogram drawn — there were no valid values')
   else
     DrawHisto (valuebuckets);
   writeln;
   writeln ('Number of out of range values : ', valuecount [OUTOFRANGE] : 7);
   writeln ('Number of invalid values : ', valuecount [ILLEGAL] : 7);
   writeln ('Number of valid values : ', valuecount [INRANGE] : 7)
end.
```

Exercises

1. Consider the following **const, type,** and **var** declarations.

```
const
    MAXLINE              = 80;
type
    SEX                  = (male, female);
    STRING               = array [1..MAXLINE] of char;
var
    bsize                : real;
    grades               : array [ 'a'..'f'] of array [male..female] of integer;
    index                : SEX;
    long                 : STRING;
    m                    : set of char;
    min                  : integer;
    result               : integer;
    stuff                : boolean;
    x                    : char;
```

Given the preceding declarations, determine which of the following are
not legal Pascal statements, and for those that are not, give the reason
why.
a) MAXLINE := result;
b) bsize := MAXLINE **div** 10;
c) result := min/100 * 10;
d) grades[x][index] := min;
e) grades[min][result] := m[x];
f) grades[long[x]][index] := bsize **div** min **mod** result;
g) stuff := (min < result) **or** (min = 0);
h) result := stuff;
i) SEX := male;
j) stuff := (min < result) < (min > result);
k) m := ['a', 'b'] * ['c', 'd', 'b'] + ['e'];
l) min := result * 0.1;
m) max := MAXLINE;
n) result := grades['c'][female] * MAXLINE;
o) x := long[bsize];
p) result := bsize **div** ord(x) + stuff;

2. Any Pascal **for** loop can instead be written using a **while** loop, or a **repeat-until** loop. Similarly, any **while** loop could instead be written using a **repeat-until** loop, and any **repeat-until** loop can be written using a **while**. For each

of the following, assume that i, m, and n have been declared as integers, and procedure S has been declared and doesn't change i, m, and n.

a) Write the following **for** loop using a **while** loop:

> **for** $i := m$ **to** n **do**
> S;

b) Rewrite the following **while** loop using a **repeat-until** loop:

> **while** $(m < n)$ **do begin**
> S;
> $m := m + 1$
> **end**;

c) Rewrite the following **repeat-until** loop using a **while** loop:

> **repeat**
> S;
> $m := m + 1$
> **until** $m > = n$;

3. One extension to the **for** loop would be the ability to "step" up the index more than a single unit at a time. Write the Pascal statements to implement the following pseudo-Pascal loop, remembering that the index of a **for** loop cannot be changed inside the loop.

> **for** $i := m$ **to** n **by** c **do**   {pseudo-Pascal}
> S ;

This statement means that i is initialized to m, and is incremented by c each time through the loop. Statement S is executed until i is greater than n.

4. Repeat the previous exercise, assuming the **to** was changed to **downto**.

5. One extension to the Pascal **case** statement would be the ability to specify a range for each case as well as an otherwise clause to be executed when none of the cases specified was true. Rewrite the following pseudo-Pascal loop as an **if-then-else** statement, assuming *next* is type char.

> **case** *next* **of**   {pseudo-Pascal}
>   'a', 'e', 'i', 'o', 'u'   : *writeln*('Vowel');
>   'b'..'d', 'f'..'h',
>   'j'..'n', 'p'..'t',
>   'v', 'x', 'z'   : *writeln*('Consonant');
>   'y'   : *writeln*('Sometimes both')
>   *otherwise*   : *writeln*('Not a letter')
> **end**

6. What does the following program produce as output? (*Hint*: Try to come

up with the answer by hand-tracing the program before typing in to see what it does.)

```
program SCOPING (input,output);
var
  a,b,c : integer;
  procedure test (var a : integer; x : integer);
  begin
    x := a;
    c := x − a;
    a := 75;
    writeln('Test: a = ', a, ' b = ', b, ' c = ', c)
  end;  {test}

  function what(huh : integer; var blah : integer) : integer;
  begin
    c := huh * b;
    blah := huh + huh;
    writeln('What: a = ', a, ' b = ', b, ' c = ', c);
    what := x − (3*blah)
  end;  {what}

begin     {main}
  a := 10; b := 20; c := 30;
  b := what(c, c);
  test(a, b);
  writeln('Main: a = ', a, ' b = ', b, ' c = ', c)
end.
```

7. Many programs spend at least part of their time either searching or sorting. Write a Pascal function called *find* which has three parameters: (1) an array to search, (2) the number of elements in the array, and (3) the value of the element you wish to find. If this value is found somewhere in the array, *find* returns the first position where it was found; otherwise, it returns an impossible position. You may determine the type of the elements in the array that *find* searches—it should be trivial to change this function to work with a different type.

8. The preceding *find* function only finds the first occurrence of the element searched for, and it always searches from the first element of the array until it finds the element or discovers that the element is not there. Modify *find* to have slightly different parameters; instead of the parameter stating the number of elements in the array, *find* should have two parameters that tell *find* where to start and stop searching in the array. How can this *find* be called so it behaves identically to the original *find*?

9. Write a Pascal procedure *count* which uses the *find* function written in the

previous exercise to count the number of occurrences of a given value in an array.

10. Write a Pascal function *TwoDimFind* which searches a two-dimensional array for a particular value and returns the row and column indexes where the value is found. Since a function may only return a single value, you must come up with a mapping of the row-column positions into a single value. Callers of *TwoDimFind* must then break up the single returned value into the row and column positions in the array. You may assume the existence of the function *find* previously mentioned in the exercises.

11. [PROGRAMMING PROJECT] Write a Pascal word counting program *WORD-COUNT* that reads the Pascal standard input file and writes out the number of lines, the number of words, the number of characters in the file, the number of control-characters, and the number of upper- and lower-case letters. What might this program be useful for?

12. Extend the word-counting program of the previous exercise so that it also computes and writes out the average length of a word, the average length of a line, and the number of characters in the longest line in the file.

13. [PROGRAMMING PROJECT] Write a program *AGES* which reads records from a file into an array, keeping the array in sorted order. (You may use one of the sorting methods in Chapter 1.) Assume the following variable declarations:

```
const
    MAXPEOPLE               = 500;
    MAXSTRING               = 30;
type
    STRING                  = array [1..MAXSTRING] of char;
    PERSON                  =
        record
            age             : integer;
            name            : STRING
        end;
var
    people                  : array [1..MAXPEOPLE] of PERSON;
```

The array should be kept in sorted order by the *age* field of each entry, with the lowest *age* as the first element in the array. When all records have been read in, write out the ages and names in order, starting with the youngest first. Part of this program needs to read the ages and names into the *people* array. Your program should behave reasonably when unexpected input is presented.

14. [PROGRAMMING PROJECT] Write a Pascal program that reads its input (a series of lines containing the sequence: any number of spaces, an operator

(either ' + ', ' − ', '*', or '/'), any number of spaces, and another integer) and prints out the result of the operator applied to the two integers. The program should verify that the input has the correct syntax and print out appropriate error messages. For example, with the input line 4*6, the program should print out the result 24. Be certain that your program handles overflow and division by zero. (This is a very simple calculator program.)

15. Extend the previous exercise to handle lines that have more than one operator. For example, lines such as 5 + 6 − 1 + 4 should be acceptable. Precedence of operators is strictly left to right. Again, validate the input before attempting to do the calculation, and be certain that overflow and division by zero are properly handled.

16. Extend the previous program to allow simple (one letter) variables. The line

$$a = 3*7 + 4$$

should assign the value 25 to the variable a without a result printed. The value of a is printed by a line containing only the variable name. Make sure to convert upper-case letters to lower-case.

17. Extend the previous program to allow multiple expressions per line separated by semicolons. The line

$$a = 3*4 + 5; b = a − 5; b$$

should print out 12. Any number of expressions should fit on a line. You can decide whether to abandon the line when an error is found, or to continue.

18. Many critics of Pascal feel the lack of built-in character string manipulation is a major drawback to the language. However, the user may implement many of these functions easily. Assuming Pascal had a data type *STRING*, the following procedures and functions would make life easier for the average Pascal programmer:

> **function** strcmp (a: STRING, b : STRING) : integer;
> {
> Returns zero if string a is equal to string b, any positive integer if string a is lexicographically greater than string b, and any negative integer if a is lexicographically less than string b.
> }

> **function** strlen (a : STRING) : integer;
> {Returns the length in characters of string a.}

> **procedure** strcpy (**var** a : STRING, b : STRING);
> {Copies the contents of the string in a, into the string b.}

Write these functions and procedures, assuming you have created your own data type STRING with the following declarations:

```
const
    MAXSTRING          = 80;
type
    STRING             =
        record
            str           : array [1..MAXSTRING] of char;
            len           : integer      {no. of valid chars in str}
        end;
```

19. Many useful programs can be written that are really quite small. They perform a simple transformation or calculation on their inputs that otherwise would be clumsy to do by hand or with a more elaborate text editor. The next few exercises suggest a series of small utility programs that can add to the usefulness of any interactive operating system. Many of these tools already exist, but it is instructive to see how they might be written, and to try writing them yourself.
    a) Write a program *HEAD* that prints out the first N lines of a file (N should be around 10–20).
    Write a program *TAIL* that prints out the *last* N lines of a file (N again should be around 10–20).
    b) Write a string searching program *STRSEARCH* that asks the user for a string. The program then searches an input file for all occurrences of that string, printing the entire line and the line number where the string is found. If your operating system allows for run-time naming of files, request the name of the file from the user also. Otherwise, assume a standard name for the input file, such as *inputfile!*

    You will have to make some assumptions about the maximum length of the string to be searched for, and the maximum length of each input line in the input file. What should be done on lines that are too long?
    c) Extend the utility of the sorting routines of Chapter 1 so that strings can be sorted. Use the technique to write a program *STRSORT* that sorts the lines in a text file. As in the previous program, make some assumptions about the maximum length of the input lines. (*Hint:* Two arrays may be compared in Pascal if they are the same type. Thus two strings can be compared.)

d) Write a program *UNIQUE* that removes duplicate lines from its input, printing only the first occurrence of each line. Provide an option for *UNIQUE* so that only duplicate lines are printed (i.e., the second and on occurrence of each line).

PROGRAM DESIGN
AND DEVELOPMENT

PROGRAM SPECIFICATION
AND DESIGN

3.1   Program Building Process

In this chapter we begin the specification and design process for a program — an interactive function plotter — that we will develop through the rest of Part II. We will complete the implementation in the next two parts. The methods we use to develop (design, code, test, verify, and so on) this program are given such names as "Top-Down Design," "Step-Wise" or "Hierarchical Refinement," "Levels of Abstraction," and "Structured/Modular Programming." They all in fact derive from a common theme: that programming is a complex and difficult problem-solving activity, and that the most effective way for people (you and me) to solve problems is to break them down into smaller and smaller subproblems until we reach a level we *can* solve, and then piece the solution back together so that the overall, larger problem is solved.

The program development process can be thought of as going through at least four phases, some quite distinct, some occurring with feedback from the others, as shown in Fig. 3.1. These phases are: Problem Statement, Functional Specification, High-Level design, and the Coding-Integrate-Test cycle.

It is from the domain of problem solving, and our ability to handle complexity (which is not too great!), that many of these current ideas in program design and programming techniques find support. In this chapter, we develop program design techniques and program coding techniques that are consistent with well-known problem-solving methods. As a result, the programming effort becomes a more organized one for us as programmers.

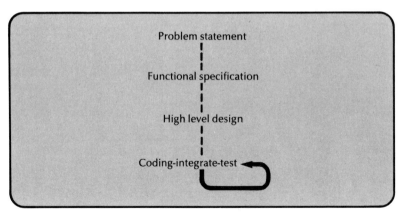

Figure 3.1. Simple diagram of program development cycle.

Problem statement

Functional specification

High level design

Coding-integrate-test

Another important reason for strict design and coding discipline is that certain formal techniques in program-correctness proofs and program verification are simpler when our structures are reduced and simplified.

Of course, the program design and development process is much more complex, and interesting, than what might be implied in a simple four-step diagram. We will try to create a program building process that has as its major effect the reduction of uncertainty on our part, as programmers, in the programming process. For many new programmers, this is perhaps the most important reason for studying, and *writing*, large programs of a wide and diverse nature: that sense that there are techniques, which usually work, that allow us to get a handle on complexity. We start the process of program building by looking at the first two stages of the program building cycle: problem statement and specification.

3.1.1 Problem Statement and Specification

Following the four-step program development cycle we'll begin the process of developing a complete, useful, and fairly substantial program: an interactive function plotter. We start with the following, fairly high-level (that is, highly ambiguous), problem statement, and then present a more detailed program specification.

Problem Statement: We would like to build a function plotter. The function plotter should allow the user to enter an equation of the form $y = f(x)$. For example, f could be a polynomial in x or a trigonometric function, but it must be a function of a single real variable x. The plotter then plots the function within an appropriate range of x and y values.

This problem statement is really rather vague. For example, must the function plotter be interactive or may the equation be entered via cards or a file? How should the output look? Should we plot to a terminal, to a line printer, to a special-purpose plotter, or should we be able to plot to many different devices? Should we do automatic scaling in x and y, or must the user specify scaling and range of plotted values? We also might want to begin asking implementation questions: How shall the data be represented? What is the maximum number of x, y pairs that can be plotted? What kind of response time do we require? Must the output be in a form that is compatible with other programs?

Of course, these and many other questions ultimately will be answered by the time the program is finished. It is desirable that we answer as many as possible before we begin the design phase, but some (relatively low-level) decisions will not be made until we actually begin coding or until we build a prototype system to test some of our ideas.

We need to specify more precisely what our function plotter should do; we need a *functional specification*. Specification development is an essential part of the overall program development process. After all, we cannot write a program to do X, unless we know what X is! But writing a specification is just one phase of the overall programming process. A functional specification should contain at least the following:

- What the program does
- The inputs expected; the processing; the outputs
- The user interface and command language forms
- Sample scenarios involving user interaction; samples of input and associated output
- The program's response to errors
- Performance criteria: response time, accuracy, storage needs

Note that the specification need not, and in fact should not, go into implementation level details. It specifies the functionality of the program and any external requirements on response time, memory requirements, and so on. It discusses, as completely as possible, *what* the program does; it does not indicate *how* the program is to accomplish these tasks. In general, specification development can be a long and elaborate process. It is not unusual in large software projects for the specification writing to take a year or longer. During the development of the specification, prototype software may also be written as a means of validating new, untried system components. We will not follow a formal specification methodology or use a formal specification language. Rather, we view the writing of a specification as an opportunity to express our ideas of what the program is to accomplish. In addition, the specification indicates the form of the input and output, the user interface, and user command language.

Often a specification for a program is given to us; it is dictated by the person or group that needs a program written. Usually our job as programmers is to take the specification and create the working program. However, the writing of a specification is often done in collaboration with prototype development, and the programming group can and does have input into the specification.

Plotter functional specification

As an example of an informal specification, we will create one for the interactive function plotter. The plotter should meet the briefly stated requirements of the problem statement. A brief functional specification for our interactive function plotter is as follows:

Input	Input is a character string representing a function of the single real variable x. The user types the function on one line of the interactive display. The function may contain the usual mathematical operations of addition ($+$), subtraction ($-$), multiplication ($*$), and division (/). The input also may contain the trigonometric functions *sin* and *cos*. The exponentiation function (e^x, indicated *exp*) and the natural logarithm (*ln*) are also to be supported. Operations may be nested to an arbitrary depth by parentheses. The usual operator precedence holds. Numbers are entered as reals, with or without a decimal place. Unary minus (e.g., -13.3) is supported. The expression may contain only the maximum number of characters that are on one line on the display. Individual numbers, functions, and operators may be separated by zero or more blanks.
Output	The output consists of a graph of the function, accurately plotted to the resolution of the output device. The plot goes from the minimum to the maximum x values specified by the user. The plot is scaled in y so that the minimum and maximum y values are plotted. The initial output device to be supported for plotting is a 25-line by 80-column CRT. x- and y-axes are included in the plot: the x-axis along the bottom of the screen and the y vertically along the left edge. [Both axes are labeled at appropriate intervals with their values.]
User Interface	The screen is divided into multiple areas, as shown in Fig. 3.2. The top area is the command and function entry area. In this area, the user enters instructions to the plotting program, indicating the function that he or she would like the

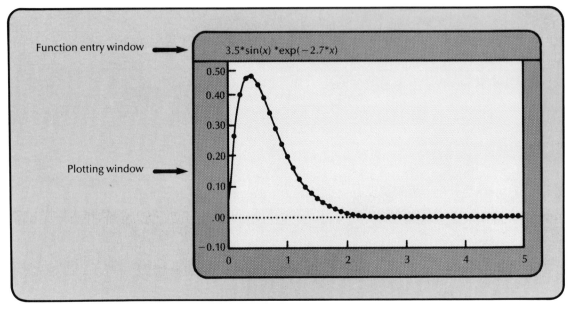

Function entry window ➞

3.5*sin(x) *exp(−2.7*x)

Plotting window ➞

Figure 3.2. Screen layout for the function plotter.

program to perform. This area is also used as a system feedback area, giving prompts and brief error messages. The top line of the screen is also the function entry line. The user types the function on this line when the system is in function entry mode. The remainder of the screen is the plotting area. Function plots occur in the plotting area.

Commands   Commands are single letters of a mnemonic nature. Commands are entered at the command entry/system feedback area. In the case of an illegal or unrecognized command, the system provides an appropriate feedback message in the feedback window and allows the user to reenter the command.

Functions   Enter function; change parameters.

Error Handling   When the user enters an illegal function, he or she is given a brief error message noting that an error has occurred. The user remains in function entry mode.

Modes   The user is usually in function entry mode. At the start, the user is prompted for a function to be plotted. After the function has been successfully parsed, the user is prompted for the range of x values to be plotted (minimum and maximum x). Then, after the table of values has been generated internally, the user is given the minimum and maximum y values and prompted for changes. The plot is then drawn to the screen.

The specification for a particular program need be no larger than is appropriate. For smaller programs, it serves as a useful guide to the design and coding processes. In fact, many of the decisions about the functions of the program — the user interface, the command language, and certainly the lower level implementation details — are not made until the program is being coded. Nonetheless, for most programs, and even for student programs, the value in developing a specification comes from both focusing on our needs early and providing a useful skeleton from which we can begin the program design process.

3.2   The Design Process

A builder starts out to build a new house; a construction crew begins the building of a bridge; an automobile factory starts the assembly of a new car; a programmer begins writing a program to plot functions. Among other things that these activities have in common, they are almost always doomed to drastic, bizarre, and catastrophic failure unless time, attention, and careful thought have been applied to the design of the structures — from the overall way in which all of the components will function, to the intermediate level of how various components will interconnect, to the lowest level details about the physical nature of the interconnections, the size, and makeup of the structures, the colors and finishes, and so on. The programming process also requires a design process, just as more mechanical tasks do, and for many of the same reasons. Obviously building a bridge or constructing a house or car requires designs and plans from which to work. We would be rather surprised if we learned that our house was built without any plans, but rather was put together by a builder based on previous experience and his or her knowledge of how various parts ought to function. What we could end up with is a structure that works perfectly on level ground in a moderate climate — how will it function if we live in the mountains with severe winters?

The obvious need to design physical structures translates into a programming corollary: design before you code! We may define program design as the process of converting a specification into the outline of a program's structure. This means that we must elaborate the data flow, the control flow, the abstract objects, and the data structures within a program. In addition, we must do this in such a way that the overall goals of good program structure are maintained; the design should lead to a program that is modifiable, efficient, and reliable. Design involves a series of refinements in the program's structure, each level of refinement providing more detail about the program's internal workings. At each level of refinement, however, we deal with objects and actions in an abstract way, independent of the actual implementation on a real processor. Of course, at some point, we must concern ourselves with the realities of an actual machine, display, or programming language (that is, the environment of our program). In fact, these notions are usually present even at the highest, most abstract, levels of design. But, as we will see later in this chapter when we design the interactive function plotter, we try to avoid any environment-dependent decisions for as long as possible.

3.2.1 Building the Design

To reduce problem complexity we pursue a decomposition strategy. We decompose a problem into (relatively) independent modules (by module, we mean a collection of routines, procedures, functions, and so on, with a related set of tasks or functions to perform). We say "relatively independent" since the degree of connection between modules will vary from application to application.

Problem decomposition has advantages beyond reducing program complexity. For team projects, decomposition allows an appropriate assignment of work to individuals or subgroups. The design and implementation strategies pursued in this book lead to decreased interdependence among modules. The strategies foster greater encapsulation of design decisions in as few routines as possible. This has a number of advantages, including easier program writing, ease of modification and extension, portability, and program verification. As we develop decomposition techniques we will see how each of these notions is influenced positively by breaking complex problems into simpler subproblems. One of our primary guidelines for decomposition and for defining a function is one of independence: Is it possible for the routine to exist, not as a procedure or function, but as a separate *program*?

Our task as program designers is to take the program's specification and convert it into a program structure that satisfies two major constraints: the requirements of the specification, obviously, and the requirements of good program design! This reemphasizes the purpose of design: to build an understandable description of the program and also to describe how the program will work.

In describing how the ultimate program works, we focus on a number of critical issues in the program building process: the control flow (that is, the modules in a program, broken down into small functional units, and their relation to each other), the data flow (that is, the communications between modules — the input and output data of each module), and eventually, the specifics of the data structures and algorithms. Since the purpose of design is to build the structure, the lowest level details (such as data structure and algorithm choices) are made only when the overall design is completed.

Design is a creative, intellectual process that often requires many iterations to complete, moving from a high-level description through finer and finer elaborations of details. As details become clearer, changes in the top-level descriptions may be needed.

By the way, we do not necessarily get "better" programs by using a top-down design strategy. What we do get, as evidence and experience have shown, are programs that are developed more quickly, at lower cost, and that are more reliable. We rely on programs to meet their specifications. If a program can be produced faster with less time in verifying, testing, and debugging, then we should make the effort to incorporate the techniques that lead to these kinds of programming efficiencies. The techniques that we develop in the next chapters are not designed to increase program efficiency in terms of execution time and storage requirements. Rather, programmer efficiency and program modifiability, extensibility, and reliability are characteristics that are improved by modern structuring techniques.[1]

At this point we can begin to develop specification, design, and even coding guidelines that will be useful in the program development cycle. Virtually every program that we write teaches us to write better code (sometimes because of hard lessons learned on what *not* to do). Perhaps one of the most important lessons is to avoid making decisions as long as possible. We want to avoid specific implementation or device-dependent decisions during the design phase. Chapter 5 elaborates on guidelines for writing

---

[1] See Brooks, F. P., Jr., *The Mythical Man Month: Essays in Software Engineering*, for the first systematic discussion of what good and bad program structuring (and organizational structuring) can do for the efficiency of the program creation process.

subroutines and deciding what should be coded directly and what should be packaged as a subroutine.

3.2.2 Designing the Program Hierarchy

Given a specification of a program we can use a number of techniques to build a design. One way is to look at the tasks in a hierarchical manner. Just as if we were constructing an outline for a paper, we begin by stating the overall goal of the program and then successively decompose the problem into subproblems, which, combined, solve the overall problem. Such a process is called functional decomposition, and it represents a process known as top-down design. As a simple example we might try building the design for a program to compute a business' weekly payroll. At the highest level, this program is represented by the hierarchical diagram in Fig. 3.3.

To process the payroll, we first need to compute gross pay; state, federal, and local taxes; and any other deductions. Then we must apply these deductions to calculate the net pay, update the employee's records and the company's books, and finally, print the checks. This next level of refinement of the program's design is indicated in the refinement of the program hierarchy diagram, shown in Fig. 3.4.

Figure 3.4 shows the modules that are called by the main payroll program. It also has an implied control structure: top to bottom, left to right. That is, the problem is decomposed into independent modules that are connected only by data that flows, one way, from one module to the other. Viewed this way, each of the modules in Fig. 3.4 is a black box that takes input data, performs some transformation on that data, and produces output data. The output of one function is then available to become the input of another. Control is sequenced by the main program. In turn, routines that are only needed by one module are defined under that module, and their control is sequenced by the routine where they are defined.

We continue in this manner, decomposing higher level modules into collections of lower level routines. When do we stop? We stop when we

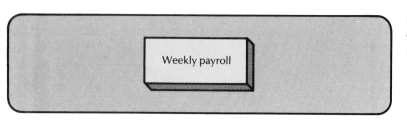

Figure 3.3. Highest level description of a weekly payroll program.

Weekly payroll

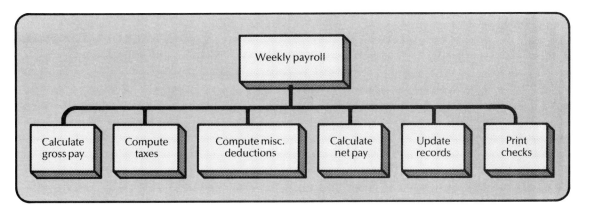

Figure 3.4. Next level of refinement in payroll program design.

have reached a point at which we could write code to implement a module, without necessarily wanting to define lower level routines. We stop when we feel we have sufficient explanatory power in the design. A design may require a number of iterations until we are satisfied that it correctly reflects the program's requirements.

In Fig. 3.4, we noticed a module labeled Update Records, but there is no box for getting the records. To compute an employee's gross pay, taxes, and miscellaneous deductions, we obviously need to get the employee's records fairly early on. In Fig. 3.5, we extend the design by adding a new module, Get Records, to reflect this change. The hierarchical design is complete to the levels shown, but we cannot begin coding yet for two reasons: further decompositions are needed in some of the modules, and we have not shown how modules communicate with each other (that is, the data flow in the structure is not shown).

3.2.3 Designing the Program's Data Flow

Since we are building modules as functional elements or transducers, we need to know the inputs required for each and the outputs generated. So for each module we will use a simple black box input-module-output diagram to show the inputs and outputs. For example, in Fig. 3.5, there is a module labeled Compute Federal Tax. Independently of all other modules in the program, we can decide the information necessary to compute federal income tax: We need employee-specific information (single, married, or head of household; number of deductions; and gross pay), and we need the federal tax tables. In Fig. 3.6(a), we show the required inputs to Compute Federal Tax.

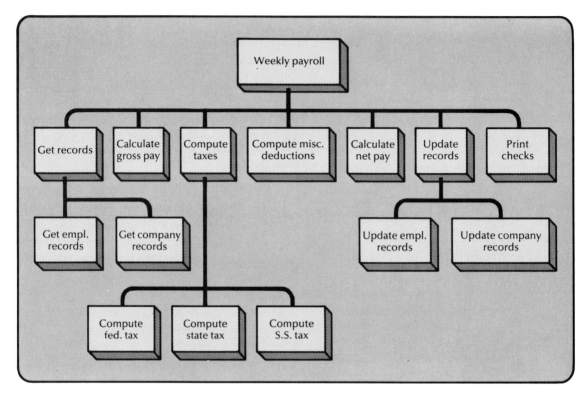

Figure 3.5. Next level of refinement of the design of Fig. 3.4, including the addition of the new module *Get Records*.

Figure 3.6. (a) Inputs needed for *Compute Federal Tax*. (b) Outputs from *Compute Federal Tax*. (c) Inputs and outputs connected to *Compute Federal Tax*.

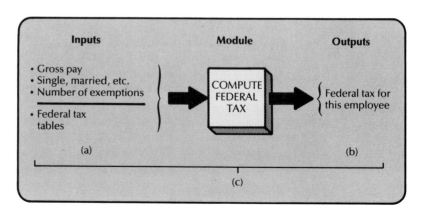

After processing, we have updated the employee's information (now, in addition to gross pay, we also show the amount of federal tax to be deducted), and we have increased the total amount of taxes to be withheld from all employees. We update both the check printing log and the payroll summary information. The outputs are shown in Fig. 3.6(b). And in Fig. 3.6(c), we show the inputs and outputs connected to the module.

After producing data flow diagrams for each of the modules in the design, we may need to iterate on the design to be certain that the data for each module is available. For example, in the payroll program this was necessary because, when we define the data required for a given module, we may not notice that a module later in the program's execution needs information that only an earlier routine can provide. In computing federal tax withholding, it is not obvious that we will need to accumulate the federal tax withheld from all employees until we look at the module that updates the general ledger.

Why not update the general ledger right then? The answer is important, one that deserves some time and consideration. We briefly mention the reasons here and elaborate on them in Chapter 4. First, such an operation might be expressly forbidden in the program's specification, or it may not make sense to do the particular operation at this point. But a more organizational reason for not doing the ledger updating when computing the tasks is *module independence* and *module coherence*. Briefly, these mean that we want our modules to be *independent* of other modules in the program. They take their inputs, perform the requisite processing on them, and produce their inputs, with the only connection being the data flow and the control sequencing. And by *coherence* we mean that a module performs a single, simple, logically complete task. In words, a single module should be describable by a simple English sentence.

We want our programs to be written with modules with these characteristics because these characteristics enhance the entire program development, coding, testing, and debugging process. They also lead to programs that have good life-time properties — maintenance, enhancements, and transporting to other environments are all simplified.

3.3 Function Plotter — The Top-Level Design

Now that we have a preliminary specification for a function plotter, and some overall ideas of the design process, we begin its design, using the techniques of the previous section. Our main considerations will be to *avoid decisions* and to indicate actions and objects in a way that is independent of any particular environment, especially independent of any underlying data representations. Specifically what kinds of decisions do we avoid? We delay as long as possible decisions relating to:

Environment	Processor; language; printer; terminal; graphics; character CRT.
Data Structures	Character arrays; integers; reals; arrays; linked lists.
Algorithms	Space/time tradeoffs; error analyses.
User Interface	Card input; screen management; feedback.
Error Handling	Stop; allow corrections by user; ignore this case; try to fix up.

At some point, of course, we must make these decisions, but we should avoid them as long as possible. We encapsulate our decisions as much as possible in separate procedures, whose implementation details are transparent to the rest of the program. To avoid decisions that will lock in choices, we will design our program and its structure to make calls upon generic routines. We discuss these decisions in terms of the function plotter.

For *environment* decisions, we make no assumptions about the nature of the processor the program will run on, nor of the language in which the program will be written. In addition, for the function plotter design we might initially assume that the program should work with input and output involving the terminal, but that procedures will be written that isolate terminal-specific components, so that with only minor changes, ouput could go to a high resolution plotter, to a simple graphics terminal, or to a high-quality color graphics terminal, if these devices are available. Normally these choices are included in the specification that we must implement. However, many environment (and other decisions) contained in the specification may have implementation alternatives.

Data structure decisions require further knowledge of available structuring alternatives, which we discuss in Part III. There we present linked structures, trees, graph representation techniques, and other structures that form a group of important and useful representations. After studying that material, we will be in a better position to make reasonable choices about the data representations.

User interface issues involve what the user sees on the screen, how the data should be presented, and what the user tells the system — the command language design. Ultimately we have to choose some method of allowing the user to indicate to the program what he or she wants done. The command language form can facilitate or hinder interaction. As with most of our design decisions, the command language interpreter will be contained within a single module or procedure, and should the choice prove unsatisfactory, we need only change that one module.

Finally, *error handling* must be viewed as a separate item to which we should give appropriate attention. A number of errors can occur in an interactive program. These include user errors, data and processing errors, and old-fashioned program bugs! Decisions about error handling require knowledge of the facilities to trap errors available in the language and run-time environment, and they also involve aspects of the user interface. We emphasize that we design for errors right from the beginning. That is, our design will be based on two assumptions: users are likely to make errors in their use of the program; and our program's internal operation is likely to contain bugs!

3.3.1 Function Plotter Design — Control Flow

The function plotter is designed using a *top-down* or *hierarchical* approach. We may think of the design as going from a fairly high-level description of the solution ("solve problem") to a realization in a programming language (Pascal), and finally, to its machine representation (fortunately this last step is accomplished by the compiler). We'll accomplish the design by using the control and data flow diagrams developed in the previous section. Initially the function plotter design can be characterized by the top-level description:

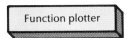

Now this doesn't really tell us very much, so we have to begin thinking about how we want the plotter to perform. The specification can give us a clue, but the internals — the data and control flow and the communication with the outside environment — are up to us as the program's designers. One technique that we can use to design the top-level description of the program's operation is to reflect on how we would go about plotting a function if we were to do so by hand.

Suppose we wished to plot the function $sin(x)/x$. The first step is to decide on the range of x values, say x_{min} through x_{max}. As an example, let's plot this function from 0 to 10 radians. Now the next thing we'd do is build a table of x,y values that we'll use for plotting, with x running from 0 to 10 (x_{min} through x_{max}). To do this, we need to provide an x increment, Δx, and then we build a table of x and y values, from 0 to 10, with an increment of Δx. Figure 3.7(a) shows the first few values with $\Delta x = 1.0$.

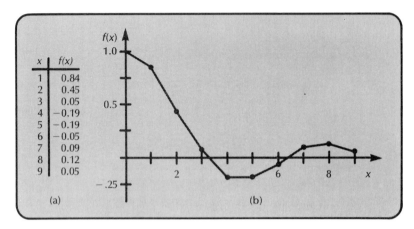

Figure 3.7. (a) Sample values from the evaluation of *sin(x)/x*. (b) Plotted points of table of Fig. 3.7(a). Line segments have been drawn connecting the points to aid visualization.

When we plot the table of values to the display, we must scale the values so that the range of x fits horizontally along the x axis, and the range of y fits the entire display vertically. Of course, we know the range of x in advance because we specified that ourselves. But we don't know the y range in advance; we have to determine that from the data. Inspect Fig. 3.7(a) and note that the range of y for this table of values appears to be from a maximum of about 0.85 to a minimum of about −0.2. We've plotted these few values in Fig. 3.7(b).

The processes needed to actually perform the Function Plotter task according to our specification and the technique of plotting that we've just described can be summarized as:

Build the Table of Values:

- Get the function from the user
- Convert to an appropriate internal representation
- Repeatedly evaluate the internal representation to build the table of values

Plot the Function:

- Scale the table of values by appropriate x and y scaling factors
- Plot the function

In Fig. 3.8 we show this top-down design graphically.

At this level in the functional decomposition of the plotter we could start coding. Our program outline as shown in Fig. 3.9 has a structure very much like that in Fig. 3.8.

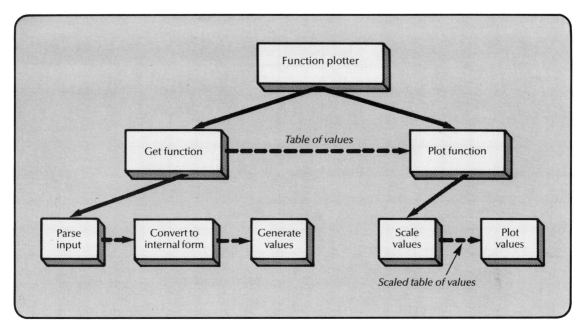

Figure 3.8. Hierarchical program structure for function plotter.

```
program FunctionPlotter (input, output);
{*************************************}
  procedure GetFunction;

  begin
    ParseInput;
    Convert;
    GenerateValues
  end; {GetFunction}
{*************************************}
  procedure PlotFunction;

  begin
    ScaleValues;
    PlotValues
  end; {PlotFunction}
{*************************************}
begin {main}
  while true do begin
    GetFunction;
    PlotFunction
  end
end.
```

Figure 3.9. Top-level code structure for the function plotter.

The main program is written as an infinite loop (**while** *true* **do**), but eventually we will decide on a more appropriate mechanism for terminating the program.

3.3.2 Function Plotter Design — Data Flow

In Section 3.2 we introduced the data flow representation of a program's design by looking at each module in the control flow representation as a black box. In this way, we'll begin the design and description of the necessary data for the modules in the function plotter. As a result of that, we could then continue the process to the point where we've defined the data structures for the entire program, down to the level of Pascal implementation. We're not quite going to do that, though. Instead, we'll describe the data in generic terms without stating explicitly how each data type is to be implemented. We'll describe abstract data objects such as ''table of values'' and ''screen array,'' and we'll note what these objects should contain. The implementation-level description may be different for different programming languages, and it may be different depending on other requirements such as response time and memory space limitations.

Referring back to Fig. 3.8, note that the program, at a high level, is decomposed into three processes: getting the function from the user, generating a table of values, and plotting a table of values to the display. From the discussion of Section 3.3.1, we know that we'll have to parse the *external expression* that the user has entered (entered as a character string) and convert it to a suitable *internal form*. The internal form will be repeatedly evaluated to generate the *table of values*. Finally, the table of values is plotted to the *display*.

Note in this written description that we have described, in very high level terms, the operation of the program, and we also have described the data that is created and communicated in the program. These abstract data structures are:

- The external expression
- The internal representation of the expression
- The table of values
- The representation of the display

Each module in the design is represented in a diagram (Fig. 3.10), showing the inputs needed (one of the four, plus other information the module needs) and the outputs. The module itself is shown as a box with its name inside. Since we can specify the design in the hierarchical representation at a number of levels, we can show the data flows at finer and finer representations of the modules also. At some point this becomes counterproductive because of the effort required to change the design. It's usually sufficient to indicate the information flow at a fairly high level.

The first module is the one that gets the expression from the user. It takes an external form of an expression (the function the user types) and converts it to an internal representation, performing error checking and feedback. So its input is an "external expression," and its output is an "internal expression." In Fig. 3.10 we show the inputs and outputs for this module, and the other modules of Fig. 3.8. (By the way, if you're wondering just what an "internal expression" is, the answer is that we will see two quite different forms. One will be a form known as a post-fix expression discussed in Chapter 9, and the other will be an expression tree, which we develop in Chapter 13.)

In Fig. 3.10 we show the modules as if they were independent entities, which of course they are. But an interesting temporal relationship exists between them, a pipeline of processes: as the inputs for a particular routine become available, that routine is able to perform its appropriate transformation, and then feed its output to the input of the next process in the pipeline.

Later in this chapter, and in Chapter 7, we will look in more detail at the exact requirements needed to make up the internal expression, the table of values, and the internal representation of the screen. At the current very high level of the design, we leave the details unspecified and think of these objects as primitives.

3.4   Piecewise Implementation

The top-level function plotter structure is quite clear at this point. The next stage is to specify the functions to be performed in greater detail. In addition, since this will be an interactive program, we need to specify the user interface in more detail — that is, the exact nature of the command language, the feedback from the system to the user, and the methods for handling incorrect user input. Many of the functions can be implemented with a wide variety of algorithms. In addition, we could specify a number of different command language forms for user input. In both cases, we try to select techniques that work and that we believe are reasonable. We will then encapsulate details of the algorithms within individual procedures. Later, if we find our choice needs refining because it is too slow, uses too much space, or is not extendable to new applications, we need merely change the individual procedures with minimal effect on the rest of the program. We saw an example of this in Chapter 1, where we used a sorting technique to find the median of an array of numbers. As we will see in Part III, there are other, more efficient sorting techniques that we may use.

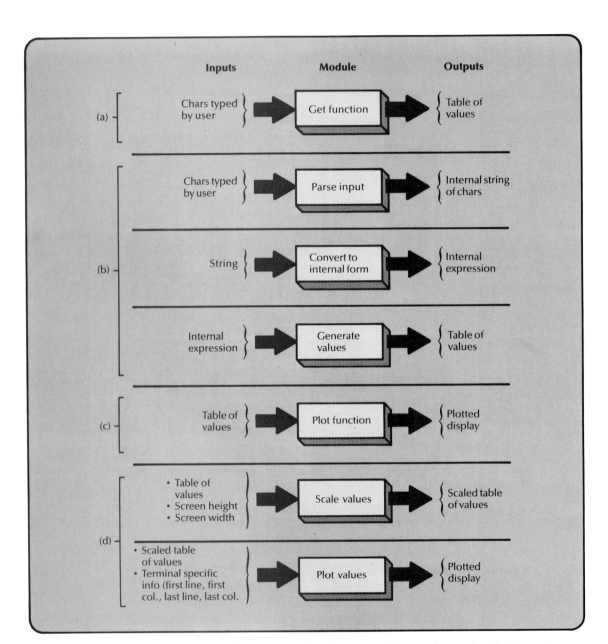

Figure 3.10. Data flow for: (a) *Get Function*; (b) modules under *Get Function*; (c) *Plot Function*; (d) modules under *Plot Function*.

It may seem unusual to attempt to design and write programs before we know thoroughly what we want to do or how to implement all of the algorithms we'll need. We will see, however, that many of the techniques are ones that we will need over and over again — they form a fundamental core of algorithms and techniques we will need for a wide range of programs. Further, it is not unusual to begin work on a program that contains unfamiliar components. Part of our task as programmers is to understand the common, familiar threads of a problem, and to apply or transfer known algorithms to unfamiliar domains.

Let's stop and look at the development process from a broad view. At first we suggested that the program would be written by the act of drawing a hierarchical representation of the program structure and module inter-connections. This was actually fairly straightforward to accomplish, and this simple step of deciding on a program structure is one of the most important ones in helping to ensure the timely, correct implementation of the code. Now, however, we will change our focus, because we must also be able to build, test, and debug a program. To do this, we need a reasonable program development and testing environment. For the function plotter, we have already suggested what that environment should be: an initial screen display and the ability to scale and plot a table of values. We are not quite ready to begin coding these first pieces; in fact, we defer the coding until Chapter 7. What we will do, however, is to suggest a com-munications environment between modules.

The means of communicating between modules comes naturally from our decisions to generate and plot a table of values. The table of values is generated by the function in Fig. 3.8 named Generate Values. That table could be passed to Scale Values as a **var** parameter or as a global variable. However, we could use a different mechanism altogether: "Generate . . ." could write its output as a *file*, then halt! "Scale . . ." could be an entirely different program that reads the file created by "Generate . . . ," transforms it, and then writes another file. Finally, Plot Function could again be another program that reads the file and actually plots the data on the screen.

The value of highly independent modules is now seen: in this case, each module takes an input stream or a file, computes a transformation, and produces an output stream or file. Modules can be written with only very limited knowledge of what other modules are doing. If this were a team project, each module could be assigned to a different member. Since the amount of information each module, and therefore each programmer, needs about others is limited, the opportunity for failure due to incorrect assumptions about data structures, values and types of variables, is greatly reduced.

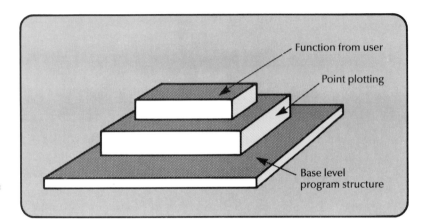

Figure 3.11. Layered design and development structure of the function plotter.

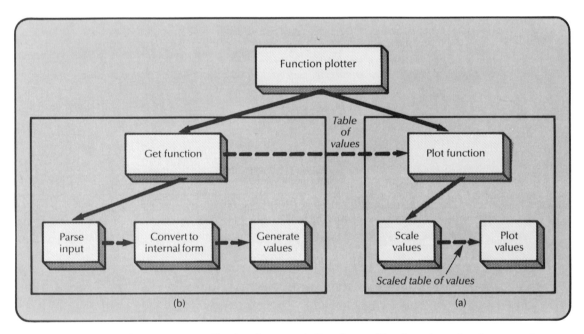

Figure 3.12. Application layers: (a) First layer, *Plot Function*, the first set of modules to be programmed. (b) Second layer, *Get Function*, the second set of modules to be programmed. Dashed lines show data coupling between modules.

Figure 3.13. Control flow for point plotting in the function plotter.

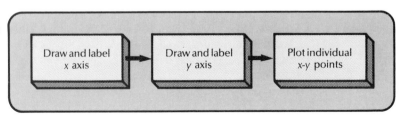

3.4.1 Layered Design

A number of routines in the function plotter can best be handled by data structures and algorithms that we have not looked at yet. How, then, do we approach the design and development of a project that contains greater complexity than we can reasonably handle at this time? The answer is, we'll build the program in layers. Each layer adds to the functionality of the plotter, but the first layer is sufficient to allow us to do real work: plotting functions. The layered notion is illustrated in Fig. 3.11. There we see that the first layer — the bottom or base layer — must be the structure on which the rest will be built. We've shown this program structure in Fig. 3.12, which repeats Fig. 3.8 while highlighting the pieces of the second (middle) and third (highest) layer.

A function plotter makes a nice case study; it has sufficient utility to be a useful tool, so that after we spend a good deal of effort building it, we'll have something useful. It can be built up from smaller pieces and, as each piece is added, the resulting program gains in utility. Most importantly, it provides the motivation for studying and implementing good program structure and design techniques and the algorithms and data structures that will become fundamental to most of the programs you will be involved with from now on.

The first thing a function plotter should do is plot values to an output device. We can do this quite simply, without needing much knowledge of how a function might be entered or how it should be converted to some internal form and evaluated by a program. Just write a little Pascal program to generate a table of x, y values, then pass the table to a point plotter.

So the first thing our plotter will do is plot points! The points will come from a program such as one that computes the values of $sin(x)/x$, the minimum and maximum values of x, and the step size in x entered during run-time, then repeatedly calls on the function $f(x)$, until x_{max} has been exceeded. The function to plot is contained in a function call, so when we want to plot another function, all we need to do is change the function, then recompile and rerun the program.

In Fig. 3.12, the Plot Function node has two subfunctions: Scale Values and Plot Values. Our first application task will be to take a table of values (a data structure that we will have to define more thoroughly), scale it, and plot the points to the display. That will be our first task after setting up the initial screen environment: scaling and plotting a simple table of values. The next layers require data structures and algorithms that we will develop in Part III.

We now have a fairly well established work plan for the further design, refinement, and coding of (at least part of) the function plotter. We'll begin with a "pseudo code," or skeleton program to perform the basic plotting of a simple function. In diagram form this will look like Fig. 3.13.

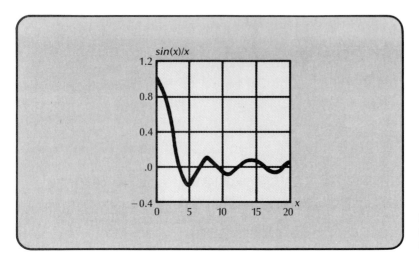

Figure 3.14. Sample output of function plotter — $sin(x)/x$ vs. x.

To draw and label the x axis and the y axis, we must examine the range of the x values and the range of the y values. At this point we do a simple scaling: the smallest value plotted will be x_{min}, and this will correspond to the y axis. The largest value, x_{max}, will be plotted at the right-most position of the x axis. We might try some sample values, plotted by hand, before writing the code to do the plotting. For example, we might try plotting $y = sin(x)/x$, for x from 0.1 to 20 radians in 0.1 radian steps. The plot should look something like Fig. 3.14. Here the axes have been drawn and labeled with appropriate ranges of x and y. Individual x, y points are plotted. The program merely plots points; it does not draw connecting line segments or attempt to fit a smooth curve to the plot. The y-axis ranges between the minimum y value and the maximum.

3.5   Plotting a Table of Values

There are at least four reasons why we want to be able to write (at least initially) a plotter that takes a table of x, y values and plots them:

- Allows for generation of plotting data by other processes
- May allow for reuseability of code
- Reduces the coupling between modules
- Increases module independence

Initially we develop the overall structure, and then the first routines we design are the ones that actually plot points. We'll do this by writing the procedure *plot,* which takes a structure representing the table of values, and plots these. We need to define more precisely what we mean by plotting, and we need to think out the table of values structure carefully. First, however, there are several other topics to cover. The first layer code is presented in Chapter 7.

3.6   Parsing the Function

The process of converting the function to its internal form is known as *parsing.* The parser can accomplish this task by pulling the expression apart and putting it back together as an internal expression. The first of these is known as *lexical scanning,* and the process is called the *scanner.* The purpose of the scanner is to break the input into individual units, or tokens. The second phase, building the internal structure, calls upon the scanner to provide it with the next token in the input, whenever needed. We'll discuss briefly the design of these processes here, but we won't implement them until later chapters.

3.6.1 Lexical Scanning

Parsing is the process of coverting the input into an appropriate internal representation and discovering errors. To parse the function we first need to break the input into recognizable units. By eye, we have no trouble doing this, but the task requires some thought if we are to have the computer do it. The expression

$$sin(x) / \quad x$$

is easily seen to involve the basic units *sin,* left parenthesis (, the function variable x, a right parenthesis), the division operator /, and another instance of the variable x. Additionally, some of the pieces are separated by blanks, others are not.

   Units that have meaning for the function plotter are *variables, numbers, functions, operators,* and *special symbols* (parentheses, etc.). These lowest level meaningful symbols are called *lexical units* or *tokens.* Our first task in parsing the function is to extract individual tokens. A routine to do this is called a *lexical scanner* (the word lexical here indicates that we are interested in extracting meaning from the input string). A *lexicon* is used to indicate the tokens (collections of symbols) that are meaningful. For the function plotter, there are four sets of meaningful tokens in the lexicon:

Numbers	Strings of digits with an optional leading sign.
Functions	The function plotter initially supports the functions *sin, cos, exp, ln* and *sqrt*.
Variables	Any string of alphabetic characters (A . . . Z, a . . . z) that is not one of the built-in functions is considered to represent the function variable (we do not restrict the variable name to be x only — any name may be used, as long as it is not one of the reserved function names).
Special Tokens	These are the single-character operators (+, −, *, and /) and other special symbols (for example, (and)).

The operation of the scanner can be represented as a finite state machine. Such a machine (an idealization of a machine, really) is used to represent the various "states" that a program is in and the possible transitions from one state to another. Initially the machine is in a start state when it begins the job of scanning for the next token in the input string. In this state, the scanner passes over blanks and tabs until a nonblank is found. A nonblank is either an *alphabetic* character (a . . . z), a *numeric* character (0 . . . 9), one of the special symbols (+, −, etc.), end of line, or anything else.

If the first character in the token is an alphabetic, we process the string on the assumption that we have either a *variable* or a *function*. If it is a numeric, we process the string as a *number* (in the same manner as we did in Chapter 1 with *NEWREADLN*). Finally, if it is one of the special symbols, we use that symbol to directly indicate the token. All of this discussion is quite succinctly summarized in Fig. 3.15, a simple diagram form of the lexical scanner process or "machine." The scanner's four legal final states as well as the error state are clearly indicated in Fig. 3.15.

When we are in the "alphabetic" state we gather characters into a string until a blank (or end-of-line, etc.) is found. This string is used to search a table of legal function names. When a match is found, the index of the location is used to index an array which gives the enumerated type associated with the found token. If no match is found, the token is a variable.

3.6.2 Converting to Internal Representation

Converting from the typed form entered by the user to an appropriate internal representation requires that the scanner be able to hand the program the next token in the input whenever needed. The tokens are stored in a

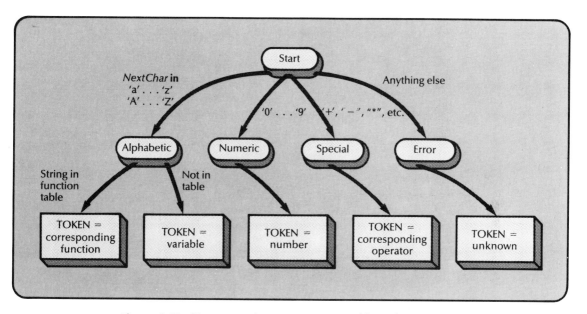

Figure 3.15. Diagrammatic representation of lexical scanner and its transitions.

way which is most efficient for the rest of the program. We could choose from a number of internal representations of the function, but the form we will use initially is the post-fix or reverse Polish notation (RPN, named after the Polish mathematician Lukysicwicz).

Reverse Polish notation is used by some commercially available calculators, and it has the advantage of being parenthesis-free. To perform an operation on two values, we give the values followed by the operation to be performed. Because the operator comes after its operands, it is called "post-fix" notation, as opposed to the usual "in-fix" notation where the operator comes in between the operands. Table 3.1 illustrates a number of in-fix and corresponding post-fix expressions.

Table 3.1. Examples of in-fix and post-fix notation.

In-Fix	Post-Fix
A + B	A B +
A + B + C	A B + C +
A + B * C	A B C * +
(A + B) * C	A B + C *
(A + B) / (C − D) * sqrt (A − B)	A B + C D − / A B − sqrt *

In Chapter 9, we will continue the implementation of the function plotter using post-fix expressions. We will use the post-fix form because that form is simple and quick to evaluate repeatedly.

The post-fix representation of the function is kept internally as a string of tokens. The first implementation layer merely plots points; our second implementation layer will include the post-fix expression entry to the plotter — expressions will be entered in post-fix form. In our top-level structure for the plotter, we note that we must convert the external form of the expression into an internal representation. Because the post-fix form of an equation is simpler to evaluate, the second layer will use the post-fix expression internally, converting numbers and operators to their appropriate tokenized form. Figure 3.11 highlighted the layered implementation. Figure 3.12(b) highlighted the second implementation that we'll pursue in Chapter 9. In that chapter we will see how to evaluate a post-fix expression for a given value of the variable x. As we have seen in the top-level design discussion, the program will generate the table of values internally by repeatedly evaluating the expression for increasing values of x. Finally, in Chapter 13 we'll handle the third-level implementation: converting the more common in-fix expression into an appropriate internal form.

Though we have covered what appear to be a few low-level issues in this chapter, we have in fact avoided the decisions we claimed we would avoid at the beginning. What we have done is to fix the information (data) and control flows of the function plotter via a straightforward control flow representation. We also addressed the issues of algorithm, data structure, and user interface choice in an implementation-independent manner. We have designed the plotter in layers, so that we may implement the design top-down. We'll implement the design in this same layered manner. We first code the overall program structure and the point plotter, a useful program in itself. In Part III, as our familiarity with the appropriate data structures and algorithms increases, we can implement the next layer, the first one in which we parse the function from the user. Finally, when we have further developed the necessary representations, we implement the last layer, the parenthesized in-fix equation parser/plotter.

Exercises

1. A number of terms were introduced in this chapter. For each of the following, give a brief definition and a reason why it is important.
    a) Problem statement
    b) Functional specification

c) Decomposition strategy
d) Device dependence
e) Command language design
f) Error handling
g) Hierarchical design
h) Piecewise implementation

We have introduced the notions of problem statement, functional specification, and hierarchical design. The following exercises will involve writing functional specifications and hierarchical design diagrams given the problem statements. Remember not to worry about low-level details. In later chapters, exercises will involve coding, testing, and debugging programs written from these functional specifications.

2. Write a functional specification and a hierarchical design diagram for a program that: Maintains an address book of names, addresses, and phone numbers. Just as we would do to a written address book, we will want to add new names, remove old ones, change addresses and names as people move or get married, and look up names when we need to make a call or write a letter.

3. Write a functional specification and a hierarchical design diagram for a program that: Plays blackjack. The program should be able to simulate the dealer playing against a number of different players, allow a person to be the dealer against a number of different players, or have a person be the dealer and the program be one of the players. Betting should be allowed, and the program should keep track of players' wins and losses.

4. Write a functional specification and a hierarchical design diagram for a program that: Simulates an extended precision calculator. The user should be able to enter very large numbers and have the program perform addition, subtraction, multiplication, and division on them without losing any precision.

5. Write a functional specification and a hierarchical design diagram for a program that: Solves "pentominoes." The user should be able to describe a board (size and whether or not it has holes in it somewhere) and the pentominoes the program should use to fill the board (how many of each kind are available). The program should then try to find all, or possibly some, of the solutions that cause the given pentominoes to fill up the given board. (There might not be a solution to a given initial situation.)

PROGRAM CODING

4.1   Structured Programming

Early in Chapter 1 we examined two programs that calculated the mean and median of an array of numbers. One we called the "good" program, the other was the "bad" one. In that chapter we gave a brief, informal explanation of why the good is better than the bad. In this chapter, we try to make those ideas more formal by introducing the program coding techniques known as *structured programming*. We can, of course, write atrocious programs using structured programming, but we will have a particularly difficult time writing good ones if we do not adhere to the structuring guidelines.

Simply stated, we encourage a coding style that uses only three *structured* statements. These statement types are:

1. *Sequential operations* (assignment, input, output, normal statement sequencing, and so on).
2. *Conditional* (also called *selection*) (**if-then-else, case**).
3. *Iteration* (**while-do, repeat-until**).

Boehm and Jacopini[1] have shown that these three statement types are sufficient for the implementation of any "flowchartable, well-behaved" program.

In Pascal, these three statement types are realized by the usual sequential control flow, assignment statements, and so on, and by the various control statements: **begin-end, if-then-else, while-do, repeat-until, for-do,** and **case.** These statements allow simple piecing together of program fragments, each fragment having the property of a single entry point and a single exit point. Figure 4.1 shows the semantics of these statements using simple diagrams. Dotted boxes have been drawn around the diagrams to indicate the one-in, one-out nature of each statement type.

The use of structured coding does not imply, of course, that programs are *guaranteed* to be better, simpler, or more comprehensible. However, their usage does give us a way to handle program complexity: by reducing the number of statement types, by ensuring that all statement blocks are single entrance–single exit, we are able to maintain better intellectual control over a program's complexity.

It may seem that these are all the statement types available in Pascal and that we are laboring a point that we cannot violate anyhow. Such is not the case, however, because Pascal supports the **goto** statement. This seemingly innocuous statement has the unfortunate effect of destroying the single entrance–single exit property of statements and blocks, and

[1] Boehm, C., and G. Jacopini, "Flow Diagrams, Turing Machines, and Languages with Only Two Formation Rules," *Communications of the ACM*, May 1966.

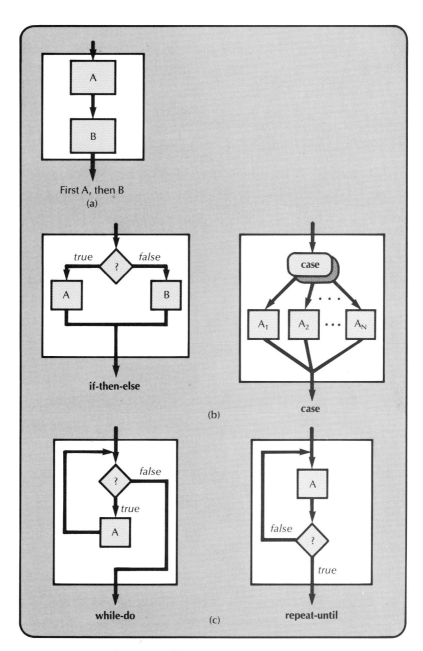

Figure 4.1. Pascal structured statement semantics: (a) statement sequencing; (b) conditional statements; (c) iteration sequencing.

consequently it may make program reading and understanding, debugging, testing, proof, and verification substantially more difficult.

In addition, Pascal variables are global to the block in which they are defined — they are available to any procedure or function declared in that block. As a result, a procedure call may change the values of variables other than those declared in the procedure's parameter list. Such changes to globals are often planned intentionally, since many programs use global flags for status information. Occasionally these changes to globals are accidental: a procedure may have (unintentional) side effects (changes to globals) that can be difficult to detect and that make testing and debugging programs more difficult.

It seems, then, that Pascal gives us just enough rope to hang ourselves. We must protect ourselves even within the highly protected environment of Pascal coding: to do so requires that we eschew the use of **goto**'s, and avoid, to as great an extent as possible, the use of side effects within procedures.

4.2   Coding from High-Level Design

The discussion and the examples in Fig. 4.1 are relatively low-level descriptions of program structure. A program's structure, of necessity, reflects the implementation language's control structures. We have tried to make at least a plausible argument that when it comes to writing code, simplicity of structures is important. We support the basic tendency to want to simplify problems and to understand complexity, by breaking problems down into simpler subproblems. However, the discussion in the previous section was at a level sufficiently low that we might not be able to actually code a large problem design without making a great effort to force the design into the mold of structured programming.

Initially the most difficult task in starting to code seems to be breaking up the design into modules, routines, and the main program control loop. At the highest levels we may write our code to follow the structure in the design quite closely, as we did in Chapter 3. Now we need to decide on an appropriate level of detail for the individual components.

One important coding goal should be device-independent, portable software. Countering these goals are low-level details related to such obstacles as language restrictions, operating system requirements, and hardware specifications. These restrictions suggest the following guideline: the factors in a program that counter portability should be isolated within language-dependent and device-dependent modules. Again, the notion is that changes in the hardware — the computer that the program runs on, the displays used for output, and so on — will require only very modest recoding effort.

A second guideline for module packaging relates to domain-specific requirements. Within any specific problem domain are primitive operations and combinations of primitives that can form a core of program building operations. For example, we have already noted that in a function plotting program, primitives include drawing axes, parsing an input equation, evaluating an equation, and so forth.

Once we have begun defining repetitive actions, domain-specific primitives, and low-level dependencies, we are in a position to further refine a program's structure. These guidelines for packaging primitives and dependencies into appropriate routines require that we identify:

■ Domain-specific primitives
■ Repetitive functions
■ Language-specific obstacles
■ Device-specific obstacles
■ Operating system–specific obstacles
■ Computer-specific obstacles (word size, memory capacity)

4.2.1 Module Characteristics

We have used the term *module* informally to mean a procedure or function, or a collection of procedures or functions, that perform a single job or function. In fact, we want our modules to have a number of characteristics:

■ Cohesiveness
■ Loosely coupled (independence)
■ Parsimony
■ Predictability
■ Small size
■ Proper error handling
■ Abstraction (portable/generalizable/extensible/device-independent)

Cohesiveness

Cohesiveness is a means of expressing the amount of internal binding between elements of a routine. In a sense, it is an informal measure of the way in which we can view a single routine as being a single, whole unit. Our goal is for high cohesiveness. One way to gauge cohesion is to examine the relationships between individual statements or blocks within a module. At the lowest level, statements (or routines, if they are also defined in a

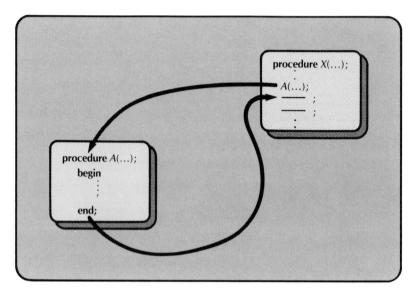

Figure 4.2. Hierarchical relationship between caller and callee.

routine's block) have no relationship with each other. They are grouped together only for the convenience of the programmer, with no regard for their role in the design and structure of the program. At the other extreme, the highest level of cohesion has been called *functional cohesion:* the routine is viewed as performing a single function. We strive for maximum cohesion in our modules.

Independence

An independent module is only very loosely coupled with the other routines in a program. Coupling between modules occurs in at least two distinct ways: control coupling and information coupling. Control coupling represents the structural relationships between caller and callee, as in Fig. 4.2, where procedure X calls procedure A.

Normally, we think of Pascal routines as being quite independent in terms of control, but the existence of the **goto** statement allows control to pass somewhat indiscriminately between routines and the main program. Specifically we may jump out of the middle of a routine via a **goto** statement, without control passing in the more formal call and return mechanisms!

Modules should also be relatively *data-independent* of each other. This implies that we view a routine in a functional sense: it takes input, performs a computation or performs some single task, produces an output (perhaps), and returns control to its caller. Another implication of data independence is that modules make no access to environment data. In other words, all data needed by a routine and returned by a routine are passed as parameters. The advantage is that we never have to worry about unexpected side effects of procedures, and the state of a routine can be described by examining the changes in the parameters. We should remember that these module characteristics lead to code that is "safer." That is, trouble is more likely to occur only within a single module, and so testing and debugging are simpler and lead to greater confidence in the code's correctness. However, we may end up with code that is unnecessarily baroque in its parameter passing, since the notion of global information is an important one that we may wish to use in some programs. As a general rule, however, use argument passing rather than globals for procedures and functions.

Parsimony

Parsimonious modules do their task in the simplest manner possible. They don't engage in coding tricks to save small amounts of memory or small amounts of execution time. Their structure is open and obvious, and clearly follows from the design. As we will see in Part III where we examine program efficiency in a formal way, all the diddling, hand tuning, and saving an instruction here and there won't do much good at all if we have selected a poor algorithm in the first place. In Chapter 1 we saw two algorithms to perform sorting (to find the median of an array of numbers). The second, "bad" program contained an algorithm that was not obvious for a number of reasons. By patient work, it could be turned into a more structured version, so that its working is clearer. But it is still, in general, a poor sorting algorithm; it has the property that sorting time goes up as the *square* of the number of values to be sorted. In Part III we will see sorting algorithms whose computing time goes up not as n^2, but as $n \log_2 n$. The moral is: Don't diddle — make your code simple and obvious, and use the most efficient *algorithm* available for the task.

Predictability

A predictable routine produces the same output with the same inputs. A random number generator, clearly, is not predictable. Neither is a routine that makes use of global variables (which are often used as environment flags). Clearly a predictable routine should be easier to test and debug, and this is another reason for establishing the *desideratum* that all information to and from routines be transmitted as parameters. Later we will discuss three specific situations when we might want to (carefully) use global variables.

Small size

If the module characteristics already discussed are actually observed, small size follows fairly naturally. That is, if a module is cohesive, independent of others, parsimonious, and predictable, it is unlikely to be very large. This is fortunate because human cognition, our ability to read and understand written materials, is quite limited as the length increases. There is no hard and fast rule, of course, about how large a routine should be, but one sheet of paper or one screen full (typically about 25 to 50 lines) is a reasonable guideline. If we think of routines as being written in a book, perhaps two facing pages would be a maximum.

It is not desirable, however, for modules to become too small, since this tends to fragment the code and thus fragment our ability to understand its structure and function. In addition, of course, excessively large numbers of procedure calls can become quite expensive computationally because of the time necessary to initialize and return from procedures.

Error handling

Errors may be handled by the routine itself or by the calling routine. There is often no strong *a priori* reason to insist on one technique or the other. However, the goal of independence would perhaps require that a minimum amount of error flag information be passed between routines, since that increases the control-level coupling. The alternative is that the routine handle the error itself according to a set of guidelines that we'll develop in Chapter 5. Our policy will be that whenever possible, a routine will detect errors, so that there need be no assumptions about correctness of inputs and so on to a module. On the other hand, to reduce mutual dependencies, a lower level module will not, in general, attempt to correct an error. Rather, an error flag will be passed to the caller, which can then take the appropriate action. We will see this in more detail in Part III when we put together data structures and useful routines on them into packages called Abstract Data Types.

Portability

One of the most important changes in coding style and notions of the past few years has been that software solutions to problems (that is, programs) be representative of solutions to a wider class of problems, the specific problem at hand merely being an instance of a more general problem area. Specifically we might ask the following questions of any piece of software we write:

What does it take to generalize the solution to larger or smaller data sets? To data of a different type?

What does it take to extend this program so that it solves other problems from a similar domain? (For example, for our program to find the mean and median, what does it take to find the variance or other statistics?)

What does it take to run this same program on another computer?

What does it take to run this program using a different set of input/ output devices?

What does it take to rewrite this program in another programming language?

4.3   Coding for Testing and Debugging

Good coding style can ease the testing and debugging process. In fact, good style generally leads to fewer bugs in the first place. We can say that good style is not "debugging" (finding and fixing existing bugs), but "anti-bugging" (bugs don't occur in the first place). One purpose of maintaining a strict coding discipline is increased predictability of program behavior. In this section we try to provide a set of guidelines that follow from well-established program development results and from desirable module characteristics of the previous section. A number of studies of the programming process have shown that design and initial coding of a program consume about 20 percent of the total program development cycle; testing and debugging over 80 percent! These results are applicable to large software projects: aerospace applications, large system software, operating systems, and so on. Generally the time spent in testing and debugging is not nearly so large in smaller application program development efforts. However, we should be aware that software implementation effort does not scale up very well — even though personal programs can be written and tested quickly, that is no indication of the efforts required in large projects. Consequently the systematic application of these development techniques may pay off in an easier debugging effort for small, personal progams, and will certainly pay off in large projects.

To increase our ability to debug programs quickly we can use four techniques:

- Use structured programming coding
- Code and test incrementally

- Provide variables trace on procedure entry and exit
- Use debugging aids and tools

Underlying these techniques are a number of assumptions about the way that programs are written, about their longevity, and about their lifetime characteristics. That is, we tacitly assume that the programs we write *will have bugs.* That is a normal, usual, human characteristic. Our programming techniques must provide the support to reduce bugs originally (anti-bugging) and to more easily detect and correct them when they occur (debugging). It is fortunate, also, that the coding techniques that reduce software errors are also those that support the top-down design and implementation notions of the previous sections.

We can think of software errors as having three conceptual sources: internal procedure (module) errors, inter-procedure communication errors, and environment errors. In Chapter 1 we gave examples of the third kind of error. In that chapter we saw that even with code that seems to be correct, interfaces to the outside world must be taken into account to protect us from hardware, data type, and user interface errors. The tools and techniques necessary to protect software from environment errors were seen to involve (at least in the case of programs running in environments that do not provide fault-tolerant interfaces) elaborate input validation on data processed by the program. Internal procedure errors relate to three fault types: the input parameters are not of the correct type; the output parameters of the procedure are not of the correct type; internal processing errors within the procedure.

Inter-procedure communication involves incorrect control flow, calling the wrong procedure from another, and so on. Of course, our programs can make higher level errors. For example, perhaps the program does not meet its specs. This may be related to our inability to understand the necessary algorithms, to inadequate design, or perhaps to inadequate or unavailable hardware or software capability. The coding styles and practices of this chapter should enable us to more quickly implement a design and to more quickly verify (that is, debug) the code.

4.4   Coding Style

We suggest four areas for stylistic guidelines. View these as suggestions, not as iron-clad rules that must be followed. No compiler will check your code to ascertain that you've followed them. Their value is in their consistency and in the constraint of written code to a narrow range of stylistic conventions. They provide, in exchange, the ability to more quickly implement a program or procedure and the ability to more quickly determine the types of variables,

```
program MYSTERY (input, output);        program GOOD (input, output);
const                                   const
   a    = 22;                              pi      = 3.14159;
   b    = 7;                            var
var                                        radius  : real;
   p    : real;                         begin
   c    : real;                            readln (radius);
begin                                      writeln (pi * sqr (radius))
p := a / b;                             end. {GOOD}
   readln (c);                                           (b)
   writeln (p * c * c)
end. {MYSTERY}
                (a)
```

Figure 4.3. Two programs illustrating use of (a) poor names, and (b) well-chosen names.

where procedures are defined, and so on. Additionally they make code more readable and consequently more understandable when it is augmented at some later time.

4.4.1 Naming Rules

Without a doubt, the largest single influence on good coding style comes from selecting meaningful variable and procedure names. Programs can become virtually self-commenting. Consider the "mystery" program in Fig. 4.3(a), and its "clear" counterpart in Fig. 4.3(b). Its function is certainly obscured in the former, while quite clear in the latter. We must remember, however, that just because a variable is named *MinimumValue*, does not make it so! We still must be certain that our code does what our variables and procedures claim it is doing!

To help select names for clarity, Pascal and most modern programming languages provide the valuable feature that names may be of arbitrary length. In addition, many environments allow for mixed-case names (upper- and lower-case). Names can then be constructed as multiple words by capitalizing the first letter of each word and removing blanks.

By using well-chosen variable names, we gain the advantage of self-documenting code. By using named constants and types, we gain the flexibility to make changes in sizes of arrays, tables, and so on merely by changing the constants used to define their bounds. Suppose we wish to declare a new type *STRING* to be a 20-character array. The declarations might be:

```
type
   STRING        =  array [1..20] of char;
var
   StudentName   : STRING;
```

Later we wish to read a single student's name:

```
for i := 1 to 20 do
    read (StudentName [i]);
readln;
```

Some time later we might wish to change the length of the string type from 20 characters to 30. The use of explicit array bounds in the type declaration and the need to repeat them in the **for** statement make this difficult to do. Rather we can declare arrays to be of named bounds whenever we suspect we might have to modify the length (which turns out to be quite frequently). In fact, any constant value used in a program should be named if it might need to be changed later. The preceding declarations for *STRING* should be declared as:

```
const
   MAXSTRING   = 20;
type
   STRING        =  array [1..MAXSTRING] of char;
var
   StudentName   : STRING;
```

Even when a constant is not likely to be changed, it may represent a value corresponding to a physical restriction in the environment. If we wish to blank out a line on a terminal with 75 characters per line, we are tempted to write a loop such as:

```
for i := 1 to 75 do
    write (' ');
```

But the meaning of the value 75 is not clear to someone reading the program, and in any event, the program might be run on a terminal of different line length. Values that we are certain are constant and fixed turn out to be modified more often than we might suspect. The **for** loop should use a named constant, (*MAXLINE*, for example) as the bounds of the iteration:

```
const
   MAXLINE = 75;
         . . .
for i := 1 to MAXLINE do
    write (' ');
```

4.4.2 Formatting Rules

Indentation style is the major concern of formatting, and there are as many differences of opinion about style as there are programmers. Perhaps more, since most of us change our minds about indentation style quite regularly. Sometimes we're not even consistent within the same program. However, indentation and other formatting considerations do enhance the readability of programs. In addition, good style makes it easier to spot certain syntactic errors relating to mismatched **begin-end** pairs, and erroneous matchings of **then**'s and **else**'s with their corresponding **if**'s. Formatting can and should follow simple rules, and this makes reformatting a program quite amenable to automatic techniques. Figure 4.4 shows a few basics. Pick a technique that seems right for you, and stick to it.

4.4.3 Procedures and Functions

Relatively new programmers often have difficulty using procedures and functions. In particular, they have difficulty deciding which type to use in a particular context. In addition, many new programmers have difficulty with the concepts of parameter passing, particularly the differences between **var** and value parameters. These concerns disappear quite quickly with even a modest amount of programming practice; more importantly, we need to understand the correct use of global variables versus parameters and local variables.

Pascal has two types of procedure parameters: **var** parameters and value parameters. **var** parameters, as we introduced in Chapter 2, have the reserved word **var** appended to their name; they are parameters whose values may change within the body of a procedure, and those changes are reflected in changes to the actual (calling) parameters. Value parameters, on the other hand, are copied to the procedure. A new copy of the parameter's value is made and passed to the procedure. Any changes made to the parameter are reflected only in the copy, not in the original (the actual or calling) parameter. Value parameters are de-allocated (they disappear) when the procedure exits. Consequently we use value parameters as input to the procedure. **var** parameters are usually used as output parameters.

Occasionally we pass large arrays to procedures as input, but we do not wish the array values to change. In the mean/median example of Chapter 1, the original array is sorted before we find the median, but we want the original array to remain unchanged. Consequently it seems appropriate to pass the array to a sort procedure as a value parameter.

> **procedure** *Sort* (*values* : *RealArray*; **var** *SortedValues* : *RealArray*; *n* : *integer*);

where *RealArray* is an array of reals. In this case, a copy of *values* is made

Compound Statement –
Indent one or two spaces
after the **begin**:

    begin
      a := c + d;
      readln (x);
      writeln ('x =', x : 5)
    end;

Loops: The **do** part of the **while**
statement may be on the same line,
or the next line:

    while $A > 0$ **do** S1;

    OR

    while $A > 0$ **do**
      S1;

If a compound statement follows an **if**
or **while**, the **begin** is often placed on
the same line with it; similarly for the
else clause in an **if** statement:

if $a < c$ **then begin**
  writeln (a : 1);
  a := a + 1
end else begin
  writeln (b : 1);
  b := b + 1
end;

If statement – The **then**
and **else** parts should be
on separate lines, indented a
space or two from the **if**:

    if $a < c$ **then**
      X (a)
    else
      Y (c);

Similarly for the **for** statement:

    for $i := 1$ **to** max **do** S1;

    OR

    for $i := 1$ **to** max **do**
      S1;

Figure 4.4. Standard formatting for various Pascal statement types.

and passed to *Sort*. Suppose, however, that *RealArray* is declared as a very large array:

    type
      RealArray   = **array** [1..50000] **of** *real*;

The copying of such a large array would be time consuming and, in any event, may consume more than the available memory. As a result, for very large structures of this type we will often make them **var** parameters:

procedure *Sort* (**var** *values* : *RealArray*; **var** *SortedValues* : *RealArray*; *n* : *integer*);

In doing this, we introduce the risk of making incorrect or unexpected changes to the array; such a change would be considered a program error. Consequently we see that the availability of value parameters aids in program correctness and robustness. We avoid using **var** parameters when we do not want the value to change. We also should not use **var** parameters when we expect a program constant to be passed as the parameter. Assignment to a constant, even when it has been passed as a **var** parameter, is illegal.

Generally we try to stick to a coding discipline that says: "Never refer to globals within procedures." Such a discipline preserves an important property of the code we write: module independence. Or, more correctly, it avoids the unfortunate possibility of undesirable side effects whenever a procedure is called. Consider the innocuous little **if** statement

if *BooleanCondition* **then**

. . .

else

. . .

where *BooleanCondition* is a boolean function. Within this function, every global variable in the program can be altered (accidentally or intentionally), and worse, because labels may be global to the entire program, the **if** statement may not even get to its **then** or **else** part! Suppose *BooleanCondition* is defined as:

```
function BooleanCondition : boolean;
begin
  BooleanCondition := true;        {assign to function name}
  a := 1;                          {change a few globals}
  done := true;
  goto 1000
end; {BooleanCondition}
```

The ability to trace the flow of control of a program using these constructs, to verify its correctness (even informally), and to debug and correct errors should (*when* is more appropriate) they occur would obviously be rather difficult. We are tempted, therefore, to take a drastic approach to the use of procedures and functions: all variables needed within the procedure must be passed as parameters or be locally declared.

However, we should consider the use of globals within procedures in three instances: when there are variables that express environment status

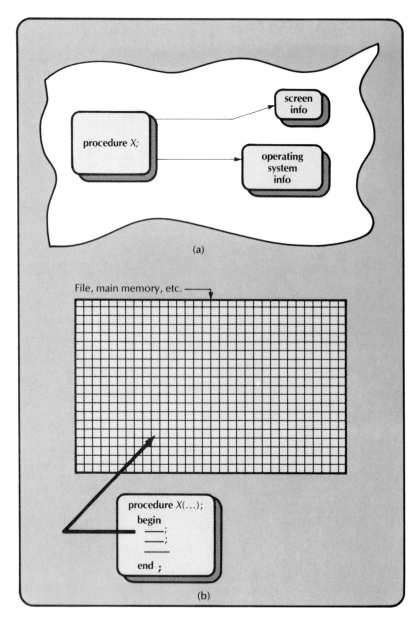

(a)

File, main memory, etc.

procedure X(...);
  begin
  ———;
  ———;
  ———
  end ;

(b)

Figure 4.5. (a) A procedure in an ether of globals, accessing the information about the local environment. (b) A procedure accessing a large global structure.

and flags; when there are variables that represent large, conceptually non-replicable structures; and when a procedure needs a "large" number of parameters, usually at program initialization.

Often a program may run in a multitude of environments. Think of a program's procedures as being embedded in an ether of status and environment information. If a procedure needs to use this information (which is considered, perhaps, static of the current environment of that procedure), an appropriate model allows the procedures to "reach" into the ether to retrieve (and perhaps modify) these values, as illustrated in Fig. 4.5(a). Again, we must be very careful that we modify only those globals that we should modify — that is, we must be certain that a change to a global name was not meant to be local to the procedure.

A different model, in which it is appropriate for procedures to manipulate a global variable or structure is when the variable represents a physical structure or device. For example, if we wish to manipulate the machine's actual memory, it seems unreasonable to pass the memory as a parameter to a procedure. This is not a conceptually clear way of handling physical structures. In any event, there may simply not be space for the copy if the variable is passed as a value parameter (see Fig. 4.5(b)). In addition, files must be passed as **var** parameters in Pascal.

Finally, it may just be that we are passing a large number of parameters to a particular function. In a number of the examples in this book we need to initialize tables of values. The size and complexity of the tables, and the fact that they remain constant (after initialization) throughout the execution of the program, indicate that we may access them in a separate initialization routine, as globals.

As the earlier example of the function *BooleanCondition* showed, an entire program's statements can be global to a procedure via jumps to globally declared labels. There are a number of restrictions on the **goto** statement, but one nonrestriction is that we may jump out of the body of a procedure into the main program (but not into the body of another procedure, nor into the "body" of a compound statement such as **if-then-else**). This is a coding style that we want to use only with the greatest of caution: it is tempting to say that **goto**'s out of procedures or blocks should never be used, but sometimes this is (almost) appropriate. The main use of this coding construct is in what is called *error escapes*. One application is handling erroneous input in processing input data. In such a case, we would like to read input, and if it is outside some appropriate range, we would like to jump to an error handling routine and then quit the program, as in the design of Fig. 4.6.

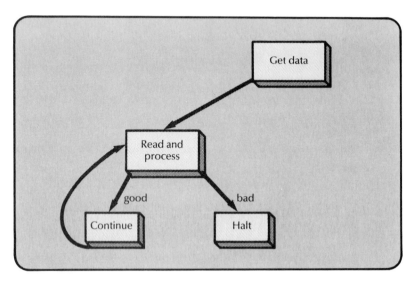

Figure 4.6. Design of a program with error-handling escapes.

Figure 4.7 is a program that implements the design of Fig. 4.6. The main program calls *GetData* and prints out the data (if all the input was valid, that is, if all input values were greater than 0). The main program code also contains the error handler, at labeled line 100, which simply prints out an error message and terminates the program.

4.4.4 Commenting Style

Comments serve a number of purposes in a program and are an important part of its documentation. With better designed languages such as Pascal, commenting requirements are fairly minimal and easy to adhere to. Perhaps the most important commenting guideline is: *Comment as you code.* Writing comments at the time the code is being written or modified is a straightforward extension of the coding process. Adding comments to an already-written program is laborious and tedious. The following few guidelines for commenting will aid in a number of aspects of program writing:

- Ease program understanding
- Document the function and workings of procedures and functions
- Ease the testing process
- Describe the input and output requirements and file characteristics
- Describe the workings of particularly obscure code

```
program GOTOTEST (input, output);
{Demonstrate error exit using goto's.}
label
  100, 200;
const
  MAXARRAY             = 100;
type
  INTARRAY             = array [1..MAXARRAY] of integer;
var
  badval               : integer;                    {global: first bad value in array}
  number               : integer;                    {number of values read}
  values               : INTARRAY;                    {input array}

  function GetData (var numbers : INTARRAY; max : integer) : integer;
  var
    i : integer;                                       {number of values read}
  begin
    i := 0;
    while not eof and (i < max) do begin
      i := i + 1;
      readln (numbers[i])
    end;
    GetData := i
  end; {GetData}

  procedure Validate (vals : INTARRAY; min : integer; n : integer);
  var
    i : integer;
  begin
    for i := 1 to n do
      if vals[i] < min then begin
        badval := vals[i];                             {global}
        goto 100
      end else
        writeln (vals[i])
  end; {Validate}

begin {main}
  number := GetData (values, MAXARRAY);
  Validate (values, 0, number);
  goto 200;
100 : writeln ('Value ', badval : 1, 'is out of range. Terminating for now.')
200 : end.
```

Figure 4.7. Program implementing the error escape design of Fig. 4.6.

Initially a comment block should be placed at the beginning of the program and at the beginning of each procedure or function. This *prologue*, like a book's preface, is designed to succinctly describe the purpose and functioning of the program or procedure. An elaborate discussion of each parameter is not usually necessary, since presumably parameter names and data type names have been chosen so that their meaning is self-explanatory. We saw, as early as Chapter 1, the use of a procedure comment prologue for the *NEWREADLN* procedure:

```
procedure NEWREADLN (var value : real; var ok : boolean);
{
Converts typed (character) input into a real number, returned in variable value.
ok is set to true if the number contains no illegal characters, false, otherwise.
}
```

The comment block is succinct; it briefly discusses the purpose of the procedure and the meanings of the parameters. In the sort procedure in Chapter 1 (the "good" program), the prologue also includes a mention of the specific sorting algorithm used. This is appropriate for routines that implement one specific algorithm out of many possible ones. As we've already seen, we could have used a number of sorting algorithms. In certain cases, the algorithm or data structure may be quite obscure. Simply naming it does not convey enough information as to its workings. In such cases, a citation to the source of the algorithm should be included.

```
procedure Sort (var numbers : INTARRAY; n : integer);
{
Sorts the array in place. Algorithm: exchange sort

INPUT:     numbers – The original array of values
           n – The actual number of values in array numbers

OUTPUT:   numbers is sorted in place, from low to high
}
```

The comment states that the array is sorted in place. That is, the original array *numbers* is *modified* by this procedure. This is also indicated by the use of a **var** parameter. An additional parameter n, the actual number of elements in the array, is also needed for this procedure, as is usually the case with Pascal procedures involving arrays, since array bounds are fixed at the time the program compiles. The additional comment indicating that the array is sorted from low to high is obviously appropriate for a sort routine.

A program prologue should include basic information about the program's function. For programs that are expected to have a life span greater than just the immediate use of the programmer, a small amount of historical information (for example, dates of creation and modification; name of writer or responsible individual) should be included. The complete case studies that we will develop in Part IV include this information. For example, the function plotter prologue might look as follows:

```
program PLOTTER (input, output);
{
Interactive Function Plotter.
DESCRIPTION:
AUTHOR:
VERSION:
DATE:
}
```

Generally, well-chosen names and a brief comment on the meaning and use of a program's data types and variables serve as part of the prologue and thus program documentation. The declarations are easier to read and easier to use if the names are in alphabetical order. As a result, we usually place each name on a separate line. Names all line up, the type separators (:) all line up, and the comment blocks all line up. Done this way, declarations form an important and useful part of the program's documentation.

Only rarely in Pascal is it necessary to comment individual statements. There is nothing to be gained by adding a comment such as:

```
repeat              {read characters until a nonblank is found}
  read (NextChar)
until NextChar <> ' ';
```

It doesn't really seem to do any harm, but an overcommented piece of code can be difficult to read; particularly with multiline comments, it becomes difficult to separate the comments from the code. In addition, we may believe that what the comment says is actually what our code is doing! We are not yet at the stage where programs can be automatically generated from comments or high-level specifications (though this is an area of active research). When in doubt about commenting a particular block or line of code, perhaps it might be better to rethink the actual coding, making its function clearer and being certain that identifier names are well chosen. Consequently comment blocks can then be used mainly for program and procedure prologues, and for succinctly describing the operation of compound blocks and those pieces of code whose function is not clear from the identifier names and program structure.

Commenting is really part of coding. The two are intertwined because comments help us understand and develop programs. But as our programs are modified, it is important to change the comments to reflect the modifications. It would be most confusing indeed if our sort routine used in Chapter 1 were replaced with one that sorted from high to low (rather than low to high, as in the original version) and we neglected to change the procedure prologue to reflect that change!

4.5   Coding the User Interface

4.5.1 Commands

Commands in interactive systems take a number of forms: function keys; full-word commands; single-letter forms; pointing, clicking, dragging with a mouse; even speech. Nonetheless, getting and interpreting commands can be performed in a single module called a command language processor (CLP), which in turn calls upon a lower level routine *GetCommand*. What makes this process command-form independent is that *GetCommand* can be written to return an enumerated type. Then the actual coding of the CLP is just a simple loop and case statement:

```
while not done do begin
    GetCommand (command);        {returns an enumerated type}
    case command of
        A : commandA;            {procedures to process each command}
        B : commandB;
        C : commandC;
        D : commandD;
        X : exitproc;
        H : help
    end {case}
end;
```

Here *GetCommand* returns an enumerated type, one of the values *A*, *B*, *C*, etc. (A rather unoriginal choice, but it illustrates the point!) Note the specific use of a procedure to handle exit (termination of program) processing (*X*) and a specific help function (*H*). Obviously this is not the only way to represent a command processor. However, we are specifically using coding style guidelines already established: a simple, compact command processing loop that uses individual procedure calls to implement a command's functions. New commands are added by four steps:

1. Include the new command's name in the type definition for the enumerated type *COMMANDS*.
2. Include the new command as one of those accepted in procedure *GetCommand*.

3. Include the new command in the **case** statement command loop.
4. Include the appropriate procedure for handling the new command.

   As input forms become more interactive (through the use of graphical I/O, pointing, touching, natural language and speech), command processors, obviously, become more complex. We have hidden this complexity, however, in the *GetCommand* procedure. It is conceivable that this procedure could process voice input, typed English, pointing and other gesticular input, etc. Any command-based program must be able to implement this function in a way appropriate to its needs. The main command loop (a call to *Get-Command* and the **case** statement) remains the same.

4.5.2 Help/Prompt

A simple help/prompt capability should be provided as part of any interactive program. Such capability can be quite simple; a mere restating of the commands available in the system and their meaning is often sufficient. If a user needs more information, he or she may be referred to a user's manual. Most incorrect use of interactive commands involves simply forgetting or confusing the command name, or confusing a command's function. The program's actions upon entering the help command can be the copying of the help file to the screen. Such a copying of one file to another (from the help file to the standard output) is surprisingly not very straightforward. A first (but wrong) attempt might be something like the following:

```
procedure ShowHelp (var HelpFile : text);
{Copy HelpFile to the standard output.   WRONG — won't work.}
var
  NextChar : char;
begin
  reset (HelpFile);        {position at start each time}
  while not eof (HelpFile) do begin
    read (HelpFile, NextChar);
    write (NextChar)
  end
end; {ShowHelp}
```

We read a character from the help file and put it on the standard output, one character at a time, and continue doing so until we reach the end of the help file. Our knowledge of Pascal is needed here to understand why this is not quite correct. When reading from *HelpFile*, the Pascal run-time environment converts the end-of-line marker (the carriage return and line feed characters) into a blank. As a result, the help file, which presumably has been neatly formatted into lines, is written as one long line on the terminal. To handle this annoyance, we must specifically test for end-of-line as well as end-of-file. When end-of-line is detected, we write a naked carriage return (via a single *writeln*) to the output; it is also necessary to continue the reading from the help file on the next line by performing a simple *readln* (*HelpFile*). (The *eoln* test remains *true* until we position the file pointer to the beginning of the next line.) The correct version of the *ShowHelp* procedure now is:

```
procedure ShowHelp (var HelpFile : text);
{Copy HelpFile to the standard output.   CORRECT VERSION.}
var
  NextChar : char;
begin
  reset (HelpFile);        {position at start each time}
  while not eof (HelpFile) do begin
    while not eoln (HelpFile) do begin
      read (HelpFile, NextChar);
      write (NextChar)
    end;
    writeln;
    readln (HelpFile)
  end
end; {ShowHelp}
```

4.5.3 Screen Management

Many programs need better screen management and positioning than what is available in just the line-oriented Pascal output. We'll discuss direct cursor positioning, erasing to the end of the current line, and erasing the entire screen. When we're done, we'll package all of the screen manipulation routines together in a file named *cursor.i*, which we can include (using the compiler directive #*include* "*cursor.i*") in any program where we need them.

To present these screen management procedures, we define a standard CRT terminal and capabilities. Virtually all currently available terminals have these functions, though each may have a different way of specifying them. Of one thing we can be certain: the following procedures are unlikely to work unmodified on your terminal. Each terminal, however, should have a means of control that is straightforward to implement. Portability of programs written using these procedures is reduced, of course, but usually only a modest effort is required to alter the individual procedures.

Figure 4.8 graphically defines the standard terminal — it is assumed to be a character-oriented CRT with 24 lines, each of 80 columns. The actual

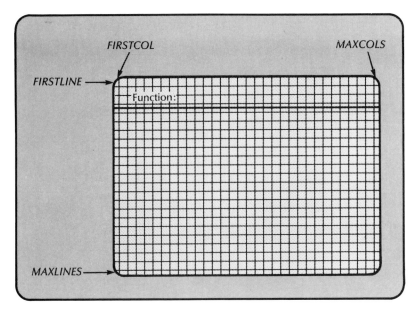

Figure 4.8. Standard terminal with origin at upper left.

size is made available in global constants *MAXCOLS* and *MAXLINES*, which must be changed for terminals of different characteristics. The top line is line 1, the left-most column is column 1, but the starting line and column numbers are also terminal-dependent and should be defined in constants *FIRSTCOL* and *FIRSTLINE*.

All of the direct screen manipulation routines use escape sequences (*ESCAPE* followed by one or more characters) to indicate screen-oriented actions. For these routines, the global *ESCAPE* is defined as:

```
var
    ESCAPE : char;              {ASCII escape character}
        . . .
    ESCAPE := chr (27);
```

That is, it is the ASCII escape character.

The first function in the screen manipulation routines is *MoveCursor*. It takes a line and column number (in screen coordinates) and places the cursor at the specified line and column. The procedure uses the global constants *FIRSTLINE*, *FIRSTCOL*, *MAXLINES*, and *MAXCOLS* to do range checking. If the line or column number is out of range, it is set to *FIRSTLINE* or *FIRSTCOL*, respectively. Note that the actual movement of the cursor is accomplished via the *write* statement: *write* (*ESCAPE*,'Y', *line*, *col*). When the terminal receives this escape sequence (the character code for *ESCAPE* followed by capital 'Y', followed by two integers), it does not actually write anything to the screen. Rather the terminal interprets this as an instruction to move the cursor to the given line and column number.

```
procedure MoveCursor (line, col : integer);
{
Positions the cursor to the indicated line and col. If line or col
is out of range, it is set to FIRSTLINE or FIRSTCOL.
}
begin
    if (line < FIRSTLINE) or (line > MAXLINES) then
        line := FIRSTLINE;
    if (col < FIRSTCOL) or (col > MAXCOLS) then
        col := FIRSTCOL;
    write (ESCAPE, 'Y', line, col)
end; {MoveCursor}
```

Two other useful screen management capabilities that most terminals have are clear to end of line and erase the entire screen. Clear to end of line erases the current line from the cursor to the end of the line. All characters to the right of the cursor are erased; those to the left are not. The cursor remains where it was originally. Clearing the screen erases all characters on the screen and then leaves the cursor at its "home" position, the first column of the first line.

Clearing to the end of the line is used for a reserved line input area. In the function plotter, we must move the cursor to a particular location on the screen, print the string "Function: ", and then wait for the user to type the function. When we do this, we'd like the previous function to be erased. We define two program constants *FUNCLINE* and *FUNCCOL* that give the line and column to move the cursor to when we wish a new function entered (typically these are line 1, column 1, but they may be different with different terminals). To position the cursor, write the string "Function: ", and erase to the end of the line, we just include the following code:

```
          . . .
MoveCursor (FUNCLINE, FUNCCOL);
write ('Function : ');
ClearEOL;

          . . .
```

Both clear to end of line and clear screen use escape sequences, as does *MoveCursor*. Again, the terminal interprets *ESCAPE* followed by a single character as a command. Here are the two routines *ClearEOL* and *ClearScreen*:

procedure *ClearEOL*;
{Erase from current cursor position to end of line. Cursor does not move.}
begin
   write (*ESCAPE*, 'K')
end; {ClearEOL}

procedure *ClearScreen*;
{Homes cursor (that is, moves cursor to *FIRSTLINE, FIRSTCOL*) and erases screen}
begin
   write (*ESCAPE*, 'H')
end; {ClearScreen}

Other procedures useful for screen management include reading the current cursor location, blinking characters, underlining characters, and defining locked fields.

    We will make use of direct cursor positioning in the function plotter. After each plot, we return the cursor to the top line, write the word "Function: ", and clear to the end of the line (so that remnants of the previous function are erased). As we noted at the beginning of this section, we've written these routines for a hypothetical CRT, using codes that are representative of many displays. However, you must find the correct codes for these functions for each terminal you use.

4.6   Style Summary and Sample Program —The Game of Life

We can summarize the style guidelines by illustrating them in a complete program. Of course, we have been following these guidelines throughout the book so far, but in this program they can be viewed and studied together. You should study this program — reading and studying the programs of others is a useful way to learn about good (and, alas, bad) coding practices. You will learn to recognize common program fragments and will gain an insight into techniques that will work well in your own programs. Many of us begin programming having a great sense of satisfaction and completion in just getting a program to compile. Later, we come to expect a program to run correctly also. More advanced programming practice also requires us to modify our own programs, and the programs of others. As our experience and abilities improve, we come more and more to appeciate and use good stylistic practices.

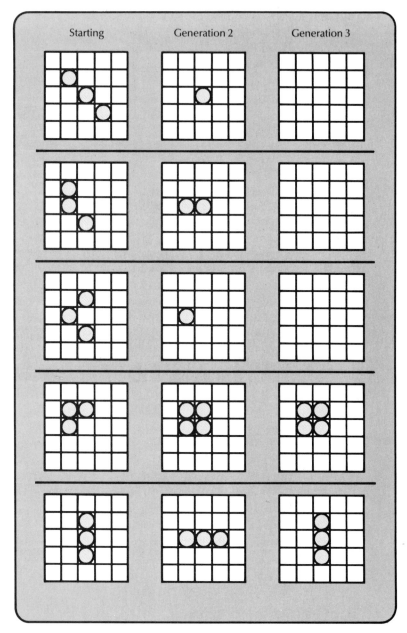

Figure 4.9. Starting and ending configurations of the *Game of Life*.

The program is a simulation of John Conway's *Game of Life*.[2] The game is designed to simulate population growth dynamics using a simple model played on a board of cells, each of which may contain a "living" token. Individuals are born, live, or die, based on three simple rules. The unit of time is a generation; all changes are considered to take place simultaneously, and the result is the next generation.

1. *Survival.* An individual survives if two or three neighboring squares (including diagonally adjacent squares) are occupied. The individual remains in the same cell.
2. *Death.* An individual dies of *overcrowding* if more than three neighboring cells are occupied, and dies of *loneliness* if fewer than two neighboring cells are occupied.
3. *Birth.* If an empty cell has exactly three occupied neighboring cells, a new individual is created. This new occupant is not considered to exist until the next generation. It can have no effect on the results for the current generation.

Various patterns and their effects on longevity have been investigated. It is amusing to find stable patterns, that is, patterns that do not end in total population annihilation and that produce either a nonempty, non-changing population, or an oscillating population. In Fig. 4.9 we see a number of initial configurations and their ultimate fate. Alas, most initial configurations lead to annihilation (a result of more than just passing curiosity).

4.6.1 Program Design

The program hierarchy is shown in Fig. 4.10. Clearly the program is spending most of its time determining the next generation from the current one. The program structurally follows a model we use in many programs: initialization routines, called once; data input routines, usually also called once; a main program loop, which continues until some internal or external event occurs; and finally post-processing or clean-up routines.

Taking the specifics of the *LIFE* program, with the program structure suggestions, the entire program will have a form very close to Fig. 4.11.

4.6.2 Data Flow Design

Each of the four modules in Fig. 4.10 will be written as an input, processing, and output transducer, and so we need to design the data flow for the

[2] See Martin Gardner's "Mathematical Games" column in *Scientific American*, October 1970.

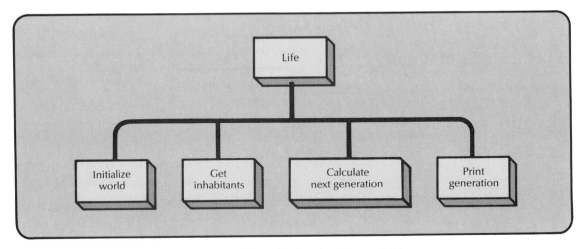

Figure 4.10. Program hierarchy for the *Game of Life.*

```
program LIFE (input, output);
begin                    {main program structure}
  InitWorld;
  GetInhabitants;
  PrintFirstGeneration;
  while living do begin
    NextGeneration;
    PrintGeneration
  end;
  TerminateProgram
end. {LIFE}
```

Figure 4.11. Top-down program structure for the *Game of Life.*

program, as in Chapter 3. The major item of data that will pass from routine to routine will be a "generation." At this point, we don't need, or want, to specify just what that is. We design the modules in terms of their processing on a generation, and after we've firmed up just what that should entail, we can select the specific representation. In terms of inputs and outputs, the modules will require, and in turn produce, the following information. In Fig. 4.12 we represent the inputs and outputs visually.

InitWorld   Takes no input; produces an empty, initialized *Game of Life* world.

GetInhabitants   Its input is an empty, initialized world. Its

	output is the initial world, with the inhabitants in their proper place.
NextGeneration	The input is a generation of life and a count of the current generation; its output is the next generation, determined according to the rules of the game, and the updated generation counter. In addition, this routine indicates whether the world has achieved static stability (two generations are identical).
PrintGeneration	Takes the current generation and the generation counter and writes to the output display. No values are returned from this routine.

Figure 4.12. Diagram representation of data flow in the *Game of Life*.

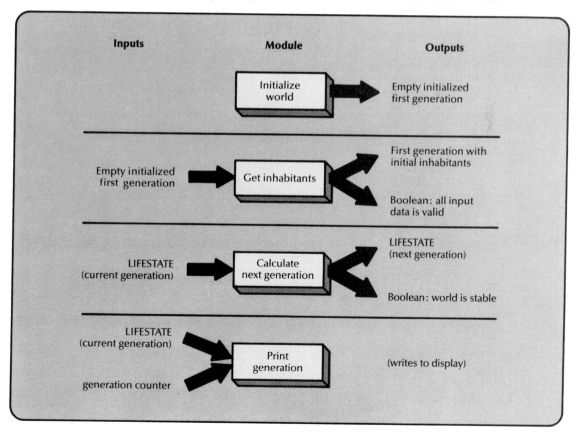

4.6.3 Data Structures and Algorithms

The world in which inhabitants live out their lives is entirely flat, so we represent it as a two-dimensional array, indexed from one up to the maximum number of columns and rows. The rules for determining the next generation from the current one require that we investigate the neighbors of each cell in the current generation. This is quite easily done, except at the borders. Conway didn't specify how a cell at a border was to be treated, so we'll make an arbitrary choice: there exists a "no-man's land" surrounding the 2D world, one cell wide, that is always empty. Then we can treat the neighbors of a border inhabitant in the same way we treat the neighbors of an inland inhabitant: we just examine their contents and process based on whether they are occupied or not. Figure 4.13(a) shows a 5 × 3 world surrounded by the unoccupied column 0, row 0, column *FakeMaxcol* and row *FakeMaxrow*. Figure 4.13(b) shows the order of examining neighbors for a cell. If the indicated cell happens to be a border cell, say, the upper left, then cells 1, 2, 3, 4, and 6 are unoccupied. No special check is needed because of the surrounding extra rows and columns.

Figure 4.13. (a) World with fake rows and columns. (b) Order of checking around current *row, col*.

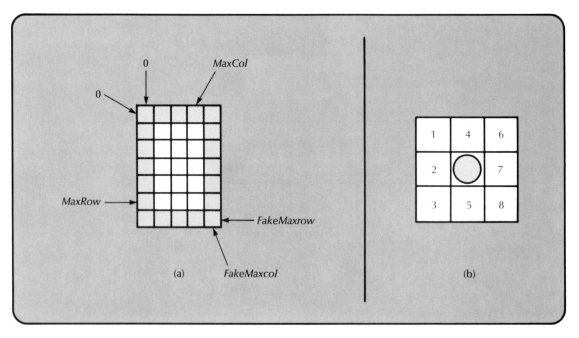

(a)

(b)

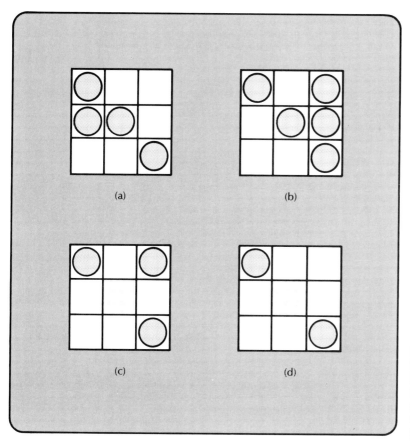

Figure 4.14. (a) Survival into the next generation. (b) Death due to overcrowding. (c) Birth in the next generation. (d) Unchanged empty cell in the next generation.

To calculate the next generation from the current, we use two versions of the world: the current one and the next. We then process the current generation from the upper left, a row at a time, running to the bottom right. For each cell, we examine its condition, and determine whether it lives, dies, or has a birth in the next generation. Indexing in the current and next generation are the same: we just work on a single cell at a time. The order of examining a cell's neighbors is not important, so we'll use the order shown in Fig. 4.13(b).

Figure 4.14 traces a number of different state changes for various cells in the current generation. In Fig. 4.14(a), the cell survives because exactly three of its neighbors are occupied. In Fig. 4.14(b), the cell dies from overcrowding because four of its neighbors are occupied. In Fig. 4.14(c), a birth occurs because exactly three neighbors are occupied. Finally, in Fig. 4.14(d), the cell remains empty into the next generation.

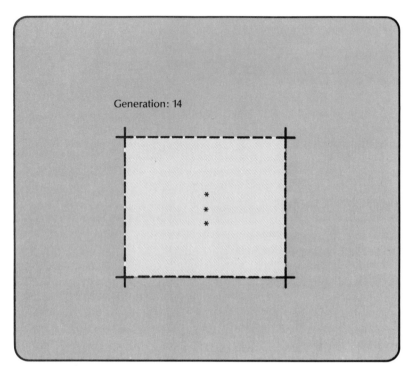

Figure 4.15. Actual screen display of a generation in the *Game of Life*.

Once the outcome of a cell in the next generation has been determined, we go to the next cell and continue column by column, row by row, until all cells have been processed. We don't determine the outcome for the no-man's land cells, however. They always remain unoccupied. Finally, we need to print the contents of the cells. One nice way to do this is to use the direct cursor movement routines of the previous section. We'll keep a generation counter at the top of the screen, which is updated just before printing the current generation. Then we move to the display area of the screen and print the entire generation, border and all. If we do this at the same screen location each time, the effect will be like an animated film; cell markers appear and disappear as births and deaths occur. The actual screen display should look similar to that in Fig. 4.15. The generation counter is at the top of the screen; the world display is beneath it.

4.6.4 The Program

The program is written so that the initial board configuration is entered from the terminal. Each line of input consists of a pair of integers, indicating the (x, y) location of a member of the population. It is assumed that these are given in "board" coordinates, that is, an x value between 1 and *MAXC*

(15 in this program) and a *y* value between 1 and *MAXR* (also 15, for symmetry). The actual board size for a game is determined at run-time, when the program requests the values from the user. The program runs until a boolean variable (*living*) becomes *false*. *living* indicates whether static stability has occurred, that is, whether a new generation and its predecessor are the same. It does not indicate *dynamic* stability, where states oscillate without ever becoming statically stable. Figure 4.16 shows an initial configuration that becomes dynamically stable. Such conditions are detected in this program visually, or by adding a generation counter and only producing the stated number of generations.

The design of the program indicated that the world is a two-dimensional plane of cells. The implementation of the world requires that we allocate

Figure 4.16. An initial configuration leading to a dynamically stable ending configuration.

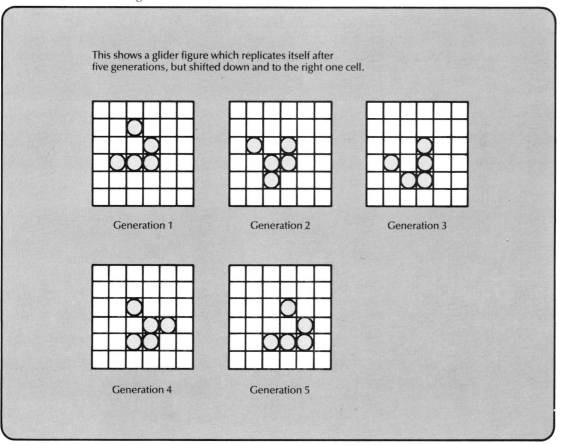

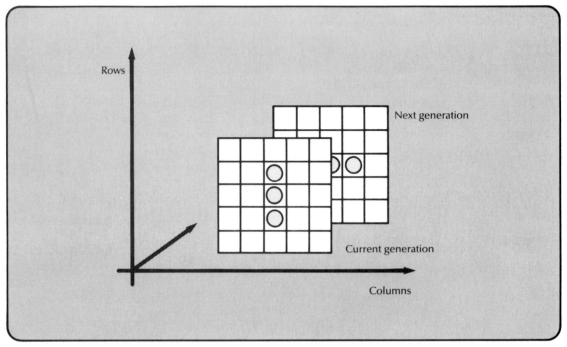

Figure 4.17. 3D array representation of current and next generation in *Game of Life*.

two of these planes: the current generation and the next. We can think of the world as being a *three*-dimensional array: the first two dimensions are the rows and columns of the world; the third dimension is the generation, current or next, as shown in Fig. 4.17.

We read the cells of the current generation and write the cells of the next. To simplify the structure, and to avoid copying arrays, we'll represent the generations using a boolean to indicate which is the current generation and which is the next generation. This flag, a generation counter, and the three-dimensional array of cells can be conveniently packaged together into a record, where the occupancy of a cell is a boolean: *true* if the cell is occupied; *false*, otherwise.

```
LIFESTATE        =
   record
      count       : integer;
      current     : boolean;
      world       : array [ROWS, COLS, boolean] of boolean
   end;
```

This now lets us define the activities of *InitWorld* and *GetInhabitants* from Fig. 4.10 more precisely. In *InitWorld*, we set all of the cells to empty, *false*. In *GetInhabitants*, we get the initial inhabitants' row and column numbers from the user and then set those cells in the current generation to occupied, *true*.

In *PrintGeneration* we first print the current generation number at the top of the screen, and then print the entire contents of the current generation.

Finally, in *NextGeneration*, we update the cells of the next generation according to the rules and the discussion in the design section. The entire program is shown in Fig. 4.18. Look at the overall program structure in the main program, then examine the individual routines. At this point, there should not be any surprises: we defined precisely the rules of the game. We then carefully designed the overall program structure, using a typical program design illustrated in Fig. 3.1. Using that design, we designed the representation and the algorithm for processing border conditions. Finally, we designed the actual data structure for the board representation.

The program requires initial output, then runs until killed (control *c* or the break key on most systems). The program asks for initial input: number of rows, number of columns, then the row and column locations of each token. On startup, the screen should clear, and the prompt "*Max-Rows:* " appears at the top of the screen. Enter the number of rows in the board, and a carriage return. You are then prompted for the number of columns: "*MaxCols:* " and you again enter the number of columns.

Now you will need to enter the location of each of the initial tokens, giving the row and column number of each. The location of each token is entered, one per line. Input ends with end of file (usually control *d*). After the starting inhabitants' locations have been entered, the program runs automatically, until either static stability, all inhabitants are dead, or the user terminates the program.

If the initial board is to look like

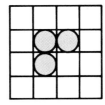

then enter the data given in Fig. 4.18(a). The program is shown in Fig. 4.18(b).

```
    MaxRows:     4
    MaxCols:     4
    DATA FOR INHABITANTS:
    2 2
    2 3
    3 2
                        (a)
program LIFE (input, output);
{
Conway's Game of Life.

DESCRIPTION:     Generates successive generations of John Conway's Game of Life, using a
                 board of MAXR by MAXC cells. See Martin Gardner's column in Scientific
                 American, October 1970.
INPUT:           The initial board configuration. The input consists of a series of lines, each
                 representing one (x, y) coordinate where an initial token is to be placed.
OUTPUT:          Successive generations are drawn on the standard output.
AUTHOR:          A. Quilici and L. Miller
VERSION:         2.1
}
const
  MAXC              = 15;                          {max allowable cols}
  MAXGEN            = 1000;                        {max number of generations}
  MAXR              = 15;                          {max allowable rows}
  TOKENSYMBOL       = '*';                         {symbol for a living cell}
type
  COLS              = 0..MAXC;
  COUNTER           = 0..maxint;
  ROWS              = 0..MAXR;
  LIFESTATE         =
    record
      count         : integer;
      current       : boolean;
      world         : array [ROWS, COLS, boolean] of boolean
    end;
var
  FakeMaxCol        : COLS;                        {one more than maximum columns}
  FakeMaxRow        : ROWS;                        {one more than maximum}
  Generation        : COUNTER;                     {number of generations}
  MaxCol            : COLS;                        {max number of columns}
  MaxRow            : ROWS;                        {max number of rows}
  ok                : boolean;                     {flag from NEWREADLN}
  state             : LIFESTATE;                   {the record of cells}
  stable            : boolean;                     {flag indicating stability}

#include "CURSOR.i";                               {direct cursor positioning}
```

Figure 4.18. The *Game of Life:* (a) sample board data; (b) program.

```
procedure InitWorld (var state : LIFESTATE);
{Initialize the world so there are no inhabitants.}
var
  col               : COLS;
  row               : ROWS;
begin
  state.current := false;
  for row := 0 to FakeMaxRow do
    for col := 0 to FakeMaxCol do
      with state do begin
        world [row, col, current] := false;
        if (row = 0) or (col = 0) or (row = FakeMaxRow) or (col = FakeMaxCol) then
          world [row, col, not current] := false
      end;
  state.count := 0
end; {InitWorld}

function GetInhabitants (var state : LIFESTATE) : boolean;
{Gets the coordinates of the original inhabitants.}
var
  c                 : real;
  col               : integer;
  cpos              : real;
  good              : boolean;
  line              : COUNTER;
  ok                : boolean;
  r                 : real;
  row               : integer;
  rpos              : real;

#include "NEWREADLN.i";                              {from Chapter 1}

  begin
    good := true;
    line := 0;
    {Get number of rows and columns}
    ClearScreen;
    write ('MaxRows : ');
    NEWREADLN (r, ok);
    MaxRow := trunc (r);
    write ('MaxCols : ');
    NEWREADLN (c, ok);
    MaxCol := trunc (c);
    FakeMaxRow := MaxRow + 1;
    FakeMaxCol := MaxCol + 1;
    {Get initial token placement}
    ClearScreen;
    writeln ('Enter row and column number (1..max) for each token.');
```

(continued)

Figure 4.18 (continued)

```
while not eof do begin
    ok := false;
    line := line + 1;
    NEWREADLN (rpos, ok);
    if not ok then begin
      writeln ('Invalid row position on line ', line : 1);
      good := false
    end else begin
      NEWREADLN (cpos, ok);
      if not ok then begin
        writeln ('Invalid column position on line ', line : 1,
          'Please re-enter both row and column');
        good := false
      end else begin
        row := trunc (rpos);
        col := trunc (cpos);
        if (row < 1) or (row > MaxRow) or (col < 1) or (col > MaxRow) then begin
          good := false;
          writeln ('Invalid coordinate on line ', line : 1,
            'Please re-enter both row and column')
        end else
          with state do
            if not world [row, col, current] then begin
              world [row, col, current] := true;
              count := count + 1
            end
      end
    end
  end;
  GetInhabitants := good
end; {GetInhabitants}

procedure PrintGeneration (var state : LIFESTATE; Generation : COUNTER);
{Print the initial state, complete with outside border.}
var
  col           : COLS;
  row           : ROWS;
begin
  if Generation = 1 then
    ClearScreen
```

```
    else
      MoveCursor (1, 1);
    writeln ('Generation : ', Generation : 1);
    writeln;
    for row := 0 to FakeMaxRow do begin
      for col := 0 to FakeMaxCol do
        if (col = 0) and ((row = 0) or (row = FakeMaxRow)) or (row = 0) and ((col = 0) or
            (col = FakeMaxCol)) or (row = FakeMaxRow) and (col = FakeMaxRow) then
          write ('+')
        else if (col = 0) or (col = FakeMaxCol) then
          write ('|')
        else if (row = 0) or (row = FakeMaxRow) then
          write ('−')
        else if state.world [row, col, state.current] then
          write (TOKENSYMBOL)
        else
          write (' ');
      writeln
    end;
    writeln
end; {PrintGeneration}

procedure NextGeneration (var state : LIFESTATE; var stable : boolean);
{Find the next generation, following the rules of the Game of Life.}
var
  col             : COLS;
  coloffset       : integer;
  neighbors       : COUNTER;
  row             : ROWS;
  rowoffset       : integer;
begin
  stable := true;
  with state do begin
    for row := 1 to MaxRow do
      for col := 1 to MaxCol do begin
        neighbors := 0;
        for rowoffset := −1 to 1 do
          for coloffset := −1 to 1 do
            if not ((rowoffset = 0) and (coloffset = 0))
                and world [row + rowoffset, col + coloffset, current] then
              neighbors := neighbors + 1;
```

(continued)

Figure 4.18 (continued)

```
            if world [row, col, current] then              {occupy only if neighbors = 2 or 3}
               world [row, col, not current] := (neighbors = 3) or (neighbors = 2)
            else
               world [row, col, not current] := neighbors = 3;
            if world [row, col, not current] then
               count := count + 1;
            if world [row, col, current] <> world [row, col, not current] then
               stable := false
         end;
      current := not current
   end
end; {NextGeneration}


begin {LIFE}
   stable := false;
   InitWorld (state);
   if GetInhabitants (state) then begin
      ClearScreen;
      Generation := 1;
      PrintGeneration (state, Generation);              {print initial configuration}
      while (Generation < MAXGEN) and (state.count > 0) and not stable do begin
         NextGeneration (state, stable);
         Generation := Generation + 1;
         PrintGeneration (state, Generation)
      end;
      if state.count = 0 then begin
         MoveCursor (1, 1);
         writeln ('All inhabitants are dead after ', Generation : 1, 'generations')
      end else if stable then begin
         MoveCursor (1, 1);
         writeln ('World is stable after ', Generation : 1, 'generations')
      end else begin
         MoveCursor (1, 1);
         writeln ('Done with last generation')
      end;
      write ('CR to exit');
      reset (input);                                    {because we tested for eof earlier}
      readln
   end
end.
```

(b)

Exercises

1. In this chapter we introduced a number of different terms. For each of the following, give a brief definition:
   a) Structured programming
   b) Domain-specific primitives
   c) Language-specific obstacles
   d) Device-specific obstacles
   e) Portable software
   f) Module cohesiveness
   g) Module independence
   h) Parsimony

2. Give two reasons why the **goto** statement is considered harmful. When does it make sense to use a **goto**?

3. In this chapter we presented a number of routines that do a primitive form of screen management which works on our mythical standard terminal. These exercises involve rewriting these routines to make them terminal-independent, as well as adding some new screen management routines.
   a) Write a function *GetTerm* which prompts the user for the type of terminal the user is on. It should present the user with a menu of terminals that the program knows about (whichever terminals you have access to in your own programming environment) and returns an enumerated type that stands for the terminal the user selects (*DUMB* if no selection is made).
   b) Rewrite the procedures *ClearScreen*, *MoveCursor*, and *ClearEOL* so that they work on all the terminals on the menu of terminals *GetTerm* presents to the user. (The terminal type should be an argument to each of these procedures.) These procedures simply write out different escape sequences depending on what terminal the user claims to be using.
   c) Write the following additional functions to manage screen input and output (the type *STRING* is a character array of an appropriate length).

   function *GetLine* (*row, col, len* : *integer*; **var** *line* : *STRING*) : *integer*;
   {
   Moves the cursor to *row, col* on the screen and attempts to read in and store up to *len* characters into the character array *line*. Returns the actual number of characters the user typed.
   }

   procedure *WriteChars* (*row, col, len* : *integer*; *line* : *STRING*);
   {
   Moves the cursor to *row, col* on the screen and writes out the first *len* characters of *line* to the screen.
   }

```
procedure EraseBox (row, col, lines, size : integer);
{
Moves the cursor to row, col on the screen and then writes size blanks
on each of the next lines lines.
}
```

4. Modify our *Game of Life* program to detect "dynamic stability," where the cycle of oscillations is less than some user-supplied maximum number of states. (You can set some reasonable limit to the user-supplied maximum number of states.)

5. Add a mechanism to our *Game of Life* program to allow the user to change the probabilities of survival of one generation to the next. For example, if a square has no neighbors, or more than three neighbors, there is a 100 percent chance that the square will become empty. The user should be able to specify the probability that the square will become empty for each rule. Then use the random number generator to return a random real in the range 0..1. If the random number is less than the associated probability, the square becomes empty, according to the appropriate rule; if the random value is greater than the probability of the rule, the square lives.

6. The function *GetInhabitants* in the *Game of Life* was unusually long because we used *NEWREADLN* for protection from illegal characters in the input values. Each call to *NEWREADLN* required a number of statements: initialize the boolean; a while loop so that we loop until the boolean is *true*, and a *write* statement to put out an appropriate message. Write a procedure *GetReal* that takes three parameters: a **var** parameter *N*, the real value returned to the caller; a value parameter *Msg* of type *STRING* (a type that must be defined in the calling program as an **array** [1..*MAXSTRING*] **of** *char*); and a third parameter *length* of type integer, the actual number of characters that are used in *Msg*. The procedure should loop, writing out the first *length* characters of *Msg*, and then call *NEWREADLN* until the boolean parameter of *NEWREADLN* is true.

7. Rewrite *GetInhabitants* of the *Game of Life* program so that it calls upon the procedure *GetReal* of the previous exercise.

8. [PROGRAMMING PROJECT]   Write a program to maintain a small database. The database has a number of records, each of which is a single Pascal array of characters and a real number. The array can have various information in it. For example, the string could be an item name, and the real number a price. The user should be able to add, change, delete, and list each record. You can use the skeleton of the command processor in Section 4.5 to help you get started. The details of implementation are left to you, but try to follow our user interface guidelines, and use good structured coding techniques. Remember to design before you code.

9. [PROGRAMMING PROJECT]   Write a program to play the game of *CRAPS*. Craps is a game played with two dice. At the beginning, you can either *win*, *lose*, or *continue*. You win if you roll a total of seven or eleven. You lose if you roll a two, three or twelve. Otherwise, you have rolled a "point." After the initial roll, if you have neither won nor lost, you continue playing, attempting to roll your point again. If you roll a seven before your point, you now lose; if you roll your point before a seven, you win. All other rolls are "no-ops," and you roll again.

Initially, you ask the user the number of games to play. Your program should generate rolls of the dice, using Pascal's random number generator, and keep statistics of the number of wins and losses on the first roll and the number of wins and losses attempting to match the point.

Use direct cursor positioning to keep, in a fixed area of the screen, a running counter of the percentage of wins and losses, the total number of wins and losses, and the total number of games played.

THE RUN-TIME BEHAVIOR
OF PROGRAMS

5.1   Introduction

While a program is running, it should have a number of properties that relate not just to the correctness of the program (Does it do what it's supposed to do?), but rather to the way in which the program handles errors. Of course, we cannot reasonably expect our programs to handle certain errors; for example, if the computer physically crashes, the survivability of the program depends on hardware issues that may be beyond the scope of the program or the programmer. But short of catastrophic failures to the physical environment, the goal of all programs during execution must be that they work reasonably and well regardless of whether they are being abused by the user, by the operating system, or by the run-time collection of functions and routines themselves. This chapter discusses these points and the particular problems of:

- Input validation
- Arithmetic problems: over/underflow; roundoff errors
- Range and type errors for built-in routines
- Who handles errors: the routine or its caller?
- Program efficiency

5.2   Run-Time Errors — Range/Validity Checking

Even the simplest programs face the problems of validity of entered data. It is the normal expectation of programmers when they first begin designing and coding a program that data values will be within the range they expect. Unfortunately this might not be the case for a number of reasons: in an interactive program, users may not understand or know the allowable data ranges; there may be a simple typing error so that a value that should have been reasonable becomes unreasonable; the hardware may make unexpected transformations to the data. Consequently *all* data that a program expects must be treated as suspect.

A simple date conversion program will illustrate the problems and some typical solutions. The techniques for validating input are straightforward, but they contain a number of hidden assumptions and have the typical side effect of greatly increasing the size of the code. As a result, the code can be less clear in its meaning and intent, and its structure can become more obscure or convoluted.

What we're going to try to do is build a little date verifier. It takes a line of input representing the date in numerical form: month/day/year, slashes and all, and simply prints it out with the month spelled out and the day and year nicely spaced. If the input is

1/3/74

```
program DATE (input, output);
{Converts a numeric date string into string with month spelled out. WARNING — HAS
BUGS!!}
const
  MAXSTRING      = 10;
type
  STRING         = array [1..MAXSTRING] of char;
var
  day            : integer;
  month          : integer;
  MonthNames     : array [1..12] of STRING;
  slash          : char;
  year           : integer;
begin {main}
  {Initialize MonthNames — pad to the right with blanks}
  MonthNames [1] := 'January     ';      MonthNames [7]  := 'July        ';
  MonthNames [2] := 'February    ';      MonthNames [8]  := 'August      ';
  MonthNames [3] := 'March       ';      MonthNames [9]  := 'September   ';
  MonthNames [4] := 'April       ';      MonthNames [10] := 'October     ';
  MonthNames [5] := 'May         ';      MonthNames [11] := 'November    ';
  MonthNames [6] := 'June        ';      MonthNames [12] := 'December    ';
  writeln ('Date converter Version 1.0');
  writeln ('Type: month (integer)/day (integer)/year (2 digit integer)');
  writeln ('Example: 12/27/45');
  write ('> ');
  while true do begin
    read (month);
    read (slash);
    read (day);
    read (slash);
    readln (year);
    year := year + 1900;
    writeln (MonthNames [month], day : 4, ',', year : 5);
    write ('> ')
  end
end.
```

Figure 5.1. The first attempt at a date formatter.

we'll print

January 3, 1974

Seems simple enough, right? Well, Fig. 5.1 is a first attempt at the solution. But don't put it into a system where you need to depend on its correctness. It handles reasonable input correctly, but if the input is out of range, or contains illegal characters, the program fails miserably. As an

```
program DATE2 (input, output);
{
Converts a numeric date string into string with month spelled out.
CAUTION — Bugs in this one too!!
}
const
  MAXSTRING     = 10;
type
  STRING        = array [1..MAXSTRING] of char;
var
  day           : integer;
  month         : integer;
  MonthNames    : array [1..12] of STRING;
  slash         : char;
  year          : integer;
begin {main}
  {Initialize MonthNames — pad to the right with blanks}
  MonthNames [1] := 'January    ';     MonthNames [7]  := 'July       ';
  MonthNames [2] := 'February   ';     MonthNames [8]  := 'August     ';
  MonthNames [3] := 'March      ';     MonthNames [9]  := 'September  ';
  MonthNames [4] := 'April      ';     MonthNames [10] := 'October    ';
  MonthNames [5] := 'May        ';     MonthNames [11] := 'November   ';
  MonthNames [6] := 'June       ';     MonthNames [12] := 'December   ';
  writeln ('Date converter Version 2.0');
  writeln ('Type: month (integer)/day (integer)/year (2 digit integer)');
  writeln ('Example: 12/27/45');
  write ('> ');
  while true do begin
    read (month);
    repeat                          {simple change that allows more free-form input}
      read (slash)
    until slash = '/';              {but note — will read forever unless '/' is entered!}
    read (day);
    repeat                          {simple change that allows more free-form input}
      read (slash)
    until slash = '/';
    readln (year);
    year := year + 1900;
    writeln (MonthNames [month], day : 4, ',', year : 5);
    write ('> ')
  end
end.
```

Figure 5.2. The second attempt at a date formatter. In this version input can be relatively free form.

exercise, try finding (and correcting!) all the bugs you can. And try thinking about ways of making it more robust.

One of the problems you'll notice right away is that input must be in a very rigid format: the month, immediately followed by a slash (no spaces!), the day, another slash (again, no spaces), and then the year. The first fix allows multiple spaces (zero or more) around the slashes. At least this frees the user from rigid input requirements.

To rectify the problem with the slashes, we just add two **repeat** loops to read characters until we read the slash, then process the next integer. This simple programming change makes the program, even without range and validity checking, substantially less error prone and easier to use. But the program is still not correct; it will crash if out of range values are entered, and it will loop forever if the user neglects to enter a slash where one is expected! This (slightly) improved version of the date converter is shown in Fig. 5.2.

The program is now somewhat more usable because the input need not stick to a rigid format. Any of the following are acceptable:

$$12/27/45 \qquad 12 \quad / \quad 27 \quad / \quad 45 \qquad 9/1/ \quad 87$$

But the program still does not do range checking. Range limits on each value are stated as follows:

Month　　　Integer in the range 1..12.

Day　　　　Integer in the range 1..31, with a value that is appropriate to the month.

Year　　　Integer in the range 0..99 (representing 1900..1999); otherwise, the value is assumed to be the actual year.

The problem is not in writing code to verify that values are within range (except for the day value, which must be appropriate to the month and must take account of leap years for February). Rather, the problem comes in deciding what to do when an erroneous, out-of-range value is found. We have a number of choices; each may be appropriate under certain circumstances. However, the following list is (more or less) in reverse order of desirability:

1. Do something wrong.
2. Stop.
3. Ignore.
4. Fix up; don't tell the user.
5. Fix up; tell the user.
6. Fix up; ask if o.k.
7. Force program into a loop until o.k.
8. Flag to exception file; replace with default, if required; and continue.

As the programs in Figs. 5.1 and 5.2 are written, they will either stop when an out-of-range value is encountered (the run-time environment produces an array access out-of-range message and terminates the program), or they will produce a clearly incorrect output value (December 89, 1927). The handling of errors is out of the programmer's control, since the run-time environment handles array range checking. The programmer must be certain that array subscripts are within bounds *before* an array reference is attempted.

In the date conversion program, a number of the listed alternatives would be acceptable. We have chosen a simple error-handling scheme that uses *default* values when an input value is out of range. These are:

Month   Set month index to *UNKNOWN*.

Day   Set day to 0.

Year   Set year to *CURRENTYEAR*.

The final version of *DATE3* is shown in Fig. 5.3. Note that this program does not handle February correctly. Additional code must be added to ascertain whether the year is a leap year. In that case, *max[February]*, corresponding to the maximum days in February, would be 29; otherwise, it should be 28. Note that the code at least doubles in size to accommodate the error checking and handling and it still may not be correct.

This program represents a substantial change from the basic outline of the first two versions of the program. We have had to delve into low-level details to write a program that is immune to most user errors. For example, since the user (as we discussed in Chapter 1) may enter illegal characters, we have written a short procedure, *ConvertToNumber*, similar in function to *NEWREADLN*, that converts characters into a corresponding integer. Since the user may type fewer numbers than needed (we need three numerical values: *month*, *day*, and *year*), we want to discontinue scanning for more data when a carriage return is typed (*eoln* is *true*).

Don't lose sight of the forest for the trees here! The purpose of this discussion is to point out the desirability of guarding against reasonable or likely user errors in interacting with a program. To do this, the simple structure and clarity of the original program has given way to an elaborately structured piece of code that accommodates both potential user errors and also oddities of the Pascal run-time environment. We can summarize the results of this exercise quite succinctly:

Programs designed with consideration of user errors are likely to be much more complex in structure, and much more lengthy, than programs that assume all input is correct in number and format.

```
program DATE3 (input, output);
{
Converts a numeric date string into string with month spelled out. Performs rudimentary error
checking. When a range error is found, the value is set to an appropriate default.
}
const
  CURRENTYEAR    = 1986;
type
  DAYS           = 28..31;
  MONTHS         = (UNKNOWN, January, February, March, April, May, June,
                      July, August, September, October, November, December);
var
  day            : integer;                              {input from user}
  max            : array [MONTHS] of DAYS;               {max days in month}
  month          : integer;                              {input from user}
  MonthNames     : array [0..12] of MONTHS;              {name for month}
  year           : integer;                              {input from user}

  procedure ConvertToNumber (var value : integer);
  {Converts the input to an integer. The converted integer is returned in value.}
  var
    minus        : boolean;                              {is the number < 0?}
    NextChar     : char;                                 {next input char}
  begin
    value := 0;
    minus := false;
    repeat
      read (NextChar)
    until (NextChar in ['−', '0'..'9']) or eoln;
    if not eoln then begin
      if NextChar = '−' then begin
        minus := true;
        read (NextChar)
      end;
      while NextChar in ['0'..'9'] do begin
        value := 10 * value + (ord (NextChar) − ord ('0'));    {similar to NEWREADLN}
        read (NextChar)
      end
    end;
    if minus then
      value := −value
  end; {ConvertToNumber}
```

(continued)

Figure 5.3. Final version of date conversion program. But note that there are still corrections and additions that could be made.

Figure 5.3. (continued)

```
begin {main}
  MonthNames [0]   := UNKNOWN;      max [UNKNOWN] := 31;
  MonthNames [1]   := January;      max [January] := 31;
  MonthNames [2]   := February;     max [February] := 28;          {what about leap year?}
  MonthNames [3]   := March;        max [March] := 31;
  MonthNames [4]   := April;        max [April] := 30;
  MonthNames [5]   := May;          max [May] := 31;
  MonthNames [6]   := June;         max [June] := 30;
  MonthNames [7]   := July;         max [July] := 31;
  MonthNames [8]   := August;       max [August] := 31;
  MonthNames [9]   := September;    max [September] := 30;
  MonthNames [10] := October;       max [October] := 31;
  MonthNames [11] := November;      max [November] := 30;
  MonthNames [12] := December;      max [December] := 31;

  writeln ('Date converter Version 3.0');
  writeln ('Type: month (integer)/day (integer)/year (2 digit integer)');
  writeln ('Example: 12/27/45');
  writeln;
  write ('> ');
  while not eof do begin
    ConvertToNumber (month);
    if not eoln then
      ConvertToNumber (day);
    if not eoln then
      ConvertToNumber (year);
    {Simple error checking}
    if not (month in [1..12]) then
      month := 0;
    if (year < 100) and (year > 0) then
      year := year + 1900
    else if (year > 2999) or (year < 0) then
      year := CURRENTYEAR;
    {verify day is valid for month}
    if (day > max [MonthNames [month]]) or (day < 0) then
      day := 0;
    writeln (MonthNames [month], day : 4, ',', year : 5);         {non-standard}
    write ('>')
  end
end.
```

5.3 Run-Time Arithmetic Errors

Arithmetic errors include over/underflow, roundoff errors, and range and type incompatibilities of built-in functions (for example, *exp* and *sin*). Some of these errors are quite subtle and rather unexpected, and they will be discussed in detail with a number of examples to illustrate the problems.

The basic flaw in computer arithmetic is that it is not real arithmetic, as we expect. The difficulty occurs as a consequence of two facts of computer number representation: finite precision and base conversion. The problems of base conversion are associated, of course, with the finite representation, but we will examine each separately.

We define *overflow* as the result of an arithmetic operation that yields a result that is too large to be represented in the normal machine representation. In Pascal, overflow occurs in integer arithmetic when an operation produces a result that would be larger than *maxint* in absolute value. For example, the arithmetic operation:

$$TooBig := 2 * maxint \textbf{ div } N;$$

produces run-time arithmetic overflow even if N is larger than two. Most of the time we do not need to worry about integer overflow, since we can usually predict in advance the range that integer variables will have in numeric computations. Such is not always the case, however, and we must resort to occasionally bizarre coding "tricks" to avoid the problem. We can often guard individual statements involving arithmetic expressions by performing simple range checks on the individual values used in the computation. Often this requires arithmetic operations of a complexity equal to or greater than the expression being guarded. Consequently program running time may suffer substantially. Since *real* arithmetic may not necessarily produce overflow when *integer* arithmetic will, we can guard against integer overflow by guarding suspect expressions with an equivalent expression using *real* arithmetic. Consider the assignment to *TooBig*, an integer variable. Suppose *EvenBigger* has been declared as a real variable. Then the following assignment could replace the previous one:

$$EvenBigger := 2.0 * maxint / N; \quad \{maxint \text{ is "widened" to a real}\}$$

We might conclude that all arithmetic should be performed using reals. Unfortunately overflow can also occur with reals, and the results are not necessarily what you might expect from observing the way a particular environment handles overflow with integers. Consider the following program:

```
program TEST (input, output);
var
    value : real;
begin
    value := 1.0e 99;
    writeln (value)
end.
```

We expect the output from the *writeln* statement to be 1.0e99. However, the output produced on a DEC VAX is 1.70141183460469e + 38, rather surprising, indeed. To understand what has happened, we must read the Pascal standard closely. The standard requires that integer arithmetic return the correct integer result, otherwise an error occurs. A result outside the range $-maxint..maxint$ is an error. Real arithmetic is specified in the standard to return an *approximation* to the correct result. The standard specifies two different techniques for handling arithmetic overflow: for integers, the program stops (an error occurs); for reals, a value equivalent to the largest real is substituted (the mythical *maxreal*), and the program continues. As we mentioned previously when discussing the techniques for handling errors, there were a number of techniques that might be appropriate. Which is correct? Which is "better"? Which do *you* prefer?

Arithmetic *underflow* occurs when an expression returns a real value that has an exponent *smaller* than the smallest (most negative) exponent available in the hardware. As we discuss in Appendix 1, this is typically about 10^{-38}. Again, most Pascal environments will replace this value with 0.0. The maximum error in this case is only one part in 10^{38}.

A more subtle, and potentially more troublesome set of errors relates to finite representation and the associated problem of roundoff error. Consider the usual rules of arithmetic on the real numbers and the associated machine operations:

Commutative	$a \times b = b \times a$
Machine	Commutativity holds.
Associative	$(a + b) + c = a + (b + c)$
Machine	Associativity does *not* hold.
Inverse	$a \times I_{mul} = a; a + I_{add} = a$
	There exists a multiplicative inverse, when $a \neq 0$, I_{mul}, and an additive inverse, I_{add}.
Machine	For any real or integer a there exists an additive inverse $-a$. A multiplicative inverse does not always exist, even when $a \neq 0$.

For the reals, the additive inverse of a is just $-a$; the multiplicative inverse is $1/a$ for $a \neq 0$; for $a = 0$, there is no unique multiplicative inverse. In machine representation, $1/a$ need not be the correct multiplicative inverse for two reasons: real division is not infinite precision; and as we've just seen, if the division produces real overflow or underflow, a substitution in value is made.

Let's examine associativity. We wish to calculate $a + b + c$. By associativity we mean that the order of operations is not important: we may perform first $a + b$, then add c to the result; or we may perform $b + c$, and then add a to the result. Examine Fig. 5.4; a, b, and c are assigned the real values as shown. When the program is run, we obtain the following output:

$$(a + b) + c: \qquad -7.13421743062672e-18$$

$$a + (b + c): \qquad -6.93889390390723e-18$$

Something strange has happened here. The real numbers are supposed to be associative under addition. Clearly computer arithmetic is not. We can more easily see the phenomenon if we shorten the machine representation. Assume that we have a decimal machine that represents reals to four significant digits: any real value with more than four significant digits is *rounded* to four digits. Let a, b, and c have the values:

$$a = 0.1234 \times 10^0$$

$$b = -0.1233 \times 10^0$$

$$c = 0.3271 \times 10^{-3}$$

Figure 5.4. Program illustrating associativity in arithmetic.

```
program ASSOC (input, output);
var
    a       : real;
    b       : real;
    c       : real;
begin
    a :=  −0.12345542345234234e 0;
    b := 0.12345542345234233e 0;
    c := 0.32741234252341234e − 17;
    writeln ('(a + b) + c : ', a + b + c);
    writeln ('a + (b + c) : ', a + (b + c))
end.
```

rounded to four significant digits. When $(a + b)$ is performed first, we obtain $(0.1234 - 0.1233) = 0.0001$, or 0.1×10^{-3}. When this value is then added to c, we obtain 0.4271×10^{-3}, the correct answer. Now, we perform the operation in the reverse order: first $(b + c)$, then add a to the result. $(b + c)$ is $(-0.1233 \times 10^0 + 0.3271 \times 10^{-3})$. The arithmetic operation is performed by "normalizing" the exponents. That is, before the addition can occur, the exponents of the two values must be the same. However, we will perform the operation with "infinite" precision, and then round the answer: $(-0.1233 \times 10^0 + 0.3271 \times 10^{-3}) = -0.0001233 + 0.0003271 = 0.0002038$. When we round the answer to four digits and renormalize, we obtain 0.2000×10^{-3}. Adding a to this gives $0.0001234 + 0.0002$, or 0.0003234. Again, rounding to four digits and renormalizing, we obtain 0.3234×10^{-3}. Note that the correct value is 0.4271×10^{-3}.

Roundoff errors are a serious problem in a large class of problems in numerical analysis. In these problems, numerical approximations are used to find the value of a function. For example, the sine of a real number is calculated by a series approximation; one approximation that may be used is the Taylor series. In this, $sin(x)$, x a real in radians, is approximated by the formula:

$$sin(x) = x - \frac{x^3}{3!} + \frac{x^5}{5!} - \frac{x^7}{7!} + \cdots$$

This formula is not exact because the Taylor series is an infinite series. When it is truncated (to four terms as shown), an error, called a truncation or finite approximation error, is introduced. The built-in functions sin, cos, exp, and ln use a series approximation to the actual function value. Consequently their accuracy may be site-dependent. However, we should expect that these routines have been written to provide accuracy to the number of significant digits supported in the real number representation in the hardware.

5.4   Error Handling

Establishing a uniform policy on handling errors within routines would be desirable. That policy would relate to the corrections or actions to be taken when errors occur, and it would also establish the appropriate place for error handling and correction to occur. When we pass values to a function or procedure, we can establish their validity before the routine is called. This is required when using the system-supplied routines, since they generally handle data errors fatally — they cause the program to halt. With some built-in routines, it may be impossible to do any error checking at all. For the *reset* function, if the parameter is the name of a file that doesn't exist, the program halts. Unfortunately, in many environments, there is no independent way to verify that a file external to the program actually exists. With routines we write ourselves, we can choose to perform validity checking before the routine is called or let the routine perform the checking. Either way has advantages and disadvantages. It is safest to require the calling party to perform validity checking. However, this can become tedious and error prone when common routines are reused regularly. It thus would appear safer for the called party to do the validity checking. Unfortunately, what appears to be an error sometimes really isn't. As we will see in Part III, when we expand the coding for the function plotter, certain operations on data structures can be viewed under some circumstances as being erroneous, and under other circumstances merely as flagging the end of processing. By insisting that the called routine perform error checking *and fix the errors*, we may be incorrectly flagging an error when none exists. It appears more reasonable to have both caller and called perform appropriate error checking. However, the called routine should not attempt to fix errors. Rather, the routine should return some appropriate flag, enumerated type, or value indicating the nature of the problem, and let the calling routine handle the error as appropriate.

One typical technique is to define a function whose job is to validate input data. If a value is valid, the function returns *true*; if it is out of range, the function returns *false*. In addition to the boolean value of the function, the function can include an additional parameter *reason* that is an enumerated type. The parameter *reason* is set to one of its values, indicating the reason for flagging the value as invalid. Typically we need to read an integer value that cannot be greater than some constant *MAXVALUE*, nor less than some other constant *MINVALUE*. In this case, we define an enumerated type *REASONTYPE*

```
type
  REASONTYPE = (VALUETOOLARGE, VALUETOOSMALL);
```

Then *valid* performs the range checking on *value*, returning the reason that *value* is out of range (if it is):

```
function valid (value : integer; var reason : REASONTYPE) : boolean;
begin
  valid := true;
  if value < MINVALUE then begin
    valid := false;
    reason := VALUETOOSMALL
  end else if value > MAXVALUE then begin
    valid := false;
    reason := VALUETOOLARGE
  end
end; {valid}
```

valid doesn't do anything with the input value if it's out of range; it merely returns the appropriate function value (*false* in this case), and sets the reason. Typically a call to *valid* is made after each data item is read. If *valid* returns *true*, normal processing continues; if *false*, control could pass to another routine, *ExceptionHandler*, which performs the appropriate action under the circumstances. In this code fragment, *NextValue* is an integer; *WhyNot* is a *REASONTYPE*:

```
                      . . .
readln (NextValue);
if not valid (NextValue, WhyNot) then
    ExceptionHandler (NextValue, WhyNot)
else
    NormalProcessing;
                      . . .
```

Note that this code fragment and the code for *valid* are self-documenting. Well-chosen variable names and the consistent use of enumerated types for passing status information greatly enhances code readability. In addition, the code is easier to write in the first place and easier to debug.

5.5 Efficiency

Writing efficient programs involves two major components: selecting the most efficient algorithms for a particular function and implementing those algorithms in a manner that minimizes execution time and space. This section briefly considers those actions that we can take to ensure that a given program/algorithm is as efficient as we can make it (given the particular language, operating system, and hardware). We also informally analyze a routine for its computing time as a function of the number of inputs it processes. In Part III we will present more formal methods for analyzing the time complexity of a number of different algorithms.

As we noted briefly in Chapter 1, and a result that we will observe from a more detailed study of algorithmic efficiency in Part III, the time differences between classes of algorithms can be quite large — so large that they swamp out almost anything that we do to fine tune or "diddle" our code. Nonetheless, careful observation of coding practices associated with efficiency and avoidance of those that are obviously inefficient can substantially improve a program's running time. We briefly discuss a few pointers here.

A word to the wise: It is almost always a mistake to sacrifice clarity and simplicity of structures and expression for running time improvements.

Some of the transformations suggested here and in Part III will have the side effect of *reducing* the structural clarity of a program. Consequently, maintaining good programming habits in terms of comments, naming conventions, and other structuring/stylistic guides of Chapter 4 become even more important.

5.5.1 Computing Time

In Chapter 1, we first saw an insertion sorting algorithm and we now should be familiar with its basic operation. We have stated that, in general, this sorting technique is not very efficient. Many programming environments provide tools that allow us to determine where a program is spending its time. Using such tools can become part of an effective way to increase the efficiency of our programs, consistent with programmer efficiency. In many applications, to have every algorithm and every line of code fine tuned to a razor's optimal edge does not really make much sense if doing so leads to code that is obscure, hard to understand, and difficult to modify when changes are needed. Recognizing programmer efficiency and overall program efficiency, we strive for the best job at writing the program, within the goals of clear structure. Then we instrument the code and determine where the program bottlenecks occur. With this notion, and after carefully monitoring the program, we gain a realistic understanding of the parts of a program that may yield to a redesign for space and time savings.

Some programming environments provide an execution profiler to show where the program has spent its time. This, in conjunction with post-execution timing statistics, can provide an indication of the efficiency of a particular program on a particular set of data. We ran the sort program of Chapter 1 on a data set of 400 integers, generated by a random number generator. The program was compiled using the Berkeley UNIX Pascal compiler and run on a DEC VAX 11/750. We argue informally as to how long this program should take to run, and we will develop more analytical techniques in Part III when we investigate alternative, more efficient algorithms.

The insertion sort routine takes the incoming number and searches the array, starting from the beginning, for the appropriate place to insert the new value. When such a place is found, the remainder of the array is shifted up one place, and the new value is placed into the newly vacated slot. There are two phases to the insertion algorithm:

1. *Find* the appropriate place to insert.
2. *Shift* the remainder of the array and insert the new value.

Initially the array is empty, and the first value is immediately inserted into it. No comparisons with any values in the array are necessary, and no shifting is done. In the general case, with the array containing $n < max$ values, the new value is compared with each value in the array in turn, until its insertion point is found. If we assume that the incoming values are randomly distributed, this new value is equally likely to belong at any of the n occupied positions of the array, or at the end. We can informally predict that on the average, comparisons will have to be made with about *half* the values in the array, that is, about $n/2$ comparisons. To insert all 400 values into the array, we expect the following number of comparisons for each new value, 1 to k to 400:

n	Number of Comparisons
1	0
2	1
$\vdots$	$\vdots$
k	$(k/2)$
$\vdots$	$\vdots$
400	200

Consequently the *total* number of comparisons is the sum of the number required for each:

$$\text{Total comparisons} = \sum_{i=1}^{N/2} i = \frac{N(N + 1)}{4}$$

For $N = 400$, this is about 40,000, a surprisingly large number, but we're still not done. After finding the insertion point, we must move the remaining values one at a time, so that we make room for the new value. The number of items that must be moved is again $n/2$ for each new value. The total number of moves is also about 40,000. (Given a random distribution of values, the total of comparisons plus moves will be about 80,000.) The insertion sort program, recoded from Chapter 1, is shown in Fig. 5.5. It has been run with a compiler that includes additional information to count the number of times each statement was executed. After executing on the randomly distributed file of 400 integers, the program was run through the Pascal execution profiler. The program profile is shown in Fig. 5.5 also. The way to read this profile is to find the statement of interest, and then move to the left to a vertical line. The number associated with that vertical line is the number of times that instruction was executed. We have highlighted the two main insertion statements of the *Insert* procedure: the one that searches for the location to insert the value and the one that does the shifting. Note that the sum of these two statements is very nearly 80,000!

For the input data, seven values could be immediately inserted at the end of the array, while a search had to be conducted for the remaining 393. With those 393, there were a total of 38,128 comparisons. Then, after finding the correct insertion point, there were a total of 41,199 shifts. The total of comparisons plus shifts is 79,327.

It is only fair to point out that this technique is not really so bad if the data is already sorted, or nearly sorted. We define nearly sorted to mean

Figure 5.5. Insertion sort routine with execution monitoring output.

```
400.─┐  procedure Insert (number : integer; var A : ARRAYTYPE; n : integer);
         {
         DESCRIPTION:        Insert number into the correct location of array A. The first
                             n elements of A are already sorted, from low to high. n is
                             initialized and incremented by the calling routines.
         INPUT:              number — the next value to insert into the array.
                             A — the array.
                             n — the number of elements already in A. The first n
                             elements of A are sorted.
         OUTPUT:             A is updated so that number is inserted into its proper
                             place. A remains sorted.
         }
         var
            i        : integer;
            j        : integer;
         begin
            i := 1;
            {quick test to see if number should go at end}
            if number > = A [n] then
     7.─┤      A [n + 1] := number                    ← INSERT AT END 7 TIMES
   393.─┤  else begin                                 ← NEED TO SEARCH 393 TIMES
   393.─┤    while (i < n) and (number > A [i]) do
 38,128.─┤    i := i + 1;                             ← TOTAL OF ALL SEARCHES: 38,128
            for j := n downto i do
 41,199.─┤    A [j + 1] := A [j];                     ← TOTAL OF ALL SHIFTS: 41,199
            A [i] := number
   400.─┤    end
         end; {Insert}
```

that no value is more than m places away from its final location, with $m << N$. This is because we inserted a special test at the beginning of the procedure to see if we could simply insert the new value at the end of the array. This test is worthless for a random file because the number of times that the test is successful is so small that we spend more time making the test than we save when the test is true. However, it is worthwhile including this test to allow us to take advantage of nearly sorted files.

The general case sorting time of this routine is so bad that we must seek substantially faster, general sorting routines, or we risk having programs that need to sort large volumes of data bog down in N^2 comparisons. Were this sorting routine part of a larger program, using the execution profiles (we can easily write our own code to count the number of times a procedure is called, and even the number of times individual statements are executed) would immediately indicate that even though *Insert* is only being called N times, the program is executing a very large number of statements within that routine. We will examine a number of alternatives in Part III.

Exercises

1. All of the programs and examples for this book were written using Berkeley Pascal running on a DEC VAX compiled with an option that accepts only standard Pascal. Therefore it should be possible to type any program in this book in on another computer, and to compile and run it with no changes. Pick any program or example in the book and try to compile and run it on your machine. Does it compile correctly the first time? Does it work correctly? What changes, if any, did you have to make to get it running on your machine? Were these changes immediately obvious?

2. Take a program (at least 200–250 lines) you've written in Pascal and try to install it on a computer other than the one for which it was originally written. What difficulties did you encounter? If you had to make changes to the original to get it working on the new machine, will the new version work on the old machine? Is it always possible to get the same program to work on computers running different operating systems and made by different manufacturers? Why, or why not?

3. If execution profiling tools are available on your computer, obtain a profile of a sizable program you've written. (Or one of the programs in the book). Where does your program spend the largest percentage of its time? Is this

where you would have guessed? Try to make your program more efficient by making whatever changes you can to the procedures that take the most time. How much of an improvement did you get? Is your program still readable? Did you have to change your algorithm, or were you able to find savings by changing little things, or reordering statements?

A particular procedure consumes a substantial percentage of a program's time for two reasons: it is quite slow or it is called a large number of times. Look for procedures that are very slow, though called infrequently, and also for procedures that are called very frequently. It may be possible to reduce the number of calls to a procedure as well as to make it faster on each call.

4. Quite often we write code that is very modularized, occasionally leading to routine calls that are just a few lines. Take a procedure or function in this book, or one that you've written yourself, that is no more than two or three lines, and code it in-line, wherever it is called. Then run your program with an available execution profiler or timing monitor. Record the absolute time improvement and the percentage time improvement between the two versions. Comment on the advantages and disadvantages of attempting this type of performance improvement.

5. Write a program that computes values for $sin(x)$, $cos(x)$, $exp(x)$, and $ln(x)$ (using the built-in Pascal functions). Run this program on different machines gathering values for $x = 0, 0.5, 1, ..., 10$. Are the values the same on all the machines? If not, by what percentage do they differ? Do you think this difference is important? Why, or why not? [*Hint:* Take an expression involving all functions with a value of the variable x that seems to give different results on different machines and compute the percentage difference in the results.]

6. In this chapter, we give a Taylor series approximation for the sine function:

$$sin(x) = x - \frac{x^3}{3!} + \frac{x^5}{5!} - \frac{x^7}{7!} + \cdots + \frac{x^n}{n!}$$

The rate of convergence of this approximation depends on whether the absolute value of x is less than or greater than 1. Implement this function with the ability to vary n. How exact is your approximation? That is, how many terms in the series are required to return a value within some epsilon of the correct value of $sin(x)$, for $|x| < 1$, and $|x| > 1$? Does the order of the computations matter?

7. A generalization of our date program is called a "date cannonizer," a program takes dates in numerous forms and places the date into a single "cannonical" form. Modify or rewrite our date program to recognize a wider variety of

dates and convert them into the form: month-day-year, for example, 2-19-1961 for February 19, 1961. Some forms of date your program should accept are:

> July 30, 1930
> 24 June 1963
> 7-20-1931
> March 4th 1963
> 1962: 7/5

You should make the forms that your program accepts as general as possible. Months with long names should allow abbreviations. (February, for example, should allow "feb" as an acceptable abbreviation.) What might this program be useful for?

8. [PROGRAMMING PROJECT]   There are some programs whose only task is error recovery. Write a spelling checker that reads in a table of words from a file (set some reasonable maximum) to use as a dictionary. Then, for a file input to the program, each word in the file is looked up in the dictionary. If the word can't be found, the program informs the user that the word is misspelled. He or she is then offered the opportunity to accept the word as is or to correct the spelling. As each word is examined, if it is found in the dictionary, it is written to a "corrected spelling" file. The corrections (or the accepted words) are also written out.

There is the interesting notion of just what a word is: you must decide how you will handle punctuation and other word separators. [*Hint:* Examine the specification for *GetToken* in Chapter 3. Try to extend the notion of a token from one that is relevant to the function plotter to one that is relevant to words in a text file.]

9. [PROGRAMMING PROJECT]   A useful tool is a generalized input validator. There are two input files for this program: a file of input data for some other program and a file containing a description of the format for the input data file. For example, the data type of each field and the values for the field that are acceptable. The output from the program is an exception list detailing all errors the verifier found. This exercise involves writing a simplified, but useful, input validator.

The description file should contain one line per field in the input data file which describes the format of that field in the input file. A format description consists of the data type description and the minimum and maximum length of the field. The valid data types are C (char), B (binary), I (integer), L (large integer), R (real number), U (unsigned integer), N (alpha-numeric), A (alpha), and H (hexidecimal). A minimum field length of 0 is an error. Blanks are assumed to separate all fields, except character fields where there is a fixed length. For example, the file containing three lines, "C 40 40", "U 1 7", and "B 8 8", describes a file where each line has three fields: the first is a group of forty characters, the second is an unsigned integer of up to seven digits (which starts in column forty-one), and the third is an eight-digit binary number.

TESTING AND DEBUGGING

6.1   Introduction

Most of us have never really had the experience of writing a program that was of critical importance: a heart monitoring machine in a cardiac care unit, an aircraft autopilot routine for landing in zero visibility, or a critical database application in which errors could cost the organization substantial financial losses. Consequently we have never directly faced the serious consequences of an incorrect program. Writing a program when we have an important stake in its correctness can be an illuminating experience.

There is the story of the professional programmer who built an elaborate statistical model of professional football, which he used to write a program to pick winners of the pro games. The picks were so successful that he began placing small wagers on the outcome (of course, this took place in a state where such wagering was legal). The wagers remained small, as befitting the general level of poverty of most programmers of the day, but the success rate was quite high: typically 65 to 70 percent of all the games he picked.

The program, unfortunately, was written in FORTRAN, and after a couple of years the programmer, having heard of structured programming, top-down design, and other current buzz words, decided to rewrite the program in Pascal. After a short recoding effort, and making some changes to the data structures to allow for greater flexibility in naming and adding new teams, he tested the new, structured program on a new season.

In the past, the program had been picking three or four games a week that were suitable for further investigation. Now, however, with his highly structured, cleanly configured, easily extendible code, the programmer was picking five to eight games a week. Well, this seemed like a windfall to our programmer. After all, if you win 2/3 of your wagers, you're better off with more wagers than with fewer. However, this logic contained one flaw: he was now *losing* more than half of the games! Finally, near financial ruin, he reran previous years' data through the new program and compared the results with what the old program had given. In addition, he carefully hand-simulated the code and compared critical mathematical results with hand-calculated answers. To nobody's surprise, the code contained a simple, and not very subtle, arithmetic mistake.

The lesson was an interesting one for the programmer. He had been programming for quite a long time and had worked on very large software systems for the government, for aerospace industries, and for computer manufacturers. Yet, here was the first time he had a true sense that something important was resting on the *correctness* of his program's code. There is a moral somewhere in this — it probably relates to a variation on Murphy's Law: "When you're absolutely sure your program is correct, don't bet on it!"

We rarely have the opportunity, as practicing programmers, to feel the critical aspects of our code. The projects we work on may be large, and the actual delivered, installed code is quite separated from the interesting design work. In some environments, testing is accomplished by a different group than the one that designed or wrote the code. The craftsman's sense of intimate involvement with his product can be missing. Unfortunately, what we learn in classroom computing may not transfer well to "real world" computing.

Perhaps the major differences are related to the size and scope of the programs written. Even though you will write substantial programs as a student, rarely is one larger than a few thousand lines of code, nor does the coding effort very often extend beyond six months to a year. Again, it is rare that a program will involve the efforts of more than one or two programmers. And, alas, quite often the code "disappears" when the original programmer leaves because changes, fixes, extensions, and so on are usually not done by anyone else.

In this chapter we develop and apply a combination of ad hoc and formal techniques for debugging code, for demonstrating the correctness of code, and for testing code. And we reexamine the benefits of good specification, design, and coding style in order to more easily build correct and easily modifiable code. These are important concerns because the testing and validation of code is often a substantial percentage of a program's total implementation cost. As early as 20 years ago, 45 to 50 percent of a project's total budget went to testing and integration in large military software projects. NASA has estimated that nearly 80 percent of the software expenditures on the Apollo moon landing project went to testing!

There are two compatible approaches to software quality: building correctness into the code initially and testing the resulting code for correctness. Testing, of course, does not introduce quality into code; it only provides a measure of a program's correctness. In addition to discovering errors in code, testing will also help us correct them.

6.2   Anti-Bugging and Debugging

Debugging means removing the bugs from a program. Nothing new in that. How do bugs get into programs in the first place? Is it possible to write bug-free programs initially? Are there techniques and procedures that will guarantee the elimination of all program bugs? If not, are there at least ad hoc procedures that are effective most of the time in eliminating bugs, and are there common critical areas that are usually associated wth bugs, so that we might look there first? Do bugs follow the "funeral" rule: kill one and ten more come to the funeral? That is, are we likely to introduce new bugs in the very process of eliminating old/known ones?

These are interesting and surprisingly tough questions that have led to important research in program correctness. It is a mark of experienced programmers that they are able to quickly, almost intuitively, generate hypotheses about where a program's difficulties lie, and correct them. We try to address these and other issues in this section by describing the experiences of programmers who have worked in large programming projects, and through illustration with short examples.

Experience and research indicate that seven broad areas are associated with most program bugs:

- Syntax errors
- Misuse of language constructs
- Logical errors in solving the problem (the algorithm is not correct)
- Incorrect approximations used in the algorithm
- Input data out of range
- Defects in the data structures (such as incorrect array bounds)
- Just plain misinterpretation of the specs

Some of these categories are "external" to the program, whereas some are programmer errors. The external ones might be incorrect algorithms, incorrect approximations in the algorithms, or misinterpretation of the problem's specifications, including inappropriately designed user interfaces. Internal (or programmer) errors relate to misuse of the language's structures and concepts, and they include syntax errors, insufficient range/validity checking on input data, and incorrect data structuring. We might also include two other external error classes: documentation errors and hardware/system errors. By documentation errors we mean that the user manuals describe one use of the program, but the program performs in a different manner. Hardware and system errors are often thought not to be the programmer's responsibility. Regrettably this is a short-sighted view, since many critical programs must still function reasonably even in the face of degraded hardware or system performance.

We'll begin by investigating internal errors — those errors that we associate with programmer mistakes. Though we have a clear idea of a problem's specification and design, and a thorough appreciation of the algorithms that are needed to implement it, we nonetheless have difficulties in actually applying all the programming language's constructs and data structures to the problem. Further, a common error is the failure to examine certain (usually rare or unexpected) cases.

Five "bug infested" categories account for virtually all of the internal (programmer) bugs. We describe each with examples and a discussion of solutions to avoid or correct them. Bugs usually associated with incorrect algorithms and data structures will be discussed in Section III when we develop dynamic data structures and a number of interesting algorithms and algorithm analysis techniques.

Sometimes we make errors because we make erroneous assumptions about the mechanics of a language and its run-time environment. Figure 6.1(a) is supposed to read an input line from the terminal, a character at a time, until a carriage return is typed (*eoln* becomes *true*). The program places the characters into the 80-character array *InputLine*, as illustrated in Fig. 6.2. The program echoes each line after it is typed, and continues until *eof* is *true*.

Immediately below the program is sample output. This program contains an error: we have neglected to reset *InputLine* to all blanks before each line is read. Consequently whatever values the elements of *InputLine* had before the new line is entered are retained unless a new character is typed at that position. We need only make the simple addition of blanking out the entire array before each line is read, just before the assignment $i := 1$, as in the following:

> **for** $i := 1$ **to** *MAXSTRING* **do**
> *InputLine* [i] := ' '

Many Pascal environments automatically initialize certain variables to default values, but this is not part of the language definition and it is not guaranteed to occur in all systems. Consequently our first potential bug in our developing bug list is:

Failure to properly initialize variables.

A pervasive and difficult-to-detect set of bugs relates to *boundary conditions*. A program can function correctly for years with no difficulties, and then suddenly failure occurs. Often a program is designed and programmed with some notion of the "general case," that is, those values of input data, array limits, and so on, that account for the usual condition. But what happens when an expected data file is empty? What happens when an array boundary is reached, when negative values are passed to procedures that normally expect positive values (such as the *sqrt* function)? As you've probably already determined, the *LINE* program in Fig. 6.1 contains a subtle bug of this type: the program will terminate with an array subscript out of bounds error if a line is longer than 80 characters! Since the program was designed to work in an interactive terminal environment where the line

```
program LINE (input, output);
{Copy input to output, a line at a time. WRONG — HAS A BUG!!}
const
  MAXSTRING      = 80;
type
  STRING         = array [1..MAXSTRING] of char;
var
  i              : integer;
  InputLine      : STRING;
begin
  while not eof do begin
    i := 1;
    while not eoln do begin
      read (InputLine [i]);
      i := i + 1
    end;
    readln;
    {Write the line}
    for i := 1 to MAXSTRING do
      write (InputLine [i]);
    writeln
  end
end.
```
                          (a)

The output from LINE:

```
Now is the time for all good men,
to come to the aid of their party.
to come to the aid of their party.
when in the course of human events,
to be or not to be, thatman events,
is the question.be, thatman events,
is the question.be, thatman events,
What is happening here?tman events,
12345678901234567890123456789012345678901234567890
Perhaps we are not9012345678901234567890
properly resetting InputLine to blanks?
```
                          (b)

Figure 6.1. (a) First attempt at a program to copy an input line to the output. (b) Sample output from program *LINE.*

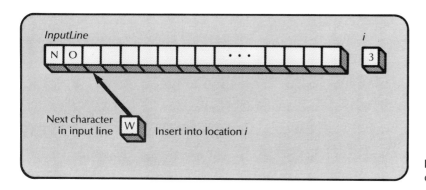

Figure 6.2. Inserting a new character into *InputLine*.

length is 80 characters, it might not appear reasonable that someone would type a line longer than 80 characters, by neglecting to type the carriage return key, for example, or by running the program on a 132-character/line terminal. We make the following straightforward changes to *LINE*, and the program now correctly handles the condition of lines longer than 80 characters. We also note a change that will make the program somewhat more efficient: rather than blank out the entire line, we "carry" along with the *InputLine* array the additional variable *count*, the actual number of characters read into the array (up to a maximum of 80, of course). Then the **for** loop used to print the array runs from 1 to *count*, rather than from 1 to 80. Now we do not have to blank out the array because we will only print the number of characters read in the current line. The final version of the program, with this change and the correct handling of lines longer than 80 characters, is shown in Fig. 6.3.

In Chapter 2 we saw that the mechanisms of a language can lead to painfully convoluted code in order to handle empty files or files without expected input values. Of course, numerous other boundary condition errors occur regularly, and they can be particularly troublesome when dealing with linked lists and pointer variables, as we will see in Part III. For now, we summarize boundary condition/special cases problem areas. Use the following checklist whenever you write programs that deal with arrays, linked lists and trees, and any other data structures that have the property that handling the general case is different from processing needed for boundary cases. Boundary conditions include:

Empty lists.   Inserting into a list that does not have any elements in it often leads to difficulty.

Beginning or end of list.   Dealing with the first or last element in a list

```
program LINE2 (input, output);
{Copy input to output, a line at a time. Dare we say it — "Bug Free"?}
const
  MAXSTRING    = 80;                    {maximum chars in a string}
type
  STRING       = array [1..MAXSTRING] of char;
var
  count        : integer;              {actual number of chars read}
  i            : integer;
  InputLine    : STRING;
begin
  while not eof do begin
    count := 0;                        {count is the number of chars actually read}
    while not eoln and (count < MAXSTRING) do begin
      count := count + 1;              {first increment, then read}
      read (InputLine [count])
    end;
    readln;
    {write the line}
    for i := 1 to count do             {only write the number read}
      write (InputLine [i]);
    writeln
  end
end.
```

Figure 6.3. Corrected *LINE* program that only prints the number of characters read (up to a maximum of *MAXSTRING*).

or file often requires special handling. Always test your code with data that will examine the case of the first or last item.

Failure to mark the end of a list or properly initialize a list. As we saw in the *LINE* program, the failure to reset the *InputLine* array to all blanks before each line was read leads to the echoed line containing characters from previous lines. We would never see this happening unless we typed a long line followed by a shorter one.

In summary:

Watch out for boundary conditions.

A large class of bugs relates to data validation. We've already discussed the necessity of tests on data for validity and reasonableness. Perhaps we can think of this as an extension of the notion of boundary condition errors: what does our program do with data not just at the boundaries, but beyond?

Certain specific errors relate to erroneous, out-of-range, or obviously implausible input data. In Chapter 5 we built a simple date converter that began with no checks on reasonableness on the input values and eventually developed into a program with extensive validity checking on the input values for day, month, and year. Without such checking, the program is perfectly satisfactory, *as long as no unreasonable data values are entered.* Many programs are written on the assumption (usually not even consciously stated) that all input data will be correct in form and within normally accepted ranges. We are often surprised to discover that errors occur the first time someone else uses a program we've written, because the new user's notion of reasonable data values may be quite different from our own. In fact, there's the old programmer's aphorism: if you want to find the bugs in your program, get your kid brother or sister to try it out! The next bug, then, in our growing exterminator's checklist, is:

Check input for validity and plausibility.

Of course, the question arises: What should we do with incorrect, out-of-range, or obviously invalid data? The answer, as has been discussed previously, is not clear cut. In general, however, we should try to *recover* from the error. If we are in an interactive environment, we should notify the user and allow the user to fix the value or to indicate the action that should be taken on the value. If we cannot induce the user to correct the value on the spot, the questionable data should be written to an exception file for special treatment later on. Figure 6.4 is a simple payroll example. The program reads a file *paydata*, formatted as shown in Table 6.1. If the hours worked is out of range or the rate of pay is out of range, the entire input line is written to an exception file, called, appropriately enough, *exceptions*. If the input data is within range, normal processing continues, and the computed information is written to the standard output. Input validation occurs in the routine *valid*, similar to the version in Chapter 5. We'd like to emphasize the use of error returns via an enumerated type within *valid*. If the input data is out of range, *valid* returns *false*. In addition, *valid* uses an enumerated type parameter *reason* to explain why the data is invalid. Note how the code becomes virtually self-explanatory with a piece of code such as

```
             . . .
     if hours > HOURSMAX then begin
        valid := false;
        reason := hourstoobig
     end;

             . . .
```

The determination that a data value is out of range is controlled by constants *HOURSMAX* and *RATEMAX*. These can be changed and the program re-compiled if different validity ranges are needed, or they can be defined as variables and entered as data to the program. The entire program is shown in Fig. 6.4. Sample input data, along with the standard output and the exception file, are shown in Table 6.1.

```
program PAY (input, output, paydata  payroll, exceptions);
{
Illustrates writing bad data to an exception file. In this program, if hours and
rate are within reasonable bounds, then gross pay is calculated. If either is
out of bounds, the record is written to file exceptions and processing
continues with the next record. Validity checking is done within function
valid.
}
const
   MAXHOURS      = 40;              {max hours w/out overtime pay}
   MAXSTRING     = 20;              {max chars in a string}
   OVERTIMERATE = 1.5;             {time and a half for overtime}
type
   ERRORTYPE     = (ratetoobig, hourstoobig, rateneg, hoursneg, ok);
   STRING        = array [1..MAXSTRING] of char;
var
   error              : ERRORTYPE;     {errors on input}
   ErrorCount         : integer;       {count of bad data}
   exceptions         : text;          {exception file}
   gross              : real;          {total gross pay}
   hours              : real;          {actual hours worked}
   i                  : integer;       {loop counter}
   name               : STRING;        {person's name}
   paydata            : text;          {input data file}
   PayHours           : real;          {hours for which person is being paid}
   payroll            : text;          {normal output file}
   rate               : real;          {actual rate of pay}
   ValidCount         : integer;       {count of valid data}

   function valid (hours, rate : real; var reason : ERRORTYPE) : boolean;
   {Determines if hours and rate are within reasonable bounds.}
   const
      HOURSMAX   = 100.0;             {100 hours maximum}
      RATEMAX    = 50.00;            {$50.00/hour max}
```

Figure 6.4. Payroll example: Out-of-range entries are written to an exception file.

```
begin
  valid := true;                    {assume data is valid initially}
  error := ok;
  if hours > HOURSMAX then begin
    valid := false;
    reason := hourstoobig
  end else if hours < 0.0 then begin
    valid := false;
    reason := hoursneg
  end;
  if rate > RATEMAX then begin
    valid := false;
    reason := ratetoobig
  end else if rate < 0.0 then begin
    valid := false;
    reason := rateneg
  end
end; {valid}


procedure ErrorHandler (error : ERRORTYPE; var ExceptionFile : text);
begin
  case error of
    ratetoobig :   writeln (ExceptionFile, 'Excessive rate of pay');
    hourstoobig : writeln (ExceptionFile, 'Excessive number of hours');
    rateneg :     writeln (ExceptionFile, 'Rate of pay less than 0');
    hoursneg :    writeln (ExceptionFile, 'Hours less than 0');
  end
end; {ErrorHandler}


procedure Initialize;
{Initialize input and output files for reading/writing.}
begin
  reset (paydata);
  rewrite (payroll);
  rewrite (exceptions);
  writeln (exceptions, 'Name          Rate   Hours   Reason');
  writeln (exceptions);
  writeln (payroll, 'Name          Rate   Hours   Pay Hours   Gross Pay');
  ErrorCount := 0;
  ValidCount := 0
end; {Initialize}
```

(continued)

Figure 6.4. (continued)

```
begin {main}
  Initialize;
  while not eof (paydata) do begin
    for i := 1 to MAXSTRING do
      read (paydata, name[i]);
    readln (paydata, hours, rate);
    {range/validity checking}
    if valid (hours, rate, error) then begin                        {normal processing}
      ValidCount := ValidCount + 1;
      if hours > MAXHOURS then
        PayHours := (hours − MAXHOURS) * OVERTIMERATE + hours {overtime}
      else
        PayHours := hours;
      gross := rate * PayHours;
      for i := 1 to MAXSTRING do
        write (payroll, name [i]);
      writeln (payroll, ' ', rate:6:2, ' ', hours:5:1, ' ', PayHours:6:1, '  $', gross:8:2)
    end else begin                                                  {exception processing}
      ErrorCount := ErrorCount + 1;
      for i := 1 to MAXSTRING do
        write (exceptions, name [i]);
      write (exceptions, ' ', rate : 7 : 2, ' ', hours : 7 : 2, '  ');
      ErrorHandler (error, exceptions)
    end
  end;

  writeln ('Processed', ErrorCount + ValidCount : 1, 'records.  ');
  writeln;
  writeln ('Valid : ', ValidCount : 5);
  writeln ('Out of Range : ', ErrorCount : 5)
end.
```

Table 6.1. (a) Sample input. (b) Normal output. (c) Exception file contents for program *PAY*.

(a) *Input:*

Martinez, Maria	10.0	10.75
Jones, Kathy	39.9	18.00
Nakano, Patti	42.0	22.75
Morgan, Vicki	45.0	6.75
Ratigliano, Sam	19.6	8.32
Martin, Dave	20.0	7.90
Vidal, Jacques	40.0	12.75
Jones, Sam	41.0	12.75
Miller, Lawrence	119.3	12.50
Quilici, Alex	23.5	51.50
Jones, Tom	14.5	27.50
McFaddan, Tom	− 5.5	12.50
Miller, Joe	87.0	49.50
Swenson, Marcy	43.0	− 12.50

(b) *Normal Output:*

Name	Rate	Hours	Pay Hours	Gross Pay
Martinez, Maria	10.75	10.0	10.0	$ 107.50
Jones, Kathy	18.00	39.9	39.9	$ 718.20
Nakano, Patti	22.75	42.0	45.0	$1023.75
Morgan, Vicki	6.75	45.0	52.5	$ 354.38
Ratigliano, Sam	8.32	19.6	19.6	$ 163.07
Martin, Dave	7.90	20.0	20.0	$ 158.00
Vidal, Jacques	12.75	40.0	40.0	$ 510.00
Jones, Sam	12.75	41.0	42.5	$ 541.88
Jones, Tom	27.50	14.5	14.5	$ 398.75
Miller, Joe	49.50	87.0	157.5	$7796.25

(c) *Exception File Output:*

Name	Rate	Hours	Reason
Miller, Lawrence	12.50	119.30	Excessive number of hours
Quilici, Alex	51.50	23.50	Excessive rate of pay
McFaddan, Tom	12.50	− 5.50	Hours less than 0
Swenson, Marcy	− 12.50	43.00	Rate of pay less than 0

```
{1}              count := 0;
{2}              while not eof (infile) and (count < max) do begin
{3}                  count := count + 1;
{4}                  read (infile, Data [count])
{5}              end;
```

Figure 6.5. Program segment that reads until end of file or until *count* exceeds *max*.

A subtle error, also associated with boundary condition difficulties, is the "off by one" error. This occurs when a loop variable is constructed in such a way that it either neglects the last value or goes one beyond the last value. This is often found in a **while** statement and usually in one with compound conditions. The example in Fig. 6.5 illustrates the problem.

The best solution is to hand-simulate the code and see what happens with the last value of the index variable. In the following example, we illustrate the internals of a *ReadInputData* procedure. In this procedure, we are to read from the input file, until either one of two stopping conditions occurs (a common coding practice). The two stopping conditions are: (1) end of file, and (2) number of records exceeds the maximum allowable in the array (1..*max*) for the data. The procedure also is to return a count of the actual number of data values read in.

Here is where the problem comes about. The input data array has been defined to be of size 1..*max*, but the number of data items actually read can be in the range of 0..*max*. Consequently it appears necessary to initialize *count* to 0, and then increment it when we are able to read another record from the file. What should the stopping condition be — do we stop when *count* = *max*, when *count* = (*max* − 1), or when *count* = (*max* + 1)? Let us carefully construct this stopping condition. We attempt to read the next value from the file; if we can do so, we should increment *count*, and assign the input value to *Data*[*count*]. This works correctly unless *count* is less than or equal to 0, or *count* is greater than *max*. The **while** stopping condition then should be constructed as in Fig. 6.5.

Note that the **while** loop (line 2) includes (*count* < *max*). Shouldn't this be (*count* <= *max*)? No, because we increment *count* at line 3 *before* the reading is done. This is necessary because *count* is initialized to 0 (we want *count* to be the *actual* number of values read).

Let's see if we can construct certain hypotheses (theorems, if you will) about the properties of *count*, and of the number of data items that are actually read in. For the **while** loop, we will do this by constructing a *loop invariant*. A loop invariant is an assertion about the relationship between variables within a loop that holds at the beginning and end of each loop iteration. In this case the loop invariant is that the variable *count* (after each iteration of the loop) is the number of data records read so far. An additional assertion that we wish to verify about this loop is that *count* cannot be greater than *max*, and thus that we will not attempt to make an illegal array access (at line 4 in Fig. 6.5). Of course, to verify that the stated loop invariant holds and to prove that our assertions are correct, we make tacit assumptions about the properties of the language, the run-time environment, and the operating system. Informally we assume that Pascal behaves at run-time the way we expect it to behave (in practice, this is not always the case, as we've seen in examining arithmetic and other run-time errors).

We argue informally that initially (before the loop is entered) *count* is the number of records already read in. Since no data has been read and *count* is zero, the relationship holds. In Fig. 6.5, the loop body itself consists of only two statements (3 and 4). In 3, we increment *count*. In 4, we read the next record and assign to *Data*[*count*]. That terminates a single loop iteration. Because the incrementing of *count* and the reading of the next data record occur together in the same compound (**begin-end**) statement, at the end of each loop iteration *count* is the number of records read. We do not read without incrementing, and vice-versa. The single-entry, single-exit properties of Pascal statements, and the assumptions of no side effects, assure this.

We must now show that we cannot read more than *max* records. The loop is controlled by the two stopping conditions. If the file contains fewer than *max* entries, the first predicate of the **while** statement (**not** *eof*(*infile*)) controls the loop, and we will not be able to read more than *max* records nor make an illegal assignment to the array. If we assume that the file contains at least *max* records, the second predicate (*count* < *max*) controls the loop. As an example, let us assume that *max* is 100. When *count* is 99, we are able to enter the loop. We increment *count* to 100. Since *Data* has been declared to be an array of 1..*max* records, we can legally make the assignment to *Data*[*count*]. At the next test at line 2, (*count* < *max*) is no longer *true*, and we do not enter the loop body. Consequently we do not make an assignment outside the bounds of *Data* within this loop.

We have informally proven two properties of this short loop: (1) the loop invariant (*count* is the number of records actually read) and (2) that no assignment outside the bounds of *Data* occurs. In so doing, we have corrected or avoided this subtle error:

Off by one.

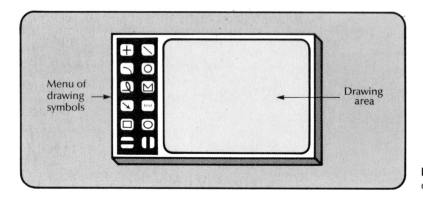

Figure 6.6. Screen layout for drawing program example.

Often related to boundary condition failures is perhaps a more general error: the failure to consider all cases. This is often associated with student programs, where there may be no well-defined a priori spec, and design consists of "code it up and see what happens."

An example that we saw first in Chapter 1 is a simple line drawing program. Suppose we wish to create a drawing program, using hardware that supports a high-resolution screen and an interactive pointing device, such as a mouse. The screen is to be divided up into functional areas as shown in Fig. 6.6.

The area on the left in Fig. 6.6 is a menu of line styles and capabilities. The major part (but not the entire part) of the screen is the drawing area. The user draws a straight line, for example, by selecting an appropriate drawing symbol from the menu area, moving to a location within the drawing area, and indicating the end points of the line segment by pressing either a key on the mouse or a function key on the terminal. At this point, the program generates a straight line between the endpoints. This is a simple and reasonable design for a program that could be used to create basic line drawings. The problem occurs, however, if an attempt is made to place one of the endpoints *outside* the drawing area, a situation that may not have occurred to the original specification writer, designer, or programmer. As in Fig. 6.7, it is clearly not appropriate to draw lines that extend beyond the drawing area boundaries. The result is an unaesthetic bug: the failure to constrain the object drawn within the drawing area.

This bug indicates that the programmer did not consider all cases when constructing the line drawing routines. The solution to the problem, however, may not be immediately obvious — it requires that the programmer have knowledge or experience in graphics programming. Before each line segment in the drawing is put onto the screen, it must be *clipped* to the appropriate

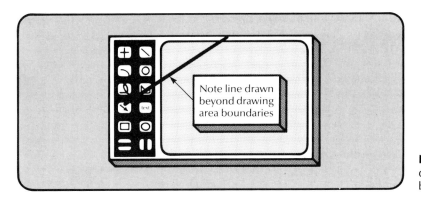

Figure 6.7. Lines incorrectly drawn beyond drawing area borders.

viewing area boundaries (called a *viewport*). Thus, in Fig. 6.7, the original line from (X_1, Y_1) to (X_2, Y_2), producing a line that extends outside the viewport, must be drawn as a line segment from (X_1', Y_1') to (X_2', Y_2'), where X_1' is the left side of the viewport, and Y_2' is the top side (see Fig. 6.8).

The intersection of the original line with the viewport boundaries determines the new points for drawing, (X_1', Y_1') and (X_2', Y_2'). Our growing list of bugs must now include:

Failure to consider all cases.

The last "internal," or programmer-based, class of errors relates to the programmer not understanding the semantics of the programming language, or having incomplete or incorrect knowledge of the run-time environment

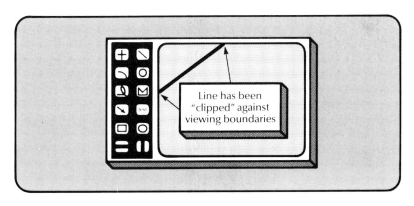

Figure 6.8. Original line clipped against viewport boundaries.

or the operating system. These types of errors are more frequent with languages whose semantics are not rigorously defined. In such cases, the program's behavior may depend on how the compiler writer interprets the language's features. A program that works perfectly well on one machine may show unexpected error behavior on another. Pascal, despite its well-designed statement semantics, does not necessarily provide adequate error handling capability and feedback. In fact, the current Pascal standard, which defines a number of error conditions, does not necessarily define what a processor is to do when such errors occur. In addition, we have seen that arithmetic results can show bizarre hardware dependencies (the example on associativity, for example), in addition to the quite different rules of integer and real arithmetic.

6.2.1 Debugging Summary

Earlier, in Chapters 4 and 5, we looked at specific coding practices that would make the debugging process easier and more straightforward. It was appropriate to present those techniques earlier, because they should and can be easily integrated into the general process of translating a design into code. We have to stress that reliable, easily tested programs are unlikely to occur unless the steps leading to coding are organized in a way that facilitates program correctness and easy debugging. We have seen in previous chapters, and have reemphasized the point in this chapter, that good design supports good programs. Those aspects of design that are most conducive to ease of implementation are related to program hierarchy, clean, coherent, loosely coupled modules, and of course, good stylistic practices in the coding process.

Programming in school is often a stress-filled, time-rushed process of just getting anything up and running and hoping that it meets some minimal specs (that is, the grader's approval). A better way to code, we have been claiming and demonstrating, is to *delay* decisions, delay the actual coding, and spend more time contemplating. The result will be programs that are less likely to have bugs initially and in which bugs are easier to detect and correct during the testing and debugging process.

The five classes of bugs that we've discussed in this chapter are as follows:

- Failure to properly initialize variables
- Boundary conditions
- Check input for validity and plausibility
- Off by one
- Failure to consider all cases

6.3 Testing

If you've followed the coding guidelines of this chapter exactly and understood the dark corners where most bugs are found, then your program is correct and bug free, and no special testing is necessary. Such is the expectation of far too many programmers. For even if these techniques are applied rigorously, including the formal verification techniques alluded to in the previous section, there are still the problems of *external* bugs, as defined earlier. Those bugs relate to failures to understand the external environment (run-time environment, operating system, and so on), or failures to properly interpret or implement the program's specifications. And, of course, late at night, an occasional bug does slip into even the most carefully written program. The purpose of program testing is to systematically probe a program to discover residual bugs. Testing does not guarantee program correctness. As the result of testing, except for very small programs, we will not be able to say conclusively that a program is bug free. Rather, testing can be a means of revealing the existence of otherwise unsuspected errors.

We test a program by constructing test cases designed to both explore a program's internal structure and by constructing tests that are oriented toward the common bugs of the last section. As test data is constructed and the program is run with that data, we gain confidence in the correctness of our code, and we discover those pieces where errors occur. Thus testing is an iterative process potentially involving further design and coding, as implied in this diagram:

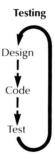

Testing

Design

Code

Test

The following discussion extends that at the end of Section 6.2. We list common bugs and discuss appropriate test case ideas to explore and probe the program for weaknesses associated with known or likely problem areas. We use these test case construction guidelines, and others, to build a set of test data for the histogram drawing program, first presented at the end of Chapter 2.

Off by one. This error is associated with loops: **for, while,** and **repeat.**
It is a subtle error to detect, since it is often associated with the

boundary conditions error. A suggestion for debugging and testing with this error in mind involves the following steps: For each loop, note the starting and ending condition of the loop variable. This is commonly 0 or 1 for the starting value, and some ending value that is often associated with the largest value in a structure such as an array. Supply test data so that loops are exercised exactly at their boundaries.

Boundary conditions.   Examine each loop, each array, and each file for upper and lower limits. Since testing boundary conditions at the upper limit can involve processing very large amounts of data, it is often effective to "artificially stress" a program by changing (during test runs) upper limits on arrays and other program constants. For example, an input line array defined initially to contain 80 characters can be redefined during testing to contain 10 characters. Under this condition, it is straightforward to generate lines with more than 10 characters. The program under test should reasonably handle this artificial line overflow test.

Unexpected cases.   By definition, this is difficult for the programmer to test. If a test can be generated for a condition that the programmer had neglected to handle, the condition would no longer be unexpected. The most appropriate way to test a program to find conditions the programmer neglected to handle is for outside parties to rigorously test the code.

Erroneous language assumptions.   As in the preceding error, this is tough for the individual programmer. Outside parties should generate test cases in the same manner as was done for tests for unexpected cases.

General cases.   In looking at boundary and other pathological cases, we may neglect to provide adequate tests of the usual, normal action of the program on its inputs. Be certain that general tests are made on any program.

6.4   Test Case Example

The first strategy in building sets of test data for the histogram program is to "walk through" the code by hand, examining all of the procedures and functions, and noting those possibilities that could lead to difficulty. In theory, this is part of the program construction and debugging phase, and if this step is carried out during program writing, using informal and formal proof techniques, we may very well be able to spot and correct errors without running the program. In doing this for the histogram, the following has been noted for this program's functions and procedures:

GetValue

Illegal values are not counted to the bucket array, rather they are counted as specific illegal values. (*Test Case:* A file containing all illegal values.) Statement: *round(inputval)*. This clearly will be an error if the input value is larger than *maxint*. A specific test case need not be created for this; rather the code should be corrected to post this value to one of the exception lists. This minor correction to *Get-Value* is as follows:

```
          . . .
else if inputvalue > maxintreal then
    valuecount [OUTOFRANGE] :=
      valuecount [OUTOFRANGE] + 1
else begin

          . . .
```

maxintreal is a real that has been set equal to *maxint*.

Count

The incoming value should go into the correct bucket. Possible illegal array reference: Can't occur because of range checking in *GetValue*. (*Test Case:* A file containing all values the same, or all values that are known to be in the same bucket. Useful in hand-checking the code.)

DrawHisto
FindMax

Finds first bucket with largest count. Assumes all counts are in the range 0..*maxint*. Hand check: Be certain that all *valuebuckets* are properly initialized to 0. *DrawHisto* performs scaling. The histogram should be aesthetically pleasing and not produce problems at scale value boundaries. (*Test Case:* A file with values that will have many values right at or near the scale value.)

On hand-checking the code, it is found that the *valuebuckets* array is not properly initialized to 0. Failure to initialize values is a potential compromise to portability and a likely cause of errors. We add the following lines at the beginning of the main program:

```
for i := 0 to MAXGROUPS do
    valuebuckets [i] := 0;              {initialize all bucket counters to 0}
```

where *i* is properly declared at the start of the program.

We used the guidelines and code notes to generate test data. The exercises contain questions that suggest additional difficulties that might occur with this program, and also suggest test cases for other example programs in the book.

All the test cases, except for the preceding one, produce correct or acceptable results. The last one shows a problem that can occur when the

Figure 6.9. Test run output from histogram program.

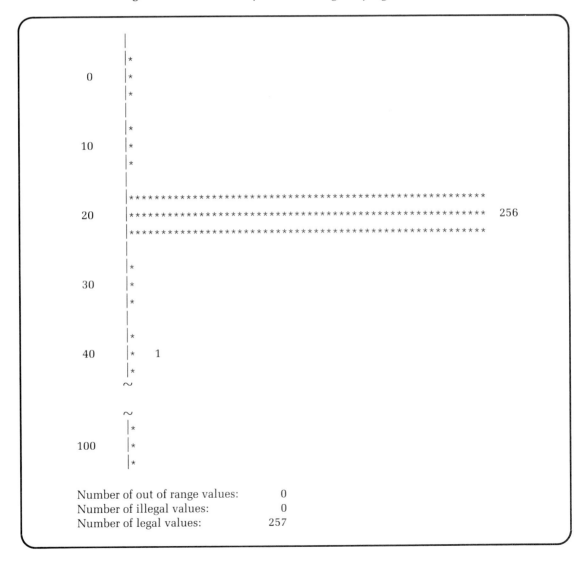

Number of out of range values: 0
Number of illegal values: 0
Number of legal values: 257

range in bucket counters is large. Because it is desirable to realistically represent the buckets' sizes, even if they contain a large count, individual bucket counts are scaled by the largest count. This scaled value is then *rounded* to produce the actual number of '*' to be printed. Clearly this scaling algorithm is not reasonable. It appears that it would be better to raise this value to the next highest integer, which can be done with this simple change:

> **while** *nextcolumn* <= *round* (*valuebuckets* [*nextbucket*] * *scale*) **do**

has been changed to:

> **while** *nextcolumn* <= *trunc* (*valuebuckets* [*nextbucket*] * *scale*) + 1 **do**

We run the new version with the same test data and produce the output shown in Fig. 6.9. This is not at all what we intended! It is clear that not only must we raise the value to the next highest integer, but we must make a special test for 0:

```
if valuebuckets [nextbucket] <> 0 then          {special test for 0}
  while nextcolumn <= trunc (valuebuckets [nextbucket] * scale) + 1 do begin
    write (VALUEMARK);
    nextcolumn := nextcolumn + 1
  end
```

And we produce, (finally!), the result we expect, as shown in Fig. 6.10.

We have used the finished version of the histogram program as our illustration of program testing. It is always reasonable to develop a test plan and apply it to a finished program, but that is not the time when testing, or thoughts of testing, should begin. Rather, the top-down, and modularly oriented program design/structuring techniques lead naturally to an incremental and top-down testing philosophy. As the highest levels of the program structure are built, lower level modules are simulated with *stubs*. Stubs are stripped-down versions of actual procedures that merely indicate that they've been called, then return to their caller. Figure 6.11 is the top-level code structure for a payroll program. It calls on the lower level functions *Initialize*, *GrossPay*, *FederalTax*, etc. We cannot test this program, however, because these procedures haven't been supplied. But we'd like to know whether the overall structure is meaningful, and we need to have the supporting structure in place as these lower level functions are written. So we begin by writing each as just a *writeln*, as in the stub for *GrossPay* in Fig. 6.12.

As each new module is integrated into the program structure (that is, as a stub is replaced by more complete code), the incrementally changed overall program can be tested at that point. In so doing, it is likely that any errors found are associated with the newly added routine. This isolation of errors to new routines is made more likely by ensuring that the routines

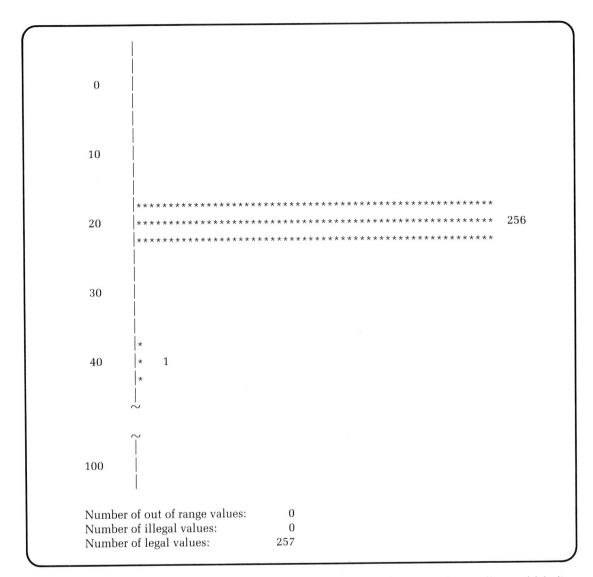

Figure 6.10. Output from histogram program after correcting scaling and labeling.

```
program PAYROLL (input, output, paydata);
{Top level structure for a payroll program.}
begin
  Initialize;
  while not eof (paydata) do begin
    ReadData;
    GrossPay;
    FederalTax;
    StateTax;
    Deductions;
    PrintCheck
  end
end.
```

Figure 6.11. Top level structure for a payroll program. The program is written as a series of function calls.

```
procedure GrossPay;
{Calculate the gross pay from hours and rate.}
begin
  writeln ('GrossPay entered')
end; {GrossPay}
```

Figure 6.12. *GrossPay*, a typical routine called from *PAYROLL*, Fig. 6.11. At first, the routine is coded as a *stub*. Later it is replaced with the completed code.

maintain the coherence and loosely coupled properties of good module design.

The completed, tested, debugged, and (we hope) correct histogram program was presented in its entirety in Chapter 2. Because of reasonable design and coding style from the start, the number of errors in the finished program was quite small. Unfortunately it is the residual errors, those that are left after all of the best design techniques and testing standards have been applied, that can be the most difficult to finally root out and correct.

6.5 Program Verification

Testing of programs can be replaced by formal verification techniques. To do this, however, we must specify very carefully and correctly the conditions within a program that must hold in order for the program to be "correct." Such an effort, it turns out, often produces a set of *verification conditions* that is longer than the original program or progamming construct to be verified. Further, formal verification can be a tedious and error-prone process.

However, this is an area of active theoretical research, and it is tempting to consider a future time when programs, or at least pieces of programs, can be automatically proven to be correct.

Even though the techniques are certainly not available for large-scale programming, we may (informally or intuitively) apply formal analysis concepts to particularly error-prone program structures as a means of assisting in the more ad hoc program testing and debugging processes. Figure 6.13 is a sort procedure, slightly modified from the first chapter's "good" program.

The procedure calls on another routine *Exchange* that exchanges the values at $A[i]$ and $A[j]$. We would like to try to convince ourselves that this procedure, embedded within a larger program, does in fact correctly sort any array of integers, with zero up to some maximum number of values. To do this, we construct a verbal statement about the values of the array A within the doubly nested **for** loops. This statement we call the *loop invariant*. In this case, the loop invariant is that, for a fixed value of i, the following relationships hold:

For $i = 1$, for any j:	$A[1] \geq \{A[2] \dots A[j]\}$
For $i = 2$, for any j:	$A[1] \geq A[2] \geq \{A[3] \dots A[j]\}$
For the general case of i:	$A[1] \geq A[2] \geq \dots \geq A[i] \geq \{A[i + 1] \dots A[j]\}$

That is, $A[1]$ through $A[i]$ is sorted, and $A[i]$ is greater than or equal to any value in the set $\{A[i + 1] \dots A[j]\}$. Consequently, upon loop exit, the entire array $A[1] \dots A[n]$ will be sorted. Note that this loop invariant is a *testable*

Figure 6.13. Sort procedure modified from Chapter 1's "good" program.

```
procedure Sort (var A : INTARRAY; n : integer);
{
Sorts the array in place. Algorithm: exchange sort.
INPUT:          A — The original array of values.
                n — The actual number of values in A.
OUTPUT:         A is sorted in place, from high to low.
}
var
   i                : integer;
   j                : integer;
begin
   for i := 1 to n − 1 do
     for j := i + 1 to n do
       if A [i] < A [j] then
         Exchange (A, i, j)
   end; {Sort}
```

```
program SORTTEST (input, output);
const
  MAX            = 1000;                      {maximum values that can be sorted}
type
  INTARRAY       = array [1..MAX] of integer;
var
  count          : integer;                   {number of values from input}
  numbers        : INTARRAY;
#include "sort.i";                            {the sorting routine}
begin
  count := 0;
  while not eof and (count < MAX) do begin
    count := count + 1;
    readln (numbers [count])
  end;
  Sort (numbers, count)
end.
```

Figure 6.14. Driver for sorting routine.

hypothesis. That is, even though we may not have the tools or mathematical ability to directly prove this assertion, it clearly suggests an instrumenting or testing operation that can be performed within the routine: at the end of each iteration through the **for** i loop, we will print i and the values of A, and we will observe whether the hypothesis holds. Again, this is not a formal proof. Rather we are using certain methods of formal proof techniques to help identify relevant test conditions. A small driver program for testing Sort is shown in Fig. 6.14. Table 6.2 shows a test data set and the program's output, after code for the output generation was added to Sort.

Table 6.2. (a) Sample input for sorting routine. (b) Output generated by sort after each iteration of the outer loop.

(a) Input Data:

15
22
19
−12
22
0
56
45
−10
9

(b) The output generated at each iteration:

i					numbers array					
1	56	15	19	−12	22	0	22	45	−10	9
2	56	45	15	−12	19	0	22	22	−10	9
3	56	45	22	−12	15	0	19	22	−10	9
4	56	45	22	22	−12	0	15	19	−10	9
5	56	45	22	22	19	−12	0	15	−10	9
6	56	45	22	22	19	15	−12	0	−10	9
7	56	45	22	22	19	15	9	−12	−10	0
8	56	45	22	22	19	15	9	0	−12	−10
9	56	45	22	22	19	15	9	0	−10	−12

Note that the output maintains the property that the first i values of the array are sorted. This greatly improves our faith in the correctness of this routine. It should still be tested for boundary conditions and potential run-time errors.

6.6 Debugging Tools

Debugging programs is easier if we have the tools that allow us to view the condition of the program as it is running. If the only way we can examine the state of a program is through the language-supplied *write* procedures, it can become difficult to trace the execution of a program and to determine where the difficulties are occurring. For one thing, the use of *write* statements requires that we have the forethought to place them in the right place initially (and our usual assumptions about the correctness of our code often cause us to neglect this), and it also means that some values are not accessible in any event: pointer (address) values may not be written using *write* procedures. Additionally, as we've seen in the earlier discussion of errors, many errors occur at places in the program that may not be adequately tested (for example, boundary conditions that may require testing the program with unusually large input values or simulating unusual dependencies in the use of the program.) Consequently we must either leave in the debugging statements, the extra *writes*, which would certainly be inappropriate in production software, or we must include them, but guard them with a state test:

> **if** *debugging*
> **then** *writeln* (...);

where *debugging* is a global boolean constant that is set *true* for compilations when debugging output is needed, and to *false* for production runs. During development runs it is common to include the debugging output (by setting *debugging* to *true*). This extra test before each *write* can affect the efficiency of a program (though an optimizing compiler, knowing that debugging is a constant, should be able to efficiently compile only the appropriate clause of the conditional, rather than having to compile in the test). Further, the amount of output can be overwhelmingly large if the *write* is contained within a loop that is repeated often or a procedure that is called often.

One technique in debugging is to produce a simple line of output when entering a procedure, stating that it's been entered, and another output line just before exiting. Figure 6.15 is a procedure *Trace* that takes two arguments: the first is a string giving the name of the routine, and the second is an enumerated type that indicates whether the caller of *Trace* has just been entered or is just about to exit. *Trace* simply writes out *ENTERING* or *EXITING* followed by the string passed as the first parameter. (Again note

```
procedure Trace (Routine : STRING; Where : ENTEROREXIT);
begin
  case Where of
    ENTER :
      writeln ('ENTERING ', Routine);
    EXIT :
      writeln ('EXITING ', Routine)
  end
end; {Trace}
```

Figure 6.15. Procedure *Trace* prints an appropriate message upon entering or exiting another procedure.

that in standard Pascal, *STRING* is not a predefined type, and so it must be declared in any program using *Trace*. We have been careful to always declare *STRING* as **array** [1..*MAXSTRING*] **of** *char*. Pascal does provide the predefined *alfa*, which is an **array** [1..10] **of** *char*.)

Exercises

1. In this chapter we have defined a number of general classes of programming bugs. List these classes and give an example of each of them. Which classes of bugs are the hardest to find? The easiest?

2. Pick a program you have recently written and do a static review of the code, paying careful attention to boundary conditions. Did you find any bugs? Would they have been likely to show up in normal use of the program?

3. Write a procedure *Assert* that takes two arguments, a boolean expression and a character array. The boolean expression represents an assertion that should be *true* at the time *Assert* is called. If the assertion is *false*, then *Assert* writes out the message. What might *Assert* be useful for? Instrument a program you have recently written with a call to *Assert* at the beginning of every procedure or function (except, of course, *Assert*). The boolean expression should represent the expected values of the parameters (and may include function calls to test things about character arrays). Did *Assert* ever write anything out? If it did, was it because your assertion was incorrectly formed, or because something you assumed to be true about the parameters wasn't?

4. Extend the *Trace* routine discussed in Section 6.6 to check if the first argument is in *DebugSet* before writing anything out. *DebugSet* should contain members of the enumerated type that represent the procedures and functions we actually want traced. If *DebugSet* is empty, no procedures are traced. Does this form of *Trace* appear to be useful? Why?

5. Write a procedure *Profile* with a single argument that is an enumerated type representing the procedures and functions we actually want traced. *Profile* simply keeps track of the number of times each procedure or function

is called. Write a procedure *DumpProfile* that prints out the procedures and the number of times they were called, sorted by number of times called. Instrument a program you have written with *Profile* and *DumpProfile* (which should be called once at the end of the program). Which procedures are being called the most often? Were they the procedures you expected? Is it possible to use *Profile* to provide statement counts of selected statements? Re-instrument a program, using *Profile*, to give execution counts for various statements.

6. Extend *Profile* to check if the first argument is in *ProfileSet* before writing anything out. *ProfileSet* should contain members of the enumerated type that represent the procedures and functions we actually want profiled. If *ProfileSet* is empty, no procedures are profiled. Does this form of *Profile* appear to be useful? Why?

7. If your Pascal has built-in clock functions, extend *Profile* to keep track of the length of time spent in each procedure. Remember that procedures can call themselves, so the desired length of time is the time actually executed for each call of the procedure, not just the entire elapsed time between entering and executing. Is *Profile* still easy to use?

8. [PROGRAMMING PROJECT] Apply *Profile*, *Trace*, and *Assert* from the previous exercises to our histogram program first developed in Chapter 2. Where could it be made more efficient? Attempt to make it more efficient. Has the code stayed readable? How much more efficient is it in actual time, and in percentage of total execution time?

9. Program *LINE* (Fig. 6.1) copied its input to its output a line at a time. Write a program that copies its input to its output a *character* at a time. What is such a program useful for? Does your operating system have a file copying utility? [*Hint:* This program is messier than it should be, because of Pascal's end of line and end of file conventions.]

   Test your program on empty files, lines with a single character, and lines that end with end of file.

10. A common programming bug is confusing **or** with **and** in conditionals with more than one clause. As an example, suppose we need to read from an input file until one of two stopping conditions occurs: the number of values read exceeds some constant *MAX*; an input value is negative. Which is the correct **while** clause:

    while (*NumberRead* < *MAX*) **and** (*NextValue* > = 0) **do**

    while (*NumberRead* < *MAX*) **or** (*NextValue* > = 0) **do**

11. The payroll program, Fig. 6.11, was designed to suggest a method of handling exceptional cases: write the exceptions to a file, then let the user fix them up at a later time. An alternative method, useful when the number of exceptions is expected to be small, is to post the record to the display and

let the user fix it up on the spot. Modify the payroll program so that it performs in this way. When an exceptional value occurs, the record is presented to the user, the user enters corrected values, and the program continues. Of course this exception handling code must also validate the data. Use direct cursor positioning (*MoveCursor*, etc.) for a cleaner, more functional user interface.

12. The error-handling routine of the payroll program is encapsulated in the procedure *ErrorHandler*, which takes an error (an enumerated type) and an output file, and writes an appropriate message. Extend the errors handled by this program to include excess total pay. Are there other errors that should be addressed? Comment on the ease of modifying this program.

13. Extend the payroll program so that it handles number of hours worked on a daily basis. Each input record consists of the person's name, the rate of pay, and the number of hours worked on each of seven days, as below.

name	rate	mon	tues	wed	thurs	fri	sat	sun
grant, rita	15.50	8.0	8.0	9.5	7.5	8.3	7.5	0.0

Compute pay based on daily overtime: 1.5 times the base rate for hours over eight; 2.0 times for any Saturday hours; 3.0 times for any Sunday hours. It will be necessary to change the definition of excess hours. For testing purposes, use 20 hours as the maximum allowed per day.

14. The following program "allegedly" converts an octal number as input into a base 10 number. Hand verify the code. State and verify the loop invariant. Run the code with an appropriate range of test conditions. Should there be any bugs, fix the code and retest.

```
program OctalToDecimal (input, output);
{Convert a string representing an OCTAL number into a DECIMAL number.}
var
  c        : char;
  sum      : integer;
begin
  while not eoln do begin
    read (c);
    sum := 8 * sum + (ord (c) − ord ('0'))
  end;
  writeln ('Decimal value: ', sum : 1)
end.
```

15. After fixing any bugs in the previous program, rewrite it so that it is a general base converter function. That is, it should take an input in any base and convert it to a number in any other base. The input and output bases are parameters to the function. The function should return *true* if the conversion is legal, *false* otherwise.

IMPLEMENTING THE FUNCTION PLOTTER — THE FIRST LAYER

7.1   Introduction

Earlier, in Chapter 3, we began the design of a useful interactive program, a function plotter. The design naturally factored into layers, and so we will implement the plotter in layers. The first of these, plotting an externally generated table of values, allows us to build the support structures of program flow and data types for later layers, as well as to perform a useful initial function. What could be better than a program that does something useful and provides a base for building something even more useful?

In this chapter we briefly review the overall design of the plotter so that we can be certain that our data structuring definitions will remain appropriate as the plotter progresses to its next layers. The concept of layered development sounds reasonable, but it implies that decisions we make in the beginning remain appropriate for the later layers also. Since these later layers involve algorithms and data structures we have not yet thought about, we must be certain that we don't make any choices that are overly limiting or idiosyncratic at this point. In the next part of the book we'll see that most actions on data structures can be described independent of the lowest level implementation, just as we can talk about arithmetic operations without being concerned whether the number system is, for example, decimal or binary.

In Chapter 6, we discussed the process of testing and verifying the correctness of our code. In this chapter we design a test plan for the layered function plotter that will help ensure the correctness of the code, and we also perform the static code review that we did on the histogram program to discover potential problems without having to perform formal tests. As we noted in the previous chapter, this static code review is quick and usually quite effective when combined with a specific checklist of things to look for. It is particularly effective when carried out by someone other than the person who wrote the piece of code in question!

7.2   Layered Design Review

Figure 7.1 reviews the design of the function plotter. In this chapter, we will build the overall structure, and the piece of the program that plots an external table of values. Figure 7.2 shows in diagrammatic form, the activities that the point plotter must perform.

The main program is written to follow the simple structure of Fig. 7.2. It performs initialization, reads the table of values from the external file *TABLE* into the internal structure *points*, performs the plotting by scaling the points to the screen structure *screen* (as developed in Chapter 4), and

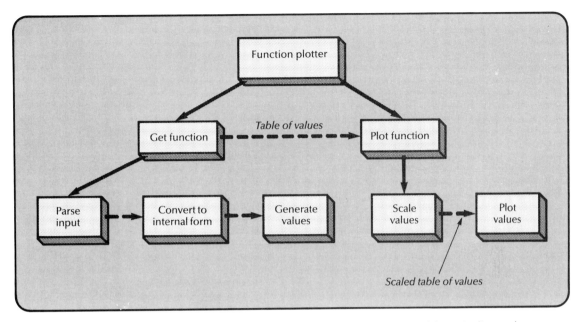

Figure 7.1. Overall function plotter design. (The dashed lines indicate data coupling between modules.)

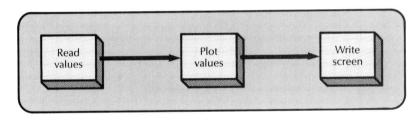

Figure 7.2. Overall structure of point plotting program.

then writes the internal screen structure to the physical display device (the terminal screen here). The entire main program is shown in Fig. 7.3.

Each of the routines *ReadPoints*, *plot*, and *WriteScreen* will be written according to the design of Chapter 3. As we saw in that chapter, only *plot* has any complexity to it. Much of the work of implementing the function

```
begin {main}
  ReadPoints (TABLE, points);
  plot (screen, points);
  WriteScreen (screen)
end.
```

Figure 7.3. Main program as a series of procedure calls for the first layer of the function plotter.

plotter was done a long time ago: making the design decisions about point plotting, deciding on a layered approach — first plotting a table of values, and so on.

7.3   Data Structures

Two data structures need to be defined and manipulated in the plotter: the internal representation for the points to be plotted (the table of values) and the internal representation of the screen. In addition, for this layer of the plotter, we need to define the external file arrangement for the values.

Table of values

The table of values will be an external text file consisting of lines of x, y pairs, one pair per line. They will be real values; the first is the x value or abscissa, and the second is the y value, or the value of the function evaluated at the given x (the ordinate[1]). To plot the values to the screen, we need to know the range of x and y values. We could insist that the range of values be available in the external file, but it is safest not to make too many assumptions about the file's structure or content. So we will have to determine the maximum and minimum values of x and y from the data. This means that all x, y pairs must be available after all the data has been read, so that scaling can be performed.

Without knowing the range of x and y in advance, the program cannot process each of the x, y pairs sequentially. As each point is read from the external file, the variables *maxx*, *minx*, *maxy*, and *miny* will have to be updated, if necessary, and the current x, y pair copied to an internal data structure. This structure, after all the points from the file have been read in, is then passed to routine *plot*, which takes the values, performs appropriate scaling, and writes them into the screen array.

We define the table of values as a Pascal **record** containing six fields:

- An array of records, each a single x, y point.
- Minimum and maximum values for x and y (four values).
- The count of the actual number of x, y points.

Since we need all the values in storage at once, we must preallocate the array of records. To do this, we have to make a reasonable guess as to the

---

[1] Someone once told me that you can tell which axis is the abscissa and which is the ordinate because the ordinate is the one with the same shape as your mouth when you say it. Try it by lingering on the "o" in ordinate.

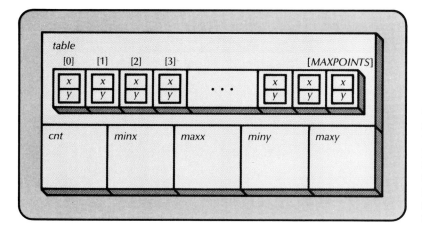

Figure 7.4. *PLOTINFO* data structure record with six fields: *table* (the array of *x*, *y* values), *cnt* (the actual number of values in *table*), and *minx*, *maxx*, *miny*, and *maxy*, the minimum and maximum values of *x* and *y* respectively.

maximum number of points that we might wish to plot. Except for functions where the range in x is quite large, most plots require only a small percentage of the maximum number of plottable points. By hand, we often create plots with only a few points (by interpolating curved lines between the points). Plots of reasonable fidelity can usually be built with a few hundred points. We define this value in the constant *MAXPOINTS*, which we have set to 500. If this value is too large, the program runs more slowly; if too small, we discard values that we should be keeping. It is a value that should be set with knowledge, obviously, of the maximum number of points likely to be in the external file.

We define the structure to be a type, *PLOTINFO*, defined under the following **type** definition:

```
type
   PLOTINFO        =
      record
         table       : POINTARRAY;      {table of points to plot}
         cnt         : POINTCNT;        {number of elements}
         minx, maxx  : real;
         miny, maxy  : real             {minimum, maximum values of points}
      end;
```

The type *POINTARRAY* is an array of x, y points, as mentioned earlier. *POINTARRAY* and *POINTCNT* are defined as follows and are shown in the diagram of Fig. 7.4.

```
         type
            POINT         =
               record
                  x, y        : real
               end;
            POINTCNT       = 0..MAXPOINTS;
            POINTARRAY     = array [POINTCNT] of POINT;
```

The screen

The internal representation of the screen must mirror the physical device used for plotting points. Think of the screen as being a two-dimensional array of points, with the origin in the upper left. For this program, a plotting surface begins with column number 1, row number 1, and runs to MAXCOL columns, MAXROW rows. A standard character CRT has 24 rows and 80 columns, indexed either from 0 or 1, so we use these values in the constant definitions of MAXCOL and MAXROW:

```
const
    MAXCOL        = 79;          {columns of screen — term specific}
    MAXROW        = 23;          {rows on screen — term specific}
```

We can use these program constants to plot to devices of different resolution. To plot to a typical line printer, we might use MAXCOL of 120 or 132, and MAXROW of 60.

We define the type SCREENARRAY to be a two-dimensional array of characters. We use a blank when there is no point to be plotted at the given location, and a special plotting symbol (an asterisk, *) when there is a point. Here is the data type for SCREENARRAY:

```
type
    COLS              = 1..MAXCOL;
    ROWS              = 1..MAXROW;
    SCREENARRAY       = array [ROWS, COLS] of char;
```

Scaling

We must take an x, y point, x and y in the range from minx to maxx, miny to maxy, respectively, and scale so that x falls in the range of 1 to MAXCOL and y falls in the range of 1 to MAXROW. Each point in the POINTARRAY structure must be multiplied by the appropriate scale factor: one for x, another for y. In Chapter 3, we saw how this is accomplished.

7.4 The Code

Figure 7.5 is the complete program for the first layer function plotter. All subsequent layers will build upon the program flow and data structures defined in this version. The main program is a series of procedure calls, as we saw in Fig. 7.3. The other routines maintain the loosely coupled, single input, single output nature of highly independent modules. In Chapter 9, and again in Chapter 13, we will add new layers to the program, keeping much of the structure and control flow developed here.

```
program PLOTTER (input, output, TABLE);
{
DESCRIPTION:        Simple function plotter driver. In this driver, the points to be plotted are
                    read from the external file TABLE, which contains lines of x, y pairs, one
                    pair per line.
INPUT:              A table of x, y pairs, one pair per line, in the file TABLE.
OUTPUT:             The function is plotted to the standard output (the display screen).
VERSION:            2.0.
AUTHOR:             L. Miller & A. Quilici.
}
const
{
A number of these constants are terminal specific, and need to be changed for different
terminals. For each terminal, the top line and left-most column may be zero or one. The
maximum number of columns and rows also varies.
}
    FuncLine        = 0;                    {first col for messages — term specific}
    FuncCol         = 0;                    {first line for messages — term specific}
    MAXCOL          = 79;                   {columns of screen — term specific}
    MAXPOINTS       = 500;                  {max points: MAXROW*MAXCOL/4}
    MAXROW          = 23;                   {rows on screen — term specific}
type
    COLS            = 1..MAXCOL;
    ROWS            = 1..MAXROW;
    POINT           =
      record
        x, y        : real
      end;
    POINTCNT        = 0..MAXPOINTS;
    POINTARRAY      = array [POINTCNT] of POINT;
    SCREENARRAY     = array [ROWS, COLS] of char;
    PLOTINFO        =
      record
        table       : POINTARRAY;          {table of points to plot}
        cnt         : POINTCNT;            {number of elements}
        minx, maxx  : real;
        miny, maxy  : real                 {minimum, maximum values of points}
      end;
var
    points          : PLOTINFO;            {table of points to plot}
    screen          : SCREENARRAY;         {screen representation}
    TABLE           : text;                {table of points}

#include "cursor.i";                       {direct cursor positioning — Chapter 4}
```

(continued)

Figure 7.5. The completely coded first layer function plotter.

Figure 7.5. (continued)

```
procedure ReadPoints (var TABLE : text; var points : PLOTINFO);
{
Reads the external file TABLE, a table of x, y pairs. Updates the values of minx, maxx, miny,
maxy, and places all of the information in the points record. This is then made available to
the plot procedures.
INPUT:              A file of x, y pairs, one pair per line. The values are reals. They do not
                    have to be in order of increasing x.
OUTPUT:             The record points is written. The table field contains the x, y values. The
                    cnt field is the actual number of values read. minx, maxx, miny, and
                    maxy are set from the data.
}
var
  count             : POINTCNT;                      {number of points read}
  maxx, minx        : real;
  maxy, miny        : real;
  x, y              : real;
begin
  reset (TABLE);
  count := 0;
  ClearScreen;
  if not eof (TABLE) then begin                      {read first pair, set minx, maxx, etc.}
    count := count + 1;
    readln (TABLE, x, y);                            {no error checking, for clarity}
    points.table [count].x := x;
    points.table [count].y := y;
    maxx := x;
    minx := x;
    maxy := y;
    miny := y
  end;

  while not eof (TABLE) and (Count < MAXPOINTS) do begin
    count := count + 1;
    readln (TABLE, x, y);                            {no error checking, for clarity}
    points.table [count].x := x;
    points.table [count].y := y;
    if x > maxx then
      maxx := x
    else if x < minx then
      minx := x;
    if y > maxy then
      maxy := y
    else if y < miny then
      miny := y
  end;
```

```
    points.cnt := count;
    points.minx := minx;
    points.maxx := maxx;
    points.miny := miny;
    points.maxy := maxy;
    ClearScreen
end; {ReadPoints}


procedure plot (var screen : SCREENARRAY; var points : PLOTINFO);
{
Places the axis and points into the screen array for later printing. The following are defined
under plot:
    PlotAxis
    PlotPoints
    ComputeScale
}
const
    NOMARK        = ' ';                    {indicates no points here}
    PNTMARK       = '*';                    {indicates point here}
    XMARK         = '–';                    {indicates x axis}
    XYMARK        = '+';                    {indicates x, y axis intersection}
    YMARK         = '|';                    {indicates y axis}


    procedure PlotAxis (var screen : SCREENARRAY);
    {Plots the axis into the screen array.}
    var
      xaxis, yaxis   : integer;
      nextx, nexty   : integer;
    begin
      yaxis := 1;
      xaxis := MAXROW;                      {default x, y axis}
      for nextx := 1 to MAXROW do
        for nexty := 1 to MAXCOL do
          if yaxis = nexty then
            screen [nextx, nexty] := YMARK
          else if xaxis = nextx then
            screen [nextx, nexty] := XMARK
          else
            screen [nextx, nexty] := NOMARK;
      screen [xaxis, yaxis] := XYMARK
    end; {PlotAxis}
```

(continued)

Figure 7.5. (continued)

```
procedure PlotPoints (var screen : SCREENARRAY; var points : PLOTINFO);
{Places the points into the screen in the correct place, first computing a scaling factor.}
var
   answer            : char;
   nextpoint         : POINTCNT;
   scalex, scaley    : real;
   yindex            : integer;
   ymin, ymax        : real;

   function ComputeScale (maxval, minval : real; DeltaS : integer) : real;
   begin
     if maxval − minval <> 0 then
        ComputeScale := (DeltaS − 1)/(maxval − minval)
     else
        ComputeScale := 0.0
   end; {ComputeScale}


begin {PlotPoints}
   scalex := ComputeScale (points.maxx, points.minx, MAXCOL);
   MoveCursor (FuncLine, FuncCol);
   ClearEOL;
   write ('MinY: ', points.miny : 7 : 1, ' MaxY: ', points.maxy : 7 : 1);
   ymax := points.maxy;
   ymin := points.miny;                          {default initialization}
   MoveCursor (FuncLine, FuncCol + 40);
   ClearEOL;
   write ('WANT TO CHANGE [Y or N]?         ');
   MoveCursor (FuncLine, FuncCol + 66);
   ClearEOL;
   readln (answer);
   if answer in ['Y', 'y'] then begin
      MoveCursor (FuncLine, FuncCol + 40);
      ClearEOL;
      write ('ymin: ');
      readln (ymin);                             {no error checking, for clarity}
      MoveCursor (FuncLine, FuncCol + 40);
      ClearEOL;
      write ('ymax: ');
      readln (ymax)                              {no error checking, for clarity}
   end;
   scaley := ComputeScale (ymax, ymin, MAXROW);
   MoveCursor (FuncLine, FuncCol);
   ClearEOL;
   write ('scalex: ', scalex : 7 : 2, ' scaley : ', scaley : 7 : 2);
```

```
      for nextpoint := 1 to points.cnt do
        with points.table [nextpoint] do begin
          yindex := MAXROW + 1 - round (scaley * (y - points.miny) + 1);
          if yindex > MAXROW then
            yindex := MAXROW
          else if yindex < 1 then
            yindex := 1;
          screen [yindex, round (scalex * (x - points.minx) + 1)] := PNTMARK
        end
    end; {PlotPoints}

begin {plot}
  PlotAxis (screen);
  PlotPoints (screen, points)
end; {plot}

procedure WriteScreen (var screen : SCREENARRAY);
{Writes out the screen array.}
var
  nextcol          : COLS;
  nextrow          : ROWS;
begin
  MoveCursor (FuncLine, FuncCol);
  for nextrow := 1 to MAXROW do begin
    for nextcol := 1 to MAXCOL do
      write (screen [nextrow, nextcol]);
    writeln
  end
end; {WriteScreen}

begin {main}
  ReadPoints (TABLE, points);
  plot (screen, points);
  WriteScreen (screen)
end.
```

By this time, the plotter should seem like a simple program to you —
that is the advantage of a highly structured approach to program design
and construction. By the end of Chapter 13, we will have built a program
of surprising sophistication in its algorithms and data structures. But we
will have done it in such a way that its design, its operation, and the
function of all its modules are open and easily testable and modifiable. In
addition, the structures turn out to be so useful that we will make use of
large portions of the code for the mini-spreadsheet program of Chapter 14.

7.5   Testing and Debugging the Code

Test cases are developed to ensure that the five classic "buggy" areas are tested. We can use the following list of bugs, repeated from Chapter 6, as a checklist to walk through the code by hand, to look for potential problems, and to build test case files.

- Failure to properly initialize variables
- Boundary conditions
- Check input for validity and plausibility
- Off by one
- Failure to consider all cases

The first potential bug develops from "failure to properly initialize variables." The main program contains the variables *points* and *screen*. *points* is the record containing the points read from the external file. The *maxx*, *minx*, *maxy*, and *miny* fields are initialized and properly set within *ReadPoints*. The table itself is not initialized. As we saw in Chapter 6, failure to initialize an array of characters leads to unexpected results when we print the array. We do not need to initialize the point values, however, because the number of points we're dealing with is carried along as an additional field in *points*: the *cnt* field.

In *ReadPoints* we use a local variable, *count*. As an aid in verifying the correctness of the code, we want to carefully specify the condition that *count* will have: it is the actual number of points read from the file *TABLE*. This is the notion of a loop invariant as discussed in Chapter 6. In *ReadPoints*, *count* is properly initialized to 0. We read points from the file within a **while** loop:

. . .

```
while not eof (TABLE) and (count < MAXPOINTS) do begin
  count := count + 1;
  readln (TABLE, x, y);              {no error checking, for clarity}
  points.table [count].x := x;
  points.table [count].y := y;
  if x > maxx then
    maxx := x
  else if x < minx then
    minx := x;
  if y > maxy then
    maxy := y
  else if y < miny then
    miny := y
end;
```

. . .

Within the **while** loop, we first increment *count*, and then we read the next x, y pair. After each iteration through the loop, *count* has been increased by one, and one more pair has been read. This hand-checking of the code gives us confidence that the reading is being performed correctly: *count* is the actual number of values read.

But suppose the file contains more than *MAXPOINTS* values. What will the value of *count* be then? Note that there are two controlling clauses in the **while** loop:

while not *eof* (*TABLE*) **and** (*count* < *MAXPOINTS*) **do begin**

When *count* is exactly *MAXPOINTS*, we do not enter the loop again. Consequently, if the file contains more than *MAXPOINTS* points, *count* will be *MAXPOINTS*, and that is the number of x, y pairs placed into *points*. Further, all the updating of *minx*, *maxx*, and so forth, is performed within the **while** loop, so those values are properly set. *ReadPoints*, at least by hand-checking, is correct.

Of course, we will perform a test case with a file of more than *MAXPOINTS* pairs (which we do by changing the constant *MAXPOINTS* to 5). But we're fairly confident that we won't have any difficulty with this case. We'll run through each of the routines, discuss potential problems against our bug checklist, and suggest test cases that will probe for difficulties.

PlotAxis	Draws the axes into the screen array. This just draws a horizontal line at the bottom of the display and a vertical one along the left side. The correctness criteria: The axes should look aesthetically pleasing!
PlotPoints	Actually places the points into the screen array. Points are scaled into the appropriate range: x between 0 and *MAXCOL*, y between 0 and *MAXROW*. In the function *ComputeScale*, note that we're dividing by (*maxval–minval*). We should guard the division to avoid division by zero, which we have done. To test that the scaling is being done properly, we should test with a file with a small number of points and hand-calculate the scaling factors. Then we should add debugging output statements to *PlotPoints*, to print the current screen array indexes. *ComputeScale* could be rewritten to

include debugging output, as follows:

```
function ComputeScale (maxval, minval : real;
    DeltaS : integer) : real;
var
    sf : real;                          {scale factor — for debugging}
begin
    if maxval − minval <> 0 then
        sf := (DeltaS − 1)/(maxval − minval)
    else
        sf := 0.0;
    ComputeScale := sf;
    if debugging then begin
        MoveCursor (FuncLine, DEBUGCOL);
        ClearEOL;
        writeln ('Scale Factor : ', sf : 6 : 2);
        writeln ('Type CR to continue');
        readln
    end
end; {ComputeScale}
```

Note that we never actually initialized *screen* in *PlotPoints*, based on the assumption that character arrays are initialized to blanks. But if we ever reuse *screen* (which we certainly will do in the later layers of the plotter), we must initialize it to blanks. The code to do this should be added to the beginning of *PlotPoints*. Try it as an exercise for yourself.

WriteScreen   We start at the top row of the screen and simply write the entire array *screen* to the display. Again, we're assuming that anything we didn't specifically write into *screen* is a blank. Anything left over from previous plots (as we saw in Chapter 6) produces anomalous output. This reinforces the need to add the additional lines of code to blank out *screen* within *PlotPoints*.

With the hand-checking of the code finished, we can write test cases that are designed to look for specific problems. However, to clarify the structure, we have specifically not put in the *NEWREADLN* code from Chapter 1. You certainly should do that for yourself when you implement the plotter. If we have a test case with illegal real values (character data,

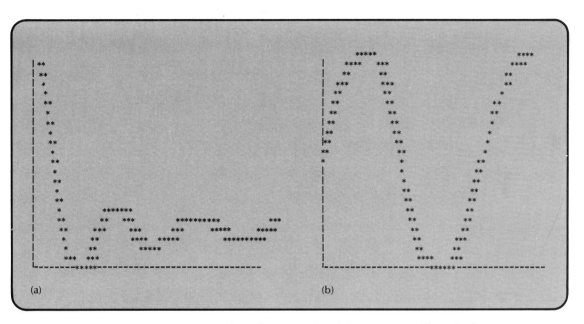

Figure 7.6. Output from function plotter for various tables of values, generated by the indicated function. (a) Plot of *sin(x)/x* for *x* from 0.01 to 20 radians. (b) Plot of *sin(x)* for *x* from 0.0 to 8 radians.

and so on), our program will crash! Of course, the plotter should work well with general case data also! In Fig. 7.6, we show the output after having plotted two different functions.

Exercises

1. Implement the function plotter on a computer you have access to, and test it by plotting a number of different functions. Remember, for each function you wish to plot, you must write a small program to generate the *x*, *y* pairs used as function plotter input. Are each of these functions plotted reasonably?
2. Add the *NEWREADLN* code from Chapter 1 to help protect the function plotter from run-time errors due to illegal characters in the input.
3. Modify the function plotter to allow different locations and methods of axes placement. Axes placement could depend on the function plotted.

When all points are negative, the axes could be placed at the top and far right of the screen. When points are spread evenly over all quadrants, the axes could be placed bisecting the screen. Should the placement of axes vary with the function plotted? Should the user be given a choice of axes placement?

4. Modify the function plotter so the user is asked for the maximum number of points to plot (*MAXPOINTS*). Plot *sin*(x) using various values for *MAXPOINTS*. Was our value for *MAXPOINTS* reasonable? Should *MAXPOINTS* vary with the screen size?

5. Modify the function plotter so that more than one function can be plotted per execution. The user should be asked for the name of a file containing the points to plot. If your Pascal environment allows a Pascal program to verify file existence and readability, your function plotter should do so.

6. Modify the function plotter so the user can specify the screen size to plot (up to some predefined maximum) before the function is plotted. There should be some reasonable default. Are functions plotted reasonably regardless of the range of points?

7. Some of the exercises of previous chapters involved the specification and design of nontrivial programs. For one of these programs, or any other program you have designed, attempt to implement those parts of the design that seem straightforward to implement. If something is confusing, it will probably be clearer after reading the next section of the book. Include debugging code, and test each piece of your program thoroughly before going onto the next piece.

8. Write a function-value generating program that builds a table of values. The program will have the function to be computed "wired in" as a function call, and should request minimum and maximum x values from the user. Make use of direct cursor positioning and the other screen management routines to make the user interface as pleasant as possible.

   Add code to the program to verify all input values for correct type and reasonableness. Make use of *NEWREADLN* from Chapter 1, and any additional validation tests that seem reasonable.

9. The current version of the function plotter does not label the x or y axes (the final version in Chapter 13 does, however). Add the code to this version of the plotter to label the axes. Because the resolution of a typical CRT display is not very high, use as few values as possible. One way to do this is to label the 0.0 value of the x and y axes, and the minimum and maximum values of each. Test your results on several different functions.

10. We can define a "normalized coordinate" system for a CRT to be a real number from 0.0 to 1.0 in both the x and y directions, with the origin at the lower left. Then any (x, y) point with coordinates from (0.0, 0.0) to (1.0,

1.0) can be plotted to the display (of course, the normalized coordinates will have to be mapped into the actual device coordinates).

Write a program that, given two points, draws a straight line between them. If the two points are not on the screen (one or more of the points is outside the range [0.0 .. 1.0]), then the line will have to be "clipped" against the screen boundaries, as discussed briefly in Chapter 6.

11. Add an option to the function plotter so that the plot can be saved to a file after the function has been plotted. If your operating system allows dynamic file naming, then ask the user for the name of the plot file; otherwise, just rewrite a wired-in name.

12. The design of the function plotter requires that all points to be plotted be written to the two dimensional array *screen* before plotting. There were two reasons for this: so the plots can be written to an external file for later plotting to another output device, and so the screen array could be written to a device that does not use direct cursor positioning. If we know that the output will always be able to make use of direct cursor positioning, the intermediate array is not needed. Modify the plotter so that output goes directly to the screen, making use of direct cursor movement, *MoveCursor*.

DATA STRUCTURES
AND ALGORITHMS

LINKED LISTS

8.1   Abstract Data Types

In this chapter we begin looking at a powerful class of data representation techniques that will greatly increase the tools and algorithms at our disposal for programming and problem solving: linked and dynamic data structures.

Throughout the last section of the book, we tried repeatedly to delay lower level implementation, representation, and data structuring decisions. When we finally had to select some one method of representing the data, or one particular algorithm, we indicated that we would not concern ourselves with finding the best. Instead, we satisfied ourselves with selecting what we thought would be a reasonable technique, did the best we could at implementing our choice, and then observed how the program performed with real data. In so doing, we were able to clearly see that some routines might be quite slow, but since they were called only rarely, they contributed little to the overall execution time of a program.

We have reached a point where we can no longer hide our structures and algorithms in lower and lower level routines. We have reached bottom, and we must now decide just exactly how data should be represented for a given problem and what particular algorithm should be used to solve the problem. Or so it seems! Actually, even when we are at the point of designing *specific* representations and selecting one *specific* algorithm, we will isolate those decisions from the rest of the program, so that only those (very few) routines that need to manipulate the structures directly need know about their actual, program/machine-dependent realization.

We do this by defining an *Abstract Data Type* (ADT), which is an idealization of the characteristics that we would like the particular data object to have. Building upon that ADT, we define a set of access procedures; then all attempts to manipulate the ADT are made through these procedures.

This part of the book is important because it gives us a new set of tools by which to implement programs (data structures). In addition, it gives us a handle on important means of using those tools (algorithms). Finally, it gives us the techniques for selecting good, even best, tools and means, and of knowing why they are good (algorithm analysis). At the end of this chapter is a *Programming Notes* section. Programming notes are designed to give added insight into real-world use of the structures and algorithms of the chapter, and to suggest ways of optimizing their use (going from "good" to "optimum").

8.2   Linear Structures

8.2.1 Linked Lists

Arrays are common structures in programs because they have the property that access to any one element in a list takes a fixed, small amount of time. Basic operations include *insert*, *delete*, and *find*. If we insert at the end of

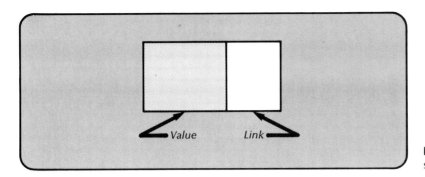

Figure 8.1. Diagram of a simple two-field node.

a list, or we always process elements of a list in turn, an array provides a fast mechanism. As we've seen, insertions or deletions from the middle of a list become painful if we must use arrays; each element in the array might have to be shifted to make room for the new element or to close up the space left by the deleted one.

An alternative structure for implementing lists and the basic operations is a *linked list.* Linked lists differ from arrays in that there is no simple addressing relationship between one element and another. To correctly implement linked lists, we need additional information contained in each element of the list—the location (or address) of the next element in the list. Each element in a linked list must have at least two fields: a field containing the value of that element and a field indicating the location of the next element. (See Fig. 8.1.) Elements of the list are hooked, or linked, together via their "link" fields. Figure 8.2 shows an array and a linked list representation for a list of integers.

Some basic terms that are used in discussing linked lists should be mentioned. First, the values are stored in a *node* of the linked list. The components of a node are called *fields.* A node has at least a *data* or *value* field, and a *link* or *next* field. The link field points to (gives the *address* of) the next node in the list. There is also a special address used to mark the end of a list. In Pascal, this end-of-list address is given the name **nil.** In diagrams, we may use either the Pascal reserved word **nil** or a slash (/). Occasionally you will see the electrical "ground" symbol used to indicate **nil.** These alternatives are shown in Fig. 8.3.

Pascal allows us to define linked lists and pointers as primitive structures. Consequently building and manipulating linked lists are straightforward. First, the declaration of an individual node:

```
type
  node      =
    record
      data    : integer;
      link    : ↑ node
    end;
```

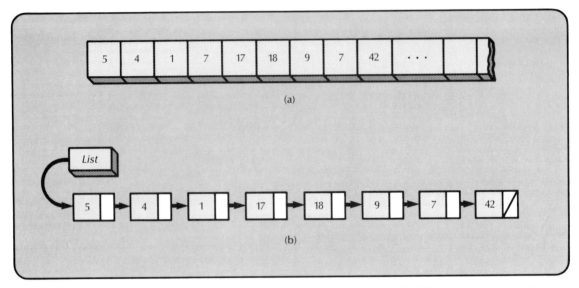

(a)

(b)

Figure 8.2. (a) Array representation of a list. (b) Linked list representation for a list of integers.

A node is defined as having two fields. The *data* field contains any standard or user defined type. Here we've used integer; later we'll use a generic type, *WHATEVER*, that can be defined for the particular application. The location of the next node in the list is contained in the *link* field. It is declared as a "pointer" type. The up arrow symbol (↑) tells the compiler that the type of this field is an address, or pointer. Since Pascal is strongly typed, a pointer may point to only one type of value. In this case the *link* field may contain only the *address*, or location, of another *node*.

To use a linked list we must declare a variable to be an appropriate type. Generally, a linked list is indicated by a pointer to the first node in the list. Subsequent nodes are then found by following the address chains.

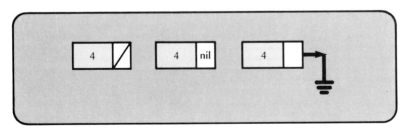

Figure 8.3. A linked list node showing alternative representations for **nil.**

A pointer to a linked list is declared in a **var** statement such as:

> **var**
> List   : ↑ node;

We haven't said anything about how these nodes are created. Since each node is a single, isolated record, it might appear that we have to declare, in a series of **var** statements, each node that we might possibly need. Fortunately such is not the case, because Pascal allows nodes to be *dynamically* allocated. That is, we do not have to declare the number of nodes that we will need in advance! Every time we need a new, empty, uninitialized node, we make a call to the built-in Pascal procedure *new*. This procedure greatly enhances the flexibility of Pascal and makes the use of linked lists reasonable. Dynamic (that is, while the program is running) storage allocation frees us from having to estimate the maximum size in advance. Instead, the run-time environment manages all free space in the machine's memory.

We illustrate these powerful new tools by building a program that takes a list of integers and places each in turn at the start of a linked list called *List*. The data types are just the ones built above. The program has one point worth noting here: the initialization of the variable *List* to the empty list. As with all variables used in Pascal programs, it is essential that pointers be properly initialized to the empty pointer **nil.** Unlike many data types, pointers are not initialized to a default value. Figure 8.4 builds the list, adding each new value to the beginning of the list.

The *new* function takes a pointer variable and finds, somewhere in memory, a block of the appropriate size. It returns, as its parameter, the address of that block. If no more memory is available, the *new* will fail fatally; the program will crash. In Fig. 8.4, *new(temp)* returns a two-word block of memory, a *node*. Both the *data* field and the *link* field are not initialized. The situation looks as follows:

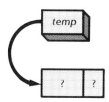

Consequently we must place the appropriate *NextValue* into the *data* field:

> temp ↑ .data := NextValue;

```
program INSERT (input, output);
{Insert values at start of a linked list.}
type
    nodeptr         =  ↑ node;
    WHATEVER        = integer;
    node            =
        record
            data        : WHATEVER;
            link        : nodeptr
        end;
var
    List            : nodeptr;
    NextValue       : WHATEVER;
    temp            : nodeptr;
begin
    List := nil;                                    {initialize to empty list}
    while not eof do begin
        readln (NextValue);
        new (temp);                                 {allocates new, uninitialized node}
        temp ↑ .data := NextValue;                  {assign the data field}
        temp ↑ .link := List;                       {link field points to head of list}
        List := temp                                {list points to new node}
    end;
    {Print list from head to end.}
    temp := List;
    while temp <> nil do begin
        writeln (temp ↑ .data);
        temp := temp ↑ .link
    end
end.
```

Figure 8.4. Program that builds a linked list by inserting new values at the start.

And we must hook the new node onto the start of the linked list:

$$temp \uparrow .link := List;$$
$$List := temp;$$

The list looks like Fig. 8.5 as we read a number of values, get a new node for each, place the value in the *data* field, and then link up the list correctly.

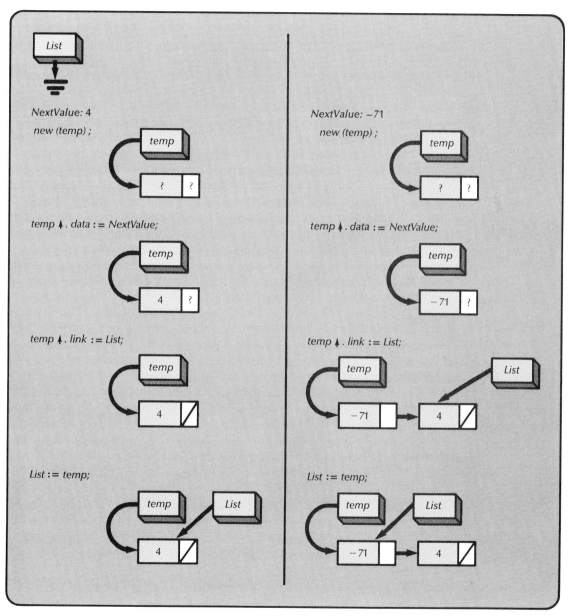

Figure 8.5. Diagram showing stages in allocating and inserting values in a list.

Linked list programming is not always very intuitive. It is important that you use whatever aids are most helpful in understanding the dynamics of list insertion, deletion, and searching. Drawings showing list changes as operations are performed are most helpful.

8.3 A Linked List Application: Insertion Sort

We're going to extend the insertion sort techniques that we first looked at in Chapter 1 by using a linked list rather than an array. To do this most efficiently, we first define the basic operations that we would need in a package of routines that deal with lists, and then we try to package them together with the appropriate data structure definitions and apply them to the task of sorting. These routines are defined in a "plain wrap" way: they are appropriate for any implementation of a linear list, whether it is an array or a linked list. Previously we saw implementations of most of these on arrays. Now we develop the routines with pointers and dynamic structures.

The first routine will be to generate an empty linked list. This is certainly a fundamental operation, so we will define a routine to do that:

```
procedure InitList (var List : nodeptr);
begin
   List := nil
end; {InitList}
```

This is not very interesting, but it is useful. But there are more complex list structures that will require a bit more work to correctly initialize them. Let's add something more interesting: we would like to insert a new node at the start of a list. We write a procedure that takes two parameters, a value of whatever type the list is using in its *data* field, and a pointer to the list, and augments the list by putting a new node at the start.

```
procedure InsertAtStart (var List : nodeptr; value : WHATEVER);
{Insert value into a new node, AT START of list pointed to by List.}
var
   temp : nodeptr;
begin
   new (temp);
   temp ↑ .data := value;
   temp ↑ .link := List;
   List := temp
end; {InsertAtStart}
```

This procedure works for both inserting at the start of an empty list (see Fig. 8.6(a)), or at the start of a nonempty list (see Fig. 8.6(b)).

Finally, we need a procedure that inserts a new node *after* the node pointed to by a node pointer. The following procedure is useful for the

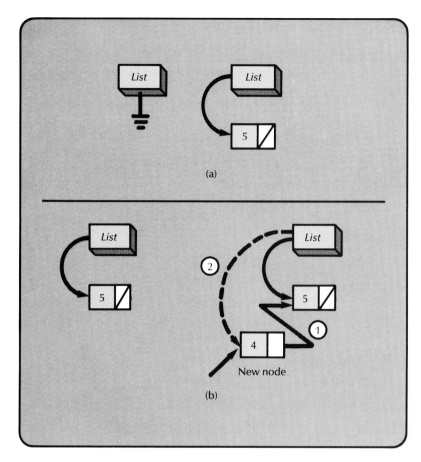

Figure 8.6. (a) Inserting at the start of an empty list (*List* = **nil**). (b) Inserting at the start of a nonempty list.

sorting program at the end of this section.

```
procedure InsertAfter (var List : nodeptr; value : WHATEVER);
{Insert value into a new node, AFTER the node pointed to by List.}
var
   temp : nodeptr;
begin
   new(temp);
   temp ↑ .data := value;
   temp ↑ .link := nil;
   if List = nil then              {Insert into empty list}
      List := temp
   else begin
      temp ↑ .link := List ↑ .link;    {1}
      List ↑ .link := temp             {2}
   end
end; {InsertAfter}
```

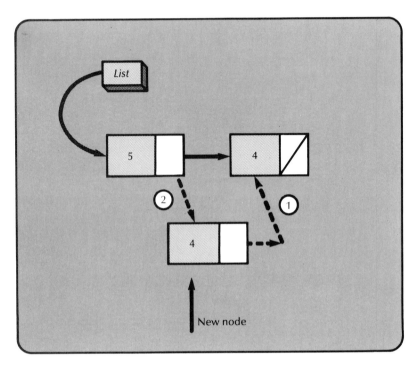

Figure 8.7. Insertion into a linked list after the node pointed to by *List*.

Because we are inserting after a given node, we have two cases to consider: *List* is pointing to **nil** (that is, we are inserting into an empty list), and the general case that *List* is pointing to a node in the linked list. Trace through the code for each of the cases by hand and see the effect of the procedure. In particular, note the order of assigning pointers for the general case, in the statements numbered {1} and {2} illustrated in Fig. 8.7.

In order to print the data in a list, we'll need a routine *PrintList*. It takes a pointer to a list and prints the *data* fields of each node in turn. We call such an operation *traversing* the list.

```
procedure PrintList (List : nodeptr);
{Write the values in each node pointed to by List.}
begin
  while List <> nil do begin
    writeln (List ↑ .data);
    List := List ↑ .link
  end
end; {PrintList}
```

We now use these routines to write an insertion sort program, this time representing the numbers in a linked list. We need one more linked list routine to do this, the one that takes an integer (or whatever) and finds the appropriate place in the list to insert the new value. As we noted in Chapter 5, this involves comparing the new value with each element in the list until we find the first one that is larger than the value. We then insert the new value *before* this element. A minor problem here. Our linked list ADT provided for *InsertAfter*. Inserting *before* a given node is a bit of a problem, because the *link* field in a node points to the next node in the chain, not back to its predecessor. To handle this, we use *two* pointers: One that points to the current node in the chain, the one we are comparing, and the other that points to its predecessor.

This is a common programming technique with linked lists, and we have a name for the predecessor pointer: it is called a *trailing link pointer*, or *trailing pointer* for short. When we wish to insert the new value into the list, the picture is as shown in Fig. 8.8. The entire procedure to insert *value* into the list pointed to by *List*, using previously defined routines, is shown in Fig. 8.9.

The code in Fig. 8.9 is worth spending some time with. First note that it uses the previously defined procedures *InsertAfter* and *InsertAtStart*. By defining these actions as separate routines, the actions of *InsertInOrder* should be clearer. However, as with many routines dealing with linked lists, note that the boundary cases are particularly irksome. We must be concerned about inserting the new value into an empty list, at the start of an existing list, or at the end of an existing list. In scanning the list to find the appropriate place to insert the new value, we note that there are in fact

Figure 8.8. Insertion of a new node just after *Previous* and just before *Current*.

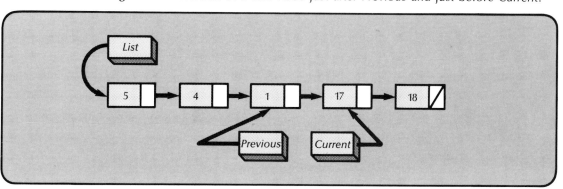

(as was the case with the array implementation) *two* stopping conditions: We have found a value in the list larger than the new value, or we have reached the end of the list. With linked list representations, each may have to be handled as a separate, special case. Consequently linked list coding requires a checklist to ensure that our code correctly handles the following cases:

- Empty list
- Start of list
- End of list
- List with a only a single node
- General case

Figure 8.9. Procedure that finds appropriate place to insert a value into an already sorted linked list, and does the insertion.

```
procedure InsertInOrder (var List : nodeptr; value : WHATEVER);
{Finds the appropriate place in List to insert value.}
var
  AtEnd      : boolean;
  current    : nodeptr;
  previous   : nodeptr;
begin
  if List = nil then
    InsertAfter (List, value)
  else begin
    current := List;
    previous := List;
    AtEnd := false;
    while (value > current↑.data) and not AtEnd do
      if current↑.link = nil then
        AtEnd := true
      else begin
        previous := current;
        current := current↑.link
      end;
    {At end of list, or found insertion place}
    if AtEnd then
      InsertAfter (current, value)
    else if current = list then              {insert at start}
      InsertAtStart (List, value)
    else
      InsertAfter (previous, value)
  end
end; {InsertInOrder}
```

```
procedure Sort (var A : ARRAYTYPE; L, U : integer);
{Sorts the elements from L to U of array A in place.}
var
   i               : integer;
   SortedA      : nodeptr;
begin
   InitList (SortedA);
   for i := L to U do
      InsertInOrder (SortedA, A[i]);
   for i := L to U do begin
      A[i] := SortedA ↑ .data;
      SortedA := SortedA ↑ .link
   end
end; {Sort}
```

Figure 8.10. Sort routine combining the various ADT list routines.

You should trace through this procedure with a number of different lists to see that it correctly functions with each of the cases using the preceding checklist. Note in particular the order in which the two pointers, *current* (the pointer used for comparisons with *value*) and *previous* (the trailing link pointer), are modified. We also need the boolean variable *AtEnd* to handle the case of inserting at the end of the list correctly.

We combine all the preceding routines in a sorting routine (Fig. 8.10) that takes as input an array A of *WHATEVER* (integer, real, and so on), and sorts $A[L]$ through $A[U]$ in place. *ARRAYTYPE* is declared as **array** $[1..MAX]$ **of** *WHATEVER*.

8.4 Deletion from a Linked List

We illustrate deleting a node from a linked list with a simple routine to remove an arbitrary node from a list. Removing a node from a linked list is a simple matter of adjusting one pointer. But when we consider the case of removing the first node of a list, or removing a node from a list with a single node, our code becomes larger and its function less clear. The deletion routine in Fig. 8.11 removes the node pointed to by T from a one-way linked list (that is, it removes $T \uparrow$). The routine also requires an additional parameter: a pointer P to the parent of the to-be-deleted node. (See Fig. 8.12.)

The routines in Fig. 8.11 include a call to the built-in Pascal procedure *dispose*. This procedure takes the space pointed to by its parameter and returns it to the free storage pool. As such, its function is the inverse of

```
procedure Delete (var List : NODEPTR; P, T : NODEPTR);
{Delete the node pointed to by T, with parent P, from List.}
var
  temp : NODEPTR;

  procedure DeleteFirst (var List : NODEPTR);
  {Remove the first node from List.}
  begin
    if List <> nil then begin              {always test for empty list}
      temp := List;
      List := List↑.link;
      dispose (temp)
    end
  end; {DeleteFirst}

  procedure DeleteAfter (var T : NODEPTR);
  {Remove the node following T.}
  begin
    if T <> nil then                       {always test for empty list}
      if T↑.link <> nil then               {test for end of list}
      begin
        temp := T↑.link;
        T↑.link := temp↑.link;
        dispose (temp)
      end
  end; {DeleteAfter}

begin {Delete}
  if T = List then
    DeleteFirst (List)
  else
    DeleteAfter (P)
end; {Delete}
```

Figure 8.11. Routines for deleting a node from a one-way linked list. *Delete* requires three parameters: the list, a pointer (*T*) to the node to be deleted, and a pointer (*P*) to its parent.

Figure 8.12. One-way list with pointer to *T* and a pointer to its parent *P*.

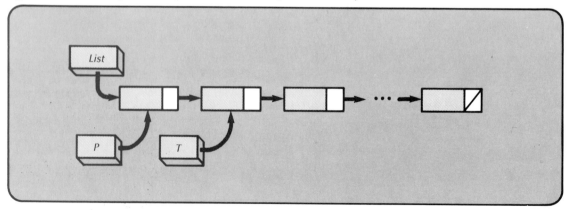

258

new. The management of such a free storage pool, however, becomes quite complex when both *new* and *dispose* are implemented. Consequently many environments do not, in fact, implement *dispose;* the procedure name is legal, it just doesn't do anything.

8.5   Additional Linear Linked Lists

Many of the operations on lists naturally require movement in both directions, such as printing (traversing) a list from back to front, finding the predecessor of a node, and so on, rather than the one-way nature of the linked lists we have just defined. A two-way linked list will have two pointer fields: one a pointer to the next node in the list and the other a pointer back to the previous node. (See Fig. 8.13.)

Such a structure is easily defined and manipulated in Pascal by extensions to the type declarations:

```
type
   TwoWayPtr        =  ↑ TwoWayNode;
   TwoWayNode       =
      record
         data       : WHATEVER;
         next       : TwoWayPtr;
         previous   : TwoWayPtr
      end;
```

With a two-way list, routines such as *InsertAfter* become a bit trickier because we must manipulate four pointer fields, and they must be done in the correct order. Figure 8.14 is the *InsertAfter* procedure that takes a pointer to a two-way linked list and a value to be inserted after the node pointed

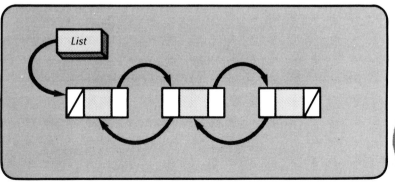

Figure 8.13. Two-way linked list.

```
procedure InsertAfter (var List : TwoWayPtr; value : WHATEVER);
{Insert value into a new node, AFTER the node pointed to by List, a two-way linked list.}
var
  temp : TwoWayPtr;
begin
  new (temp);
  temp ↑ .data := value;
  if List = nil then begin                    {insert into empty list}
    List := temp;
    temp ↑ .next := nil;
    temp ↑ .previous := nil
  end else begin
    temp ↑ .next := List ↑ .next;             {1}
    if List ↑ .next <> nil then
      List ↑ .next ↑ .previous := temp;       {2}
    temp ↑ .previous := List;                 {3}
    List ↑ .next := temp                      {4}
  end
end; {InsertAfter}
```

Figure 8.14. *InsertAfter* procedure using a two-way linked list.

to. Again, note the special test for insertion into an empty list (**if** *List* = **nil**). The four steps for this insertion are diagrammed in Fig. 8.15.

Step 2 in Fig. 8.14 seems most curious (*List* ↑ .*next* ↑ .*previous* := *temp*). It is clear what we are trying to do: the *previous* field of the node following *List* should point back, not to *List*, but to the new node *temp*. First, we identify this node following *List*. It is *List* ↑ .*next*. Its *previous* field may be specified in one expression as *List* ↑ .*next* ↑ .*previous*. The assignment to this field is made in line 2.

A major advantage of two-way lists is that we do not need a trailing pointer, and we may move freely in either direction throughout the list. Since a two-way list is symmetric with respect to direction of motion, it seems appropriate to associate two pointers with a two-way list: a pointer to the head of the list and another to its tail as in Fig. 8.16.

Our final linear linked structure is the *circular* linked list. This completes the notion of symmetry in a linear list by having the *link* field of the last node point back to the first node in the list. Circular lists can be implemented as one-way or two-way lists. Figure 8.17 shows a one-way list. Note that the special properties of the first and last node (no node points to the first,

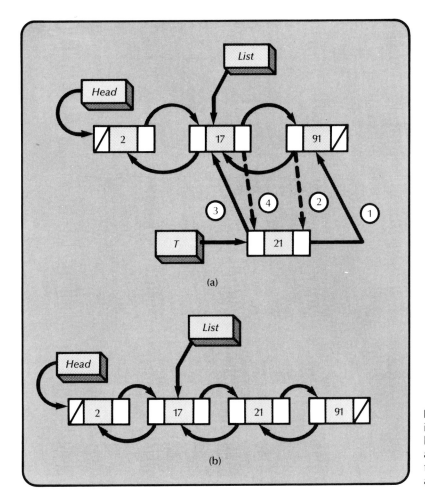

(a)

(b)

Figure 8.15. Four-step insertion into a two-way linked list. (a) Before adjustment. (b) After all four links have been adjusted.

Figure 8.16. Two-way list with two pointers, one to the head, the other to the tail.

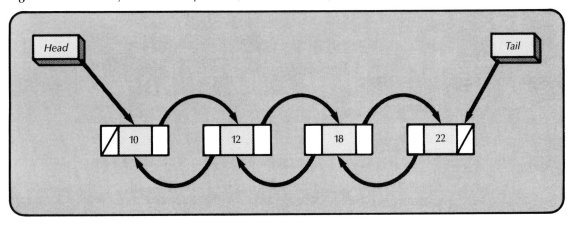

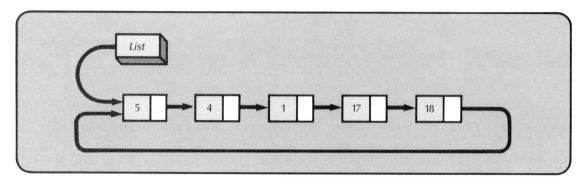

Figure 8.17. One-way circular linked list.

Figure 8.18. Insertion at start of a one-way circular linked list. (a) Empty list. (b) General case.

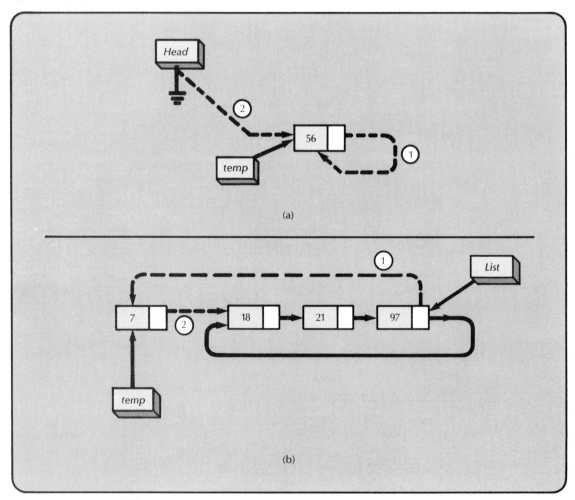

(a)

(b)

and the last node points to **nil**) no longer hold. Any node in the list can be distinguished as the head.

Inserting at the start of a circular linked list might seem particularly troublesome, since it appears that we must go to the end of the list so that the *link* field of the last node may point back to the new head. To avoid this difficulty, we require that the pointer that we usually use to point to the head of the list actually point to the *last* element in the list. In this case, inserting at the beginning is a trivial matter of inserting at the end! This is shown in Fig. 8.18 and in a rewrite of the procedure *InsertAtStart* (Fig. 8.19) for a one-way circular linked list.

Even though there is never a **nil** pointer in any node in a circular list, the initial value of the list pointer, *List*, is **nil** to indicate an empty list. Each of the earlier procedures for usual one-way or two-way linked lists can be modified to handle circular lists:

InitList,
InsertAtStart,
InsertAfter,
Delete,
InsertInOrder,
PrintList
Sort

Figure 8.19. Routine to insert a value at the start of a circular linked list.

```
procedure InsertAtStart (var List : nodeptr; value : WHATEVER);
{
Insert value into a new node, AT START of list pointed to by List. We assume that List points
to the LAST node of a one-way, circular linked list.
}
var
   temp : nodeptr;
begin
   new (temp);
   temp ↑ .data := value;
   if List = nil then                          {insert into empty list}
     List := temp
   else
     temp ↑ .link := List ↑ .link;
   List ↑ .link := temp
end; {InsertAtStart}
```

Programming Notes

Header Nodes

Many of the routines for dealing with linked lists required extra code specifically for handling the notoriously error-prone boundary/empty list conditions: inserting into an empty list, deleting from an empty list, handling a list with only a single node, and so on. Many of the linked list routines were substantially increased in size just to handle these special cases. An alternative solution to this problem, and one you should consider using when writing your own programs to manipulate these linear linked structures (and the nonlinear trees of Chapter 10), is the use of a dummy, or header, node, as illustrated in Fig. 8.20. In this way, a list is *never* empty. We will show an example and code for manipulating a simple one-way linear list. The other linked list routines can be modified to deal with lists with dummy nodes. Figure 8.20 shows the usual one-way linked list, but with a dummy header node added.

Figure 8.20. Diagram of one-way linked list with header node: (a) general case; (b) empty list.

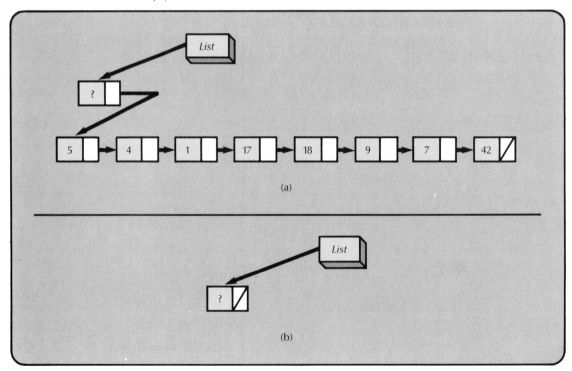

First we note that the header node looks just like an ordinary node, except that it does not contain any data. In Fig. 8.21 we've rewritten the routines *InitList* and *InsertAfter*, and a routine *PrintList* that prints the *data* field of each node in the list. We've written a complete driver program that reads integers and inserts them at the beginning of the linked lists. Examine the main program carefully, because it does not appear to depend at all on the fact that the list is a one-way list with a dummy node! And, in fact, the main program does not need to know about the underlying representation at all. The advantage of thinking and implementing lists as abstract objects

```
program DUMMYTEST (input, output);
{
Driver program for building linked lists using a one-way list with a dummy header node.
Integers are read and added to the front of a one-way linked list. Notice in the main program
that all of the calls to the list routines make use of abstract LIST operations: it is irrelevant to
the main program whether the list is an array, or one of the various linked lists.
INPUT:              A list of integers, one per line.
OUTPUT:             The list is printed in reverse order.
}
type
  WHATEVER          = integer;
  NODEPTR           = ↑ NODE;
  NODE              =
    record
      data            : WHATEVER;
      link            : NODEPTR
    end;
var
  L                 : NODEPTR;
  Next              : WHATEVER;

  procedure InitList (var List : NODEPTR);
  {Initialize List to the empty list.}
  var
    temp : NODEPTR;
  begin
    new (temp);              {get the dummy node}
    temp ↑ .link := nil;     {set its link to nil}
    List := temp
  end; {InitList}                                          (continued)
```

Figure 8.21. Procedures *InitList*, *InsertAfter*, and *PrintList* modified to use a dummy header node, with a driver program that illustrates their use.

Figure 8.21. (continued)

```
procedure InsertAfter (var List : NODEPTR; value : WHATEVER);
{Insert value into a new node, AFTER the node pointed to by List.}
var
   temp : NODEPTR;
begin
   new (temp);
   temp ↑ .data := value;
   temp ↑ .link := List ↑ .link;
   List ↑ .link := temp
end; {InsertAfter}

procedure PrintList (List : NODEPTR);
{Print the data fields of the list pointed to by List.}
begin
   List := List ↑ .link;          {skip over the dummy node}
   while List <> nil do begin
      writeln (List ↑ .data);
      List := List ↑ .link
   end
end; {PrintList}

begin {main}
   InitList (L);                   {create an empty list}
   while not eof do begin
      readln (Next);
      InsertAfter (L, Next)        {insert new value into L}
   end;
   PrintList (L)                   {print the contents of L}
end.
```

is that the programs that need lists can be written without regard to how they're implemented. The main program will work equally well whether we implement the routines using linked lists or arrays.

Exercises

1. In this chapter we introduced the most common operations performed on linked lists. This exercise asks you to write some of the other relatively common linked-list operations. Write the following functions, assuming

one-way linked lists:

a) *Count (list)*—returns a count of the number of elements in *list*.

b) *Nth (list, n)*—returns a pointer to the nth element in *list*, or **nil** if there aren't at least n elements.

c) *Last (list)*—returns a pointer to the last element in *list*, or **nil** if *list* is empty.

d) *Sort (list)*—returns a pointer to *list* sorted in increasing order.

e) *StripValue (list, value)*—returns a pointer to a list which is formed by removing all elements of *list* whose contents are equal to *value*.

f) *Shrink (list, SourceList)*—returns a pointer to a list created by deleting all elements of *list* with the value of any element in *SourceList*, another list.

g) *CountValue (list, value)*—returns the number of elements in *list* whose value is *value*.

2. Repeat Exercise 1, assuming these functions operate on doubly linked lists.

3. Repeat Exercise 1, assuming these functions operate on singly linked, circular lists.

4. Write a function *CopyList* that takes a list and makes a copy of it, returning a pointer to the newly copied list.

5. Write a function *Merge(L1, L2, L3)* that merges two already-sorted lists *L1* and *L2* to produce a third sorted list, *L3*.

6. Consider the following structure representing a linked list (assuming that *node* represents the standard node in a singly linked list):

```
type
   LISTPTR          = ↑ list;
   NODEPTR          = ↑ node;
   list             =
      record
         head, tail    : NODEPTR;
         count         : integer
      end;
```

Repeat Exercise 1, assuming each of these functions are passed *LISTPTR*'s instead of *NODEPTR*'s.

7. Write a procedure *Delete(list, value)* that takes a pointer to a doubly linked list and a value, and removes any element with that value from the list.

8. Repeat Exercise 7, assuming *Delete* is given a pointer to a singly linked circular list.

9. Repeat Exercise 7, assuming *Delete* is given a pointer to a doubly linked circular list.

10. Sets are a familiar data type of Pascal, and they are sometimes implemented

using a sorted linked list. Here is one possible type declaration for sets:

```
type
    ASETPTR    = ↑ ASET;
    NODEPTR    = ↑ node;
    ASET       =
      record
        count    : integer;
        nodes    : NODEPTR
      end;
```

Treating sets as an abstract data type, and remembering that sets can have no duplicate elements, write the following set operations. Remember that the type of data in a set is determined by the type of the *data* field of a node.

a) *Create (setptr)*—creates a set and initializes it to the empty set.

b) *AddElement (setptr, element)*—adds *element* to the set given by *setptr*.

c) *DelElement (setptr, element)*—deletes *element* from the set given by *setptr*.

d) *Member (setptr, element)*—returns *true* if *element* is in the set given by *setptr* and *false* otherwise.

e) *Cardinality (setptr)*—returns the number of elements in the set given by *setptr*.

f) *Union (sp1, sp2)*—a function that creates a new set which is the union of the sets given by *sp1* and *sp2*, and returns a pointer to it.

g) *Intersection (sp1, sp2)*—a function that creates a new set which is the intersection of the sets given by *sp1* and *sp2*, and returns a pointer to it.

h) *Difference (sp1, sp2)*—creates a new set which is the set difference of the sets given by *sp1* and *sp2*, and returns a pointer to it.

i) *IsEmpty (setptr)*—returns *true* if the set given by *setptr* is the empty set and *false* otherwise.

11. Write a procedure *Reverse (list)* that takes a pointer to a linked list and reverses the pointers in the nodes. If the list originally looks like:

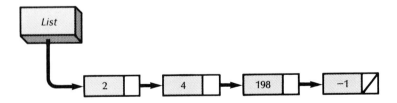

then after the procedure is called, it will look like:

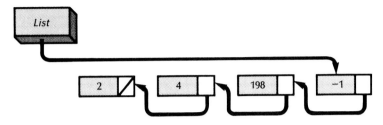

12. Modify the insertion sort routine, Fig. 8.10, so that it uses a doubly linked list. Use this in a program that reads values from the input (until *eof*), then sorts them with the modified insertion sort. After sorting, request the order of output: low to high or high to low. Then print the values in the indicated order.

13. Modify the insertion sort routine, Fig. 8.10, so that it sorts character strings (defined as **array** [1..*MAXSTRING*] **of** *char*). Write a program that reads input lines and sorts them using the modified insertion sort routine, then prints them in order.

    The following exercises explore the use of dynamic storage allocation for arrays (rather than records). They illustrate how arbitrarily long strings can be stored and manipulated in Pascal.

14. Given the following declarations, write a program that reads a string and stores it in the dynamically allocated array *Line*, then prints the string.

    ```
    const
        MAXSTRING      = 100;
    type
        STRING         = array [1..MAXSTRING] of char;
        STRINGPTR      = ↑ STRING;
    var
        Line           : STRINGPTR;
    ```

15. Extend the previous exercise so that it reads an arbitrary number of strings, each stored in a dynamically allocated array, and inserts each in turn at the end of a linked list. Each node in the list will contain two pointers, one a pointer to a string, the other a pointer to the next node in the list.

16. Now write a program that allows for arbitrarily long strings (an arbitrary number of characters terminated by a carriage return), by storing each N character piece of the string in a node (using the technique of the previous exercise). N can be around 10 or 20. You will need some way of marking the end of the last piece of the long string. After the long string is entered and stored, it should be printed out.

DATA STRUCTURES USING LISTS: QUEUES AND STACKS

Certain specific list structures have proven to be valuable for implementing a number of important algorithms. Two of these structures, *stacks* and *queues*, are so important that we will look at them in detail, and examine some useful applications. We will examine the queue in the first section, and the stack (also called a "pushdown stack," but usually referred to as just a "stack") in the next. The stack structure will also allow us to continue the layered construction of the function plotter. In this chapter, we'll build the pieces that take a post-fix function from the user, build the internal representation, repeatedly evaluate that representation in order to build the internal table of values, and, of course, plot the table.

9.1   Queues

Perhaps the most common restriction on a linear list, certainly the one that we have the most direct, human experience with, is the *queue*. When we line up for a movie, wait our turn at the bank, submit jobs to be run in a computer center, we are directly or indirectly manipulating a linear list through the limited access techniques allowed: join the line at the rear, leave from the front. These restrictions define a queue, a list restricted to making insertions only at the end and removals only from the front.[1]

First person
in movie queue

Last person
in queue

[1] The word "queue" has an interesting etymology, since the primary meaning of the word (now obsolete) is "...the tail of a beast." One occasionally applies such a definition to debugging and other joys of programming.

With people waiting in line to see a film, the queue discipline is maintained by the good manners and expectations of the members of the queue. Other than by the force of our verbal skills in patiently explaining the mechanisms by which movie lines are restricted access linear lists, there is no external formal mechanism for maintaining the queue. We will see how we define and maintain a queue in Pascal (using, of course, the available structures: arrays and linked lists). We know that in Pascal, as in life (!), the queue can only be maintained by the discipline and common agreement among the routines that need to access it. To protect all the code that needs a queue for its own purposes, we define a queue as an abstract data type (ADT), with a limited set of operations. Consequently all accesses to a program's queues are allowed only through this set of routines. As with all other ADTs we have defined and will define, we carefully assess the access requirements, and then write the routines in such a way that their internal operations are disguised from the calling routines. It will make no difference to outsiders whether the queue is maintained as an array or a linked list (or, for that matter, some obscure combination of file reads and writes). Consequently, for those languages that do not support the initial implementation, we need only rewrite the direct queue manipulation routines (for insert and delete as well as the utilities to create the queue, test various characteristics, and so on), to port our programs to a new environment.

This description of our (programming) view of a queue contrasts with queues as a problem representation and solving tool. As with the stacks we develop in the next section, we should realize that these structures did not come to us fully formed. Rather, they have proven to be important, useful objects for representing processes and solving certain classes of problems. Queues have a long and rich mathematical history. Queueing[2] theory examines the mathematical properties associated with queues as an intermediate structure for servers and jobs awaiting service. One important question is how large a queue must be for a particular application. The answer requires a detailed mathematical analysis of the number of servers and the rates at which they can service the queue; the number and interarrival rates of jobs needing service, and so on. For the design of a movie line, the size of the queue also depends on the quality of the film: for some films, the queue will be very short; for the latest space or science fiction epic, the queue will have to be quite long. Since queue overflow can occur, we also need to concern ourselves with the discipline of handling arrivals to an already full queue.

---

[2] The word "queueing" is an interesting one, by the way, because it appears to be the only word in the English language with five successive vowels (u e u e i)!

The basic operations we need to perform on a queue are:

Enqueue(Q, V)
: Boolean function that inserts V at the rear of Q. If the queue was full before the attempt to insert V, the function returns *false*; otherwise, *true*. (In the linked representation of a queue, overflow is not expected. In any event, using the Pascal *new* procedure causes a fatal error when it fails.)

Dequeue(Q, V)
: Boolean function that returns the front of the queue in V. If the queue is empty, the function returns *false*; otherwise, *true*.

InitQueue(Q)
: Returns a new, empty queue.

IsFull(Q), IsEmpty(Q)
: Boolean functions that return *true* if the queue is full (or empty), as appropriate.

These are not necessarily the only operations we will ever have to perform on a queue. With the linked representations, some of these are so trivial that they suggest in-line code rather than procedure/function calls. We will, however, write both linked and array implementations for each, because there are enough differences to warrant the attention. The linked list queue will look like Fig. 9.1(a), and the array representation looks like Fig. 9.1(b).

9.1.1 Queue as Linked List

Since we access the queue at two locations (insert at *rear*, remove from *front*), it appears necessary to have two pointers for a queue. For the linked representation we assume the following data type declarations:

```
type
  QPTR            = ↑ QueueElement;
  QueueElement    =
    record
      value       : WHATEVER;
      next        : QPTR
    end;
  QUEUE           =
    record
      Front       : QPTR;
      Rear        : QPTR
    end;
```

WHATEVER is declared to be the appropriate type for the data represented in the queue. Note that the queue itself is a record containing two pointers:

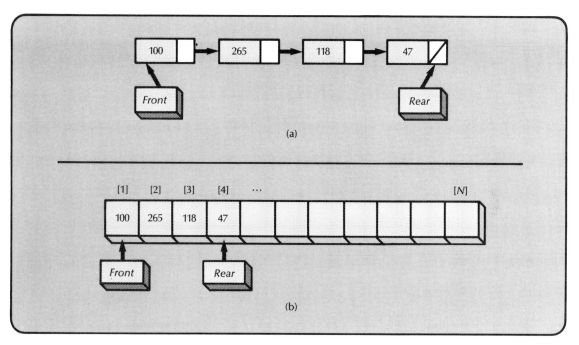

Figure 9.1. Two diagrams of a queue: (a) as a linked list; (b) as an array. Each has two pointers, *Front* and *Rear*.

Front, a pointer to the front of the list (from which elements are removed or dequeued), and *Rear*, a pointer to the end, where elements are added or enqueued. We can simplify the definition of a queue and only require one pointer if we use a *circular* linked list, as shown in Fig. 9.2.

As usual, we must be careful to perform the operations correctly when inserting into an empty queue, or removing from a queue with a single

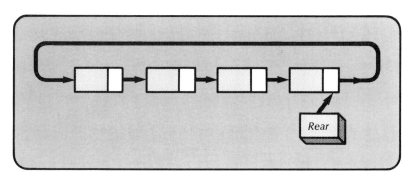

Figure 9.2. Diagram of a queue as a one-way circular linked list. In this case, all insertions are made after *Rear*, and deletions are made by removing the node following *Rear*.

```
function IsFull (Q : QUEUE) : boolean;
begin
  IsFull := false                                {assume no overflow with linked lists}
end; {IsFull}


function IsEmpty (Q : QUEUE) : boolean;
begin
    IsEmpty := Q = nil
end; {IsEmpty}


procedure InitQueue (var Q : QUEUE);
begin
  Q := nil
end; {InitQueue}

function Enqueue (var Q : QUEUE; V : WHATEVER) : boolean;
begin
  if IsFull(Q) then
    Enqueue := false
  else begin
    if IsEmpty(Q) then
      InsertAtStart(Q,V)
    else begin
      new(temp);
      temp↑.value := V;
      temp↑.next := Q↑.next;
      Q↑.next := temp;
      Q := temp
    end;
    Enqueue := true
  end
end; {Enqueue}

function Dequeue (var Q : QUEUE; var V : WHATEVER) : boolean;
var
  Front : QUEUE;
begin
  if IsEmpty(Q) then
    Dequeue := false
  else if Q↑.next = Q then begin;              {queue with one element}
    Dequeue := true;
    Front := Q;
    V := Q↑.value;
    Q := nil
    dispose(Front)
  end else begin                                {remove from general queue}
```

Figure 9.3. Basic operations on the queue ADT.

```
    Dequeue := true;
    Front := Q ↑ .next;
    V := Front ↑ .value;
    Q ↑ .next := Front ↑ .next;
    dispose(Front)
  end
end; {Dequeue}
```

element. In a circular list, the data types are simplified and we show them here:

```
type
  QPTR              = ↑ QueueElement;
  QueueElement      =
    record
      value         : WHATEVER;
      next          : QPTR
    end;
  QUEUE             = QPTR;
```

With this simpler structure, we now look at the straightforward code for the queue ADT. The following routines make use of the previous type definitions, and of the procedure *InsertAtStart* defined in Section 8.5 (Fig. 8.19). That procedure inserted a value of type *WHATEVER* at the beginning of a one-way, circular linked list. However, it took a list parameter of type *nodeptr*. For a queue, we need a list of type *QUEUE*. Consequently, because of Pascal's strong typing, we must change the declaration of this procedure to:

procedure *InsertAtStart* (**var** List : *QUEUE*; *value* : *WHATEVER*);

Figure 9.3 shows the basic operations for the queue ADT.

9.1.2 Queue as Array

In Fig. 9.1(b), we saw a diagram representing a queue in an array. For arrays, there is no way to avoid requiring two indexes: one for the front and another for the rear. The problem with the array representation is that queues gobble up memory: when we insert into the queue, we must increment the rear pointer; when we delete, we also increment the front pointer. Eventually all of the array will be used, yet the queue might very well not be full, or it may even be empty, as we see in Fig. 9.4.

An elegant solution to this annoyance[3] is to view the array in terms of modular arithmetic: in this case, the array of N elements is continuous from

[3] A favorite word of mine: much in programming involves finding solutions to minor environment- and language-induced annoyances.

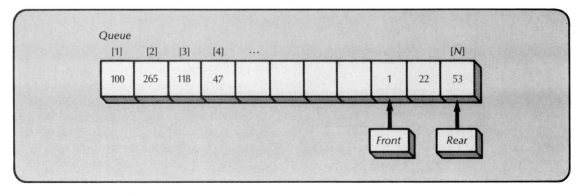

Figure 9.4. Queue as array gobbling up all of memory. Here the queue has only three elements, but there is no room for more.

Q[0] to Q[N − 1], with the successor of Q[N − 1] being Q[0]. We call such a structure a *circular queue*, shown in Fig. 9.5. We will show the *Enqueue* routine for the circular queue. The other routines are straightforward and are left as exercises. Because of the problem of filling the queue array when the queue itself is not full, you should always use a circular queue when implementing a queue in an array.

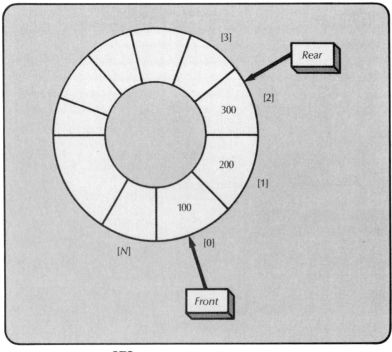

Figure 9.5. Diagram of a circular queue.

The alternative to the use of the circular array is to use a shift procedure that moves all the elements of the array back to the start whenever the rear pointer reaches the end of the array. Such a technique is not recommended because of the extra time required to shift all the elements. The following routine requires neither shifting nor additional inserting or deleting work. It does, however, require that at least one element in the array always be empty (or that there be an extra flag) to distinguish a full queue from an empty one.

The code is quite direct, except for the case when we are inserting or deleting across the "array boundary." In this case we use the Pascal **mod** function so that all indexes are in the range 0 to $N-1$. Thus, changing the front and rear pointers is accomplished via:

$$Front := (Front + 1) \bmod N;$$
$$Rear := (Rear + 1) \bmod N;$$

Figure 9.6 shows various states during insertion and deletion from a circular queue of size N. Note, in particular, the initial values of the front

Figure 9.6. Insertion into and deletion from a circular queue: (a) *Rear* points to the next empty cell. (b) after a series of insertions and deletions.

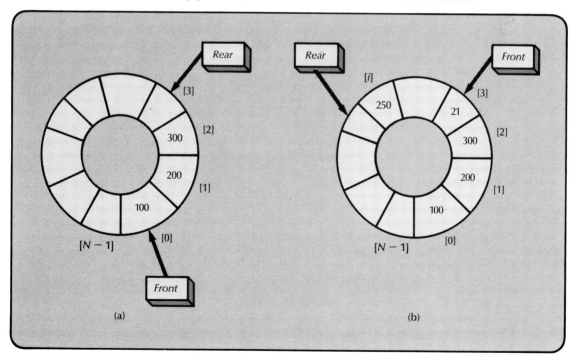

```
const
  MAXQUEUE     = 99;                    {max size of queue}
type
  QUEUEINDEX   = 0..MAXQUEUE;
  QUEUE        =
    record
      Front      : QUEUEINDEX;
      Rear       : QUEUEINDEX;
      value      : array [QUEUEINDEX] of WHATEVER
    end;
```

Figure 9.7. Data definitions for a circular queue.

and rear pointers, and that when the queue is full, in fact, one location is unused.

First we need the data type definitions of Fig. 9.7 to define the array representation of a queue. Then we can present a function, Enqueue(Q, V) in Fig. 9.8, which puts V at the rear of Q.

We cunningly have neglected to include the function IsFull. You are encouraged to try it for yourself (see the exercises for a suggestion). Remember that it is always useful in dealing with these data structures to use diagrams and trace through a series of insertions. In this case, you should use an artificially small queue of five elements or so. In the function Enqueue(Q, V), note also that the rear pointer is incremented *before* the insertion is made. Now you should be able to write the function Dequeue(Q,V), and the function it will need: IsEmpty(Q).

Figure 9.8. Enqueue procedure for a circular queue.

```
function Enqueue (var Q : QUEUE; V : WHATEVER) : boolean;
begin
  if IsFull(Q) then
    Enqueue := false
  else
    with Q do begin
      Enqueue := true;
      Rear := (Rear + 1) mod MAXQUEUE;    {first increment}
      value[Rear] := V                    {then insert}
    end
end; {Enqueue}
```

9.2 Stacks

Formally, a stack is a list, but with restrictions on the elements that can be examined, and the order in which they are placed in and removed from the list. A stack's restricted access allows additions and deletions only at the beginning of the list. Even though internal elements of the stack can be examined (we could hardly prevent it in any event with the usual Pascal environment), we will only allow new elements to be placed at the beginning (also called the top). Similarly, removals may be made only from the beginning. Since a stack discipline is equivalent to "last in, first out," it is also known as a LIFO queue. One effect of a stack is that if we place the elements into the stack in some order, they are removed in reverse order. Figure 9.9 illustrates the stack as a restricted access list.

Now, nothing in this restriction on a list requires that a stack be implemented as a linked list, and in languages that do not support dynamic data structures, such as FORTRAN, stacks must be implemented using arrays. But the applications for stacks that we investigate use stacks in such a dynamic way (that is, with both additions and removals) that a dynamic, linked implementation seems the most reasonable.

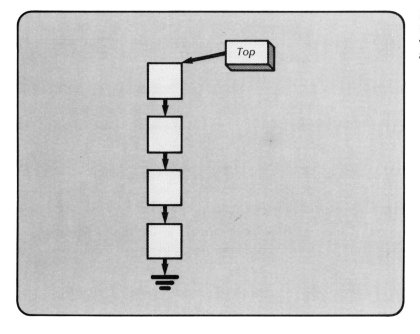

Figure 9.9. Stack as restricted-access linked list; we insert and remove only at the top.

Since actions occur only at the top of the stack, the addition and removal routines have been given special names, reflective of the mechanical model of a stack such as a stack of plates, with its bottom disappearing into a spring-loaded hole. Inserting onto the top of the stack is called *pushing*, removing from the top is called *popping*. A stack as an ADT will need to implement these two routines, *pop* and *push*. Pushing onto a stack requires that we dynamically allocate a new node, then hook it in properly to the stack. No overflow can occur in a dynamic implementation unless the *new* procedure fails. Popping from the stack involves returning the element found at the top to the caller. We should also be good citizens and return the space used by the top node to the free storage pool (via the *dispose* procedure). Unfortunately popping from a stack has a built-in error potential: how do we pop from an empty stack? Following the error-handling guidelines of Chapter 6, we will write the popping routine as a function that returns a boolean: *false* if we attempt to pop from an empty stack; *true*, otherwise. The calling party can use this information as it needs. In this chapter we build the post-fix expression evaluation using a stack. In that routine you will see how the caller uses the information that a stack is empty.

As we have seen already, a linked list is implemented as a series of nodes, each of which contains at least two fields: a data field, and a pointer to the next node in the list. A stack is implemented in just this way: the pointer to the head of the list is called the *stack pointer*. For any stack, the stack pointer is initialized to **nil**. Subsequent additions to the stack (pushing onto the stack) are made by acquiring a new node, placing the appropriate information into its data fields, then inserting the node at the start of the list.

Popping from the stack requires that we return the data fields of the head of the list (assuming the list is not empty), then remove the head (a rather vivid description, to say the least!).

We show the routines *Push* and *Pop*, the appropriate data structures, and a small program that reads a line of text and prints it out backwards.

Figure 9.10. Data types for the ADT stack.

```
type
    WHATEVER    = char;
    STACKPTR    = ↑ STACKNODE;
    STACKNODE   =
      record
        data      : WHATEVER;
        link      : STACKPTR;
      end;
    STACK       = STACKPTR;
```

```
procedure Push (var S : STACKPTR; V : WHATEVER);
var
  temp : STACKPTR;
begin
  new(temp);
  temp↑.data := V;
  temp↑.link := S;
  S := temp
end; {Push}

function Pop (var S : STACKPTR; var V : WHATEVER) : boolean;
var
  temp : STACKPTR;
begin
  if S = nil then
    Pop := false
  else begin
    Pop := true;
    V := S↑.data;
    temp := S;
    S := S↑.link;
    dispose(temp)
  end
end; {Pop}
```

Figure 9.11. *Push* and *Pop* routines for the stack ADT.

First, we define the data structures we'll need for stack manipulation in Fig. 9.10.

Figure 9.11 shows the two stack routines, *Push* and *Pop*.

Combining the preceding routines and their data types, we write the following routine to reverse the first N characters of a string.

```
procedure Reverse (var C : STRING; N : integer);
var
  i             : integer;
  CharStack     : STACKPTR;
  ok            : boolean;
begin
  for i := 1 to N do
    Push(CharStack, C[i]);
  for i := 1 to N do
    ok := Pop(CharStack, C[i])
end; {Reverse}
```

We don't use the value returned from *Pop* because we only pop the number of elements pushed onto the stack. Figure 9.12 traces the routine with the string "Too Hot to Hoot." If all the blanks are removed from this string, it reads the same forwards and backwards. This is called a *palindrome*; it's amusing to find nontrivial ones of your own (like "Madam, I'm Adam", which requires that the apostrophe and the blanks be removed).

We finish the introduction to stacks by noting that there are other operations that can be performed on a stack as an ADT, just as there were other utilities needed for general linked lists. Since we implement a stack as a linked list, we list these routines, but do not provide complete procedures:

Initialize(Stack)	Initializes *Stack* to the empty stack.
IsEmpty(Stack)	Returns a boolean indicating whether *Stack* is empty or not.
ExamineTop(Stack,value)	A function which returns the top of *Stack* in *value*. The function is *true* if the stack was not empty, *false* if it was.

Figure 9.12. Trace of pushing and popping in order to reverse a character string.

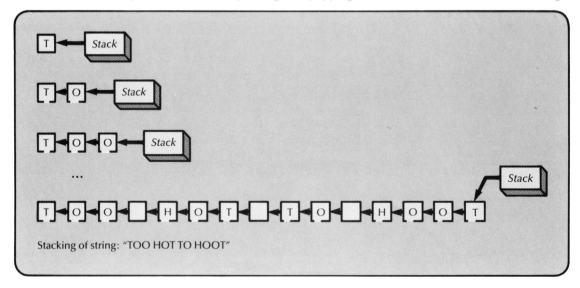

Stacking of string: "TOO HOT TO HOOT"

9.3   Expression Evaluation—The Next Layer in the Function Plotter

Back in Chapter 7 we built the first layers of the plotter: we could take a file representing a table of values and plot the values to the display. In the first version, the table must be generated by another program. In the next layer the table is generated internally. The user enters the function of x to be plotted, and the program generates the table by repeatedly evaluating the function at increasing values of x. As we first noted in the plotter design in Chapter 3, parsing and evaluating a function that follows arithmetic precedence rules, handles parentheses, and so on, is a rather complex task. Instead of attempting to build such a capability immediately, we'll use the intermediate form of post-fix, or reverse Polish notation (RPN).[4]

Those who have RPN calculators know that expressions are entered without parentheses to indicate the order of operations. The process of converting from the normal notation (called in-fix because the operators come in between their operands) uses the usual arithmetic precedence rules and the expression's parentheses to determine the order of calculations.

First we examine the problem of determining the order of evaluating an expression. Take as an example, the expression $5 + 4 * 10$. How should this simple expression be evaluated: is it 90 or 45? If we always evaluate expressions from left to right, 90 is correct. If we always evaluate from right to left (as does the programming language APL, for example), 45 is correct. It is also correct if we follow the usual arithmetic rules of precedence: first do the highest precedence operations, then the lower ones. What, then do we do about $18*9/27$? Is this $(18*9)/27$, or $18*(9/27)$? That is, for operations of equal precedence, which do we perform first? The normal rules of arithmetic indicate that operators of equal precedence should be evaluated from left to right. In this case, the order of evaluation doesn't affect the results (except for the potential associativity problems discussed in Chapter 5). Let's look at exponentiation: is $2^{3^2} = (2^3)^2$ or $2^{(3^2)}$? The first evaluates to 8^2 or 64, the second to 2^9 or 512. So order of evaluation is clearly important. With exponentiation, we evaluate from right to left. Previously we indicated that operations of equal precedence are evaluated left to right.

These precedence rules seem more complex than what we can accommodate in Pascal race track diagrams, and in fact we'll use a set of recursive procedures for doing the conversion. First, however, we examine post-fix in order to appreciate its advantages as an intermediate form for representing an expression.

[4] This isn't an ethnic joke! RPN is named after the Polish mathematician Lukasiewicz, who invented, actually, pre-fix notation. RPN reverses the sense of the symbols. Hewlett-Packard calculators use RPN notation for entering calculations.

In-Fix	Post-Fix	Pre-Fix
Table 9.1. Examples of in-fix, post-fix, and pre-fix expression forms.		
A/B	$A\ B\ /$	$/\ A\ B$
$A+B-C$	$A\ B\ +\ C\ -$	$-\ +\ A\ B\ C$
$sin(X)/X$	$X\ sin\ X\ /$	$/\ sin\ X\ X$
$sin(X)+A*cos(B*X)$	$X\ sin\ A\ B\ X\ *\ cos\ *\ +$	$+\ sin\ X\ *\ A\ cos\ *\ B\ X$
$A+B/C$	$A\ B\ C\ /\ +$	$+\ A\ /\ B\ C$
$(A+B)/C$	$A\ B\ +\ C\ /$	$/\ +\ A\ B\ C$

9.3.1 Post-Fix Evaluation

The post-fix form of an expression places the operator after the operands on which it works (rather than between them). To add A and B, we write:

$$A\ B\ +$$

We can build up more complex expressions from this basic rule. In Table 9.1 we show a number of in-fix expressions, and their equivalent post-fix form. There is an equivalent form, known as pre-fix, which places the operator *before* the operands. Expressions represented in pre-fix form have a particularly nice analog in Pascal function calls. For example, $A+B$ is represented in pre-fix as $+\ A\ B$. The '$+$' can be thought of as a function, *PLUS*, which acts on its two operands. The pre-fix form, $+\ A\ B$, is equivalent to the functional form *PLUS(A,B)*. We'll implement the post-fix form, however, because it is somewhat simpler and is found in commercially available RPN calculators. The evaluation of pre-fix forms is left as an exercise.

Note that the post-fix form of the expression does not use parentheses. The elimination of parentheses is an important reason why we are interested in this form of an expression. In post-fix the order of evaluation is unambiguous.

9.4 Evaluating a Post-Fix Expression—The Next Layer of the Plotter

The post-fix form gives the operator preceded by its (one or two) operands. To evaluate an expression we must temporarily store the operands until we reach the operator. We then apply the operator to the required number of operands. Suppose we are evaluating $5\ 7\ +$. When we first see the 5, we do not know whether the operator is a unary one (such as sin) or a binary one, such as $+$. (A unary operator is one that requires only one operand; a binary operator requires two.) We temporarily set aside the 5. The next token in the expression string is the 7. Again, we do not know what is to be done with this until we see its associated operator. We set aside the 7. Finally, the next token is the operator $+$. Since this token is a binary operator, it requires that we take the previous two operands and apply the operator to them: $5 + 7$.

The structure for "temporarily setting aside" the operands is a stack: as each operand is seen, we push it onto the top of the operand stack. When the next token is an operator, we pop the requisite number of operands (one for unary operators, two for binary operators) from the stack, apply the operator to these operands, and then push the result back onto the top of the stack.

This last step, pushing the result back onto the stack, can best be appreciated by working out a few short examples. We'll trace out the two expressions:

$$
\begin{array}{llll}
(A+B)*C & = & A\,B + C\,* & \{1\} \\
A+B*C & = & A\,B\,C\,*\,+ & \{2\}
\end{array}
$$

for $A=5$, $B=3$, and $C=2$. The first should evaluate to 16, and the second to 11. Figure 9.13 traces through the steps, showing the status of the operand stack as each token is seen.

Tracing through the first post-fix expression, $A\,B + C\,*$, we stack the first token (A, or 5), because it's an operand. The next token, 3, is also stacked. The next token is the operator $+$. We pop the stack twice, and sum the two values: this result is 8, and we push that back onto the stack. The next token is C, or 2. We push that onto the stack. The last token is $*$, and the operand stack, just before the application of the $*$ operator, looks like this:

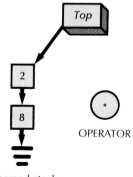

Operand stack

The algorithm repeats: the next token is an operator—we pop the stack twice, returning first the 2, then the 8, and apply the operator (*) to the two operands. The result is 16, and this is pushed onto the stack. Were there more tokens in the expression string, we would continue in the same way. When we reach the end of the expression, the stack should contain just one element, and this value is the value of the expression.

In this example, the stack never contained more than two (intermediate) values. For the next example, $A B C * +$, we again push operands onto

Figure 9.13. Trace of post-fix evaluation on two expressions. (a) $A B + C *$. (b) $A B C * +$.

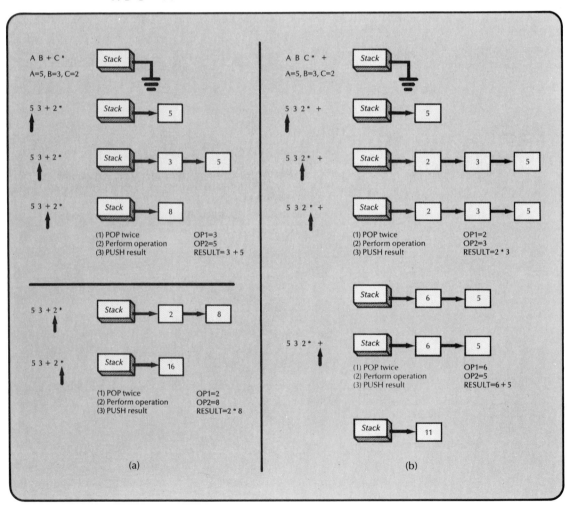

(a)   (b)

the stack, then pop the required number of operands when the current token is an operator. First, we push the 5, then the 3, and then the 2. Just before applying the *, the stack looks like the following.

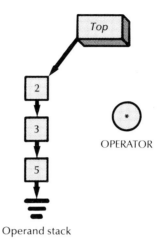

Operand stack

To perform the multiplication, we pop the stack twice, multiply the two values, and push the result back onto the stack. The stack now looks like this.

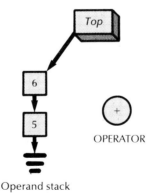

Operand stack

Finally, the next token is the +, and we apply it in the same way: pop twice, evaluate, and push the result back onto the stack. This is, of course, 11.

The algorithm for evaluating a post-fix expression is straightforward. We give it here in skeletal form. Then we develop the detailed Pascal procedures to do it correctly, consistent with the data structures and specifications of the function plotter. We discuss errors, their detection and correction, in more detail when we present the code. The evaluation algorithm is a simple process that centers around the appropriate action to perform with the next token:

1. Get the next token. No more? Go to step 4.
2. OPERAND? Push onto stack. Go back to step 1.
3. OPERATOR? Pop the stack once or twice, as appropriate. Apply the operator to the two operands. Push the result back onto the stack. Go back to step 1.
4. NO MORE TOKENS? Top of the stack is the value of the expression.

We summarize this as "push operands; pop and evaluate operators." We must account for a few subtleties. One is the order of evaluation. If we evaluate the simple expression 10 5 /, the stack contains both the 10 and the 5 at the time the / is seen, as shown here.

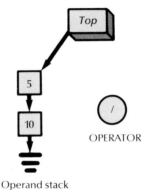

Operand stack

Upon seeing the division operator /, we pop the stack twice and apply the operator. We'll let *firstop* be the result of the first pop, so *firstop* is 5. *secondop* is the result of the second pop, or 10. To perform the division, we must do it in the correct order: 10 divided by 5, or *secondop* divided by *firstop*. Order of evaluation is important for both subtraction and division because these are not commutative. In addition, we should protect ourselves from division by zero:

> **if** *firstop* $<>$ 0 **then**
>   *result* := *secondop* / *firstop*
> **else**
>   *defined* := *false*

where *defined* is a boolean returned by the routine that evaluates the expression, indicating whether or not the evaluation was defined. Other potential errors that our code must guard for are log of a number less than or equal to zero and square root of a negative value.

9.4.1 Evaluating the Post-Fix Expression—The Design

To incorporate this algorithm into the function plotter, we need to flesh out the design, including specifics of data structures, user interface, error handling, and intermodule communication.

Expressions are to be entered in post-fix form. Reviewing the specifications from Chapter 3, the allowable operators are the binary operators +, −, *, and /, and the unary operators *sin*, *cos*, *exp*, *ln*, and *sqrt*. The user will be presented with a prompt at the function entry line for the next function:

Function:

The function is then entered by the user. After successfully parsing the function, the user is prompted for the minimum and maximum x values:

xmin: xmax:

Since the design remains the same as we developed in Chapter 3, we must be certain that our new algorithms and data structures for this next layer of implementation correspond to the first layer's. After the function has been entered, and the minimum and maximum values of x have been obtained, the program will generate an internal table of values with the *same* structure as the table built when the values are read from an external file — that is, a record of six fields: the x, y array of points, the count of the number of points, and the minimum and maximum values of x and y (four values).

The new routines for this layer of the program are *BuildTokenList* (which calls on *GetToken*), which builds the internal post-fix string, and *Evaluate*, which evaluates the post-fix expression. In Chapter 3 we designed *GetToken*. Now we'll examine *BuildTokenList* and *Evaluate* closely.

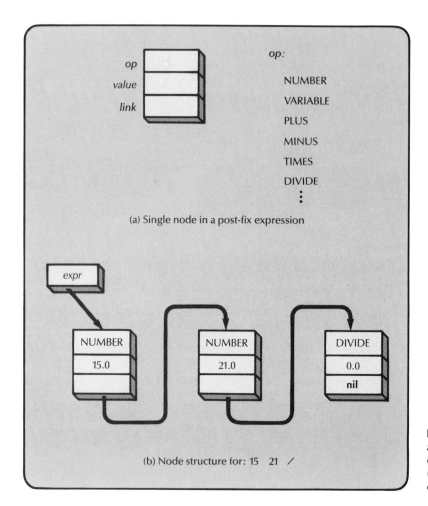

(a) Single node in a post-fix expression

(b) Node structure for: 15   21   /

Figure 9.14. An expression as a tokenized list. (a) The contents of a single node. (b) The list representation of the expression.

Figure 9.15. Diagram of linked token representation of *x sin* 3.2 *x* ∗ /.

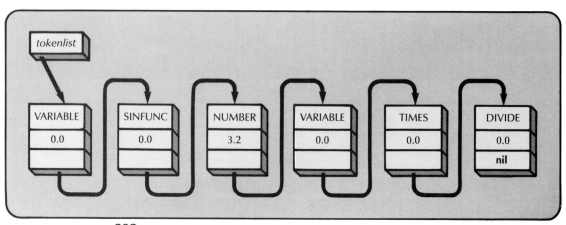

9.4.2 Building the Expression in the Function Plotter

Internally a post-fix expression can be represented as a linked list of tokens, along with enough information to describe the value of the token if it is a real number. In converting the typed string of characters into a list of tokens, each token in the string is replaced by an enumerated type (of type *TOKEN*) that names the token. The allowable tokens for this layer of the plotter are the various unary and binary operators and functions, a token indicating a variable, a token indicating a constant real number, and special tokens indicating the end of the list and an error condition. For this layer, *TOKEN* is defined as:

type
    TOKEN = (*SINFUNC, COSFUNC, EXPFUNC, LNFUNC, SQRTFUNC, PLUS,*
       MINUS, LEFTPAREN, RIGHTPAREN, TIMES, DIVIDE, VARIABLE,
       NUMBER, NOMORE, UNKNOWN);

A *VARIABLE* is a token that represents the function variable x. A *NUMBER* is a constant real value. The fields within a node in the expression list need the token type, its value if it is a *NUMBER*, and a pointer to the next node in the list.

If we have an input function such as:

$$15 \quad 21 \quad /$$

which represents the in-fix expression:

$$15 \ / \ 21$$

we'd represent this in the tokenized list as in Fig. 9.14. Part (a) shows the make-up of a single node; part (b) shows the entire list for the expression.

The data structure supporting this list is a basic one-way linked list. Each node contains the three fields: *op*, *value*, and *link*:

type
  NODEPTR   = ↑ *NODE*;
  NODE   =   {token list node}
    record
      op   : *TOKEN*;
      value   : *real*;
      link   : *NODEPTR*
    end;

A more complex expression such as "x sin 3.2 x * /" (which is the post-fix form of *sin(x / 3.2 * x)* is represented by the linked list of six tokens of Fig. 9.15.

Now we need the routine to build this list from the array of characters that the user enters. Because many interactive environments do not allow the program to see the characters that the user types until a carriage return is entered, we simply take each character as it is typed and enter it into an internal array of characters called *userinp*. Routine *BuildTokenList* repeatedly calls on *GetToken* to return the next token in *userinp* (see Fig. 9.16).

As long as *GetToken* returns a legal token (and does not return NOMORE, indicating that the end of the input line has been reached), *BuildTokenList* just builds the new node, with appropriate values of *op* and *value* fields. We need an additional pointer, *lasttoken*, that points to the end of the token list so that the new node can be hooked in at the end properly (see Fig. 9.17). We could also have used a circular list, and then we would only

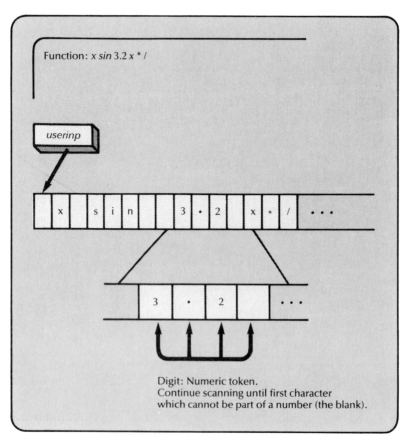

Figure 9.16. Diagram of extracting characters from *userinp* to build the token list.

Function: *x sin* 3.2 *x* * /

userinp

| x | | s | i | n | | | 3 | • | 2 | | x | * | / | • • • |

| 3 | | • | | 2 | | • • • |

Digit: Numeric token.
Continue scanning until first character
which cannot be part of a number (the blank).

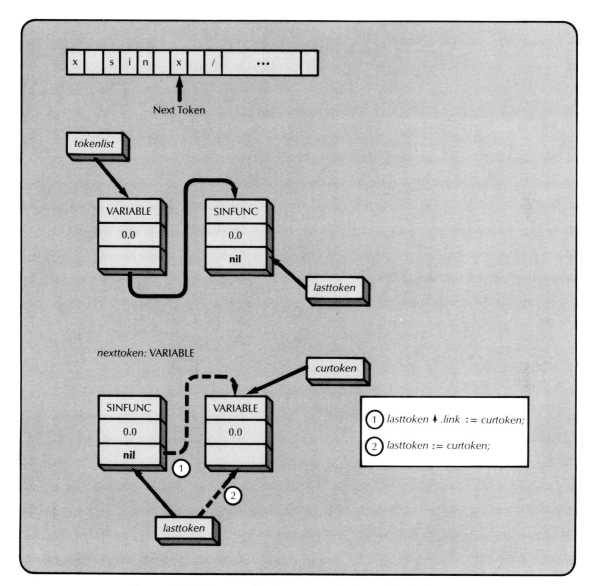

Figure 9.17. Diagram showing new node being hooked in at *tokenlist*.

have needed a single pointer. *BuildTokenList* is shown in Fig. 9.18. Its structure and construction are made virtually trivial because of the use of the *GetToken* routine. Such a partitioning of tasks, as we've emphasized, makes the overall program construction process much more straightforward.

```
function BuildTokenList (var tokenlist : NODEPTR;
                         var userinp : INPUTTYPE) : boolean;
{
Builds a list of tokens by repeatedly calling GetToken until we have
processed all of the tokens. Returns true if all tokens read in are legal,
and false if we get an unknown token.
}
var
  currtoken        :NODEPTR;
  lasttoken        :NODEPTR;
  nexttoken        :TOKEN;
  num              :real;
begin
  tokenlist := nil;
  BuildTokenList := true;
  while GetToken (userinp, nexttoken, num) <> NOMORE do
    if nexttoken = UNKNOWN then
      BuildTokenList := false
    else begin              {make node and insert at end of list}
      new (currtoken);
      currtoken ↑.op := nexttoken;
      currtoken ↑.value := num;
      currtoken ↑.link := nil;
      if tokenlist <> nil then
        lasttoken ↑.link := currtoken
      else
        tokenlist := currtoken;
      lasttoken := currtoken
    end
end; {BuildTokenList}
```

Figure 9.18. *BuildTokenList*—a routine that builds a list of tokens corresponding to a post-fix expression entered by the user.

GetToken is an important and useful routine that we'll expand upon and use in further examples. The concept of a token extracting routine is an important one that should be in every programmer's arsenal.

For completeness, we give the entire GetToken function so that its use of data types and the values it returns can be seen in detail. In Chapter 3, we developed the requirements for a token extracting routine, using a finite state machine model to indicate that the process of extracting tokens from the input involves determining (by examining the first character in the token) whether the token is a special symbol (+ , − , and so on), a numeric token (a real number), or an alphabetic token. If the token is alphabetic, we must further determine whether the token is one of the legal functions (*sin*, *cos*, and so on) or is the function variable.

Figure 9.19 is the complete *GetToken* function. We have written it modularly, so that it calls on additional routines *GetChar*, *UnGetChar*, and *SkipBlanks*. *GetChar* gets the next character from the input array (as long as the total number of characters actually in the line has not been reached). *UnGetChar* (an unusually named procedure indeed!) puts the last character back into the input line (by decrementing the count of characters seen). We need to do this because we can't determine that a given character is the last one in the token until we see the first character that can't possibly be part of the token. In processing 237.3x, for example, we don't know that we've reached the end of the number (273.3), until we see the x. We put the x back, finish the processing of the number 273.3, and are then ready to begin with the x as the next token. Finally, *SkipBlanks* just does as it says: skips over blanks to find the start of the next token.

```
procedure GetChar (var userinp : INPUTTYPE; var ch : char);
{
Places the next character in the input array into ch, or if at the end of the array, a blank.
Called by GetToken to get the next character in the input token.
}
begin
   if userinp.last < userinp.length then begin
      userinp.last := userinp.last + 1;
      ch := userinp.line [userinp.last]
   end else
      ch := ' '
end; {GetChar}


procedure UnGetChar (var userinp : INPUTTYPE; var ch : char);
{
Undoes the last GetChar so we can get the character over again later. If the character is a
blank, then there is no need to put it back, we would only skip it later. Called by GetToken.
}
begin
   if ch <> ' ' then
      userinp.last := userinp.last − 1
end; {UnGetChar}
```
(continued)

Figure 9.19. Completely coded *GetToken* routine for the interactive function plotter.

Figure 9.19. (continued)

function *SkipBlanks* (**var** *userinp* : *INPUTTYPE*) : *boolean*;
{
Skips blanks, and returns *true* if at the end of the line, and *false* otherwise. The *last* pointer
is set to the first nonblank character.
}
var
  blank : *boolean*;
begin
  blank := *true*;
  while (*userinp.last* < *userinp.length*) **and** *blank* **do begin**
    userinp.last := *userinp.last* + 1;
    if *userinp.line* [*userinp.last*] <> ' ' **then**
      blank := *false*
  end;
  if not *blank* **then**
    userinp.last := *userinp.last* − 1;
  SkipBlanks := *blank*
end; {SkipBlanks}

function *GetToken* (**var** *userinp* : *INPUTTYPE*; **var** *nexttoken* : *TOKEN*;
                var *num* : *real*) : *TOKEN*;
{
Places the type of the next token in the user input line into *nexttoken*, and if that token is a
number its value into *num*. Uses *GetChar* to get characters as it builds up tokens. Since we
don't know if we are done with a token until we have read one character past the end of it,
we use *UnGetChar* to put that character back. *SkipBlanks* is used to skip any blanks before
the current token. If there are no more characters in the line, the token *NOMORE* is returned,
and if we can't figure out what token this is, the token *UNKNOWN* is returned.
}
var
  ch   : *char*;
  DIGITS   : **set of** *char*;
  IDCHARS   : **set of** *char*;
  OPERATORS   : **set of** *char*;
  tokenval   : *ID*;

```
procedure SimpleToken (ch : char);
{Token is one of the one-symbol tokens.}
begin
  case ch of
    '+' : nexttoken := PLUS;
    '−' : nexttoken := MINUS;
    '*' : nexttoken := TIMES;
    '/' : nexttoken := DIVIDE;
    '(' : nexttoken := LEFTPAREN;
    ')' : nexttoken := RIGHTPAREN
  end
end; {SimpleToken}


procedure Alphabetic (var ch : char);
{
Token is alphabetic (either a built-in function, or a variable). A character string is built up
into global tokenval, then this is used to find a match in the global array funcdesc.
Otherwise, the token is assumed to be VARIABLE.
}
var
  next       : integer;                    {next character in token}
  nextfunc   : TOKEN;                      {next function in function table}
begin
  for next := 1 to MAXIDLEN do            {blank out token holder}
    tokenval[next] := ' ';
  next := 0;
  while ch in IDCHARS do begin            {build the alphabetic token}
    next := next + 1;
    if next <= MAXIDLEN then
      tokenval[next] := ch;
    GetChar (userinp, ch)
  end;
  UnGetChar (userinp, ch);               {read too much here}
  nexttoken := VARIABLE;
  for nextfunc := SINFUNC to SQRTFUNC do  {search the function table}
    if funcdesc [nextfunc] = tokenval then
      nexttoken := nextfunc
end; {Alphabetic}
```

(continued)

Figure 9.19. (continued)

```
procedure Numeric (var ch : char);
{
Token = NUMBER. This procedure builds the value by converting characters into
appropriate numeric form. The method is the same as in NEWREADLN (Chapter 1). The
value is passed in global num.
}
var
   factor          : real;
   frac            : real;
begin
   nexttoken := NUMBER;
   factor := 0.1;
   frac := 0.0;
   num := 0.0;
   while ch in DIGITS do begin
      num := num * 10 + (ord(ch) − ord('0'));
      GetChar (userinp, ch)
   end;
   if ch = '.' then begin
      GetChar (userinp, ch);
      while ch in DIGITS do begin
         frac := frac + (ord(ch) − ord('0')) * factor;
         factor := factor * 0.1;
         GetChar (userinp, ch)
      end
   end;
   UnGetChar (userinp, ch);
   num := num + frac
end; {Numeric}

begin {GetToken}
   nexttoken := UNKNOWN;
   OPERATORS := ['+', '−', '/', '*', '(', ')', '='];
   IDCHARS := ['a'..'z', 'A'..'Z'];
   DIGITS := ['0'..'9'];
   if SkipBlanks (userinp) then
      nexttoken := NOMORE
   else begin
      GetChar (userinp, ch);
      if ch in OPERATORS then            {'simple' token}
         SimpleToken (ch)
      else if ch in IDCHARS then         {'variable' or 'function' token}
         Alphabetic (ch)
      else if ch in DIGITS then          {'numeric' token}
         Numeric (ch)
   end;
   GetToken := nexttoken
end; {GetToken}
```

9.4.3 Evaluating the Expression in the Function Plotter

Once the expression has been built as a linked list of tokens, evaluating it just requires that we implement the code for evaluating a post-fix expression. As we noted earlier, this requires that we stack operands and intermediate results. We'll write a function, *Evaluate*, which defines the operand stack within it, including the basic operations *Push*, *Pop*, *IsEmpty*, and *InitStack*. To actually build the table of values, we need the minimum and maximum values of x, so we ask the user for them. After doing this, we repeatedly evaluate the function in steps from *minx* to *maxx*. The step size we use is given by the maximum number of values our table of values can hold: *MAXPOINTS*. We just set a delta x (which we call *large*) of about (*maxx* − *minx*)/*MAXPOINTS*. To build the table of values we first evaluate the function at its minimum x value, *minx*. We then increment by delta x, and continue this way until x is greater than *maxx*.

We use the current value of x for those nodes that contain the token *VARIABLE*. A *VARIABLE* is an operand, and its value gets stacked. What we stack, however, is not the *value* field of the node (which is used only for constants), but rather the current value of the variable x. Figure 9.20 shows an intermediate state in the evaluation of x *sin* x / (*sin*(x)/x), using the current value of x of 2.0.

To evaluate the expression list we'll need a function that takes the list as input, along with the current value of the function variable (2.0 in the case of Fig. 9.20), and returns the result of evaluating the expression with that value. As we noted earlier, we must also be careful about illegal operations (division by zero, square roots of negative numbers, and so on), so we also return a boolean flag, *defined*, which will be *true* if the expression could be evaluated; *false*, otherwise. Here is the function header for evaluating the post-fix expression.

> **function** *Evaluate* (*tokenlist* : NODEPTR; *nextvalue* : *real*;
> **var** *defined*, *error* : *boolean*) : *real*;

When we look at the evaluation algorithm, we note two cases that can cause the algorithm to fail:

1. Attempting to pop from an empty stack.
2. A stack with more than one element, or with no elements, at the end.

The first error occurs when we have a post-fix string such as 3 + . The latter occurs with expressions such as 3 7 9 + or 7 x *sin*.

If an illegal string is entered, we want to detect this immediately. Since building the internal post-fix expression essentially involves repeated calls on *GetToken*, we do little error checking until the end of the input string. At this point, we call on *Evaluate* to detect errors in the expression. As we

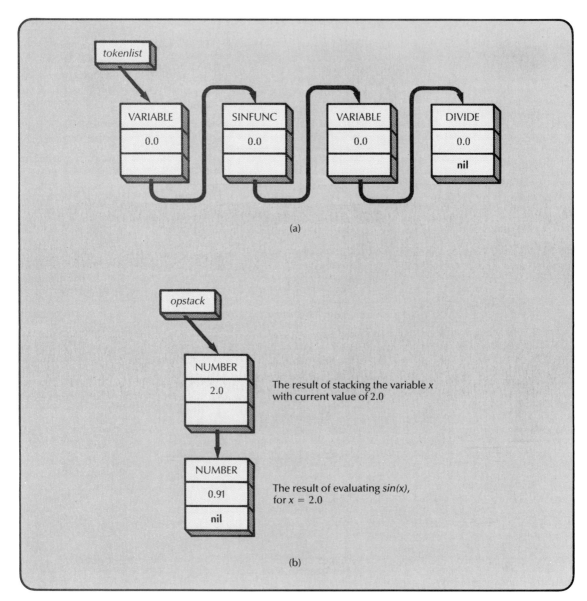

Figure 9.20. (a) Linked list token string of *x sin x* /. (b) Stack when we've just pushed the second *x* (at *x* = 2.0).

might expect, adding code to *Evaluate* to check for illegal expressions increases its size substantially and obscures the fundamentals of the algorithm.

We should, however specify in advance the manner in which our routine will handle these errors. Then the requirements of this specification can be incorporated into the routine's design. It seems reasonable for this application, a function plotter, that when either of the errors occurs, we return an appropriate error message to the user and place the user back into command entry mode. That is, we discontinue the processing of the current function.

We show the function *Evaluate* in somewhat abbreviated form in Fig. 9.21, which highlights the components of the algorithm and the way in which the linked list is manipulated. We have not shown the complete **case** statement, since most of the entries are quite similar. Note, by the way, that we use the *include* file mechanism to read in the stack ADT operations. The file *stack.i* includes the routines *IsFull*, *IsEmpty*, *Push*, *Pop*, and so on. For this application, the type of the value in the stack (that is, the type of *WHATEVER*) is *NODEPTR*, which we define in the main program.

```
function Evaluate (tokenlist : NODEPTR; nextvalue : real; var defined, error : boolean) : real;
{
Evaluate the tokenlist using a stack, assuming tokenlist represents a list of tokens entered for
a post-fix expression. It is noted if the point is undefined, or if there is an error.
}

type
   WHATEVER        = NODEPTR;
var
   firstop         : real;
   IGNORED         : set of TOKEN;
   OPERANDS        : set of TOKEN;
   opstack         : STACKPTR;
   result          : real;
   resultnode      : NODEPTR;
   secondop        : real;

#include "stack.i";                                    {operations on the stack ADT}

                                                                      (continued)
```

Figure 9.21. Post-fix expression evaluation.

Figure 9.21. (continued)

```
function GetOperand (var operandvalue : real) : boolean;
{Pops the stack and gets the operand if possible.}
var
   valuenode          : NODEPTR;
begin
   GetOperand := true;
   if Pop (opstack, valuenode) then
      if valuenode↑.op = VARIABLE then                      {variable}
         operandvalue := nextvalue
      else                                                  {number}
         operandvalue := valuenode↑.value
   else
      GetOperand := false
   end; {GetOperand}

begin {Evaluate}
   Evaluate := 0;
   InitStack (opstack);
   IGNORED := [LEFTPAREN, RIGHTPAREN];
   OPERANDS := [VARIABLE, NUMBER];
   defined := true;
   while (tokenlist <> nil) and not error do begin
      if not (tokenlist↑.op in IGNORED) then                {ignore parens}
         if tokenlist↑.op in OPERANDS then                  {operands are pushed}
            Push (opstack, tokenlist)
      else begin
         if not GetOperand (firstop) then                   {get one or two operands}
            error := true
         else if tokenlist↑.op in [PLUS, MINUS, TIMES, DIVIDE] then
            if not GetOperand (secondop) then
               error := true;
         if not error then begin                            {perform operation}
            result := 0;
            case tokenlist↑.op of
               PLUS : result := firstop + secondop;
               DIVIDE :
                  if firstop <> 0 then
                     result := secondop / firstop
                  else
                     defined := false;
               NUMBER, VARIABLE : result := firstop;
               SINFUNC : result := sin (firstop);
               COSFUNC : result := cos (firstop);
               EXPFUNC : result := exp (firstop):
                  . . .
            end;
```

```
                new (resultnode);
                resultnode ↑ .op := NUMBER;
                resultnode ↑ .value := result;
                Push (opstack, resultnode)
            end
        end;
        tokenlist := tokenlist ↑ .link
    end;
    if not error then begin
        if GetOperand (result) and IsEmpty (opstack) then
            Evaluate := result
        else
            error := true
    end
end; {Evaluate}
```

9.4.4 The Function Plotter with Post-Fix Expressions—The Code

We've built up the pieces necessary to handle the post-fix expressions for the function plotter. All we need to do is incorporate the new routines into the structure from Chapter 3, and we'll have an interactive function plotter. An interactive plotter, one that allows the user to both enter and plot functions, is much more useful than just a plotter alone. We got to this point by carefully building the preliminary pieces, which, fortunately, also perform a useful function. Now, with a bit of patience from the user (in entering expressions in post-fix form), we can quickly plot useful functions.

The plotter, however, still lacks the usual in-fix expression entry, which we'd like to provide as a front end more attuned to the way most of us think about mathematical expressions. In Part IV, we'll use a set of highly recursive routines to parse an in-fix expression and build an alternative intermediate representation known as an expression tree. Recursive expression building is such a powerful and general technique that we'll be able to use the code, with only minor modification, to build a useful interactive spreadsheet (computed fields) program, called MiniCalc, in Chapter 14. Our greatest lesson in the examples that we build in this book is that we build structures in an abstract way, and with pieces that we borrow and reuse from other programs. Figure 9.22 is the completely coded interactive post-fix expression plotter. We have not repeated the code for actually doing the plot (that is, the procedure Plot and the routines that it calls) because they are the same as in Chapter 7. Similarly, the routine to draw the plot to the screen, WriteScreen, is not repeated.

program *PLOTTER* (*input, output, HELPFILE*);
{
Interactive post-fix function plotter.
DESCRIPTION: A simple post-fix function plotter. Users can plot functions or get help on
                using the program. The functions plotted are arbitrary post-fix expressions
                of one variable.
AUTHOR: A. Quilici & L. Miller
VERSION: 2.1
}
const
    {Many of the following constants are TERMINAL SPECIFIC, and must be changed for
    different terminals.}

    CMDERRLINE   = 23;   {screen row to write errors on — term. specific}
    CMDLINE   = 22;   {screen row to get command on — term. specific}
    FUNCCOL   = 0;   {screen column to start output}
    FUNCLINE   = 0;   {screen row to get function}
    MAXCOL   = 77;   {number of columns on screen — term. specific}
    MAXIDLEN   = 10;   {longest identifier/function name}
    MAXLINE   = 80;   {longest input line}
    MAXPOINTS   = 500;   {max number of points plotted}
    MAXROW   = 19;   {number of rows on screen — term. specific}
    MINCOL   = 0;   {lowest numbered column — term. specific}
    MINROW   = 0;   {lowest numbered row — term. specific}
    PLOTLINE   = 1;   {row to start plot on — MINROW + 1}
    RANGELINE   = 1;   {screen row to get range from — term. specific}

type
    COLS   = MINCOL..MAXCOL;
    ROWS   = MINROW..MAXROW;
    COUNTER   = 0..*maxint*;
    LINETYPE   = **array** [1..MAXLINE] **of** *char*;
    INPUTTYPE   =
      record
        line   : LINETYPE;   {user input line}
        length   : COUNTER;   {number of characters}
        last   : COUNTER   {last character looked at}
      end;
    ID   = **array** [1..MAXIDLEN] **of** *char*;
    POINT   =
      record
        x, y   : *real*
      end;
    POINTCNT   = 0..MAXPOINTS;

Figure 9.22. Interactive, post-fix expression plotter.

```
POINTARRAY          = array [POINTCNT] of POINT;
SCREENARRAY         = array [ROWS, COLS] of char;
SCREENDESC          =
   record
      pnts               : SCREENARRAY;                    {internal rep. of screen}
      maxcols            : COLS;
      maxrows            : ROWS
   end;
PLOTINFO            =
   record
      table              : POINTARRAY;                     {points to plot}
      cnt                : POINTCNT;                        {number of points to plot}
      minx, maxx         : real;
      miny, maxy         : real
   end;
USERMSGS            = (CMDPROMPT, CMDLIST, FUNCPROMPT, NOFUNC, MINPROMPT,
                        BADFUNC, BADLINE, TOOMANY, TOOFEW, BADEXPR, NOFACTOR);
TOKEN               = (SINFUNC, COSFUNC, EXPFUNC, LNFUNC, SQRTFUNC, PLUS,
                        MINUS, TIMES, DIVIDE, VARIABLE, LEFTPAREN, RIGHTPAREN,
                        NUMBER, NOMORE, UNKNOWN);            {various input tokens}
COMMANDS            = (HELP, PLOTFUNC, QUIT, BAD);          {plotter commands}
NODEPTR             = ↑ NODE;
NODE                =                                       {expression stack node}
   record
      op                 : TOKEN;
      value              : real;
      link               : NODEPTR
   end;

STACKPTR            = ↑ STACKNODE;
STACKNODE           =
   record
      data               : NODEPTR;
      link               : STACKPTR
   end;
STACK               = STACKPTR;
var
   command            : COMMANDS;                           {possible commands}
   FirstFunction      : boolean;                            {true for first function}
   funcdesc           : array [SINFUNC..SQRTFUNC] of ID;    {function name table}
   HELPFILE           : text;                               {help information file}
   lastfunc           : NODEPTR;                            {last function plotted}
   points             : PLOTINFO;                           {points to plot}
   screen             : SCREENDESC;                         {screen representation}
```

#include "cursor.i" {direct cursor positioning routines}

(continued)

Figure 9.22. (continued)

```
procedure WriteUser (msg : USERMSGS; line : integer);
{Goes to line on screen, blanks it out and writes the message there.}
begin
  MoveCursor (line, FUNCCOL);
  ClearEOL;
  case msg of
    BADEXPR :        write ('Bad expression given');
    BADFUNC :        write ('Bad function given');
    BADLINE :        write ('Bad input line (too long or short)');
    CMDLIST :        write ('Commands : p(lot), h(elp), w(rite), q(uit)');
    CMDPROMPT :      write ('Command : '):
    FUNCPROMPT :     write ('Function : ');
    MINPROMPT :      write ('Enter Xmin, Xmax : ');
    NOFACTOR :       write ('Unrecognized token in expression');
    NOFUNC :         write ('No function has been plotted yet');
    TOOFEW :         write ('Too few points');
    TOOMANY :        write ('Too many points')
  end
end; {WriteUser}


function GetInp (var userinp : INPUTTYPE) : boolean;
{
Get a line of input from the user, storing it in userinp. We return true if we get any input, false
otherwise. The number of characters read is placed in length field. Called by Plot to get the
function, GetPoints to get the minimum and maximum values to plot, and GetCommand to get the
next command.
}
var
  ch : char;
begin
  userinp.length := 0;
  userinp.last := 0;
  if eof then
    GetInp := false
  else begin
    while not eoln do begin
      read (ch);
      if userinp.length < MAXLINE then begin
        userinp.length := userinp.length + 1;
        userinp.line [userinp.length] := ch
      end
    end;
    readln;
    GetInp := true
  end
end; {GetInp}
```

procedure *GetChar* (**var** *userinp* : *INPUTTYPE*; **var** *ch* : *char*);

procedure *UnGetChar* (**var** *userinp* : *INPUTTYPE*; **var** *ch* : *char*);

function *SkipBlanks* (**var** *userinp* : *INPUTTYPE*) : *boolean*;

function *GetToken* (**var** *userinp* : *INPUTTYPE*; **var** *nexttoken* : *TOKEN*;
                 var *num* : *real*) : *TOKEN*;

  procedure *Alphabetic* (**var** *ch* : *char*);

  procedure *Numeric* (**var** *ch* : *char*);

function *BuildTokenList* (**var** *tokenlist* : *NODEPTR*; **var** *userinp* : *INPUTTYPE*) : *boolean*;

function *Evaluate* (*tokenlist* : *NODEPTR*; *nextvalue* : *real*; **var** *defined*, *error* : *boolean*) : *real*;

  function *GetOperand* (**var** *operandvalue* : *real*) : *boolean*;

function *DoPlot* (**var** *points* : *PLOTINFO*; **var** *screen* : *SCREENDESC*;
           expr : *NODEPTR*) : *boolean*;
{
Actually do the plot. Gets the x range from the user, calculates the points for the given expression, and then plots the points into an array representing the screen.
}
var
  error   : *boolean*;
  pointsplotted   : *COUNTER*;

function *GetPoints* (**var** *points* : *PLOTINFO*; *expr* : *NODEPTR*; **var** *error* : *boolean*) : *integer*;
{
Reads in points, saving them in an array so they can be printed out later. Also gathers information about the points, including the maximum and minimum values for x and y, as well as the number of each value greater and less than zero. The number of points actually read is returned, as well as being placed into the *points* data structure.
}
const
  DIVFAC   = 4;   {MAXPOINTS/DIVFAC are generated}
var
  defined   : *boolean*;
  large   : *real*;
  nextx   : *real*;
  nexty   : *real*;
  pcnt   : *COUNTER*;
  range   : *real*;

(continued)

Figure 9.22. (continued)

```
procedure UpdateRange (var minval, maxval : real; nxtval : real);
{
Updates the current minimum and maximum values, depending on whether or not nextval is
the smallest or largest value so far.
}
begin
  if nextval < minval then
    minval := nxtval
  else if nxtval > maxval then
    maxval := nxtval
end; {UpdateRange}

function GetRange (var small, large : real) ; boolean;
{Get range of x values from the user, checking to make sure the input is valid.}
var
  nexttoken    : TOKEN;
  rangeinp     : INPUTTYPE;
  realnum      : REAL;

function GetNumber (var rangeinp : INPUTTYPE; var realnum : real) : boolean;
{Get a number from the user, allowing a sign. Return the value in realnum.}
var
  numtoken     : TOKEN;
  sign         : real;
begin
  sign := 1;
  numtoken := GetToken (rangeinp, nexttoken, realnum);
  if numtoken = MINUS then begin
    sign := -1;
    numtoken := GetToken (rangeinp, nexttoken, realnum)
  end;
  GetNumber := (numtoken = NUMBER);
  realnum := sign * realnum
end; {GetNumber}

begin {GetRange}
  GetRange := false;
  WriteUser (MINPROMPT, RANGELINE);
  if GetInp (rangeinp) then
    if (rangeinp.length > 0) and (rangeinp.length < = MAXLINE) then begin
      if GetNumber (rangeinp, small) then
        if GetNumber (rangeinp, large) then
          if GetToken (rangeinp, nexttoken, realnum) = NOMORE then
            GetRange := true
    end
end; {GetRange}
```

```
begin {GetPoints}
  pcnt := 0;
  error := false;
  if GetRange (nextx, large) then begin
    range := abs ((large − nextx)/(screen.maxrows * screen.maxcols/DIVFAC − 1));
    while (nextx <= large) and not error do begin
      defined := true;
      nexty := Evaluate (expr, nextx, defined, error);
      if not error then begin
        if defined then begin
          pcnt := pcnt + 1;
          if pcnt <= MAXPOINTS then begin
            if pcnt = 1 then begin
              points.maxx := nextx;
              points.minx := nextx;
              points.maxy := nexty;
              points.miny := nexty
            end else begin
              UpdateRange (points.minx, points.maxx, nextx);
              UpdateRange (points.miny, points.maxy, nexty)
            end;
            points.table [pcnt].x := nextx;
            points.table [pcnt].y := nexty;
            points.cnt := pcnt
          end
        end;
        nextx := nextx + range
      end
    end
  end;
  GetPoints := pcnt
end; {GetPoints}

procedure Plot (var screen : SCREENDESC; var points : PLOTINFO);
{Places the axes and the points of the function into screen for later printing.}
{Same as in Chapter 7.}

  procedure PlotAxis (var screen : SCREENDESC);
  {Not shown—same as in Chapter 7.}

  procedure PlotPoints (var screen : SCREENDESC; var points : PLOTINFO);
  {Not shown—same as in Chapter 7.}

begin {Plot}
  PlotAxis (screen);
  PlotPoints (screen, points)
end; {Plot}
```

(continued)

Figure 9.22. (continued)

```
begin {DoPlot}
  DoPlot := false;
  pointsplotted := GetPoints (points, expr, error);
  if error then
    WriteUser (BADEXPR, CMDERRLINE)
  else if pointsplotted > MAXPOINTS then
    WriteUser (TOOMANY, CMDERRLINE)
  else if pointsplotted = 0 then
    WriteUser (TOOFEW, CMDERRLINE)
  else begin
    Plot (screen, points);
    DoPlot := true
  end
end; {DoPlot}



procedure WriteScreen (var screen : SCREENDESC);
{Writes out the array representing the screen onto the terminal screen.}
{Not shown — Same as in Chapter 7.}



procedure DoHelp;
{
Writes a help message for the user. This message is kept in HELPFILE and contains
instructions on the use of the program. Since no provision for paging is made, the file
should be less than a screen page long.
}
var
  ch : char;
begin
  ClearScreen;
  reset (HELPFILE);
  while not eof (HELPFILE) do begin
    while not eoln (HELPFILE) do begin
      read (HELPFILE, ch);
      write (ch)
    end;
    writeln;
    readln (HELPFILE)
  end;
  write ('Press RETURN to continue.');
  readln;
  ClearScreen
end; {DoHelp}
```

```
function GetFunction : NODEPTR;
{
Get a function from the user, returning a pointer to a list of tokens representing the function if
there are no errors.
}
var
  tokenlist      : NODEPTR;
  userinp        : INPUTTYPE;
begin
  WriteUser (FUNCPROMPT, FUNCLINE);
  if GetInp (userinp) then
    if (userinp.length > MAXLINE) or (userinp.length = 0) then
      WriteUser (BADFUNC, CMDERRLINE)
    else if BuildTokenList (tokenlist, userinp) then
      GetFunction := tokenlist
    else
      GetFunction := nil
  else
    WriteUser (BADLINE, CMDERRLINE)
end; {GetFunction}


function GetCommand (var command : COMMANDS) : boolean;
{Get a single-letter command, making sure it is in the set of valid commands.}
var
  ch             : char;
  userinp        : INPUTTYPE;
begin
  GetCommand := false;
  command := BAD;
  if GetInp (userinp) then begin
    GetCommand := true;
    if not SkipBlanks (userinp) then begin
      GetChar (userinp, ch);
      if SkipBlanks (userinp) then
        if ch in ['p', 'P', 'h', 'H'] then
          case ch of
            'p', 'P' : command := PLOTFUNC;
            'h', 'H' : command := HELP
          end
        else if ch in ['q', 'Q'] then
          GetCommand := false
    end
  end else
    WriteUser (BADLINE, CMDERRLINE)
end; {GetCommand}
```

(continued)

Figure 9.22. (continued)

```
procedure Initialize;
begin
   funcdesc [SINFUNC] :=      'sin       ';     {pad each to MAXIDLEN (10) chars}
   funcdesc [COSFUNC] :=      'cos       ';
   funcdesc [EXPFUNC] :=      'exp       ';
   funcdesc [LNFUNC] :=       'ln        ';
   funcdesc [SQRTFUNC] :=     'sqrt      ';
   screen.maxrows := MAXROW;
   screen.maxcols := MAXCOL;
   FirstFunction := true;
   ClearScreen
end; {Initialize}

begin {main}
  Initialize;
  WriteUser (CMDPROMPT, CMDLINE);
  while GetCommand (command) do begin
    case command of
       HELP :
         begin                              {print messages to user}
           DoHelp;
           if not FirstFunction then        {re-draw display if function plotted}
             WriteScreen (screen)
         end;
       PLOTFUNC :
         begin                              {get a function from user and plot it}
           MoveCursor (CMDERRLINE, MINCOL);
           ClearEOL;
           lastfunc := GetFunction;
           if lastfunc <> nil then
             if DoPlot (points, screen, lastfunc) then begin
               WriteScreen (screen);
               FirstFunction := false       {we've plotted a function}
             end
         end;
       QUIT : halt;
       BAD : WriteUser (CMDLIST, CMDERRLINE)
    end;
    WriteUser (CMDPROMPT, CMDLINE)
  end
end.
```

9.5 Testing the Post-Fix Function Plotter

In Chapter 7 we tested and debugged the first layer of the plotter, and we're reasonably content that it correctly plots a table of values. In hand-checking the code, however, we noted a couple of points that might lead to difficulty in the interactive versions of the plotter. These included:

- Failure to initialize the screen array, *screen*, to blanks
- Failure to use *NEWREADLN* when reading reals from the external file

As we can see in this new layer of the program, both of these problems have been corrected. The first is necessary because we reuse the screen array for each subsequent function to be plotted. If we do not reset *screen* to blanks before each new plot, the old plot will remain as the new one is written (but the scale factors between the two will be different). The second problem is handled in *GetToken*, in the routine that reads numeric tokens. There, we read the input string as characters and convert to a real. If an illegal character (nonnumeric) is found in the number string, *GetToken* assumes that the character cannot be part of a numeric token, and it finishes processing the current number. In the routines where we get the minimum and maximum x values, we use a method similar to *NEWREADLN*.

9.5.1 Testing the Building of the Token List

Testing the new plotter now involves testing the new modules that have been added in this layer: parsing the input, building the internal post-fix tokenized list structure, and evaluating the post-fix expression (that is, internally building the table of values). In addition, we must be concerned about the data communication between these new parts and the old part of the program.

In reviewing Chapter 7 and looking at the new code for this version of the plotter, we see that the work of plotting the value table is done in *PlotPoints*. But this routine is unchanged from the first layer. If the table of values is generated correctly in *Evaluate*, the function will be correctly plotted. Our testing must ensure that the table generated by *Evaluate* is the same as would have been generated by a program written to build the table externally, as we had to do with the first layer. To do this, we must first ensure that the internal list is being built correctly.

The correctness criteria for the internal post-fix representation of the function is that the tokens correspond to those entered by the user, and that the *value* field be properly set to the real value if the token is *NUMBER*. We modified *BuildTokenList* to include debugging statements. The entire function, with the new debugging statements, is shown in Fig. 9.23.

```
function BuildTokenList (var tokenlist : NODEPTR; var userinp : INPUTTYPE) : boolean;
{
Builds a list of tokens by repeatedly calling GetToken until we have processed all of the
tokens. Returns true if all tokens read in are legal, and false if we get an unknown token.
}
var
    currtoken       : NODEPTR;
    lasttoken       : NODEPTR;
    nexttoken       : TOKEN;
    num             : real;
begin
    tokenlist := nil;
    BuildTokenList := true;
    while GetToken (userinp, nexttoken, num) <> NOMORE do
      if nexttoken = UNKNOWN then
        BuildTokenList := false
      else begin      {make node and insert at end of list}
        new (currtoken);
        currtoken ↑ .op := nexttoken;
        currtoken ↑ .value := num;
        currtoken ↑ .link := nil;
        if tokenlist <> nil then
          lasttoken ↑ .link := currtoken
        else
          tokenlist := currtoken;
        lasttoken := currtoken;
        {if debugging, write out the new token}
        if debugging then begin
          writeln ('NEXT TOKEN : ', nexttoken);
          writeln ('VALUE : ', num : 8 : 2);
          writeln
        end
      end
end; {BuildTokenList}
```

Figure 9.23. *BuildTokenList* with additional debugging output added.

We ran the plotter with debugging turned on, and saw that the internal list correctly matched the function as entered by the user. In Fig. 9.24, we show two examples, one with legal input, and one with illegal input, and the debugging output generated by *BuildTokenList*.

Much of the work in *BuildTokenList* is being done in *GetToken*, and as we have learned, processing input from the terminal is often associated with bugs: lines that are too long, failure to reset a line array to blanks, or failure to reset a length counter to zero. To test for the "failure to test boundary conditions" case, we tested the plotter with lines that were longer than *MAXLINE* (80) characters, and found, to our horror, that the program was terminating with a subscript out-of-bounds error, trying to access past the end of the input array. We quickly noted that in *SkipBlanks*, we loop

Input: x *sin* 3.2 x * /

NEXT TOKEN: variable
VALUE: 0.00

NEXT TOKEN: sinfunc
VALUE: 0.00

NEXT TOKEN: number
VALUE: 3.20

NEXT TOKEN: variable
VALUE: 0.00

NEXT TOKEN: times
VALUE: 0.00

NEXT TOKEN: divide
VALUE: 0.00

(a)

Input: 3.27 x + +

NEXT TOKEN: number
VALUE: 3.27

NEXT TOKEN: variable
VALUE: 0.00

NEXT TOKEN: plus
VALUE: 0.00

NEXT TOKEN: plus
VALUE: 0.00

(b)

Figure 9.24. (a) Legal post-fix expression and the debugging output of *BuildTokenList*. (b) Illegal expression and the debugging output.

until we reach the end of that array (until *userinp.length*). The *length* field of *userinp* was being set to the total number of characters that the user typed, rather than to *MAXLINE* if we exceeded that number. We also should have discovered the bug when looking at the code of *GetInp* and constructing an appropriate loop invariant: the *length* field should always be the number of characters in the *line* field (the actual array of characters). We corrected *GetInp*, hand-verified the code, and ran again with lines longer than *MAXLINE* characters. This time, the program was correct![5] Look back at the complete code in Fig. 9.22, and see where *GetInp* has the additional code to be certain that *userinp.length* is never greater than *MAXLINE*.

Next we want to incorporate and test the post-fix expression evaluation, the procedure *Evaluate*. We do this with the confidence that the token list has been correctly built.

9.5.2 Testing the Evaluation of the Token List

From our testing and hand-verification (and corrections!) of *BuildTokenList*, we have confidence that a correct token list, representing a post-fix expression, is passed to *Evaluate*. *Evaluate* builds the table of values, which is then passed to *PlotPoints*. (See Fig. 9.25.)

Evaluate performs correctly if the table contains the correct function evaluation for all values of the function variable, from the user-specified minimum to the user-specified maximum, with the number of values given by *MAXPOINTS*, and a uniform interval. Additionally the table must contain the correct values for the minimum and maximum x and y values, and the correct count of the number of values actually in the table.

In addition, *Evaluate* must perform reasonably if the post-fix token list is malformed, or if the user specifies inconsistent values for *minx* and *maxx* (such as the minimum being greater than the maximum).

In testing *Evaluate*, we added debugging conditionals, so that if we're in debugging mode, we will see the table of values generated on the screen. We compare these with hand- or program-generated values as a means of gaining confidence in the correctness of the routine. We also wrote code into *Evaluate* that specifically tests for malformed expressions, and we did this in an interesting way. To determine if an expression is malformed, we do a "test" evaluation (setting the value of the variable to 0.0). If during the course of evaluation, we need to pop the stack, and there are not sufficient operands, we have a malformed expression (an expression such as 17.3 + 141, while a correct in-fix expression, is not a valid post-fix

---

[5] We confess our sins under the assumption that seeing the mistakes of others — how they were found and corrected — makes it easier to see the errors in our own code.

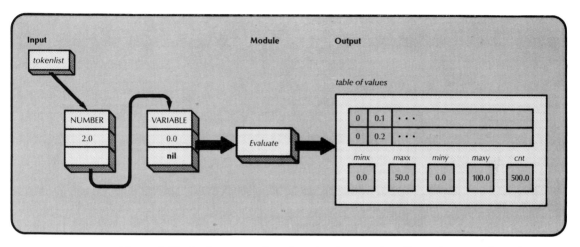

Figure 9.25. *Evaluate* as a function: it takes a token list as input and produces a table of values as output.

expression). In addition, when we reach the end of the list, *exactly* one value must be on the stack. If none or more than one are there, we have a malformed post-fix expression. We notify the user of that fact, and invite him or her to enter another function.

With the testing of *Evaluate* complete, we are now confident (but not completely assured) of the correctness of the current implementation of the plotter. We have an interactive, useful tool for viewing functions, and most of the pieces are in place for the final version in Chapter 13, evaluating an in-fix expression.

Programming Notes

Looking at the code for this first interactive layer of the plotter you should note that we've used a simple single-letter command form. A prompt is presented at the bottom of the screen, and the user enters a single letter indicating the operation. Of course, the number of commands at this level is quite small — plot, help, and quit. Though we've discussed command-based interactive programs before, we want to emphasize the way the commands are built and parsed, and how new commands can be easily added.

First, we define a command as an enumerated type, so that we have all of the commands identified in one place, with names that clearly indicate their function.

```
type
    COMMANDS  = (HELP, PLOTFUNC, BAD, QUIT);          {plotter commands}
```

Next, we include a routine, *GetCommand*, which parses the input, and maps the characters (in this case, just a single character) into the command name. Basically *GetCommand* is a **case** statement that takes the command as typed and returns the corresponding enumerated type. If the user types a command that is not known, a special command name *BAD* is returned.

```
function GetCommand (var command : COMMANDS) : boolean;
{
Get a single letter command from the user,
making sure it is in the set of valid commands.
}
var
    ch          : char;
    userinp     : INPUTTYPE;
begin
  GetCommand := false;
  command := BAD;
  if GetInp (userinp) then begin
    GetCommand := true;
    if not SkipBlanks (userinp) then begin
      GetChar (userinp, ch);
      if SkipBlanks (userinp) then
        if ch in ['p', 'P', 'h', 'H'] then
          case ch of
            'p', 'P' : command := PLOTFUNC;
            'h', 'H' : command := HELP
          end
        else if ch in ['q', 'Q'] then
          GetCommand := false
    end
  end else
      WriteUser (BADLINE, CMDERRLINE)
end; {GetCommand}
```

Finally, the main program contains the command processing loop, calling on *GetCommand* and performing the appropriate action in a **case** statement based on the command returned.

```
begin {main}
  Initialize;
  WriteUser (CMDPROMPT, CMDLINE);
```

```
while GetCommand (command) do begin
  case command of
    HELP :
      begin                                    {print messages to user}
        DoHelp;
        if not FirstFunction then              {redraw display if function plotted}
          WriteScreen (screen)
      end;
    PLOTFUNC :
      begin                                    {get a function from user and plot it}
        MoveCursor (CMDERRLINE, MINCOL);
        write (' ' : MAXCOL);
        MoveCursor (CMDERRLINE, MINCOL);
        lastfunc := GetFunction;
        if lastfunc <> nil then
          if DoPlot (points, screen, lastfunc) then begin
            WriteScreen (screen);
            FirstFunction := false             {we've plotted a function}
          end
      end;
    QUIT : halt;
    BAD : WriteUser (CMDLIST, CMDERRLINE)
  end;
  WriteUser (CMDPROMPT, CMDLINE)
end
end.
```

Adding a new command is a simple process that requires five steps.

1. Give the command a name and enter it in the type definition of *COMMANDS*.
2. Associate the command with an appropriate single letter that the user types or with action taken, to indicate the command.
3. Modify *GetCommand* to recognize the new command string or action, and extend the **case** statement so that the new command name can be returned.
4. Write the routine to perform the appropriate action.
5. Extend the **case** statement in the main command loop so that when *GetCommand* returns the command, the new routine is called.

In the exercises for this chapter, and in the exercises for the completed plotter in Chapter 13, you will be asked to extend the plotter's functions. Use this five-step process to add the new commands.

Exercises

1. Rewrite the queue routines of Fig. 9.3 for a queue implemented as an array, but not as a circular array. When the queue is full, call on a routine that moves all queue elements back to the beginning of the array.

2. The definition and implementation of a circular queue in Section 9.1.2 required that there be an unused location in the array in order to distinguish a full queue from an empty queue. Show that this is in fact the case with the definitions of that section, and the code of the *Enqueue* routine of Fig. 9.8.

3. Extend the implementation of a circular queue by writing the routines *IsFull*, *IsEmpty*, and *Dequeue*.

4. Modify the declaration of a stack to include a *count* field that contains the number of elements currently on the stack. Then modify the existing stack operations (*Push, Pop, IsEmpty,* and *InitStack*) to update or use this *count* field, where appropriate. Finally, write a function *COUNT* that returns the number of elements currently on the stack.

5. Implement the *ExamineTop* routine suggested at the end of Section 9.2.

6. Write a procedure *REVERSE* that reads an arbitrarily long line of characters and prints them out in reverse order. Assume the existence of the stack operations mentioned in this chapter.

7. Write a procedure *INVERT* that, given a pointer to a stack, returns a pointer to the same stack with its elements inverted. For example, if the stack originally had the elements in the order 3, 6, and 9, *INVERT* would return a pointer to the same stack, whose elements would now be in the order 9, 6, and 3. Again, assume the existence of the stack operations mentioned in this chapter.

8. Write a procedure *IsBalanced* that given an arbitrarily long string of characters, returns *true* if the parentheses and brackets are balanced appropriately, and *false*, otherwise. The following rules should be used to determine whether or not the string is balanced:

   a) A right parenthesis balances a single preceding left parenthesis. For example, the expressions (), ((())), and ()()() are balanced.

   b) If no unbalanced preceding left bracket exists, a right bracket balances all preceding unbalanced left parenthesis. For example, the expressions ((((([and (())((([are balanced.

   c) Otherwise, if an unbalanced left bracket exists, a right bracket closes that left bracket, and all unbalanced left parentheses following that left bracket. For example, the expressions (((([([)], [(([, and ((([[([]]]] are balanced.

   d) An expression is unbalanced if any right parenthesis or right bracket follows a balanced expression, or if any right parenthesis follows an unbalanced left bracket. For example, (())), [[[]]]], ()(), and [) are unbalanced.

9. A two-level queue contains two simple queues, one for high-priority items and one for low-priority items. All high-priority items are removed from the queue before any low-priority items are removed. Implement the following operations:

   a) *TwoLevelCreate* — creates a new two-level queue.

   b) *TwoLevelEnqueue* — enqueues an item on the two-level queue. One of the arguments to this procedure is the priority of the item (either low or high).

   c) *TwoLevelDequeue* — dequeues an item from the two-level queue. All high-priority items are dequeued before any low-priority items are dequeued.

   d) *TwoLevelEmpty* — returns *true* if the two-level queue is empty, and *false*, otherwise.

   e) *TwoLevelHigh* — returns the count of high-priority items on the two-level queue.

   f) *TwoLevelLow* — returns the count of low-priority items on the two-level queue.

10. The stack used in evaluating the post-fix expressions was implemented using linked lists, and will not overflow unless the *new* function fails. Implement the stack routines *InitStack*, *IsEmpty*, *IsFull*, *Push*, and *Pop* using an array representation rather than linked lists. Then implement *Evaluate* so that it handles the case of stack overflow in a reasonable way. Given that the maximum length of an expression will be one line of the input and that we intermix both pushing and popping operations, suggest and use an "appropriate" maximum size of the stack.

11. Add a new command, F, to the plotter that causes the current plot to be written to a file. The program may define an external file, *PlotFile*, and the current plot is added to the end of this file.

12. Add a new command, T, that writes the table of values for the current function to an external file *PlotTable*.

13. Modify the function plotter so that it will plot a table of values, in the manner that the first layer of Chapter 7 did. You will need to add a new command that indicates that a plot is desired from an external file, rather than generating the table internally.

MULTILINKED STRUCTURES:
TREES AND GRAPHS

10.1   Introduction

In the previous two chapters we examined linear lists and their applications in two very useful structures, queues and stacks. In this chapter we extend the notion of lists to *nonlinear* structures. We look at general and binary trees, including a formalization of some of their important and useful properties into an appropriate abstract data type (ADT). Trees, particularly binary trees, have applications in numerous areas, including sorting and searching.

In the second part of this chapter we look at a more general structure called a graph. We will see how graphs occur as a natural representation in scheduling problems, in communications networks and many other applications.

As in the previous chapter, we build upon good design and coding practices of Part II, but now with emphasis on both applications and the stronger notions of information hiding and data abstraction. Consequently trees and graphs are representational objects, used to model the structures in the problem being solved. As such, the choice of tree versus linked list should remain hidden from the rest of a program. Additionally these structures are themselves ADTs, and so their exact representation within a program should also be hidden from all other routines except for those that directly manipulate them. Consequently we examine both linked and array representations for trees, and both a linked and a two-dimensional array representation for graphs. We hope that you will not shy away from exploring the formal and mathematical properties of these structures and their utility as models for many interesting problems. Trees, and particularly the more general graph structures, have been studied and applied for almost 400 years! They have certainly earned their place as important, useful, and interesting problem representation schemes.

We begin the chapter with trees, and through them a review of recursion and a look at the programming techniques (and to some extent, thought processes) needed to write recursive routines. We do this because, as we have noted in the last chapter, the linked data structures can be defined *recursively*.

10.2   Trees

Adam and Eve, it is reputed, did their thing, and begat the whole human race. Of course, they didn't really do that. What they did, presumably, was to beget just one or more offspring. These offspring, in turn, begat more offspring, and so in addition to the human race, recursion was invented! We represent their begetting in the form of a diagram, with A & E at the top and all their progeny branching downward from them in Fig. 10.1.

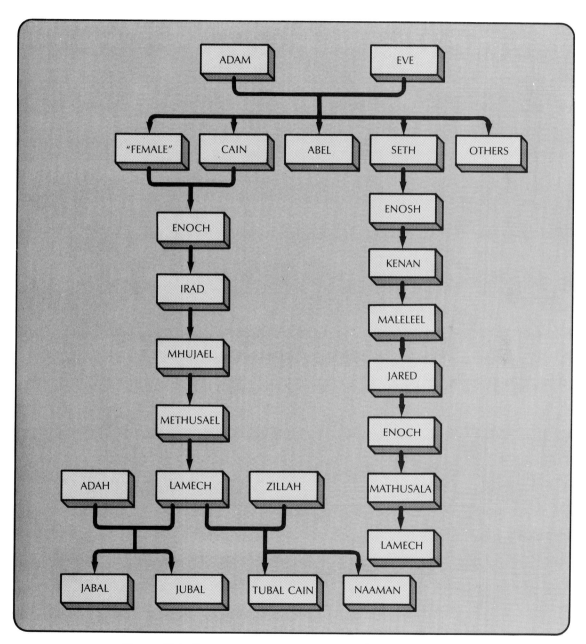

Figure 10.1. Tree structure representation of Adam and Eve and a few generations of their offspring.

Figure 10.1 represents the traditional family tree, with the most distant ancestors at the top and all their progeny cascading downward from them. Such structures are familiar to us from everyday experience. These tree structures are also quite useful in representing, or modeling, a number of processes and problems for programming purposes.

Trees are familiar to us through family trees, and through other familiar uses. One of these is a *game tree*. We represent the current state of a game as the top-most node in the tree (called the *root*), and all possible moves available from that board position are shown as branches (offspring, to use the family tree terminology; more formally, *subtrees*) of the root. A simple game familiar to most is Tic-Tac-Toe. The object of the game is to fill three squares horizontally, vertically, or diagonally with your symbol (X or O). We represent the game in terms of a starting configuration, and all the possible counter moves available from that position, the counter moves to the counter moves, and so on. We show the game tree for Tic-Tac-Toe in Fig. 10.2, with a starting position representing an intermediate point in the game.

We formalize some of the terminology on trees, and look at the typical actions we might want to perform on them. This allows us to define a reasonable Pascal representation and a package of routines needed to define the tree ADT. First we formally define a tree:

Definition: A *tree* is finite set of one or more nodes such that:

1. There is one anointed (special) node called the *root* of the tree.
2. The remaining nodes are partitioned into $m \geq 0$ disjoint sets T_1, T_2, ..., T_m, each of which is in turn a tree. These trees are called *subtrees* of the root.

We see that this defines a tree as a recursive structure. That is, the definition of tree refers to other trees. The definition is meant to formalize what we already know informally about trees, and it does not contain any surprises. There is a special type of tree, the *binary tree* (a tree with at most two subtrees of each node), which we will spend some time with in the next section. Most of our attention, in fact, will be focussed on binary trees since they are particularly useful in a number of important areas. The algorithms dealing with binary trees are some of the most elegant, powerful, and efficient ones that we will examine, yet they are simple to understand. The binary tree algorithms are fun to work with, are intellectually stimulating, and involve powerful recursive procedures available in Pascal. In all, they introduce a class of algorithms well worth study and application.

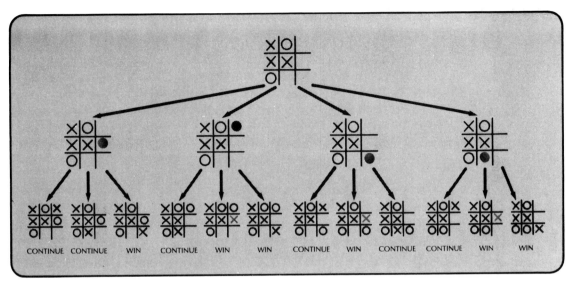

Figure 10.2. Game tree for Tic-Tac-Toe.

10.2.1 Binary Trees

A binary tree is a special kind of tree and we define it formally as follows:

Definition: A *binary tree* is a finite set of *zero* or more nodes such that:

1. There is one anointed node called the *root* of the tree.
2. Each node has two subtrees, distinguished as the *left* and *right* subtrees.

Figure 10.3 shows examples of a number of different binary trees. The first is called an expression tree, a particular kind of tree that we will look at quite closely in Part IV. The second and third are trees containing integer values. They both have two nodes, but they are *not* the same at all, for a binary tree distinguishes between its left and right subtrees. In the second, the root has no left subtree; in the third, it has no right subtree.

We'll define a few basic terms dealing with binary trees. The two subtrees of a node are distinguished as the *left* and *right* subtrees of the node. Continuing the botanical terminology, a node with no subtrees is called a *leaf node*. Nodes with one or two subtrees are called *interior nodes*. A collection of two or more trees is called a *forest*.

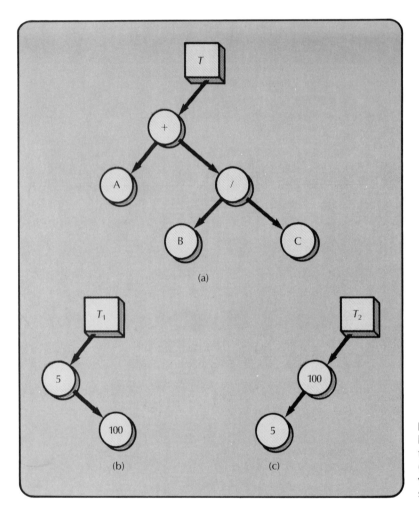

Figure 10.3. Examples of binary trees. (a) Expression tree for $A + B/C$. (b) and (c) Two trees with integer values, which are *not* the same binary tree.

Continuing the family tree nomenclature, nodes immediately beneath a given node are called its *offspring*, or *children*. Those on the same level as a given node are called *siblings* of the node. Nodes above a given node are called its *ancestors*, and the node immediately above a given node is called its *parent*. All nodes have a single parent, except the *root*, which has no parent. Occasionally the masculine terms, *father*, *son*, *brother*, and so on are used. We prefer the previous genderless terms.

The *height* of a binary tree is the length of the longest path from the root to a leaf node, plus one. By this definition, a tree with a single node has a height of one. We define the height of the empty tree to be zero. The height of some sample binary trees is shown in Fig. 10.4.

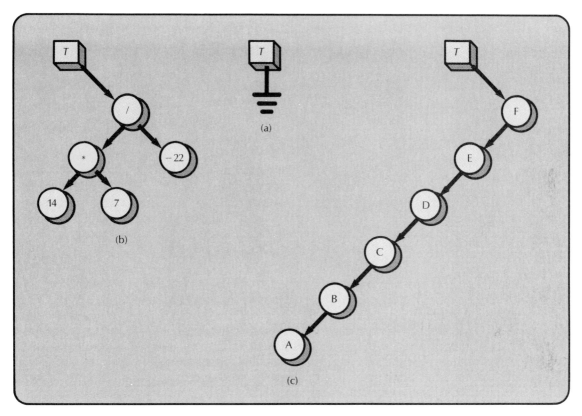

Figure 10.4. Binary trees of different height. (a) Height 3. (b) Empty tree, height 0. (c) Height 6.

The number of nodes in a tree of a given height depends on the shape of the tree. Obviously the maximum height of a tree with n nodes is n. More interesting is the minimum height of a tree with n nodes. Such a tree is called a *complete* binary tree, since it has the property that all nodes have exactly two subtrees, except nodes at the two lowest levels of the tree. A complete binary tree such that all levels are full is called a *full* binary tree. Both full and complete binary trees are illustrated in Fig. 10.5.

The height of a full binary tree of n nodes is then $\log_2(n + 1)$. Conversely the *maximum* number of nodes in a binary tree (which will be a full binary tree) of height H will be $2^H - 1$. It also follows that the maximum number of nodes at any given level of the tree must be 2^{H-1}. By this property, more than half the nodes in a full binary tree are at the lowest level (that is, in a full binary tree, there are 2^{H-1} nodes at the lowest level and $2^H - 1$ total

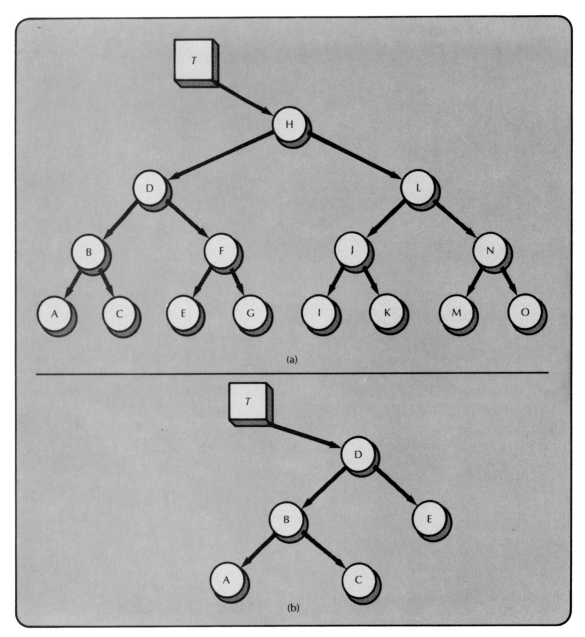

Figure 10.5. (a) *Full* binary tree of height 4. (b) *Complete* binary tree of height 3.

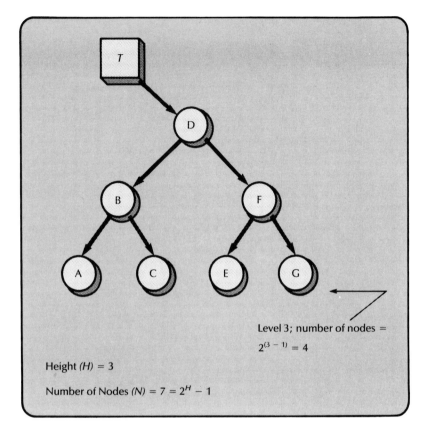

Level 3; number of nodes =
$2^{(3-1)} = 4$

Height $(H) = 3$

Number of Nodes $(N) = 7 = 2^H - 1$

Figure 10.6. Diagram showing mathematical relationships in a tree.

nodes in the tree). These relationships are easier to visualize with the help of diagrams, as in Fig. 10.6. Finally, a tree whose nodes all have only one subtree (except the last) is called a *degenerate* tree, shown in Fig. 10.7.

10.2.2 Binary Tree ADT

We will build a basic set of routines and data definitions for a binary tree that we can package as a binary tree ADT. As with our previous attempts to build an ADT, we make no claim that these are the only operations; rather we view them as a useful starting point for a package of access operations, defined in a manner that is not dependent on the underlying language or machine representation for the tree. In fact, at this point, we have not looked in detail at how a tree could be represented. We'll delay

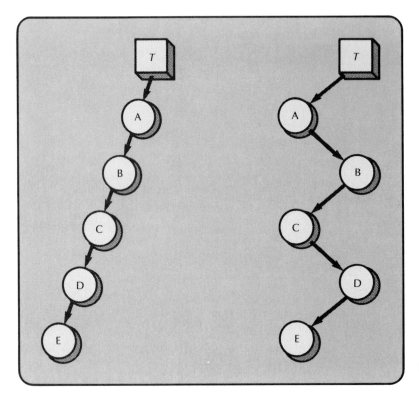

Figure 10.7. Degenerate binary trees.

(as is our custom) the implementation decisions until we examine specific operations on trees.

During the building phase of a binary tree, we need to be able to move through the tree, taking a left branch or a right branch, depending on the requirements of the algorithm. Additionally we may need to move up the tree, going from a node to its parent. Occasionally we may need to move from a node to its sibling. And, of course, we would like to be able to initialize a tree to the empty tree. Some, but by no means all, of the primitive routines include:

InitTree(T)	Initializes *T* to be an empty binary tree.
Parent(N)	Returns the parent of a given node *N*.
LeftChild(N)	Returns the root node of the left subtree of *N*.
RightChild(N)	Returns the root node of the right subtree of *N*.

Traverse(T)	"Visits" each node in the tree in some prespecified order.
TreeInsert (value, T)	Inserts value into the binary tree pointed to by *T*.
Delete(T, P)	Deletes the node pointed to by *P*, from the binary tree *T*.

Representation

Binary trees are most easily represented in Pascal using pointers. We may also use a nondynamic, or nonlinked representation, similar to that used for linear linked lists. We defer this second representation to the exercises, however. The basic node in a tree (shown in Fig. 10.8) will be a record containing at least three fields:

■ A data field of type *WHATEVER* (which, as before, can be any pre-defined or user-defined data type, including pointers to other structures)
■ A pointer to the node's left subtree (which may be **nil**)
■ A pointer to the node's right subtree (which may be **nil**)

In some applications it may be desirable to have additional pointers in each node, including pointers to the node's parent, pointers to the node's siblings, and so on. However, the two pointers to a node's left and right subtrees will suffice for our initial applications. For other applications,

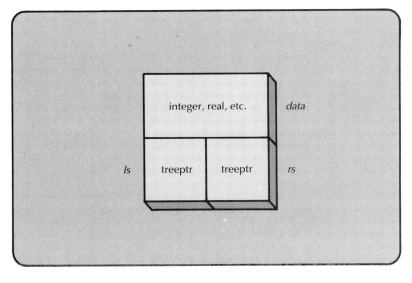

Figure 10.8. Diagram of a binary tree node showing three fields.

where different processing of the nodes may be required, we will not hesitate to include the additional pointers when they are needed.

In Pascal, the node as diagrammed in Fig. 10.8 is defined as a record:

```
type
    TREEPTR      =  ↑ TREENODE;
    TREENODE     =
    record
        data      : WHATEVER;
        ls        : TREEPTR;
        rs        : TREEPTR
    end;
```

Note that the data definitions are virtually the same as for a two-way linked list. It is not the data type definition that distinguishes a linear list from a binary tree. Rather, it is the way that nodes are processed in the structure. In the following sections we discuss some of the more useful, important applications of binary trees, which will allow us to develop the binary tree operations just defined.

10.2.3 Traversing a Binary Tree

The applications we'll look at in this chapter require that, after the binary tree is built, we "visit" or process the nodes of the tree in some regular order. In the case of linear lists, a natural processing order exists: head to rear. No such natural ordering exists in binary trees, except that it seems reasonable to begin processing at the root. In most applications, however, three natural orderings of the nodes occur. We look at these orderings in terms of an expression tree. Figure 10.9 is the tree for the expression $(A + B) * C$.

Evaluating an expression tree is really quite simple: first we evaluate the left subtree of T (no matter how complex), next the right of T, and then we apply the operator at the root to the results returned from evaluating the left and right subtrees. We call such an order of evaluation the *post-order* traversal of the tree T. We can define the post-order traversal in an informal, recursive manner:

Traverse $(T ↑ .ls)$;   {1}
Traverse $(T ↑ .rs)$;   {2}
Visit (T);   {3}

Let's apply this pseudo-procedure to the expression tree of Fig. 10.9(a), defining *Visit(T)* to mean "print the token at T." In so doing, we produce

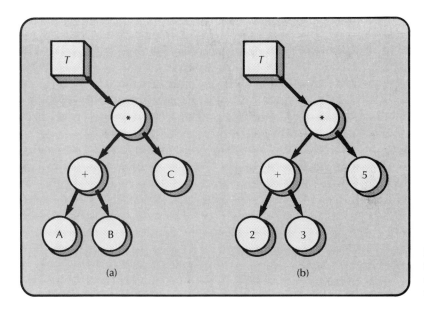

Figure 10.9. (a) Expression tree for $(A + B) * C$. (b) Using $A = 2$, $B = 3$, $C = 5$.

the string:

$$A\ B + C *$$

Surprise! The post-order traversal of the tree is just the post-fix form of the original expression!

Two other permutations of the preceding three statements produce important traversal orders of the nodes of the tree. These are defined as the in-order traversal and the pre-order traversal. Table 10.1 shows the three

Traversal	Code	Output from Fig. 10.9(a)
Table 10.1. Traversal order, code, and output from Fig. 10.9(a).		
Post-order	Traverse(T ↑ .ls); Traverse(T ↑ .rs); Visit(T);	$A\ B + C *$
In-order	Traverse(T ↑ .ls); Visit(T); Traverse(T ↑ .rs);	$A + B * C$
Pre-order	Visit(T); Traverse(T ↑ .ls); Traverse(T ↑ .rs);	$* + A\ B\ C$

permutations and the result of applying them to the expression tree of Fig. 10.9(a).

A delightful surprise of these traversals is that they produce as output a string corresponding to one of the intermediate forms for representing expressions that we saw in Chapter 9: the in-order traversal corresponds to the in-fix form of the expression, post-order to post-fix, and pre-order to pre-fix. Consequently a binary tree representation of an expression appears to be more general than one of the three linear string forms.

If we assume that an empty binary tree consists of a single pointer to **nil** (as shown here)

and the nodes of a nonempty tree have pointers to their respective left and right subtrees, or to **nil** if the respective subtree is empty (as shown here),

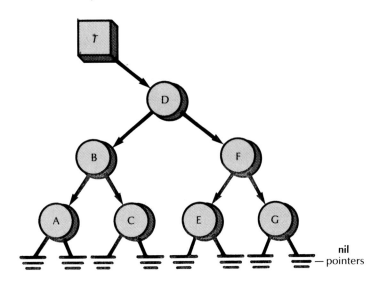

then the code for any of the three traversals is an extremely simple recursive Pascal procedure:

```
procedure Traverse (T : TREEPTR);
begin
  if T <> nil then begin
    Traverse(T ↑ .ls);                {1}
    Visit(T);                         {2}
    Traverse(T ↑ .rs)                 {3}
  end
end; {Traverse}
```

This is the *in-order* traversal; appropriate permutations of the three statements 1 through 3 yield the other two traversals. This procedure will prove to be quite fruitful given careful study and attention. For those who might be a bit mystified by recursion (and it is certainly a powerful mechanism for dealing with these inherently recursive structures), we will develop a nonrecursive version of the in-order traversal in the *Programming Notes* at the end of the chapter: it is larger and will require an auxiliary stack. The recursive versions are elegant, compact, and virtually certain to compile and work correctly.

The *Visit* routine depends on the particular application. In the case of expression trees, *Visit* is a routine that applies the operator at the node to the values returned from the left and right subtrees of the node. It returns a value in an appropriate parameter, which is then passed back up as the value of the node's entire tree.

Later in this chapter we look at an entirely different use of a binary tree: sorting and searching. The algorithm for building the tree is quite different from that used to build the expression tree, yet the same traversal techniques are used. (Expression trees are covered in Chapter 13.)

10.3 Applications of Trees

In this section we look in detail at an important application of binary trees. It is useful because it indicates the great utility that trees have as problem and data structure representations. The application we look at is binary search trees/insertion and deletion.

10.3.1 Binary Search Trees

We look at binary search trees in detail. This is our first look at a sorting algorithm that is substantially faster than the insertion sort techniques we first examined in Chapter 1. Recall that the insertion techniques required a computing time, for randomly distributed values, proportional to n^2, where n is the number of values to be sorted. We saw that as n became large, the computing time became prohibitively expensive. Binary tree sorting requires computing time proportional to $n\log_2 n$. We will informally prove this result later and examine the computing time with sample input files of 200, 400, 800, and 5000 randomly distributed values.

Building the tree

We will build a binary tree with values in each node. The values in the tree must be such that an ordering exists: one of the Pascal predefined types of integer, real, boolean, or character, or a user-defined type on which an ordering is implied. The rule for building the tree is simple: at any node, we want to guarantee that all values in the *left* subtree of the node are less than or equal to the value of the node. Similarly, we want all values in the *right* subtree to be greater than the value of the node. If this condition holds, it is simple to prove that the *in-order* traversal of the tree, beginning at the root, will produce the values in sorted order (this proof is left as an exercise). A tree with this property is called a *binary search tree (BST)*, which is shown in Fig. 10.10. For this application, we may define the routine *Visit* as one that prints the value of the node. (A BST might not allow duplicate values depending on the specific application.)

Building this tree is surprisingly simple. We show this by writing a procedure that takes two parameters: a binary tree that already has the BST property and a new value to insert at the appropriate place in the tree. To see how to accomplish this, we first note that the empty tree trivially maintains this property. When we read the first value, we insert it as the root of the tree. Now we have a tree with a single node — the BST property again trivially holds in this case, since we have **nil** left and right subtrees. As we insert additional values, we must decide where they are to go in the tree. Our decision process for moving to the left or right subtree of a given node is quite simple. We compare the new value with the value of the node. If the new value is *less than* (or *equal to*) the value at the node, we move *left*. If the new value is *greater than* the node, we move *right*. Finally, when the appropriate subtree of the node is empty, we attach a new node, with the new value, as the left or right subtree, as appropriate, to the existing node. The process is easier to visualize than to explain! We trace the insertion of the values 4, 19, -7, 49, 100, 0, 22, and 12 into an initially empty binary search tree T in Fig. 10.11.

The first value always becomes the root of the tree: this is 4. The next value, 19, is compared with 4. Since it is larger, we move to the right subtree of 4; the right subtree is **nil,** so we attach a new node with 19 as

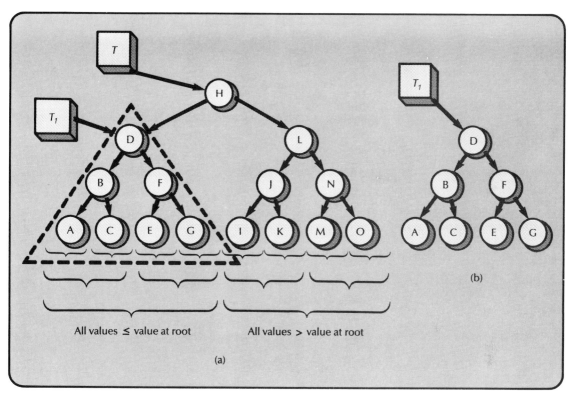

Figure 10.10. Recursive property of binary search tree. (a) Each node partitions the tree into two subtrees; the left contains only values ≤ node, the right contains only values > node. (b) The BST property holds recursively for any node in the tree.

the right subtree of 4. The next value, -7, is compared with the root, and is less than the value there, 4 — we move left. The left subtree of the root is **nil,** so we attach a new node with -7 as the left subtree of 4. The completed tree is shown in Fig. 10.11(c).

Obviously, this is becoming repetitive and it is not necessary to describe the process further. The procedure in Fig. 10.12 inserts a new value at the appropriate place in the binary search tree T. To properly attach the new node as the left or right subtree of the parent, we use two pointers as we move down the tree (as was the case with linear linked lists): the *current* and *previous* pointers. Figure 10.12 assumes the earlier data type declarations for a binary tree.

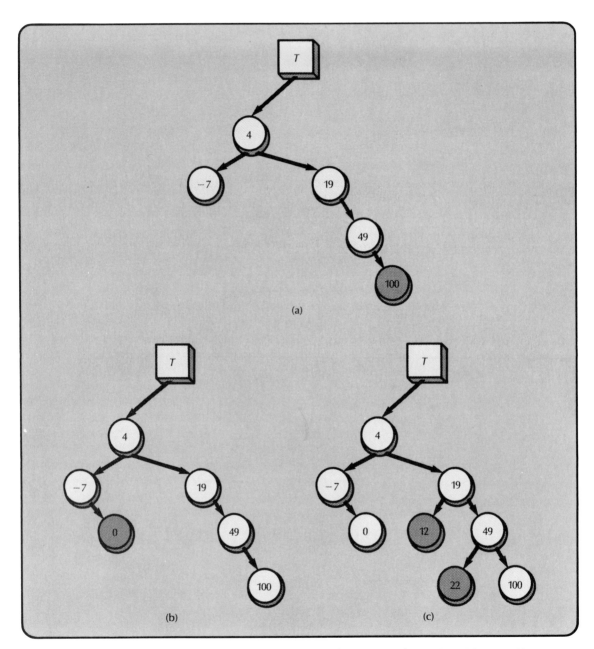

Figure 10.11. Trace of insertion into a binary search tree *T*. (a) Insert 100. (b) Insert 0. (c) Insert 22 and 12.

```
procedure TreeInsert(value : WHATEVER; var T : TREEPTR);
{Insert value into the binary tree pointed to by T.}
var
    current         : TREEPTR;
    previous        : TREEPTR;
    temp            : TREEPTR;
begin
    {Find where to move. Watch out for empty tree.}
    previous := T;
    current := T;
    while current <> nil do
        if value <= current↑.data then begin        {move left}
            previous := current;
            current := current↑.ls
        end else begin                              {move right}
            previous := current;
            current := current↑.rs
        end;

    {
    At this point, we've found the insertion point, OR we are inserting into empty tree.
    Empty tree occurs ONLY when T = nil.
    }
        new(temp);                                  {get the new node}
        temp↑.data := value;
        temp↑.ls := nil;                            {set subtrees to nil}
        temp↑.rs := nil;
        if T = nil then                             {inserting into empty tree}
            T := temp
        else if value <= previous↑.data then
            previous↑.ls := temp
        else
            previous↑.rs := temp
    end; {TreeInsert}
```

Figure 10.12. Procedure to insert a new value into an existing binary search tree.

The code is compact and clear in its functioning. Again, we have to be careful about the initial insertion into an empty tree (which could be eliminated by using a header node as discussed at the end of Chapter 9). The final version of the tree, with the preceding values, is shown in Fig. 10.11(c).

If we now apply an in-order traversal to this tree, we obtain the values

Table 10.2. Sorting times for binary tree sort.		
n	Time (sec)	*k*nlog$_2$*n*
200	0.7	0.64
400	1.5	1.44
800	3.1	3.20
5000	23.9	26.00

in the nodes in numerical order, from low to high. We ran this sorting algorithm on randomly generated files of integers on a DEC VAX 11/780, using the Berkeley Pascal compiler. The files contained 200, 400, 800, and 5000 integers. The program included a simple driver to read values from the standard input, to call *TreeInsert* until end of file, and then to call the recursive in-order traversal procedure, *Traverse*. The execution times are shown in Table 10.2, along with the values for $k$nlog$_2$n, where k has been computed from the data to be 0.00040. That is, the value 0.00040 nlog$_2$n, will be quite close to the total computing time (in seconds).

These results are really quite astounding. They indicate that the computing time (unlike the insertion sort algorithms of Chapter 1, which grew in time proportional to the square of the number of inputs) now grows in proportion to n, the number of inputs, times the log to the base 2 of n. As we begin to understand the meaning of such execution time properties and the reasons for their comparatively low values, we are on the way to emerging out of the realm of struggling programming students into that of practicing programmers. We have taken our first step from merely finding an algorithm, any algorithm, that performs a task (sorting in this case), to finding good, efficient algorithms. Reviewing the results of the insertion sort schemes of Chapter 5, we begin to appreciate that there are classes of algorithms that, no matter how tricky we get with our coding, always get very bad as the number of inputs grows. It has taken an entirely different approach to the problem to break out of this curse of large numbers of values. We investigate other interesting and important classes of algorithms in Chapter 11, and we see how we can formalize our notions of algorithmic efficiency.

Of course, we have cheated a bit in this algorithm because we have assumed that the values are randomly distributed and that the integer files generated for Table 10.2 were produced with a random number generator. What happens if the numbers are not randomly distributed? For example, assume the values are *already* sorted. Let us apply the BST insertion algorithm on the values 1, 3, 5, 7, 9, 11, 13, 15, and 17. In this case we end up with the following BST.

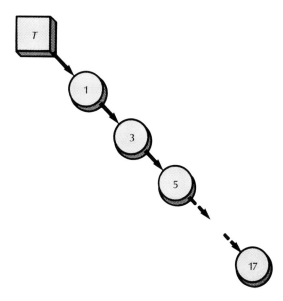

We don't seem to have a tree at all! This looks exactly like a one-way linear linked list, and so we expect that the time to sort an already sorted list does not grow as $n\log_2 n$, but rather as n^2. In assessing this and other sorting algorithms, we must be concerned about both the average and the worst case performance.

We have not proven, of course, that binary tree sorting takes time proportional to $n\log_2 n$. We should certainly wonder where a computing time expression such as this comes from. Actually the result is quite simple to see if we verify it informally. A thorough, analytical proof requires probability mathematics, beyond the reasonable scope of this book. Nonetheless, such mathematics does verify formally the result we develop informally. We start by assuming that the values are randomly distributed. That is, given n values to be inserted, any of the $n!$ possible permutations of the values is equally likely. More importantly, this assumption means that at each comparison step in the insertion algorithm, we are equally likely to decide to move left as right. Consequently, at any given state in the building of the tree, we should have the property that the number of nodes in the left subtree of the root is approximately equal to the number of nodes in the right subtree. This is shown in Fig. 10.13.

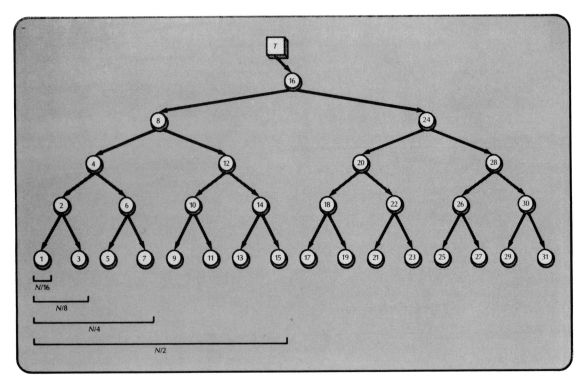

Figure 10.13. BST with equal numbers of nodes in left and right subtrees.

The recursive property of the tree should ensure that this property of equal number of nodes in each subtree holds for *each* node of the tree. Counting nodes in each subtree, and assuming m nodes in the tree already, we expect about $m/2$ nodes in the left subtree and $m/2$ nodes in the right. For the tree whose root is the left child of the root of the tree, we expect $m/4$ nodes in its left subtree and $m/4$ in its right; similarly for the left and right children of the right child of the root.

Using the mathematical results described earlier, the average path length to the insertion point for the new value in the tree is about the height of the tree. For a tree that grows in such a way that it is nearly complete, this path length is about $\log_2 m$, when m nodes are already in the tree. We must repeat this process for each of the n values to be inserted. That is, the number of comparisons is bounded above by $n\log_2 n$.

Combining all of this, we can expect the total computing time for all n insertions, under ideal conditions of randomly distributed keys, to be about n times the log to the base 2 of n. Analytical results investigating all possible combinations of $n!$ permutations of n values indicate that the BST is expected to deviate by at most about 40% (on the average) from this ideal figure. We saw this result supported in Table 10.2's computing times for our test values. In Chapter 12 we will examine a number of other sorting techniques, generally with the $k n \log_2 n$ computing time property, that have a smaller constant k and that are able to avoid the problems of n^2 computing time when the values are already sorted.

We should, however, be very pleased with the BST technique. It has a number of valuable properties: it is conceptually simple, and thus easy to program; it is dynamic (that is, the tree can be built and the values sorted, without needing all n values initially); it is simple to remove values from the tree, while retaining the desirable balanced shape of the tree (which we discuss next); and searching, or determining whether a given value is in the tree, can be accomplished quickly and efficiently (as we will see in Chapter 11). All in all, binary trees are a wonderfully powerful programming structure that can prove useful in many applications.

Deleting from a BST

It is quite simple to delete a node from a binary tree; it is another matter to delete a node and maintain the BST property. There are at least two methods of deleting a node: one leaves the tree quite unbalanced, and the other preserves the original balance to a greater degree. We briefly describe and illustrate one technique and leave the other as an exercise.

First, we start with an existing BST (possibly empty) and a pointer to a node that we wish to remove from the tree. There are three cases (illustrated in Fig. 10.14) in the deletion of the node pointed to by N:

1. Node N is a leaf.
2. Node N has a **nil** left or right subtree.
3. Neither (1) nor (2) hold.

The removal of a leaf node is trivial: set the left or right subtree of its parent (as appropriate) to **nil.** The following piece of a *Delete* procedure accomplishes this:

```
            . . .
if (N ↑ .ls = nil) and (N ↑ .rs = nil) then begin
  temp := Parent(N);
  if (N ↑ .value <= temp ↑ .value) then
    temp ↑ .ls := nil
  else
    temp ↑ .rs := nil
end else begin

            . . .
```

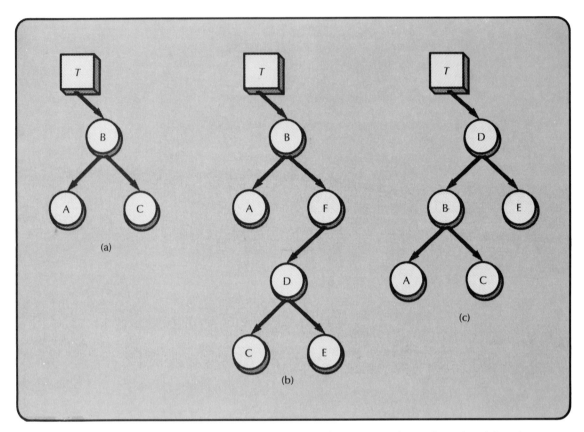

Figure 10.14. Sample BST *T* showing three cases of a node to be deleted.
(a) Delete 'C': **nil** subtrees. (b) Delete 'F': only one **nil** subtree. (c) Delete 'B':
both subtrees non-**nil.**

Of course, with a little bit of extra thought, we see that cases (1) and
(2) are handled in the same way: if we wish to delete a node with either
or both subtrees **nil**, we just attach its parent to its non-**nil** subtree (and if
both are **nil**, just set the appropriate subtree of the parent to **nil**). This is
illustrated in Fig. 10.15.

The code to accomplish both these cases is shown below:

```
        . . .
    if (N ↑ .ls  =  nil) then begin
      temp := Parent(N);
      if (N ↑ .value <=  temp ↑ .value) then
        temp ↑ .ls := N ↑ .rs
```

```
else
    temp ↑ .rs := N ↑ .rs
end else begin
if (N ↑ .rs = nil) then begin
    temp := Parent(N);
    if (N ↑ .value <= temp ↑ .value) then
        temp ↑ .ls := N ↑ .ls
    else
        temp ↑ .rs := N ↑ .ls
end else begin

        . . .
```

Finally, we reach the case that the node has non-**nil** left and right subtrees. Now we use a fundamental property of the BST: if a node has non-**nil** left and right subtrees, its successor (following the in-order traversal) will have a **nil** *left* subtree. We then find the successor of the node, exchange its data with its successor, and then delete the successor node. Again, this

Figure 10.15. Removal of a node with **nil** subtree. (a) Before. (b) After.

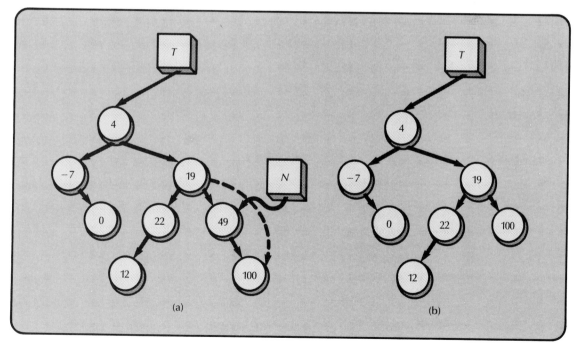

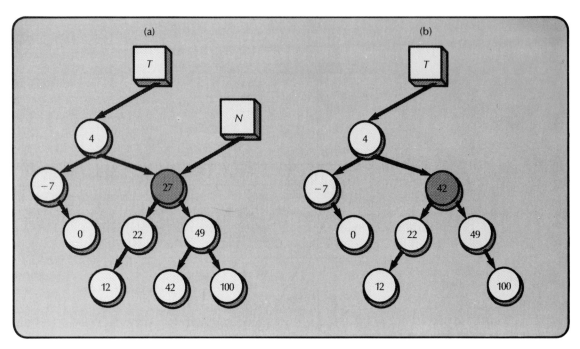

Figure 10.16. (a) Binary tree *T* before removal of node *N*. (b) Binary tree *T* after removal of node *N*.

is easier visualized than explained, and Fig. 10.16 illustrates the deletion of node N: first find its successor, then exchange data, and finally delete the successor node. The successor is found by moving right once, then all the way left, as shown in the following:

```
procedure Successor (T : TREEPTR; var P, S : TREEPTR);
{
T is a pointer to a node with non-nil left and right sub-trees.
RETURNS:  S, a pointer to the in-order successor of T.
          P, the parent of S.
}
begin
  P := T;
  S := T↑.rs;
  while S↑.ls <> nil do begin
    P := S;
    S := S↑.ls
  end
end; {Successor}
```

This technique for removing nodes from a tree generally leaves the tree with the same shape as before the deletion. Another technique also makes use of the fact that the successor of a node with non-**nil** left and right subtrees will have a **nil** left subtree. This second technique deletes the node by attaching the left or right subtree of the parent (as appropriate) to the node's *right* subtree, then attaching the node's left subtree as the *left* subtree of its successor. You are asked to program the second deletion technique in the exercises.

10.4 Graphs

Graphs are generalizations of the trees we've been looking at in the previous sections. We may think of them as representing objects or actions; locations such as cities, processors, and so on; and the relations and connections between them. The study and analysis of graphs has interested mathematicians for many centuries and represents a highly refined branch of combinatorial mathematics. Many elegant and efficient algorithms have been developed for manipulating or processing graphs and for discovering certain connectivity properties of a given graph. Obviously the field is far too broad to cover in a short section here. But we would be surprised if such a long-studied, rich branch of mathematics did not yield important representation schemes and efficient algorithms for processing them and, in fact, such is the case. We will examine graphs, their utility in representing interesting problems amenable to computer solution, and their representations. We will begin the design of a modest case study that uses a directed graph for determining the order of processing: a mini-spreadsheet program. By representing the spreadsheet as a directed graph, we can easily determine the correct order of evaluation. The complete program comprises Chapter 14.

10.4.1 Basics

Figure 10.17 is a map of the United States showing certain cities and the cost of an airline flight between them. We are interested in finding the lowest fare between two given cities based on the hypothetical fare information between a number of cities.

We will represent the map by a data structure known as a *graph*. Formally, a graph is a collection of two sets: *vertices* (the cities here) and *edges* (here the air routes connecting various cities). The edges constitute a set of pairs of vertices (here indicating that there is a nonstop flight between the cities). If there is a *cost* or *weight* associated with each edge, we call the graph a *weighted graph* (here the weight is the price of the nonstop flight between

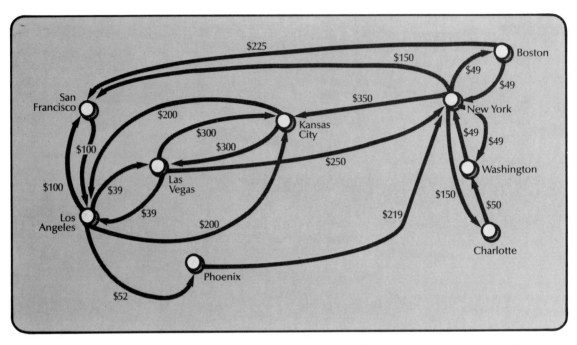

Figure 10.17. Airline route map of the United States showing costs for flights between a few cities.

the cities). If the edges are directed (that is, there may be an edge from vertex i to vertex j, but not the other way), the graph is called a *directed graph* (Fig. 10.17 represents a directed graph because some city pairs have a flight in one direction only, and because the cost of a flight from city A to city B is not always the same as the cost from B to A). If direction is not important (that is, there is no distinction between A to B versus B to A), the graph is an *undirected graph*.

If there is an edge from A to B, we say that A is *adjacent to* B and B is *adjacent from* A (in Fig. 10.17 Las Vegas is adjacent to New York, but New York is not adjacent to Las Vegas). In an undirected graph, the existence of an edge between A and B means that each is adjacent to the other. If it is possible to reach B from A via one or more edges, we say that there is a *path* from A to B. If the path does not pass through any vertex more than once, it is called a *simple path*. If there is a path of length two or greater (usually we require three or greater for undirected graphs; can you see why?), which begins and ends at the same vertex, the graph is said to contain a *cycle*. A graph without any cycles is called *acyclic*.

In Fig. 10.17 we see that Charlotte is not adjacent to New York, but there is a *path* from Charlotte to New York (through Washington). There are a number of cycles in the graph; for example, the path from Los Angeles to Las Vegas to Kansas City to Los Angeles.

There is the interesting problem of finding the lowest cost flight from city *A* to city *B*. As we can easily see from Fig. 10.17, the lowest cost fare between some cities is not always the nonstop flight. For example, there is a nonstop flight from Kansas City to Las Vegas for $300. But the airlines all have special fares to the bigger cities, and a traveller could take the nonstop to Los Angeles for $200 and then the gamblers' special to Las Vegas for $39, for a savings of $61.

The solution to this problem of finding the lowest cost (or shortest, or fastest) path between two vertices in a graph is an important algorithm in graph theory, and we will look at it in a bit. First we take up the problem of representing a graph such as Fig. 10.17 in Pascal. Then we use the representation to solve problems such as finding the lowest cost path.

10.4.2 Representation

We first shorten Fig. 10.17 to a smaller graph shown in Fig. 10.18.

There are two standard techniques for representing a graph *G* (such as in Fig. 10.18): the *adjacency matrix* and the *adjacency list*. The adjacency matrix *M* is a two-dimensional array representing the connections between

Figure 10.18. Simplified graph of Fig. 10.17.

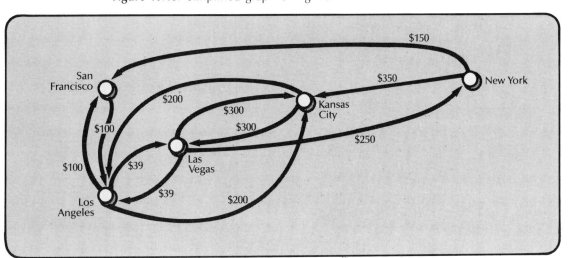

pairs of vertices. The columns and rows represent the graph's vertices. If there is an edge from i to j (that is, vertex i is adjacent to j), the cost (or weight) of the edge from i to j is entered; if there is no edge from i to j, an entry of $+\infty$ is made (that is, the cost of flying from i to j is $+\infty$). We assume that the cost of flying from i to i is 0, so the diagonal of M is set to all 0's. (For clarity, we do not show these values in the following matrix.) If G is an unweighted graph, an entry of 1 is made if there is an edge from i to j; 0, otherwise. If G is an undirected graph, the matrix is symmetric: $M[i, j] = M[j, i]$. Here is the adjacency matrix for Fig. 10.18:

	SF	LA	LV	KC	NY
SF		100			
LA	100		39	200	
LV		39		300	250
KC		200	300		
NY	150			350	

The second common method for representing graphs, useful when a graph has many vertices and few edges, is the *adjacency list*. In this representation, we use a linked list for each vertex v in the graph that has other vertices adjacent *from* it. The entire graph is represented as an array of head nodes (as we discussed at the end of Chapter 9) which either are **nil** (the vertex is not adjacent to any other) or point to the first node in the list of vertices that v is adjacent to. The graph in Fig. 10.18 is represented in the following adjacency list:

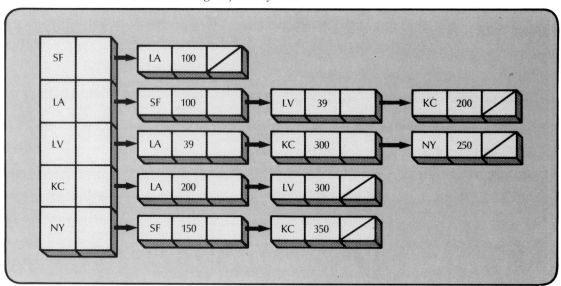

```
const
  infinity        = maxint;
  MAXV            = 100;                          {or whatever is appropriate}
type
  VERTEX          = 1..MAXV;
  GRAPH           =                               {adjacency matrix}
    record
      size          : VERTEX;
      cost          : array [VERTEX, VERTEX] of COSTS
    end;
                                    (a)


type
  COSTS           = 0..infinity;                  {non-negative costs only}
  VERTEXPTR       = ↑ VERTEXNODE;
  VERTEXNODE      =
    record
      id            : VERTEX;
      cost          : COSTS;
      link          : VERTEXPTR
    end;
  GRAPH           =                               {adjacency list}
    record
      size          : VERTEX;
      cost          : array [VERTEX] of VERTEXPTR
    end;
                                    (b)
```

Figure 10.19. Two representations for a graph. (a) Adjacency matrix. (b) Adjacency list.

The choice of representation depends on the particular algorithm being implemented and whether the graph is "sparse" or "dense." A sparse graph is one in which the number of vertices N is much greater than the number of edges E. In a dense graph the number of edges approaches the maximum ($N^2 - N$; because we do not allow a vertex to be adjacent to itself, the diagonal is always 0). Some algorithms are better designed using both representations, or a hybrid combination of the two. Some perform better with a highly specialized representation for that particular problem. Graphs and graph algorithms give you the opportunity to experiment and devise alternative representations that can have a significant effect on computing time. However, these two representations, the adjacency list and the adjacency matrix, will prove satisfactory in most applications.

Figure 10.19(a) shows typical declarations for an adjacency matrix, and Fig. 10.19(b) gives typical declarations for an adjacency list.

10.4.3 Applications

The first graph application we look at is the one we've been discussing in relation to Fig. 10.18, finding the lowest cost path between two vertices, A and B. One solution to this problem was developed by E. Dijkstra[1] and is called Dijkstra's algorithm. It actually does more for us than just finding the lowest cost path between A and B—for the same amount of effort, it finds the lowest cost paths from A to *all* other vertices. In this collection of paths will be the lowest cost path to B. The problem is thus called the single source, shortest path problem.

Discussion

The algorithm uses a simple technique that at first seems naive, but that works correctly here: a locally optimal solution is part of a globally optimal solution. Such an algorithm picks the best it can do at any given point and assumes that that selection, which is good locally, is part of the over-all best solution. Such an algorithm technique is called a *greedy* algorithm. If we begin our path from vertex A, we pick the shortest edge adjacent from A. Let's assume this is the edge from A to i. Now we would like to find the shortest path from the set S = {A, i} to a vertex outside this set, say, vertex j. Such a path must either go direct from A, or go through one or more of the vertices in this set. To find the next shortest path, we compare the sum of the costs of going from each of the vertices currently in S to each of the vertices not in S. We add the vertex with the lowest cost to S, and continue. To keep track of the accumulation of total costs from A to each of the other vertices, we use an auxiliary array *PathCosts*. As a new vertex j is entered into S, the cost of getting there from i is accumulated in *PathCosts[j]*.

If you're having trouble distinguishing A's, i's, j's, and S's, Fig. 10.20 should help establish these points. Remember what we're trying to show: that a locally optimal solution is part of the globally optimal one.

The original graph is shown in Fig. 10.20(a), with the source being vertex A. The first step finds the shortest vertex from A to all other vertices. This is the edge from A to B, with a cost of 100 (Fig. 10.20(b)). The set of selected vertices is now A and B. We now look for the shortest edge from {A, B} to all other edges, which is B to E (cost 20). The cost of the path from A to E is now the minimum of the direct cost of the edge (200) and the cost from A to B to E (120), Fig. 10.20(c). In Fig. 10.20(d) we add the next edge, A to D, and the various costs are updated.

[1] Dijkstra, E., "A note on two problems in connexion with graphs," in *Numerische Mathematik*, V. 1, pp. 269–271 (1959).

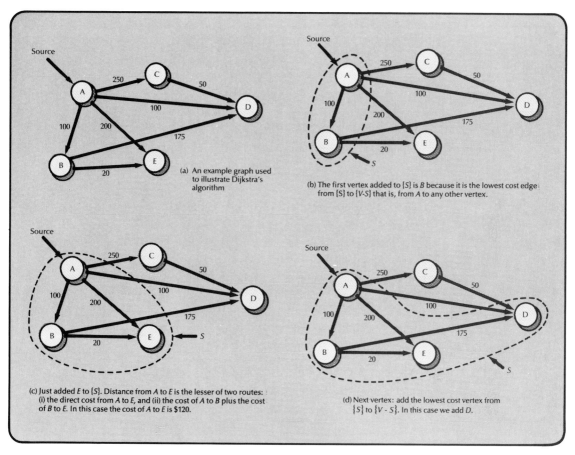

Figure 10.20. Stages in Dijkstra's algorithm.

We are assuming that all edge weights are nonnegative. If we allow negative weights (an airline pays us for flying that route!), Dijkstra's algorithm will not necessarily pick the lowest cost path.

The algorithm has just three steps and we present it here. The code is shorter than the written description! We assume that we are beginning at vertex $v0$.

1. Initialize $PathCosts[i]$ to $Cost[v0, i]$. $PathCosts[i]$ will be the cost of the shortest path from $v0$ to $v1$. Initialize S to $v0$.
2. Choose vertex v in $\{V - S\}$ such that $PathCosts[v]$ is the minimum of all $PathCosts[i]$. $\{V - S\}$ empty? Done. Otherwise, put v in S.
3. For each u in $\{V - S\}$, update the costs by setting $PathCosts[u] = MIN(Costs[u], PathCosts[v] + PathCost[v, w])$. Go to step 2.

In closely examining this algorithm and the code in Fig. 10.21, you'll note a major step involves finding the minimum cost edge in the graph,

procedure *ShortestPath* (**var** *G* : *GRAPH*; *N* : *VERTEX*; *v0* : *VERTEX*;
                          var *PathCosts* : *COSTARRAY*);
{
Finds shortest path from *v0* to each of the *N* vertices in *G*, represented as an adjacency matrix. The costs are returned in *PathCosts*, an array of integers.

N is ≤ *MAXV*.
GRAPH is an adjacency matrix of nonnegative costs.
COSTARRAY is **array** [1..*MAXV*] **of** *integer*.
}
type
  VERTEXSET   = **set of** *VERTEX*;
var
  CurrentVertex   : *VERTEX*;
  S   : *VERTEXSET*;
  V   : *VERTEXSET*;
  w   : *VERTEX*;

  function *FindMin* (*V* : *VERTEXSET*; **var** *PathCosts* : *COSTARRAY*) : *VERTEX*;
  {Finds a vertex *w* in *V* such that *PathCosts*[*w*] is a minimum.}
  var
    CurrentVertex   : *VERTEX*;
    MinCost   : *COSTS*;
  begin
    MinCost := *maxint*;
    FindMin := 0;
    for *CurrentVertex* := 1 **to** *N* **do**
      if *CurrentVertex* **in** *V* **then begin**
        if *PathCosts*[*CurrentVertex*] <= *MinCost* **then begin**
          MinCost := *PathCosts*[*CurrentVertex*];
          FindMin := *CurrentVertex*
        end
      end
  end; {FindMin}

  function *MIN* (*A*, *B* : *integer*) : *integer*;
  begin
    if *A* <= *B* **then**
      MIN := *A*
    else
      MIN := *B*
  end; {MIN}

Figure 10.21. Dijkstra's algorithm for finding the shortest path from one vertex to all others in a graph.

```
begin {ShortestPath}
  S := [v0];                                        {S is initially v0}
  V := [ ];                                          {V is initially empty set}
  PathCosts[v0] := 0;
  for CurrentVertex := 1 to N do begin
    if CurrentVertex <> v0 then
      PathCosts[CurrentVertex] := G.cost[v0, CurrentVertex];
    V := V + [CurrentVertex]                         {set union operation}
  end;
  while S <> V do begin
    w := FindMin(V − S, PathCosts);
    S := S + [w];
    for CurrentVertex := 1 to N do
      if CurrentVertex in V − S then
        PathCosts[CurrentVertex] := MIN(PathCosts[CurrentVertex],
                                   PathCosts[w] + G.cost[w, CurrentVertex])
  end
end; {ShortestPath}
```

between vertices in S and {V − S}. Such a process requires that we search the entire row of the adjacency matrix for each vertex, an amount of time proportional to V, the number of vertices in the graph. Since we must ultimately do this for *each* vertex in the graph, the total time for the routine will be proportional to V^2. If we double the number of vertices in the graph, the algorithm will run about four times as long; quadruple the number, about 16 times as long, and so on.

10.4.4 Generalizations of Traversals

Graphs are a generalization of trees, in that a tree can be defined as a restriction on directed graphs. Since traversals are so important in the tree algorithms, we'd like to generalize the idea to arbitrary graphs. When we perform a typical traversal, such as pre-order, on a given binary tree, we first visit the node, and then visit its left subtree. We repeat this process recursively, visiting and moving down the left branch. Such an operation is called a "depth-first" visit or depth-first search of the tree. Only when a given branch is empty do we back up to the previous node and attempt to visit its right subtree.

We can generalize this notion to a graph if we think of a graph in terms of a tree. This makes sense, of course, only when we can designate some

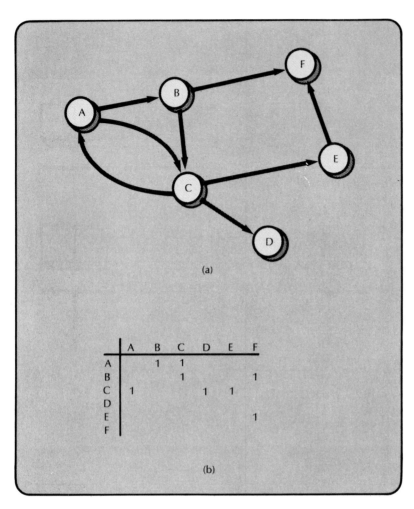

(a)

	A	B	C	D	E	F
A		1	1			
B			1			1
C	1			1	1	
D						
E						1
F						

(b)

Figure 10.22. (a) Sample graph illustrating depth-first search. (b) Adjacency matrix for graph of part (a).

vertex as being the first one visited, that is, the "root" of the graph. Then we recursively visit all the vertices that can be reached from this first vertex.

As an example, consider the graph G of Fig. 10.22(a) with vertices with character names, represented by the adjacency matrix of Fig. 10.22(b)

If we start at A in the depth-first search of G, we first visit A, and from there we go to B, since that is the first nonzero entry in A's row. Then we go to B's row. From B we go to C, from there to D (because we continue from C's row), then to E, and then to F.

That finishes the rows of C, D, E, and F, but when we go from C to F on B's row, we find that we need to visit F again. We must mark each vertex as having been visited the first time we examine it so that we avoid the problems of multiple vertices pointing to a single vertex, and we avoid infinite loops in graphs with cycles.

360

As usual, the verbal description of the process is more complex than the program to implement it. We just need an auxiliary array *Visited* that is initialized to *false*, and that we set to *true* upon visiting a vertex. The procedure *DepthFirstSearch* is shown in Fig. 10.23(a). It assumes that the

```
procedure DepthFirstSearch (var G : GRAPH; V: VERTEX);
var
   i : VERTEX;
begin
   visited[V] := true;
   writeln(V);
   for i := 'A' to G.size do
       if G.cost[V, i] and not visited[i] then
       DepthFirstSearch(G, i)
end; {DepthFirstSearch}
```
                                    (a)

```
program DFSTEST (input, output, graphdata);
{
Performs the depth-first search on a graph.
INPUT:      The vertices and edges in a graph, represented as an adjacency matrix.

OUTPUT:     The depth-first traversal of the graph.
}
type
   COSTS      = boolean;
   VERTEX     = char;
   GRAPH      =
      record
         size      : VERTEX;
         cost      : array [VERTEX, VERTEX] of COSTS
      end;
var
   answer     : char;                              {indicates existence of edge}
   FirstVertex : VERTEX;                            {vertex to start search}
   G          : GRAPH;                             {the graph}
   graphdata  : text;                              {file with vertices and edges}
   i          : VERTEX;                             {loop counter through vertices}
   NextVertex : VERTEX;                             {loop counter through vertices}
   Visited    : array [VERTEX] of boolean;          {marks vertices as visited}
```
                                                              (continued)

Figure 10.23. (a) Routine to perform depth-first search on a graph represented as an adjacency matrix. (b) Driver program illustrating the use of depth-first search on a graph represented as an adjacency matrix. (c) Input graph data, and output when starting at vertex *B*.

```
#include "DFS.i";                                    {file contains procedure DepthFirstSearch}

begin {main}
  with G do begin                                    {get the graph's vertices and edges}
    reset(graphdata);
    readln(graphdata, size);                          {maximum vertices in this graph, a char}
    for NextVertex := 'A' to size do begin
      for i := 'A' to size do begin
        read(graphdata, answer);                      {does an edge exist?}
        cost[NextVertex, i] := answer in ['Y', 'y']
      end;
      readln(graphdata)
    end
  end; {with}
  readln(graphdata, FirstVertex);
  for NextVertex := 'A' to G.size do
    Visited[NextVertex] := false;
  DepthFirstSearch(G, FirstVertex)
end.
```

(b)

Input File: **Output:**
F   B
nyynnn   C
nnynny   A
ynnyyn   D
nnnnnn   E
nnnnny   F
nnnnnn
B

(c)

vertices are given character labels, and the graph is represented as an adjacency matrix. In Fig. 10.23(b), we've written a small driver program which reads an external file *graphdata* containing information on the vertices and edges in the graph, initializes *Visited* to *false*, and then makes the initial call to *DepthFirstSearch* on the designated first vertex. You should try running this code on the sample graph of Fig. 10.22, using different starting vertices; when you do this you'll get different orderings of the vertices. In Fig. 10.23(c) we show the contents of file *graphdata* for the graph of Fig. 10.22, and the output generated by the program when we start at vertex *B*.

Programming Notes

Nonrecursive Tree Traversal

The recursive procedures for traversing a binary tree are elegant and simple. However, they may entail substantial system overhead in calling and parameter passing. Additionally, recursive procedures require that the run-time environment maintain a stack of calls and return addresses. As an alternative, we may perform the traversals nonrecursively by maintaining a stack ourselves, and save the expense of additional procedure calls. We gain a potential program speedup at the expense of greater complexity in the routines. However, these are important and interesting techniques which are valuable when we are trying to minimize running time or space, and so they should be in every programmer's recipe kit.

When we traverse a binary tree using an in-order traversal, we begin at a node, but must save it for later processing. Then we move to the left subtree of a node and do the same: save the node for further processing and move left. The structure we use for "saving for later processing" is a stack: stack a node when we come to it, then move left and repeat, as we see in Fig. 10.24. We finally stop this process when we can't move left any further. At such a time, we pop the stack, visit the node there, and then move *right* to get the next node, repeating the stacking and moving left process. The algorithm terminates when there are no more nodes on the stack.

Of course we don't need to push the entire node on the stack; rather the stack will contain *pointers* to the nodes. The algorithm is expressed in the following four-step process:

1. Let the current node be the root.
2. Is the current node **nil**? If so, go to step 4. Otherwise, go to step 3.
3. Push the current node onto the stack. Then the current node is set to its *left* subtree. Go to step 2.
4. Pop the stack. Is the stack empty? Done. Otherwise, set the current node to the popped node, and "visit" the current node. Go to step 2.

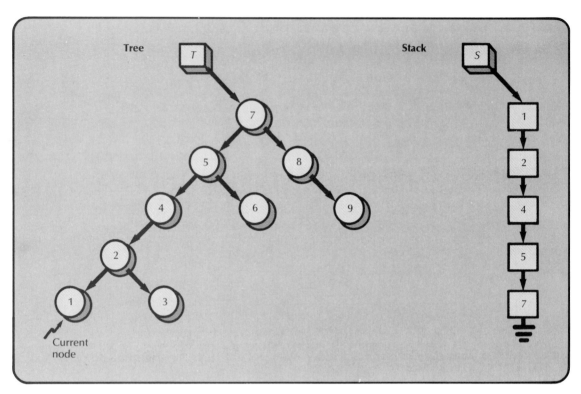

Figure 10.24. Stacking nodes in in-order traversal. What gets stacked is not the value of the node, but a pointer to it.

Figure 10.25 briefly traces the operation on a small tree, where "visit the node" means print the *data* field of the current node.

Figure 10.26 is a procedure, *Traverse*, that implements a stack-based, nonrecursive, in-order traversal of a binary tree pointed to by *root*. We've shown the procedure making calls to the usual stack routines *Push* and *Pop*, which are defined in the include file *stack.i*. These routines are the same as defined in Chapter 9. Since those routines used parameters of type *STACKPTR* and *WHATEVER*, we redefine those types within the body of *Traverse* for this particular application. In this way, we are able to use already written and debugged routines, an important consideration in the rapid building of correct programs.

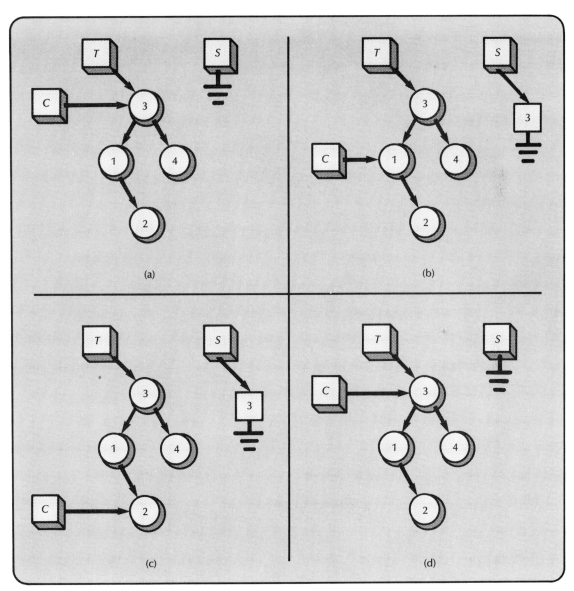

Figure 10.25. Trace of using a stack for a nonrecursive in-order traversal. (a) Initial configuration. (b) Stack C, move left. (c) **nil** left subtree: print C, move right. (d) **nil** right subtree: print C, then set C to *Pop(S)*.

```
procedure Traverse (root : TREEPTR);
{
This is the nonrecursive (stack-based) in-order traversal. All stack definitions, Push, Pop,
and so on, and data types are defined within this procedure. Thus the internals of trav are
hidden from its callers.

    DEFINED under Traverse :
      Stack abstract data type
      Push
      Pop
}
type
  WHATEVER     = TREEPTR;              {pointer to a binary tree node}
  STACKPTR     = ↑STACKNODE;          {stack of return nodes}
  STACKNODE    =
    record
      data       : WHATEVER;
      link       : STACKPTR
    end;
  STACK        = STACKPTR;
var
  S            : STACK;
  T            : TREEPTR;

#include "stack.i";                   {stack ADT routines}

  function FirstNode (T : TREEPTR) : TREEPTR;
  {
  Takes a node, T, and returns a pointer to the first node in the in-order traversal. Stacks up
  nodes visited along the way. Returns nil if T is nil.
  }
  begin
    if T = nil then
      FirstNode := nil
    else begin
      while T↑.ls <> nil do begin
        Push(S, T);
        T := T↑.ls
      end;
      FirstNode := T
    end
  end; {FirstNode}
```

Figure 10.26. Procedure for nonrecursive in-order binary tree traversal.

```
function Successor (T : TREEPTR) : TREEPTR;
{Finds the in-order successor of T, manipulating the global stack, S.}
var
   top : TREEPTR;
begin
   if T ↑ .rs <> nil then
      Successor := FirstNode(T ↑ .rs)
   else begin
      if not Pop(S, top) then
         halt                              {error condition}
      else
         Successor := top
   end
end; {Successor}

begin {Traverse}
   S := nil;                              {initialize the stack to empty}
   T := FirstNode(root);
   while T <> nil do begin
      writeln(T ↑ .data);
      T := Successor(T)
   end
end; {Traverse}
```

Exercises

1. There is the well-known story of the counterfeit coins: A dealer comes across a collection of twelve apparently quite valuable gold coins — except that one is counterfeit. The dealer knows that one is counterfeit, but doesn't know which one. She does know, however, that all the coins weigh exactly the same except the counterfeit one, which is either lighter or heavier, she doesn't know which. The dealer has at her disposal an old balance scale that she can use to compare the weights of coins. The scale can tell only that coins in the two arms weigh the same or that one pile is heavier than the other.

   What is the minimum number of coin weighings necessary to determine the counterfeit coin? Show, using diagrams, an order of weighing the coins that will always guarantee finding the counterfeit one.

2. Generalize the results of the previous exercise so that there are N coins, with one counterfeit. How many weighings are required in this case to find the counterfeit coin?

3. Is it possible to use the procedure in Exercise 2 if there are M bad coins, each of which is heavier than the legal ones (M known)? Suppose that there are M bad coins, any of which may be lighter or heavier (but all the same amount lighter or heavier) than the legal ones. Is it still possible to devise a series of weighings that will always guarantee finding the bad coins?

4. Prove that the in-order traversal of a binary search tree will visit the nodes in sorted order. (That is, given a BST built using procedure *TreeInsert* of Fig. 10.12, traversing the tree in-order will yield the values of the nodes sorted from low to high.)

5. Given a BST built using *TreeInsert* of Fig. 10.12, describe the ordering of the values produced using a *post-order* traversal; describe the ordering of the values produced using a *pre-order* traversal.

6. Write a version of *TreeInsert* that builds a BST for a binary tree with a dummy head node. The head node contains no data, and its left subtree is always **nil.** The dummy's right subtree is **nil** if the tree is empty; otherwise, it points to the root node.

7. Write a recursive procedure to perform the in-order traversal of a binary tree with a dummy head node, as described in Exercise 6.

8. *TreeInsert* of Fig. 10.12 is a nonrecursive procedure that inserts a new value into its appropriate place in a BST. Write a recursive version of *TreeInsert* that performs the same function. (*Hint:* Think recursively: we compare the value with the root; if it is less than the root, we "insert" it into the left subtree; if it is greater than or equal to the root, we "insert" it into the right subtree.)

   Test the routine with a driver that reads values, one per line, from the standard input, and inserts them as they are read into a BST. Your program should use the data types as specified in this chapter, defining the type *WHATEVER* as integer. Upon completion of input, print the values in the tree using an in-order traversal.

9. The operation *Parent* is a relatively expensive operation. Write a version of *Delete* that doesn't require the use of the *Parent* operation.

10. If we know in advance the maximum size that a binary tree can be (both in number of nodes and expected height) we can use an array to store the nodes. The root node is at array location 1, the root's left and right subtrees at 2 and 3 respectively, and in general, the left and right children of a node at location i will be found at locations $2i$ and $2i + 1$, respectively (see Fig. 10.27). The advantage of this representation is that we can find the parent of a node just as quickly (what is it?). Write a routine that uses an array

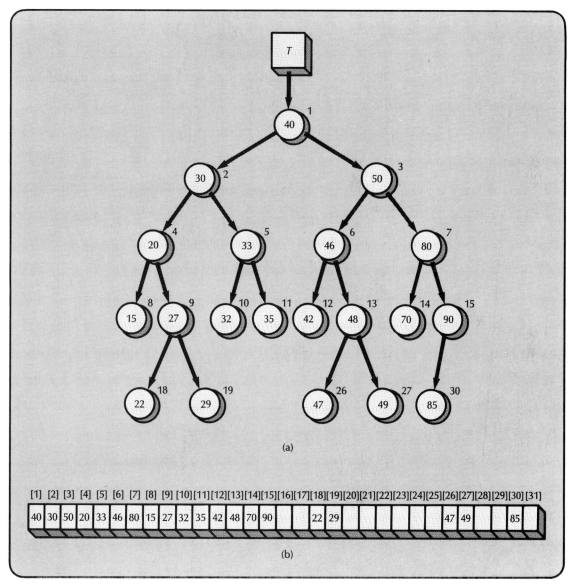

Figure 10.27. (a) A binary tree. (b) The same tree represented as an array.

representation of a binary tree as described here, and finds the in-order successor of its argument node. The procedure has three parameters — the tree (represented as an array), the index of the given node, and the index of its successor (a **var** parameter). You may assume that the array is large enough so that the index of the successor will not be out of bounds.

11. Implement nonrecursive versions of the pre-order and post-order traversals, using the stacking mechanisms suggested in the Programming Notes. Note that a fundamental operation in the in-order traversal is finding the in-order successor of a given node via calls to the function *Successor*.

12. In this chapter we have introduced some of the more common operations performed on binary trees. Write some of the other relatively common operations performed on binary trees. None of these functions requires the creation of new nodes. Write the following functions:

    a) *Count(tree)* — returns a count of the number of elements in *tree*.

    b) *Leaves(tree)* — returns a count of the number of leaves in *tree* (a leaf has **nil** left and right subtrees).

    c) *BST(tree)* — returns *true* if *tree* satisfies the properties of a binary search tree, *false* otherwise.

    d) *Height(tree)* — returns the height of *tree*. A tree with no nodes has height zero.

    e) *StripValue(tree, value)* — returns a pointer to a tree formed by removing all elements from the BST *tree* whose contents equal *value*.

    f) *Shrink(tree, sourcetree)* — returns a pointer to a tree created by deleting all elements from the BST *tree* with the value of any element in *sourcetree*.

    g) *CountValue(tree, value)* — returns the number of elements in the BST *tree* whose value is *value*.

13. Write a procedure that prints the values of the nodes of a binary tree in level order. That is, all of the nodes at level i are printed, then all the nodes at level $i + 1$, and so on. The argument to the procedure is a pointer to the root of a binary tree.

14. One of the exercises of Chapter 8 is the implementation of sets with lists. Sets can also be implemented as binary search trees. Here is one possible type declaration for sets (*node* refers to a node in the BST):

```
type
    asetptr         = ↑ aset;
    nodeptr         = ↑ node;
    aset            =
        record
            count       : integer;
            nodes       : nodeptr
        end;
```

Treating sets as an abstract data type, and remembering that sets can have no duplicate elements, write the following set operations:

a) *Create* — creates a set, initializes it to the empty set, and returns a pointer to it.

b) *AddElement(setptr, element)* — adds *element* to the set given by *setptr*.

c) *DelElement(setptr, element)* — deletes *element* from the set given by *setptr*.

d) *Member(setptr, element)* — returns *true* if *element* is in the set given by *setptr*, *false* otherwise.

e) *Cardinality(setptr)* — returns the number of elements in the set given by *setptr*.

f) *Union(setptr, othersetptr)* — creates a new set that is the union of the sets given by *setptr* and *othersetptr*, and returns a pointer to it.

g) *Intersection(setptr, othersetptr)* — creates a new set that is the intersection of the sets given by *setptr* and *othersetptr*, and returns a pointer to it.

h) *Difference(setptr, othersetptr)* — creates a new set that is the set difference of the sets given by *setptr* and *othersetptr*, and returns a pointer to it.

i) *Empty(setptr)* — returns *true* if the set given by *setptr* is the empty set, *false* otherwise.

15. [PROGRAMMING PROJECT] Write a program to print a visual representation of a binary tree. For simplicity of presentation, nodes contain integers. Experiment with different visual representations, including horizontal and vertical presentations.

16. There are two common methods for searching graphs. The first, *depth-first search*, searches down a path of the graph until the end of the path, where it backs up to its most recent choice point. Such a search technique is a generalization of a pre-order traversal in a binary tree. The second, *breadth-first* search, searches level by level. In Section 10.4 we implemented depth-first search. Write a routine to implement breadth-first search. Your program has to keep track of the nodes that have been visited along the way. (*Hint:* Consider using a queue; also, see Exercise 13.)

17. [PROGRAMMING PROJECT] Write a program that runs a maze. A maze is a rectangular array of 0's and 1's. A mouse (or token) is placed at a starting point in the maze (which must be a 1), and must find a connected path of 1's that leads to some designated ending point (see Fig. 10.28). In the simplest rules, the mouse may move only horizontally and vertically; more complex variations allow diagonal or even nonadjacent moves. Consider representing the maze as a graph, with the edges connecting 1's for which a legal move is possible. Use the direct cursor movement routines of Chapter 4 so that your mouse will run the maze visually.

```
                    0  0  0  S  0  1  0

                    0  0  0  1  0  1  0

                    0  0  1  1  1  1  1

                    0  0  0  1  0  0  0

                    0  0  0  1  1  1  0

                    0  0  0  0  0  1  1

                    0  1  1  1  0  1  0

                    E  1  0  1  1  1  0
```

Figure 10.28. Sample maze of 0's and 1's. The cell marked S is the starting point; the one marked E is the exit point.

18. Write a program that reads the costs of flights between cities, using the data of Fig. 10.18, then use these costs on Dijkstra's algorithm to find the lowest cost airfare between the following city pairs:
    a) New York to Las Vegas.
    b) Kansas City to Charlotte.
    c) Phoenix to LA.
    d) San Francisco to Washington.
19. Dijkstra's algorithm gives only the costs of the shortest path between a starting vertex and all other vertices. Extend the algorithm so that it retains the edges that make up the lowest cost path. Then for each of the city pairs in Exercise 18 determine the edges that make up the lowest cost path between the cities.
20. Develop an algorithm to discover whether a graph is acyclic.
21. Another abstract data type is known as a "Priority Queue." It is used to implement operations where each item in the queue is tagged with a priority. Items are placed into the queue as they arrive, but are removed according to their priority. When an item is removed from the queue it is not necessarily the first one entered (as with an ordinary queue), or the last one (as with a stack); rather it is the item with the highest priority. The abstract operations on a priority queue are at least:

    ■ *CreatePQ* — Create a new empty priority queue
    ■ *InsertPQ* — Insert a new item into a priority queue
    ■ *DeleteMax* — Remove the item with the highest priority

    Use linked lists to implement the priority queue operations, assuming the priorities are positive integers.
22. A priority queue can also be represented as a *heap*. A heap is a binary tree with the restriction that the value of a node is larger than or equal to the

values in its subtrees (see Fig. 10.29). Compare this with a BST, where a node partitions the tree into subtrees less than or equal to the node, and greater than the node.

a) Write the routine *InsertPQ* that inserts a new value into an existing (possibly empty) heap.

b) Write the routine *DeleteMax* that removes the item with highest priority from a heap. (*HINT*: Consider using an array representation for the heap as suggested in Exercise 10.)

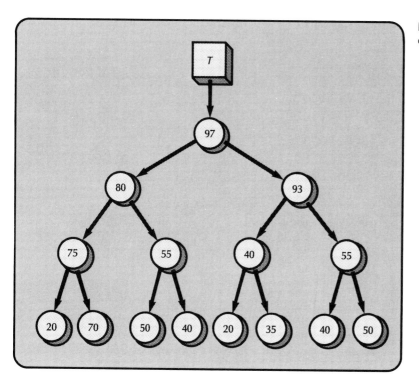

Figure 10.29. A binary tree organized as a heap.

ALGORITHMS: SORTING

Chapter 1 introduced you to the benefits of good programming style, and we have maintained a strong sense of good program design and coding style throughout the book. We have been claiming all along that the advantages of these good practices are many, including easier program construction, better and more thorough testing, easier debugging, and advantages that accrue further in time: a more comprehensible program that simplifies extensions, modifications, and portability to other machines or devices.

We have also alluded from time to time to a further advantage of good programming habits: the abstraction of operations, data structures, and algorithms in such a way that their internal behavior is totally hidden to all but those parts of the program that access them directly. In this section we have finally had to face directly the techniques of actually implementing our low-level decisions. We have looked at a collection of useful, important, powerful data structures, and along the way have discovered perhaps the most important lesson in program construction: all implementation decisions involve tradeoffs such as memory space versus execution time versus programmer time. In this chapter and the next we complete our examination of program implementation. We look in detail at important algorithms and classes of algorithms, and we more completely develop the tools and techniques to analyze the space and time complexity of various algorithms. In so doing, we complete the study of programming and problem solving in a top-down manner—we develop good design and coding techniques in the same way that we should develop individual programs.

We examine in detail two classes of algorithms: sorting and searching. Sorting and searching combine to provide both a rich, diverse collection of intellectually stimulating problems and puzzles, and an important vehicle for understanding the techniques by which efficiency can be designed, analyzed, and refined. For the mathematically and analytically inclined, they include complex, interesting combinatorial problems that should satisfy the puzzle lover in all of us. For the implementor, there has been a long, detailed study of techniques and so there is always an opportunity to find just the "right" algorithm for a particular task.

11.1   Computing Complexity

We define computing *time complexity* as the amount of time a program (or routine or algorithm) takes as a function of the number or size of its inputs. Similarly we define an algorithm's *space complexity* as the amount of memory required as a function of the inputs. These definitions are not quite as simple as they might seem. For example, we must distinguish between the *worst case* space or time required, the *average* space or time, and the *best* space or time. And we must always concern ourselves with how an algorithm performs with one given set of inputs. In Chapter 5 we saw how various arrangements of input values can change the time complexity of a sorting routine. In that chapter we examined an insertion sort routine in some detail. We saw that the computing time of the routine increased as the *square* of the number of inputs (which gets bad very fast). But if the input was already sorted, we saw that the time increases only *linearly* in the number of inputs. In this chapter we usually refer to the *average* performance of a particular algorithm; but when its performance is substantially different in the best and worst cases, we also note that fact.

Many algorithm selection decisions involve tradeoffs. One of our roles as programmers is not necessarily to select an algorithm that is best for all possible cases (since this is highly unlikely in any event). Rather, we must have broad knowledge of many classes of algorithms, and of basic algorithm analysis techniques, so that we can make a reasonable choice and avoid catastrophes. When our programs are constructed, we use available program monitoring tools or include instruction counting code to determine where our programs are *actually* spending their time. We use this experimental evidence to guide us in fine tuning a piece of code.

As we stated before, we define an algorithm's *time complexity* as the amount of time it takes to complete as a function of the number or size n of its inputs. Suppose we have a sorting algorithm with time complexity $t(n)$ given by:

$$t(n) = C f(n) + k,$$

where C and k are constants independent of n. We will examine algorithms with time complexity functions $f(n)$ such as n^2, and $n\log_2 n$; in addition, $f(n)$ could be 2^n, $n^3 + n^2 - n$, and so on. The two constants C and k depend on the particular computer, language, compiler, and overhead required for algorithm initialization. For small values of n, the computing time may be dominated by external considerations, encompassed in the constant k. Consequently we are more interested in an algorithm's *asymptotic* performance: How does its computing time change as n increases, in the limit as n gets large? We define this more formally by defining a notation, called the "Big Oh" notation, that describes the behavior of a function, such as $t(n)$, when n gets large. If $t(n)$ grows as n^2 as n gets large, we say that $t(n)$ is $O(n^2)$. Formally we define the Big Oh notation as: $t(n)$ is $O(f(n))$ if there exist two positive constants C and n_0 such that $Cf(n)$ bounds $t(n)$ from above (that is, it is greater than $t(n)$) whenever n is greater than n_0.

Many functions can bound the time complexity from above. In general we are interested in the tightest bounding function, though quite often we will be able to prove that a given function is an upper bound, but not that it is the *best* (that is, the *least*) upper bound. Big Oh tells us that the time complexity behaves in a certain way, for number of inputs n larger than some number n_0. The advantage of the Big Oh notation is that it incorporates all of the language, machine, startup transients, and other implementation details in the two constants C and n_0. Consequently it gives us a mechanism for describing how an algorithm will perform asymptotically, and it allows for a comparison between algorithms. The algorithms we examine in this chapter generally have a simple time complexity, usually one of $O(n)$, $O(n^2)$, or $O(n\log_2 n)$.

We now examine the first sorting routine from Chapter 1 to determine its time and space complexity more formally. In so doing, we make some assumptions about the machine on which the code ultimately runs. These assumptions are not necessarily descriptive of any one actual computer. Rather, they generalize the properties of most sequential computers. The exact timing characteristics of a particular computer and the efficiency with which a given compiler can translate a piece of code into machine language do not affect the overall asymptotic behavior of an algorithm (that is, the Big Oh description of its time complexity is insensitive to these differences— they are subsumed in the two constants C and n_0).

Figure 11.1 contains the sorting routine first seen in Chapter 1. It is called an exchange sort. It functions by comparing the first element of the array with each of the subsequent elements. When it finds an element that is smaller than the first, the two are exchanged. The (temporarily) smallest

Figure 11.1. Exchange sort.

```
procedure Sort (var A : ARRAYTYPE; L, U : integer);
var
    i               : integer;
    j               : integer;
    temp            : WHATEVER;
begin
    for i := L to U − 1 do                          {1}
        for j := i + 1 to U do                      {2}
            if A[i] > A[j] then begin               {3}
            {exchange them}
                temp := A[i];                       {4}
                A[i] := A[j];                       {5}
                A[j] := temp                        {6}
            end                                     {7}
end; {Sort}
```

i	Statement 2
1	n
2	$n - 1$
3	$n - 2$
$\vdots$	$\vdots$
$n - 1$	1

Table 11.1. Number of times statement 2 is executed for increasing values of *i*.

element is now in the first array position. The algorithm continues, comparing and exchanging if necessary, until the end of the array. This constitutes one pass over the array, and the smallest value now is in the first array location. We repeat the process, this time beginning at the second location. Upon completing the second pass, the second smallest value is in the second location. Finally, after $n - 1$ passes, the array is completely sorted. In Chapter 6 we investigated the code in some detail, including an investigation of a formal verification technique that led us to believe that the code was correct: it will always sort the first n values into ascending order.

In Chapter 5 we demonstrated experimentally that the algorithm increased in computing time proportional to the *square* of the number of values to be sorted. We now are going to see why this result holds by actually counting the number of times each statement is executed in the procedure, as a function of n, the number of values to be sorted.

The comparisons are performed at statement 3. If the values are out of order, statements 4 through 6 are performed (exchanging the two values). Otherwise, we drop immediately to 7, the end of both loops. Statement 1 is performed n times. When i is 1, statement 2 is performed n times. When i is 2, statement 2 is performed $n - 1$ times. Finally, when i is $n - 1$, 2 is executed n times. Statement 3, where the comparison is performed, is executed one less time than 2, for each value of i. We will discuss statements 4 through 6 in a moment. For now, let's count the number of times statement 2 is performed, as shown in Table 11.1.

The total number of times statement 2 is executed is then $\Sigma_{i=1}^{n} i$, and in closed form, this is $n(n + 1)/2$ or $(n^2 + n)/2$. Statement 3 is executed $(n^2 - n)/2$ times. We are now able to determine the total computing time of this routine. We just add up the times for each of the statements 1 through 7. But how much time does a **for** statement take to execute? How much time for an **if** statement? An assignment statement? These questions cannot be answered without a better knowledge of the compiler and the machine on which the program runs. With this precise information, we can determine the exact computing time of this routine on a given array of n elements. This is important information, obviously, but it is too narrowly focused. Instead, we would like to know the properties of this routine that are not machine- and implementation-specific. To do this, we make a simplifying assumption: all statements in the procedure, as long as they are simple (that is, not compound, **begin-end** statements), take the same amount of time to execute, and we call this one unit of time. As a result, the total execution time of a routine is the total number of statements executed, which we show for exchange sort in Table 11.2.

Table 11.2 indicates that statements 4 through 6 will be executed a variable number of times. The actual number of times depends on properties of the original ordering of the array. If the array is already sorted, the **if** test of 3 always fails, and so statements 4 through 6 are never executed. If the array is reverse ordered, 3 always succeeds, and 4 through 6 are executed the same number of times as 3: $(n^2 - n)/2$. The total number of statements executed in this routine, and thus the total time required to sort the array, is the sum of the times for the individual statements. This is $(n - 1) + (n^2 + n)/2 + (n^2 - n)/2 +$ (something in the range from 0 to $(n^2 - n)/2$). Summing up, this is $n^2 + n + X$, where X is between 0 and $(n^2 - n)/2$. This expression for the computing time involves terms of degree 2, plus terms of lesser degree. The n^2 term dominates: that is, as n gets large, the computing time goes up as n^2. That is, the computing time is $O(n^2)$.

Now it may seem that the term involving n would cause the time complexity to be larger than $O(n^2)$. To see that it is in fact $O(n^2)$, we must find two constants C and n_0, such that the actual function of the computing time, $t(n) = n^2 + n + X$, is less than Cn^2 for all n greater than n_0. Any value of C and n_0 will do, as long as the inequality is met. Let us select C to be 10, and n_0 to be 1. Then it is straightforward to show that $10n^2$ is greater than $t(n)$, for all n greater than 1. We have shown that the computing complexity of exchange sort is $O(n^2)$. This is independent of whether the

---

Table 11.2. Statement number and number of times executed for exchange sort.

Statement	Times Executed
1	$n - 1$
2	$(n^2 + n)/2$
3	$(n^2 - n)/2$
4–6	variable —
	Max: $(n^2 - n)/2$
	Min: 0

	Sorting Time (sec)			
	Machine 1		Machine 2	
N	Compiler 1	Compiler 2	Compiler 1	Compiler 2
100	6.2	1.3	3.1	0.7
200	22.8	4.6	11.9	2.5
400	90.0	19.0	44.3	10.7
800	360.0	74.0	180.8	40.0

Table 11.3. Comparison of sorting times on two machines and two different compilers.

array is already sorted, sorted in reverse order, or by some random ordering of the n values. It will always have the property that the computing time grows proportional to the *square* of the number of values. $t(n)$ is dominated by its highest order term: $t(n)$ contains a term involving n^2 plus terms of lower order, and is $O(n^2)$. In the exercises, you are asked to generalize this result: any polynomial of degree i (that is, it contains a term involving n^i plus terms of lower degree) is in fact $O(n^i)$. It is also amusing to note that the characteristics of t before n_0 are not of interest. It is only a function's behavior beyond n_0 that determines its Big Oh properties. Similarly the function need not be continuous nor even defined at all points, either before or after n_0.

We ran the procedure of Fig. 11.1 on two different computers and two different Pascal compilers on each machine. The total computing time for each is shown in Table 11.3, where we sorted 100, 200, 400, and 800 random integers (each in the range 1 to 10,000). Though the total computing time across machines and compilers differs substantially, the relationship within one evironment across number of values is as we expected: time to sort is proportional to n^2.

We also plotted the time for the four conditions and four different numbers of inputs, and these are shown in Fig. 11.2. A single graph was used to represent all four conditions. It is clear from this figure that the time complexity is indeed $O(n^2)$, regardless of the environment in which the program runs.

In the next section we investigate several other sorting techniques, and we use the instruction counting method to determine their computing time. We should realize, of course, that asymptotic performance is really the first cut at computing time. It provides a means of avoiding seriously poor methods, but is not sufficiently fine-grained to compare two different programs implementing the same algorithm. We will see, in fact, that a number of

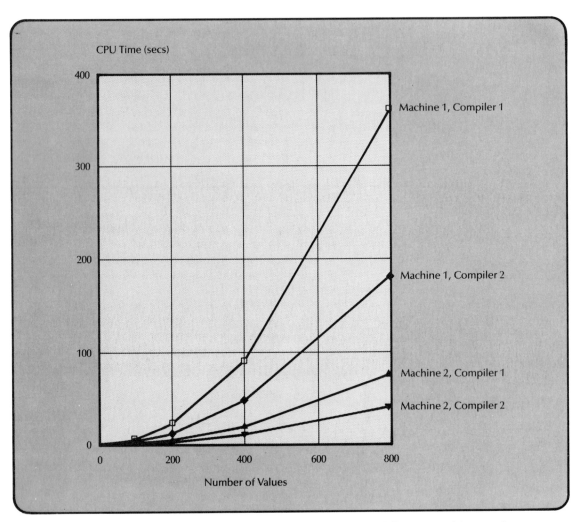

Figure 11.2. Computing time versus n, for two different machines and two different compilers.

steps can be taken with many of the sorting algorithms to make them substantially faster: they may still appear as $O(n^2)$ or $O(n\log_2 n)$, but the constant of proportionality can be reduced substantially. But let's keep the big picture in sight here: only when running time is critical will we have to take steps to reduce a given algorithm's computing time to the minimum.

We have already seen algorithms that grow as $O(n)$, $O(n\log_2 n)$, and so on. We should remind ourselves how these functions grow as a function of n. These functional relationships are shown in the graphs of Fig. 11.3.

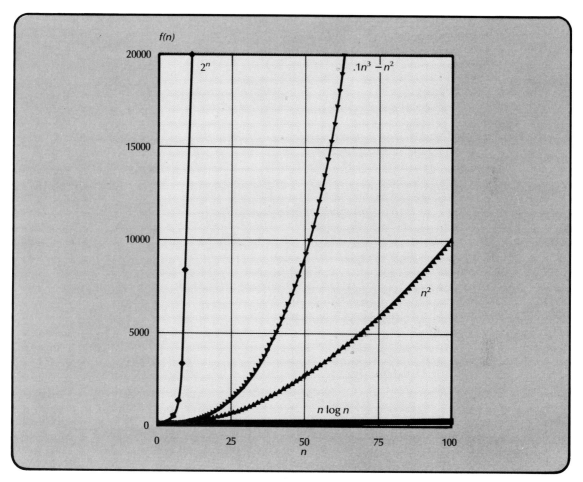

Figure 11.3. Graphs of various functions of computing complexity.

11.2   Sorting

We will look at several sorting techniques in this section. When we are finished, you will know more about sorting than you probably thought you'd care to. Sorting, as much as any other class of algorithms, allows us to indulge our fascination for puzzles and games. Most of the routines are short; many of them gain substantial time improvement through coding tricks and "diddling," as we will see; and they allow us to explore the benefits of thinking about the common threads that make good techniques good and poor ones poor. They represent a stimulating introduction to issues in the theory of computation.

We divide our study of sorting into three broad classes:

1. *Exchange techniques*, such as bubble sort and insertion sort that we've already seen in earlier chapters, that are generally $O(n^2)$ in time complexity.
2. *Tree-based techniques*, such as binary tree sorting, which are $O(n\log_2 n)$.
3. *Recursive techniques*, which are also $O(n\log_2 n)$, but with additional benefits of compact coding and (potentially) better performance than other techniques.

Within each of the subsections, we present only one or two representative techniques. We are not presenting a cook book on sorting recipes; rather, we examine broad classes for their core technique, and try to understand where their time and space complexity come from and how they function.

Each of the sorting routines is presented as a procedure with three parameters (as we saw in Fig. 11.1). The first is the array A of values to be sorted. The values can be integers, reals, characters, strings, and so on. We define a data type in the main program, called *WHATEVER*, that defines the type of the values. The array is defined as **array** [1..*MAX*] **of** *WHATEVER* and is passed as a **var** parameter. It is sorted "in place." Because of the recursive nature of some of the routines, which work on only a piece of the array, we also include two additional parameters, L and U, giving the lower and upper bounds within the array A. All the routines are given the same name, *Sort*, so that any program that needs to do sorting need only call the generic routine *Sort*. We reinforce the abstract data type/abstract operation notions of sorting in such a way that the main program need not know about the internals of the sorting routine.

Each of the routines uses the same procedure header:

procedure *Sort* (**var** A : *ARRAYTYPE*; L, U : *integer*);

To illustrate the functioning of each routine, we have written a simple driver that reads values from the standard input and assigns them to an array called *Values*. The actual number of values read from the input is counted in a variable called *number*. The array is sorted by the call to *Sort* with parameter *Values*, from 1 to *number*: *Sort*(*Values*, 1, *number*).

Figure 11.4 is the driver we used for debugging and gathering timing data. Note that the actual sorting routine is defined using an *include* statement. Many Pascal compilers provide such a mechanism to specify the name of a file (containing procedure or function definitions) that is read in at the time the program compiles.

```
program SORTTEST (input, output);
{General purpose sorting driver.}
const
  MAX           = 1000;                {maximum size of array to be sorted}
type
  WHATEVER      = integer;             {or char, real, etc.}
  ARRAYTYPE     = array [1..MAX] of WHATEVER;
var
  i                : integer;          {index for output}
  NextValue        : integer;          {from input}
  number           : integer;          {actual number of values read in}
  Values           : ARRAYTYPE;        {input array}

#include "bubblesort.i";               {or whatever routine is being used}

begin
  number := 0;
  while not eof and (number < MAX) do begin
    readln(NextValue);
    number := number + 1;
    Values[number] := NextValue
  end;
  Sort(Values, 1, number);
  for i := 1 to number do
    writeln(Values[i])
end.
```

Figure 11.4. General-purpose sorting driver.

11.2.1 Exchange Sorting
Bubble sort

The first sorting technique we examine is perhaps the best known of the exchange sorting techniques — bubble sort. It is given this catchy name because in successive iterations through the array, the smaller values bubble up to their appropriate place. This is the algorithm that we used in Chapter 1 and that we analyzed earlier in this chapter. In Chapter 5, we used a formal proof technique to verify that the code does in fact sort the array. Table 11.4 gives the CPU time in seconds to sort arrays of n randomly distributed integers. We have already noted that this is an (n^2) algorithm, and this property is demonstrated in these sorting times. These, and all other times in this chapter, were gathered with programs compiled using

Table 11.4. Bubble sort times.

Bubble Sort (CPU time in sec)	
n	Average Case
100	1.3
200	4.6
400	19.0
800	74.0

the Berkeley Pascal compiler running on a DEC VAX 11/750. The timing data includes the time to read the values from a file, but not the time to write them.

Insertion sort

Bubble sort is not suitable because its computing time is so slow. We need a technique that uses only very little additional space, but is faster than bubble sort. One effective technique is insertion sort, first examined in Chapter 1. In that version, we sorted an array by building a second array into which values from the first were inserted in their proper order. If we needed to insert into the middle, we had to shift other values to make room for the new value. In Chapter 8 we examined a version that built a secondary linked list. In this case, no shifting was needed, but we still had to search the list until we found the place to insert the new node. Again, this technique requires additional space for the sorted linked list, plus the time to copy the list back into the original array. Why not try to develop a routine that sorts the array in place, without the need of a second array or linked list? All we need to do is modify the code just a bit so that "input" comes from the array itself, and so that the shifting terminates at the current location in the array. Figure 11.5 is the complete procedure.

Table 11.5 gives the sorting times for the random files of integers as with bubble sort. We also repeat the times for bubble sort for comparison. For small arrays of characters, reals, integers, and so on, insertion sort is the $O(n^2)$ technique of choice.

11.2.2 Tree Sorting

The $O(n^2)$ sorting routines in Section 11.2.1 are computationally prohibitive as n gets much above a few hundred. If the values to be sorted are large

```
procedure Sort (var A : ARRAYTYPE; L, U : integer);
{Insertion sort.}
var
    i, j, k          : integer;               {loop indexes}
    found            : boolean;               {found place to insert A[i]}
    temp             : WHATEVER;              {for exchanging}
begin
    for i := L + 1 to U do begin
      j := L;
      found := false;
      while (j < i) and not found do
        if A[i] < A[j] then
          found := true
        else
          j := j + 1;
      if found then begin                     {shift and insert A[i]}
        temp := A[i];
        for k := i - 1 downto j do
          A[k + 1] := A[k];
        A[j] := temp
      end
    end
end; {Sort}
```

Figure 11.5. Insertion sort.

arrays or records, insertion sort and bubble sort become even more expensive because each requires a substantial amount of moving (exchanging, shifting) of values. Even though in Pascal we can assign entire arrays or records in one statement, at the machine level this is almost always accomplished one word at a time (it takes twice as long to assign a two-word array as it does

Table 11.5. Comparison of n^2 sorting techniques.

Comparison of Sorting Times (in sec)

n	Insertion Sort	Bubble Sort
100	0.7	1.3
200	3.0	4.6
400	9.3	19.0
800	35.8	74.0

a one-word value). To avoid the "curse of large numbers" and the excessive movement of values, we must find a different way to sort.

Binary tree sort

One technique for sorting that is quite fast is binary tree sorting, first seen in Chapter 10. Given an array to be sorted, we build a binary search tree, then use the in-order traversal to return the values, sorted from low to high. The computing time for such a procedure includes the time to build the tree plus the time to traverse the tree. But as we have already studied in Chapter 10, the time to build the tree (on average) is $O(n\log_2 n)$, and the time to traverse the tree is $O(n)$. We must be careful, however, in understanding that this is the *average* time. If the array is already sorted, the binary tree is in fact a one-way linked list, and binary tree sorting degenerates to insertion sorting.

In addition to this technique's time complexity, we must be concerned about the amount of memory required for binary tree sorting. We build a binary tree with a number of nodes equal to the size of the original input. Each of these nodes also requires space for the subtree pointers. In many applications, the space for each of these pointers will be one full word. Consequently, if we are sorting single-word records, binary tree sorting requires an additional amount of space equal to *triple* the input array! If the records are quite large, however, the additional space required by pointers is a smaller fraction of the total for the data. Consequently binary tree sorting is most applicable when the amount of data to be sorted is not too large, and more so when the records are relatively large.

The binary tree sorting routine is similar to the routines of Chapter 10. We show only the skeletal procedure *Sort* in Fig. 11.6. In Table 11.6 we give the computing time for arrays of size 100, 200, 400, and 800, as before. Compare these times with those for the best n^2 technique we've seen: insertion sort. The times given in Table 11.6 are really very satisfying. They progress on the order of $n\log_2 n$, as we expected, so that for $n = 800$ the sorting time is better than a factor of 10 faster than insertion sort!

Binary tree sorting has another nice property: once the tree is built, we can obtain the values sorted either from low to high or from high to low. To obtain the values from low to high, we perform an in-order traversal. If we define a "reverse-order" traversal as traverse the *right* subtree, "visit" the node, and then traverse the *left* subtree, we obtain the values in the nodes in reverse order. As noted in Chapter 10, permutations of the three statements in procedure *Traverse* would yield different orderings of the

```
procedure Sort (var A : ARRAYTYPE; L, U : integer);
{
Sorts the elements from L to U of A, using binary tree sort.

Defined under Sort:

  TreeInsert   Inserts the next value into the binary tree. (From Chapter 10.)
  Traverse     Traverses the binary tree, returning the values to A. (From Chapter 10.)
  Various binary tree data types.
}
type
  TREEPTR        = ↑ TREENODE;            {pointer to a binary tree}
  TREENODE       =                        {node in a binary tree}
    record
      data       : WHATEVER;              {integer, real, char, etc; declared in main program}
      ls, rs     : TREEPTR
    end;
var
  i              : integer;               {index into A}
  SortTree       : TREEPTR;               {the binary sorting tree}

#include "TreeInsert.i";                  {insert into binary search tree}
#include "Traverse.i";                    {in-order traversal; return values to A}

begin
  for i := L to U do
    TreeInsert(A[i], SortTree);           {build the tree}
  i := L;                                 {first element of A}
  Traverse(SortTree)                      {traverse the tree}
end; {Sort}
```

Figure 11.6. Binary tree sort.

Table 11.6. Binary tree sorting times.

	Binary Tree Sort (CPU time in sec)	
n	Average Case	Already Sorted
100	0.4	1.0
200	0.7	2.6
400	1.5	9.5
800	3.1	37.9

nodes. Here is *Traverse* with the statements permuted to yield the reverse-order traversal.

```
procedure Traverse (T : TREEPTR);
{Recursive reverse-order tree traversal.}
begin {Traverse}
  if T <> nil then begin
    Traverse(T ↑ .rs);              {first the right subtree}
    A[i] := T ↑ .val;              {A and i are global to this procedure}
    i := i + 1;
    Traverse(T ↑ .ls)             {then the left subtree}
  end
end; {Traverse}
```

11.2.3 Recursive Sorting

The fastest we can hope to sort with the usual sequential processors is $O(n\log_2 n)$. What we are seeking, then, are optimal $n\log_2 n$ techniques. Two that are particularly interesting are merge sort and quick sort. The catchy name of quick sort is appropriate; it appears to be the fastest general-purpose sorting routine known.[1] Merge sort is also quite fast and has the advantage of being compact to code. Both of the techniques are coded in a highly recursive manner, because they are much easier to understand, implement, and debug that way.

Quick sort

Think of sorting an array of values by imagining the array as being partitioned into two subarrays: one with all the values less than or equal to a certain central value, and another with all the values greater than the central value. For purposes of this discussion, the "central value" can be any arbitrary value in the array. In quick sort, we call this value the *pivot*. For simplicity, we may let the first element in the array be the pivot. The first step is to partition the original array into two subarrays as shown in Fig. 11.7.

An important property of the relationship between the two subarrays is that each element in the left subarray is guaranteed to be smaller than each element in the right subarray. This is a very exciting property, because we can repeat the same process on each of the two subarrays, partitioning each into two more subarrays in the same manner as with the entire array. (See Fig. 11.8.)

---

[1] Quick sort was first discovered/invented/developed (take your pick) by C. A. R. Hoare.

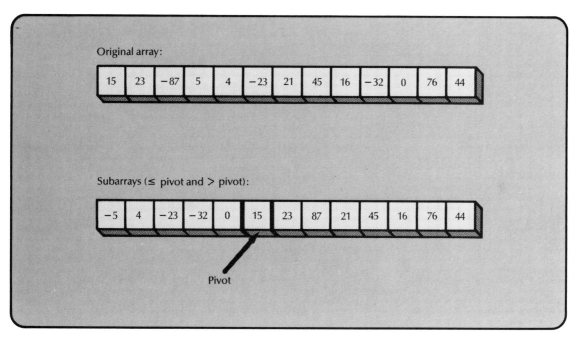

Figure 11.7. An array of integers partitioned into two subarrays. The left is less than the pivot; the right is greater than the pivot.

Continuing recursively on the subarrays eventually sorts the entire array. In pseudo-code, this can be expressed as:

```
procedure Sort (var A : ARRAYTYPE; L, U : integer);
begin
   if U > L then begin
      "Rearrange A into two subarrays such that A[i] ≤ A[Mid] for every
         i in the left subarray, and A[i] > A[Mid] for every i in the right."
      Sort(A, L, Mid − 1);
      Sort(A, Mid + 1, U)
   end
end;
```

The entire array is sorted via the call *Sort* (*Values*, 1, *number*). We need to write the procedure that implements: "*Rearrange A...*" We'll call this routine *Partition*; it has the job of altering *A* so that it is divided at location *Mid* into two subarrays. As we've just defined, all values in *A* to the left of *Mid* will be less than or equal to *A*[*Mid*], whereas all values to the right will be greater than *A*[*Mid*].

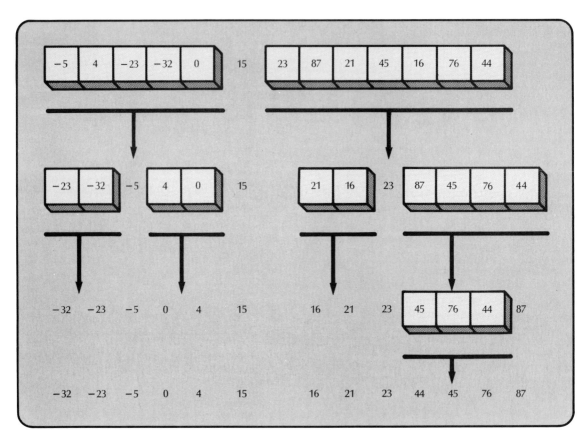

Figure 11.8. After the first partitioning (using 15 as the pivot) we partition again, using a pivot of -5 on the left and 23 on the right. The process continues recursively until the array is sorted.

The partitioning is done in two steps: first select an appropriate value to use as a pivot, then partition the array into subarrays. Any value in the array can be used as the pivot, but if the array is already sorted, the pivot will divide the array into two arrays, one of size 0, the other of size $n - 1$; not very efficient indeed. On the other hand, if we are lucky the pivot will divide the array into two equal-size pieces. In this case the pivot is the *median* of all values. However, finding the median, as we saw in Chapter 1, appears to be as computationally expensive as sorting the entire array! Instead we'll use a pseudo-median; it will just be the middle element of the array. This is not as good as picking the actual median, but unless we are very unlucky it will avoid the time-consuming process of repeatedly partitioning the array and only reducing its size by one element each time.

Partitioning is accomplished by using two pointers: L representing the smaller values in A, and U, the larger values. We begin by setting L to the lower limit of the array and U to the upper limit. Then we just compare $A[L]$ to the pivot and increment L if $A[L]$ is smaller. When finally $A[L]$ is larger than the pivot, we begin comparing $A[U]$ with the pivot. We continue comparing and *decrementing* U until we find an $A[U]$ smaller than the pivot. At this point we exchange $A[L]$ and $A[U]$ and continue the process until U passes L heading south (or more formally, until U is less than L). As usual, the process is easier to visualize than explain, and we show it in detail in Fig. 11.9. In all cases, the pivot has been selected as the middle element in the array, and has been placed into the first element of the array.

Figure 11.9. Diagrams of the partition process of quick sort.

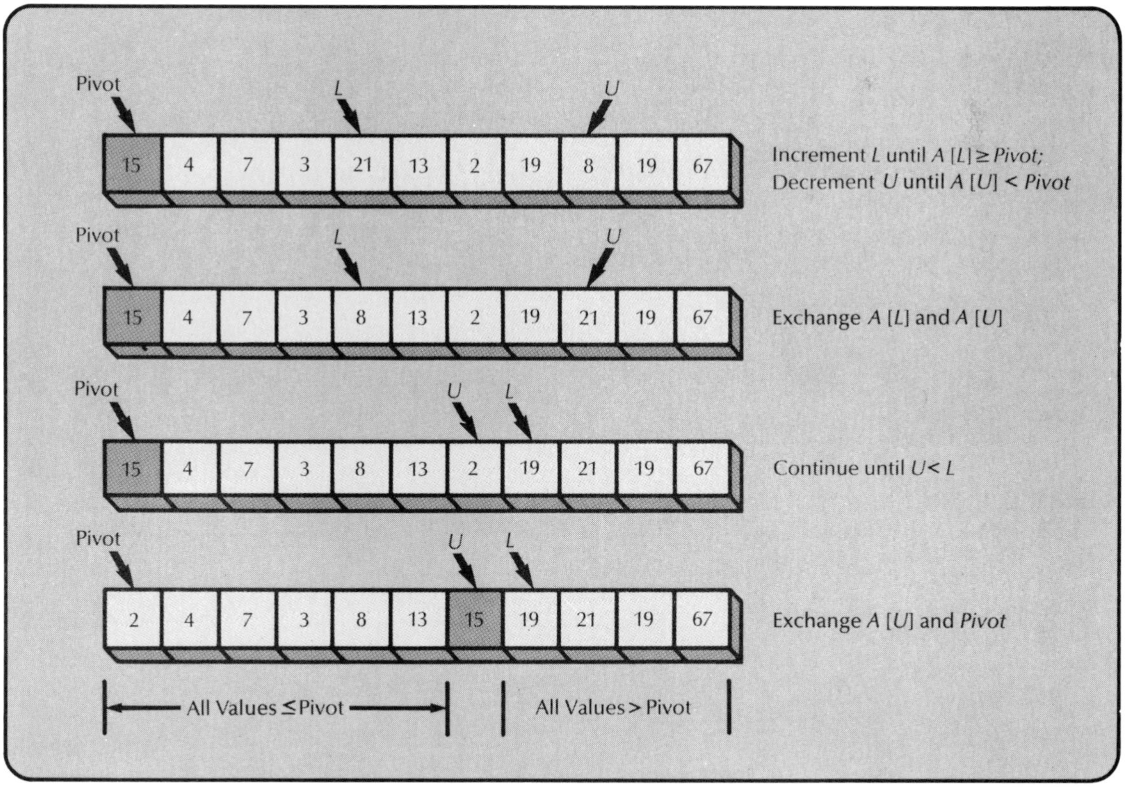

The code should be traced by hand on these example arrays to see its operation. It is a bit trickier than it seems, and most people, given a description of the algorithm, have some difficulty getting it to work correctly. As we like to do with all routines, this one should be tested for boundary conditions, off-by-one errors, empty arrays, and so on. The partitioning procedure is shown in Fig. 11.10.

---

procedure Partition (**var** A : ARRAYTYPE; L, U : integer; **var** P : integer);
{
Partition A so that $A[L..P - 1] \leq A[P]$ and $A[P + 1..U] \geq A[P]$. This is where the work is done in quick sort.

Defined under Partition:
  GetPivot : Gets the pivot value.
}
var
    LowerLimit   : integer;   {original value of L}
    Pivot   : WHATEVER;   {pivot value}
    temp   : WHATEVER;   {for exchanging two values}

    procedure GetPivot;
    {
    Gets the appropriate pivot from A. All values are global to this procedure for efficiency.
    Places the pivot in $A[L]$.
    }
    var
      Mid   : integer;   {the middle index of A}
      temp   : WHATEVER;   {used for exchanging values}
    begin
      Mid := $(U + L)$ **div** 2;
      Pivot := $A[Mid]$;
      temp := $A[L]$;
      $A[L]$:= $A[Mid]$;
      $A[Mid]$:= temp
    end; {GetPivot}

begin {Partition}
  LowerLimit := L;
  GetPivot;
  L := $L + 1$;   {start partitioning at next element}

Figure 11.10. Partitioning procedure of quick sort.

```
while L < U do begin
   while (A[L] <= Pivot) and (L <= U) do
      L := L + 1;
   while (A[U] >= Pivot) and (L <= U) do
      U := U - 1;
   if L < U then begin                        {exchange them}
      temp := A[L];
      A[L] := A[U];
      A[U] := temp
   end
end;
{Exchange pivot with proper location in A.}
if Pivot > A[L] then begin
   temp := A[L];
   A[L] := A[LowerLimit];
   A[LowerLimit] := temp;
   P := L
end else begin
   temp := A[U];
   A[U] := A[LowerLimit];
   A[LowerLimit] := temp;
   P := U
end
end; {Partition}
```

Partition requires a substantial amount of bookkeeping[2] and this can be quite time consuming when the subarrays are small. We have already seen sorting routines that are quite good when the number of values is small. Consequently, when the size of the array is less than *MIN* (we'll use five initially), we will not continue to do further partitioning. Instead we will directly sort this small subarray with one of the $O(n^2)$ techniques. In the following code, we have called this generic $O(n^2)$ routine *DumbSort*. (For the timing data that follows, we used bubble sort; insertion sort produces similar results.)

The complete quick sort routine is somewhat more sophisticated than the basic outline in the pseudo-code procedure because of the steps we have taken for efficiency and to avoid the problem of already sorted arrays: we used the middle element of the array as the pivot, and we replaced the

[2] This word, and its derivatives, are the only ones in the English language with three double letters (*oo, kk, ee*) in a row!

calls to *Partition* when the size of the array is smaller than *MIN*. Figure 11.11 is the final procedure for quick sorting. In Table 11.7 we show the timing data on our usual files of 100, 200, 400 and 800 randomly distributed integers. We also include the time to sort a list of 5000 values for comparison. In addition, to show the effect of using the middle element pivot, we also include times for sorting already sorted arrays.

The times are slightly faster when the array is already sorted because the selection of the middle element always guarantees that the subarrays are of (approximately) equal size. In addition, no exchanges are required in *Partition* because values are never out of order; in the random file of 400 integers, for example, there were 576 exchanges. Compare these times with binary tree sort: quick sort is about 16 percent faster.

```
procedure Sort (var A : ARRAYTYPE; L, U : integer);
{
Quick sort. Sorts the elements from L to U of A, in place.

Defined under Sort:
    DumbSort    Exchange sort called when size of A is less than MIN.
    Partition   Partitions the array into two subarrays.
}
const
    MIN = 5;                                      {use DumbSort when less than MIN}
var
    Mid : integer;                               {returned from Partition}

#include "DumbSort.i"
#include "Partition.i"

begin
    if U - L > 0 then                            {0 or 1 element — just exit}
        if U - L + 1 < MIN then                  {too few — use DumbSort}
            DumbSort(A, L, U)
        else begin
            Partition(A, L, U, Mid);
            Sort(A, L, Mid - 1);                 {sort the lower}
            Sort(A, Mid + 1, U)                  {sort the upper}
        end
end; {Sort}
```

Figure 11.11. Quick sort.

Table 11.7. Quick sort times.		
Quick Sort (CPU time in sec)		
n	Average Case	Already Sorted
100	0.3	0.3
200	0.6	0.6
400	1.3	1.2
800	2.6	2.3
5000	17.6	15.6

Clearly, quick sort appears to be the $n\log_2 n$ algorithm of choice when sorting collections of more than a few dozen values. It can be made to run even faster, and with less depth to the recursion, by further fine tuning of the code, as we show in the *Programming Notes* and as suggested in the exercises. Quick sort does involve a large number of exchanges, and so may not be suitable for sorting values which are part of large records. Figure 11.12 traces the routine on an array of 19 elements.

Merge sort

Suppose we have two files that are already sorted: we would like to combine them into one large sorted file. The process is straightforward, and it forms the core of an important sorting technique known as merge sort. The process of merging two already sorted arrays is shown in Fig. 11.13. We use two pointers, one for each array, plus a third array to contain the merger of the two input arrays. We merely compare the two values at the current locations within the input arrays and copy the *smaller* of the two into the next location of the output array. We must be careful that we handle the case of one or both arrays being empty, and we must be certain that we finish the copying correctly when one array is smaller than the other.

The code (Fig. 11.14) is less clean and longer than we would expect, primarily because we are careful to handle the case of the combined size of the two arrays being larger than the maximum size of an array (MAX). Counting lines of code, we see that the procedure is $O(m + n)$, where m is the number of elements in the first array and n is the number in the second. Consequently we call this an $O(n)$ algorithm.

Sorting an array using repeated mergings can be accomplished if we view the process recursively: first sort the left half of the array, next sort

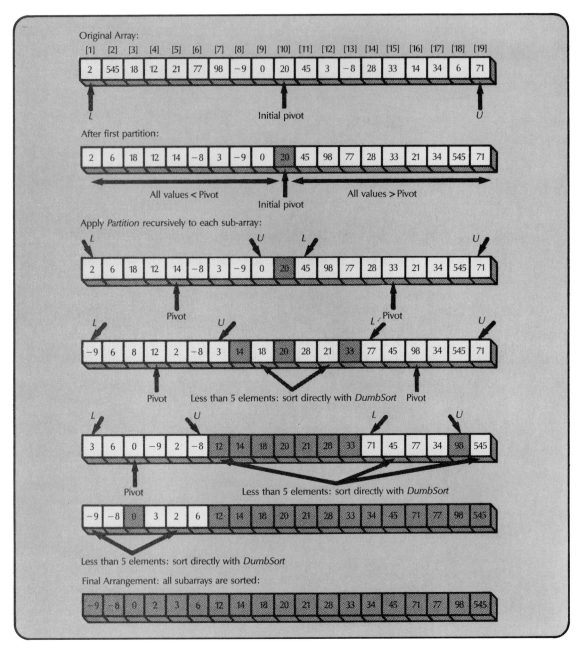

Figure 11.12. Trace of quick sort: recursively partition subarrays until a subarray has fewer than 5 elements, then apply *DumbSort*.

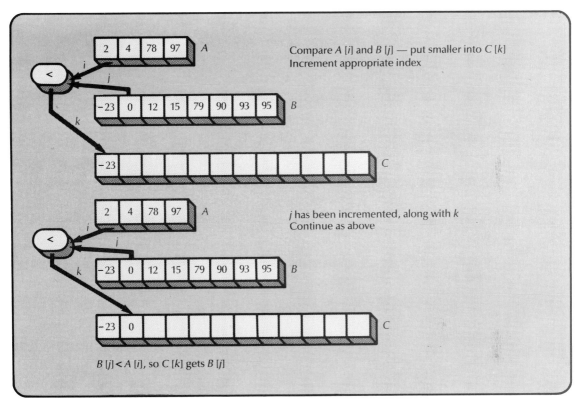

Figure 11.13. Merging two already sorted arrays into a third.

the right half of the array, and then merge the two. We repeat this process recursively on the two halves, eventually stopping the recursion when the size of a subarray is less than or equal to one (since an array with one element is already sorted). The code is surprisingly clean and compact. We present it in Fig. 11.15 along with timing data on our usual sample files (Table 11.8). We will see in a moment how to compute its time complexity. Merge sorting does require additional space, as we've already noted, so it is not appropriate when internal space is critical.

We have not shown the time to sort an already sorted array because it is the same as for a random file: merge sort does the same amount of work regardless of the original ordering of the values.

```
procedure Merge (A : ARRAYTYPE; L1, U1 : integer; B : ARRAYTYPE; L2, U2 : integer;
                 var C : ARRAYTYPE; var k : integer; MAX : integer);
{
Merges the two arrays A and B (L1 to U1 from A, L2 to U2 of B) into C.

INPUT:              Two original arrays, and their lower and upper bounds.
OUTPUT:             Merged array, and the actual number of values (k). If the combined sizes
                    of the two input arrays is greater than MAX, then only MAX elements
                    are merged into C.

}
var
  i, j : integer;
begin
  i := L1;
  j := L2;
  k := 0;
  while (i <= U1) and (j <= U2) and (k < MAX) do
    if A[i] <= B[j] then begin                    {copy from A}
      k := k + 1;
      C[k] := A[i];
      i := i + 1
    end else begin                                {copy from B}
      k := k + 1;
      C[k] := B[j];
      j := j + 1
    end;
  {Copy out the rest of A or B (not more than MAX elements)}
  if i > U1 then begin                            {copy out B}
    i := j;
    while (i <= U2) and (k < MAX) do begin
      k := k + 1;
      C[k] := B[i];
      i := i + 1
    end
  end else begin                                  {copy out A}
    j := i;
    while (j <= U1) and (k < MAX) do begin
      k := k + 1;
      C[k] := A[j];
      j := j + 1
    end
  end
end; {Merge}
```

Figure 11.14. Procedure to merge two sorted files into a third.

```
procedure Sort (var A : ARRAYTYPE; L, U : integer);
{Merge sort.}
var
  i                    : integer;              {index for copying back to A}
  mid                  : integer;              {middle of current subarray}
  result               : ARRAYTYPE;            {intermediate array for merging subarrays}
  size                 : integer;              {size of the two merged subarrays}

#include "merge.i";                            {procedure Merge}

begin
  if U - L >= 1 then begin                     {single element — just exit}
    mid := (U + L) div 2;
    Sort(A, L, mid);                           {sort recursively on two subarrays}
    Sort(A, mid + 1, U);
    merge(A, L, mid, A, mid + 1, U, result, size, MAX); {merge the two subarrays}
    for i := L to U do                         {copy back to original}
      A[i] := result[i - L + 1]
  end
end; {Sort}
```

Figure 11.15. Merge sort.

Informally we can analyze the time complexity of merge sort by tracing its behavior on an example array (Fig. 11.16). We see that merge sort is always dividing the array into subarrays, each of which is half the size of the original array. The number of times that we must divide an array of size n in half is $\log_2 n$. But for each division, we must put the whole array back together again by merging two subarrays into one larger array. Each of these operations is $O(n)$. Thus the total time is proportional to $n\log_2 n$ or $O(n\log_2 n)$. The following experimental data confirms this $O(n\log_2 n)$ time complexity.

Table 11.8. Merge sort times.

Merge Sort (CPU time in sec)	
n	Average Case
100	1.3
200	2.4
400	5.0
800	10.0

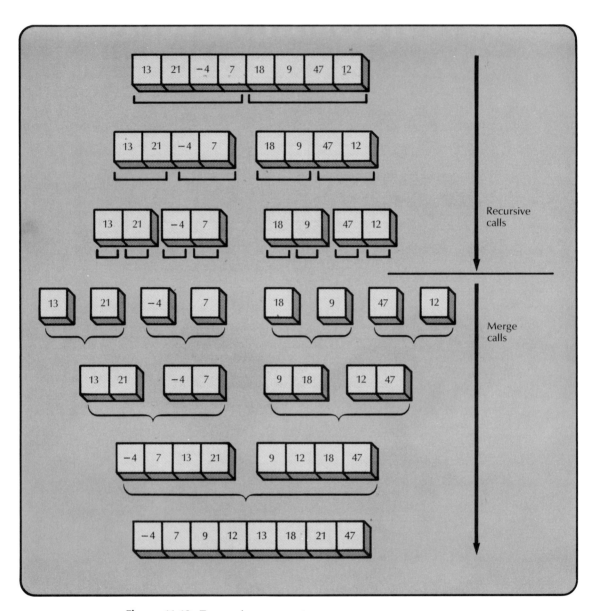

Figure 11.16. Trace of merge sort.

Though merge sort is about four times slower than quick sort for large arrays and uses an auxiliary array equal in size to the original one, it has certain properties that make it useful in some situations. That is because the "heart" of the algorithm is the merging of two sorted arrays into one larger, sorted array. Such an operation becomes essential when we are sorting a number of values that is too large to be contained in main memory at one time.

11.2.4 Comparison of Sorting Techniques

Even the n^2 techniques have their place in the selection of an appropriate sorting technique. When the number of values to be sorted is small (less than 100, say), insertion sort yields times only about twice as slow as quick sort: 1.3 seconds versus 0.7, which generally is not substantial enough to be important. Since insertion sort is compact and easy to code, and requires little movement of records, why not use it as the technique of choice when sorting small files? In addition, we've seen that even the vaunted quick sort includes an n^2 technique buried within it when the size of the current subarray is less than *MIN*.

As the number of values becomes large, however, we must abandon the n^2 routines and investigate the $n\log_2 n$ techniques. Quick sort should be the routine of choice, unless we suspect some special characteristics of the data might suggest one of the others. Quick sort's basic structure is clean and compact, and by using the routines of this chapter, will work for any sortable data types. All that needs to be done is to modify the procedures to handle the sorting of records based on a *key* field.

All the data from the timing tables is summarized in Fig. 11.17. Here we have plotted the sorting times for bubble sort, insertion sort, binary tree sort, merge sort, and quick sort. The gap between the n^2 techniques and the $n\log_2 n$ techniques is apparent. The differences between the various $n\log_2 n$ routines is rather small.

11.3 Divide and Conquer (or Where *n*log₂*n* Comes From)

We should begin to wonder if there are common threads among some of the algorithms we've examined, particularly in our ability to gain such enormous time improvements by finding $n\log_2 n$ algorithms in place of n^2 ones. One way to describe sorting algorithms such as quick sort, merge sort, or the binary tree algorithm is "divide and conquer." These algorithms have a simple, common control structure: if the size of the problem is small

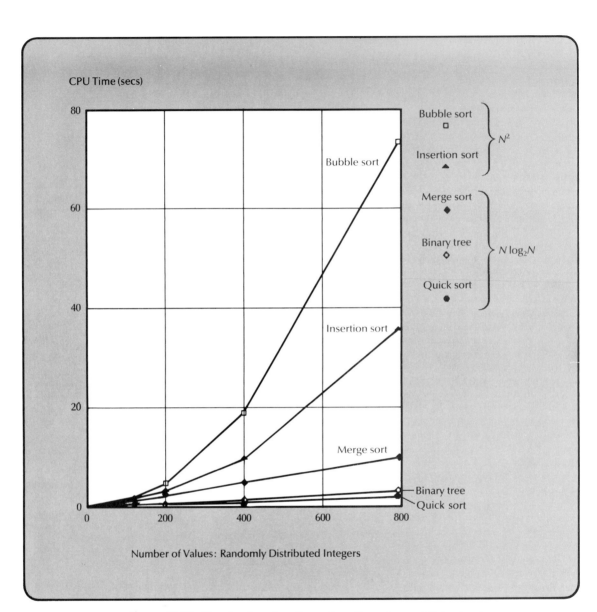

Figure 11.17. Graph of sorting times for all routines of this chapter.

enough, solve it directly; otherwise, divide the input into two (we hope, about equal) pieces, and apply the algorithm recursively to the two pieces, combining the result into the solution. We express this in the form of a pseudo-Pascal procedure, *DivideAndConquer*, which takes three parameters: an input array *A*, and its lower and upper bounds, *L* and *U*.

```
procedure DivideAndConquer (var A : ARRAYTYPE; L, U : integer);
begin
  if (U − L) < MINSIZE then
    SolveDirectly(A, L, U)
  else begin
    Partition(A, L, U, M);
    Combine(DivideAndConquer(A, L, M), DivideAndConquer(A, M, U))
  end
end; (DivideAndConquer)
```

The important property of divide and conquer is that if we divide a larger problem into smaller problems, solve the smaller problems, and then combine the solutions, we *may* gain computing time efficiency. Let's briefly reexamine a particularly poor sorting technique, bubble sort, to see if we might be able to apply the philosophy of divide and conquer to gain efficiency.

From what we now know about sorting, we'll call this generic n^2 technique *DumbSort*. We begin with a particularly simple notion of applying divide and conquer. First, divide the original array into two subarrays at the midpoint. Then call *DumbSort* on each of the subarrays in turn. Finally, combine the two sorted subarrays with a call to *Merge*. The complete procedure is shown in Fig. 11.18.

At first this might appear to be compounding our problems: we call a bad routine twice and then we need the additional work of merging the two subarrays (an additional $O(n)$ procedure). Let's apply our algorithm analysis techniques directly and see what the computing time will be.

We make two calls to *DumbSort*, each with an array of size (approximately) $n/2$. The computing time of each of these calls is:

$$\frac{n/2(n/2 + 1)}{2} = \frac{n^2/4 + n/2}{2}$$

Consequently the total time for both calls is:

$$2\frac{n^2/4 + n/2}{2} = n^2/4 + n/2$$

$$= 1/2\, n^2/2 + \frac{n}{2}$$

```
procedure Sort (var A : ARRAYTYPE; L, U : integer);
{Sorts A from L to U.}
var
   B                  : ARRAYTYPE;          {auxiliary array for merging}
   Bsize              : integer;            {number of elements in B}
   mid                : integer;            {middle index of A}

#include "DumbSort.i";                      {some O(n²) sort}
#include "merge.i";

begin
  mid := (U + L) div 2;
  DumbSort(A, L, mid);
  DumbSort(A, mid + 1, U);
  merge(A, L, mid, A, mid + 1, U, B, Bsize, MAX);
  A := B           {copy B back to A}
end; {Sort}
```

Figure 11.18. Divide and conquer sorting.

which, as n becomes large, is half the computing time for sorting the entire array using a single call to *DumbSort!* We must also add the additional time ($O(n)$) to merge the two subarrays. We thus predict that using a simple divide and conquer, involving a notoriously poor sorting technique, improves our computing time by about 50 percent.

Table 11.9 shows the CPU times in seconds for arrays of various sizes. As before, it includes the time to read the values from the input file, but not the time to write them. The column for *DumbSort* is repeated from Table 11.4. Even though the percent savings are greater than 50 percent, this reflects differences in the run-time environment at the time the programs

Table 11.9. Divide and conquer sort times.

		Divide and Conquer Sort (CPU time in sec)	
n	DumbSort	Recode using Divide and Conquer	Time Savings (percent)
100	1.3	0.8	38
200	4.6	2.3	50
400	19.0	8.7	54
800	74.0	32.8	56

were run; the actual time differences, averaged over many runs, would be closer to 50 percent.

If we divide the initial array into four equal pieces, sort each separately, and then recombine the pieces, we would expect the time to be about 25 percent of the original. If we divide into 10 equal pieces, the computing time should go down to about 10 percent of the original! We have not really applied our divide and conquer prototype because we have not called the routine recursively. All we did was divide the array into a fixed number of pieces, and then sort each piece separately. The divide and conquer prototype would have us continue the process until each array is "small." What happens if we continue all the way until each subarray is just a single element? In that case, the calls to *DumbSort* are not needed at all, and we have merge sort! This is an interesting and important result: divide and conquer applied to an initially poor technique has yielded an optimal technique.

We finish this divide and conquer discussion by suggesting a solution to the problem first posed in Chapter 1: finding the median of a list of values without sorting. We use divide and conquer as we just have, except that we use the fact that we may ignore the subarray that does not contain the median. We use the same technique as in quick sort. First, we partition the array into two subarrays, one with all elements less than the pivot, the other with all elements greater than the pivot. If we are lucky, the size of the two subarrays is the same, in which case the pivot is the median. In general, however, one subarray is larger than the other, and so the median is in one or the other. Now the median is the "middle" value — the one that, when the array is sorted, divides the array into two equal pieces. If the array originally contains n values, the median is located at $n/2$.

When the array is partitioned, the median will always be in one or the other. We continue the partitioning on the subarray that will contain the median. Eventually, through repeated partitioning, the subarray containing the median will consist of just a single element. This is when we stop the recursion. Figure 11.19 demonstrates the process on an array of 24 elements.

The code is quite similar to quick sort, except that there is only one recursive call in the procedure. We have also chosen to implement the call in such a way that an outer procedure *Median* initializes the variable *Middle*, which gives the index where the median will be in the sorted array, and then makes the initial call to *FindMedian*. Upon returning from *Median*, the array will *not* be sorted. However, we can say for certain that the median of the values in the array will be found at location *Middle*. In the exercises, you are asked to verify additional facts about the array after returning from *Median*, and about the space and time complexity of the routine.

We hope that this routine will be particularly pleasing, because it represents the end of a journey that began in Chapter 1 (when the problem

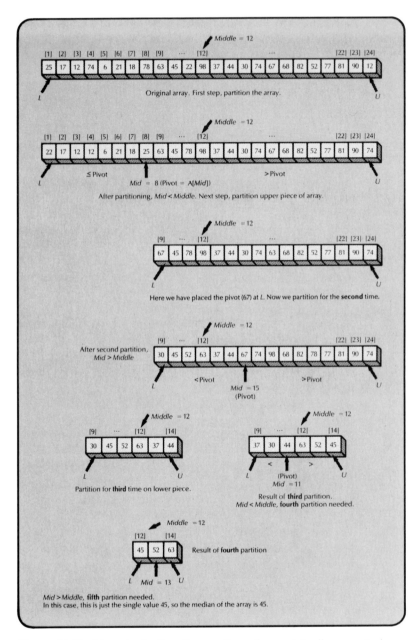

Figure 11.19. Steps in finding the median of an originally unsorted array.

was first posed), passed through the second part of the book (program design and development), and ended at this part (data structures and algorithms). We hope that your appreciation for this procedure is far greater than its small size, that it represents an appreciation and understanding of efficiency in terms of the space and time complexity of an algorithm, and that it will stimulate your interest and fascination in both the practical and theoretical aspects of algorithm development. Fig. 11.20 is the code.

```
procedure Median (var A : ARRAYTYPE; L, U : integer);
{
Finds the median of A. Uses partitioning technique of quick sort.
Upon returning, the median will be at the middle location of A ((U + L) div 2).

Defined under FindMedian :
  Partition   Partitions the array into two subarrays.
}
var
  Middle      : integer;

  procedure FindMedian (var A : ARRAYTYPE; L, U : integer);

  var
    Mid       : integer;

#include "partition.i";                        {same procedure as in quick sort}

  begin
    if U − L > 0 then begin                     {0 or 1 element — just exit}
      Partition(A, L, U, Mid);
      if Mid <> Middle then
        if Middle > Mid then                    {median is in upper piece}
          FindMedian(A, Mid + 1, U)
        else
          FindMedian(A, L, Mid − 1)             {median is in lower piece}
    end
  end; {FindMedian}

begin {Median}
  Middle := (U + L) div 2;
  FindMedian(A, L, U)                           {the median will be at location Middle}
end; {Median}
```

Figure 11.20. Procedure to find the median of an array of values.

Programming Notes

Efficiency

It may seem as if we're stretching the point quite a bit to still be concerned about sorting efficiency. After all, as we saw in Fig. 11.17 (graph of comparison of sorting times), quick sort and other $O(n\log_2 n)$ routines have given us substantial performance improvements over the first sorting routines of

```
procedure Sort (var A : ARRAYTYPE; L, U : integer);
{
Quick sort. Sorts the elements from L to U of A, in place.
Recursive call eliminated via 'tail recursion elimination.'

Defined under Sort :
    DumbSort  Exchange sort called when size of A is less than MIN.
    Partition Partitions the array into two subarrays.
}
label
    100;
const
    MIN = 5;
var
    Mid : integer;

#include "DumbSort.i";              {exchange sort called when less than MIN values}
#include "partition.i";             {partitioning step in quick sort}

  begin
  100 :
    if U − L > 0 then                { 0 or 1 elements — just exit}
      if U − L + 1 < MIN then        {too few — use DumbSort}
        DumbSort(A, L, U)
      else begin
        Partition(A, L, U, Mid);
        Sort(A, L, Mid − 1);         {sort the lower}
        L := Mid + 1;                {reset the lower bound}
        goto 100                     {second recursive call replaced by goto}
      end
  end; {Sort}
```

Figure 11.21. Quick sort recoded to eliminate tail recursion.

Chapter 1. But seeking efficiency is a natural goal of all programmers, and sometimes even a few percentage points of saving can have substantial cumulative effect. We must be certain, however, that our efforts are justified and guided by techniques that are likely to lead to time savings.

Quick sort was written initially to be about as fast as we could make it: we used the middle value of the array as the pivot to avoid the catastrophe of n^2 time if the list is already sorted, and we used a simple exchange sorting technique when the size of the list was small to avoid excessive recursive procedure call overhead. We can do even better, however, in procedure call overhead by eliminating the last recursive call to *Sort* altogether. This call is equivalent to a **goto** to the first statement in the procedure, with the value of the lower bound, *L*, changed to *Mid* + 1. This process is called "tail recursion elimination," and should yield some time savings, since the overhead of procedure call linking, parameter passing and returning, is eliminated for the second call. We show the entire procedure, along with its calls to *Partition* and *DumbSort* in Fig. 11.21. We ran this recoded version on our file of 800 randomly distributed integers: we required about 2.37 seconds to sort the array, versus 2.6 (see Table 11.7) for the original version — a savings of about 9 percent. Tail recursion elimination will almost always yield a speedup, but this is at the price of reduced clarity in the code: for example, the natural "divide and conquer" description of the routine is more difficult to see. We urge that routines be developed and written in the high-level manner consistent with the abstract data types of this part. Only after the code is running correctly, and only when and where speed has been demonstrated to be important, should we spend the additional effort to gain time improvements.

Exercises

1. Order the following time-complexity functions from most preferable to least preferable, for $n = 10$. (*Hint:* Plug in values for *n*.)
   a) $10n$
   b) n^2
   c) 2^n
   d) $n^2 + n$
   e) n^3
   f) $n \log_2 n + n$
   g) $2^n + n \log_2 n$
   h) $n \log_2 n + 10 \log_2 n$

2. Repeat Exercise 1 with $n = 25$. With $n = 50$. Some of these functions will be very large, even with such small n's. Consider these as a single group for ordering.

3. What is the order, in Big Oh notation, of the functions in Exercise 1?

4. What is the minimum number of comparisons needed to sort two elements? three? five? seven? What appears to be the order of the number of comparisons needed to sort n elements? Can you prove it?

5. Implement insertion sort for sorting strings of characters, rather than integers, as in this chapter. If your compiler does not support strings, define a string to be an array of characters.

6. Which sorting method discussed in this chapter would be best for a nearly sorted list? A nearly sorted list can be defined as a list in which no element is more than k units out of place. (*Hint*: Try each sort on a 10 element nearly sorted list with $k = 5$, and count comparisons.) Which sorting method would be worst?

7. How do each of the sorts discussed in this chapter behave on already sorted lists? Can this be improved? If so, does the improvement change the order of the sort?

8. Modify insertion sort to sort using a linked list rather than an array, so no physical shifting of array elements needs to be done. How much of an improvement does this make in running time? Suppose that the records to be sorted consist of five fields, containing numerical and character string data. Does this affect the running time of insertion sort?

9. Min-Max sorting sorts by finding the maximum and minimum elements in the list of elements to sort and removing them, and repeating the process until the list is sorted. What is the time complexity of this sort?

10. Implement a nonrecursive version of merge sort. Does this improve the running time? If so, by how much?

11. Repeat Exercise 10 with quick sort. That is, remove the recursive call in the version of quick sort in the *Programming Notes*. (*Hint*: You will need to use a stack.)

12. All of the sorting routines in this chapter are order of n times something: $n\log_2 n$ or n^2. If the n values to be sorted are elements from a (small) finite set (such as integers between 0 and 100,000), there is a technique that will sort them in $O(n)$, known as radix sort. Radix sort works by sorting the values a "column" at a time: first sort on the least significant digit, then the next most significant, and so on until the most significant digit (all values are considered to be "padded" to the left with 0's).

The sorting is accomplished a digit at a time by placing each value into a queue for its particular digit: any value with a 0 in the current column is placed into the 0 queue; a value with 1 is placed in to the 1 queue, and so on. When all the values have been enqueued, the values are sorted again, on the next most significant column, by first dequeuing the 0's, then the

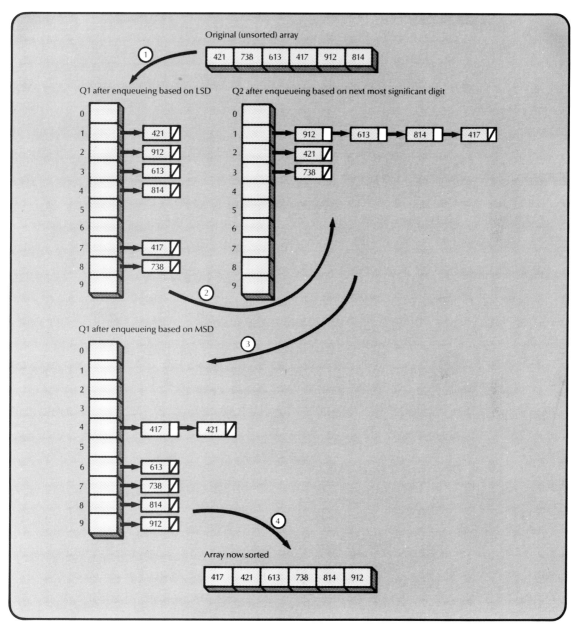

Figure 11.22. Trace of radix sort on three-digit numbers. We always sort on the least significant digit first.

1's, and so on through the 9's. The routine requires two queues, plus the original array, so you must be careful about using calls to *dispose* as well as *new*. In Fig. 11.22, we show a trace of radix sort on six three-digit numbers. On the first pass, we sort based on the least significant digit (LSD).

On the second, we dequeue from Q1 and enqueue into Q2, based on the middle digit. Finally, on the last pass we sort back to Q1 based on the most significant digit (MSD). We then dequeue from Q1 back to the original array. Write a radix sort routine that will sort seven-digit integers. Compare its time with the time to sort using the other routines in this chapter. Actually the computing complexity is $O(Dn)$, which is $O(n)$ if $n >> D$, where D is the number of digits used for sorting.

13. Perhaps the fastest of the exchange sorts is due to Shell, called Shell sort, and uses the idea of first exchanging far separated pairs of values, then decreasing the increment of separation, exchanging again, until the increment is one on the last pass. Implement Shell sort using distance d of 1, 4, 13, 40, 121, ..., n (n is the number of values in the array). d takes on values of 1, then is incremented to $3d + 1$, and so on. Start with the largest value of d that is less than or equal to n first, then calculate the next value of d as

$$d := d \ \mathbf{div} \ 3;$$

Empirically determine the time complexity of Shell sort. You may find that your results do not fit a neat formula such as n^2 or $n\log_2 n$. Shell sort has not been analyzed thoroughly, but appears to have time complexity of about $n^{1.25}$.

14. Use divide and conquer to write an algorithm to find the kth largest element in a set of elements. Empirically determine the running time of your algorithm. Note that if k is $n/2$, where n is the number of elements in the set, we find the median.

15. Use divide and conquer to write an algorithm to multiply two n-bit numbers. Assume n is a power of two. Empirically determine the running time of your algorithm.

16. Which of the sorts presented in this chapter could most easily be adapted to sorting elements from a file on disk, where it is impossible to have all elements in memory at the same time? Either make changes to one of our sorts, or write your own sort, to sort a disk file.

ALGORITHMS: SEARCHING

Hand in hand with the design of sorting algorithms is the design and use of *searching* algorithms. We may define the abstract data type *search table* as a collection of records. The records themselves contain at least one field, the *search key*, but usually contain additional fields associated with the key: the *data* fields. Typical examples include phone books (the search key is the person's name and the data are the address and phone number) or symbol tables for compilers (the key is an identifier and the data are the value or location). Search tables are such widely used objects that their properties have been studied both experimentally and analytically for some time. There are many techniques for implementing them. As with all the abstract data types we have defined, the differences are related to time complexity and space used.

12.1 Search Table ADT

We can define in abstract terms the types of operations that we typically perform when we search a table for information, and when we build the search table in the first place. We need at least the following basic operations; more can be added as the need arises.

InitTable	Initialize the search table to the empty table.
InsertTable	Insert a new value into the search table. Report if the value already exists or if the table is full.
TableSearch	Search the table for the existence of a value. Report if the value is in the table and what its location is.
DeleteTable	Remove a value from the search table. It is not required to report if the table is empty or if the value was not in the table.
SortTable	Sort the table.
PrintTable	Print the entire contents of the table.

Of course, we haven't defined what a search table is! In a real sense, we don't have to! These operations *define* a search table. As programmers we must make data structure decisions about the most efficient way to implement these operations, and we briefly examine five different techniques here; two of them (open and closed hashing) will be new; the others have been covered in earlier discussions of data structures and will only be briefly reviewed. We describe the search table operations and provide procedures for implementing them. We also briefly analyze their time and space complexity. Many of the specifics of timing depend on the details of the operations we perform on the table. For example, inserting and searching operations may be substantially different if duplicate keys are allowed, and the low-level implementation of the data structures will be different if we allow deletions as well as insertions from the table.

12.2 Sequential Search

Perhaps the simplest and most direct way to implement a search table is as a *list*, that is, a sequential arrangement of records, using either an array or a linked list. As shown in Fig. 12.1, we use records with two fields: *key*, a name, and *data*, a phone number.

To simplify the presentations of the alternative search table representations, we assume that we are building the tables out of records with just a single field, the key. Obviously, in real applications, more fields are used, and the definitions and procedures are modified accordingly. The data

Figure 12.1. Sequential list of records. (a) Linked list. (b) Array.

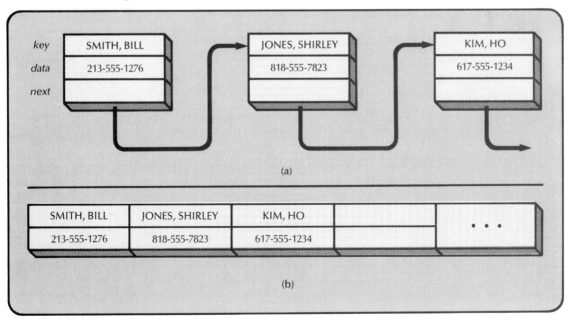

```
const
    MAXTABLE        = 1000;              {or whatever is needed}
    MAXSTRING       = 30;.              {no. of chars in a string}
type
    STRING          = array [1..MAXSTRING] of char;
    WHATEVER        = STRING;
    TABLEARRAY      = array [1..MAXTABLE] of WHATEVER;
    SEARCHTABLE     =
      record
        Number      : integer;          {no. of occupied locations}
        data        : TABLEARRAY
      end;
```

Figure 12.2. Data definitions for a search table implemented as a linear array.

definitions for a search table implemented as a linear array of string keys are shown in Fig. 12.2.

Initializing the table to the empty search table is accomplished by setting the number of occupied records (the *Number* field) to zero.

```
procedure InitTable (var Table : SEARCHTABLE);
{Initialize Table to the empty table.}
begin
    Table.Number := 0
end; {InitTable}
```

Given a key that we wish to insert into the table, and assuming we do not allow duplicate keys, we must first search the table for the existence of the key. If the key is found, we return a boolean indicating a duplicate key. If the key is not found, we insert the key into the table (if there is room), updating the *Number* field, the actual number of values in the table. The procedure *InsertTable* is shown in Fig. 12.3; it uses the global *MAXTABLE* to test for overflow.

Since we search the list to determine if the key is a duplicate, the time to insert into an unordered list, whether it is represented as an array or a linked list, is $O(n)$, where n is the number of entries in the table. If we do not check for duplicates, then inserting into an unordered list takes constant time regardless of the size of the list. Such constant time complexity is said to be $O(1)$.

```
procedure InsertTable (var Table : SEARCHTABLE; key : WHATEVER;
                   var duplicate, overflow : boolean);
{
DESCRIPTION:      Put key into Table. overflow is set to true if the table is already full, false
                  otherwise.
INPUT:            The search table and the key
OUTPUT:           The key is entered into the table, if there is room.
                  duplicate — set to true if the value is already in the table, false otherwise.
                  overflow — true if the table is full, false otherwise.
}
var
  location : integer;
begin
  overflow := false;
  duplicate := false;
  with Table do
    if Number = MAXTABLE then
      overflow := true
    else begin
      location := 1;                      {search for duplicate}
      while (location <= Number ) and not duplicate do
        if data [location] = key then
            duplicate := true
        else
          location := location + 1;
      if not duplicate then begin
        Number := Number + 1;             {first increment...}
        data [Number] := key              {...then insert}
      end
    end
end; {InsertTable}
```

Figure 12.3. Insertion into a linear, sequential table.

12.3   Binary Search

If the list is kept sorted, we can do surprisingly better than $O(n)$ in searching a list using a technique known as *binary search*. Binary search is used on *sorted* arrays and works by constantly splitting the search space in half. We begin by comparing the key, not with the first element in the table, but with the one at the middle. If the key is less than the middle, we know that it must be in the left half of the array; if it is greater than the middle

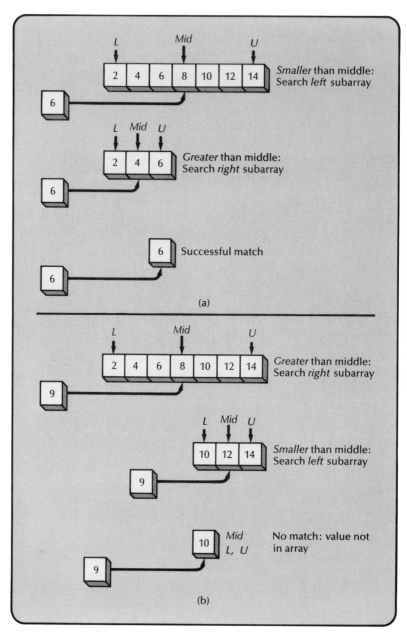

Figure 12.4. (a) Example of successful binary search. (b) Example of unsuccessful binary search.

value, it must be in the right half; and if it equals the middle value, we have found the key in the table. The operation of binary search on an array of integers is illustrated in Fig. 12.4 for both successful and unsuccessful searches.

Obviously we need to know if the search is successful or not, and we would also like to return the location of the key in the array if it is found. We'll write binary search as a recursive function that returns *true* if the key is found in the table; *false*, otherwise. This is certainly not the most efficient way to write a binary search routine, however, and you are asked to recode it nonrecursively in the exercises. (*Hint*: it's a little messier than it might first seem.)

Since binary search operates by repeatedly cutting the search space in half with each recursive call, its time complexity, for both successful and unsuccessful searches, is $O(\log_2 n)$, an important improvement over searches in an unordered list. The complete function is shown in Fig. 12.5.

Figure 12.5. Binary search procedure.

```
function Search (var A: SEARCHTABLE; L, U : integer;
                 key : WHATEVER ; var mid : integer) : boolean;
{
DESCRIPTION:    Binary search on the sorted array A.
INPUT:          L and U are the initial lower and upper bounds of A.
OUTPUT:         mid is the location where key is found.
RETURNS:        true if key is found in A; false otherwise.
}
begin
  if U < L then
    Search := false
  else begin
    mid := (U + L) div 2;
    if A [mid] = key then
      Search := true
    else if key < A [mid] then
      Search := Search (A, L, mid − 1, key, mid)
    else
      Search := Search (A, mid + 1, U, key, mid)
  end
end; {Search}
```

We call binary search on an entire table by:

if Search (Table, 1, Number, key, where) **then**...

If *key* is found in the table, the function returns *true*, and *where* is set to the index of *key* in *Table*. If *key* is not found, the function returns *false*, and *where* is meaningless. In examining the code in Fig. 12.5, note that there is no check for duplicates; the function returns *true* when it finds any occurrence of *key*.

Both the unordered and the ordered list representation of a search table can be useful for many applications. If the size of the table is relatively small (say less than a few hundred records) and the frequency of access is low, unordered tables are reasonable. They can be built quickly, and their searching time is not unreasonable. If we know in advance all the values that will be in the table, and we also know their frequency of occurrence (as would be the case with a table of reserved words in Pascal), we can place the most frequent keys at the beginning of the table, and this will have the effect of substantially speeding up the time for successful searches (of course, it does nothing for unsuccessful searches). In addition, if insertions are rare but searches are frequent, it is worth the effort to keep the table as a sorted array and use binary search for relatively fast access. As new entries are made to the table, a simple insertion sort is appropriate.

12.4   Binary Search Trees

In Chapter 10 we introduced binary trees as a useful representation scheme for a number of different problems. In Chapter 11 we were reminded that binary trees can yield an efficient sorting technique. Not surprisingly, they are also useful for search tables. The binary tree is built in the same way that binary tree sort builds its internal sorting tree. We compare the value to be inserted with the root of the tree. If the key is less than the root, we move to the *left* subtree; if the key is greater than the root, we move to the *right*; and if the key equals the root, we have a duplicate key. The operations required in searching the tree for a given key are identical. Since (well-shaped) binary trees have a height on the order of $\log_2 n$, where n is the number of records in the tree, both the time to insert a new key and the time to search for a given key (either successfully or unsuccessfully) are $O(\log_2 n)$.

Binary search trees have a major advantage over unordered lists: we get sorting virtually for free. All we need to do is perform the in-order traversal of the tree. Consequently, because of their efficiency in inserting, searching, and sorting, binary search trees are the method of choice for many applications. In addition, deletion from a binary search tree, though a bit messy, can be performed in $O(\log_2 n)$ time (including the time to search for the key), as we saw in Chapter 10. We must be concerned, of course, with the possibility of a degenerate binary tree if the keys are already in order before the tree is built. In that case we have a linear list, with its associated time complexity.

12.5 Hash Tables

If all keys were guaranteed to be small integers, say, in the range of 1 to m, then searching would be a trivial task: we just define an array of records and the key is the index into the array. As an example, if we keep a search table for student information for one class, then the keys might be a student ID number in the range from 1 to 30. When we enter information for a student or search the table for information about a student, the student's ID allows us to retrieve records in a fixed amount of time [$O(1)$]. (See Fig. 12.6.)

Obviously we would choose such a search table technique if we could guarantee that there are few keys and that they fall into a narrow range. If we extend the notion to an entire school's student body, such an implementation becomes impractical. Typical student ID's may be 10 or more digits. Just to store the keys, let alone the additional information for each student record, would require 10^{10} elements in the storage table, an amount clearly beyond the internal storage capacity of most current systems. Nonetheless such an idea is quite appealing because of its fast insertion and search properties. If we are to use such a technique, we obviously require search tables much smaller than the entire range of possible keys. To make use of the key itself as an index into the search table, we need some way to map the (large) key into a (smaller) index. In Fig. 12.7, we present in diagram form what the operation should be like.

Such a process is known as *hashing*, a term that probably derives from the way large keys are cut up (hashed) into smaller values to index the table. For this technique to work effectively, we must address two requirements of a hashing process: the selection of a good *hash function* and the *collision resolution strategy*.

12.5.1 Hash Functions

A good hash function takes a key and maps it into a valid table index. The hash table itself may be represented as an array of size m, indexed from 0 to $m-1$. Appropriate hash functions have been studied for quite awhile,

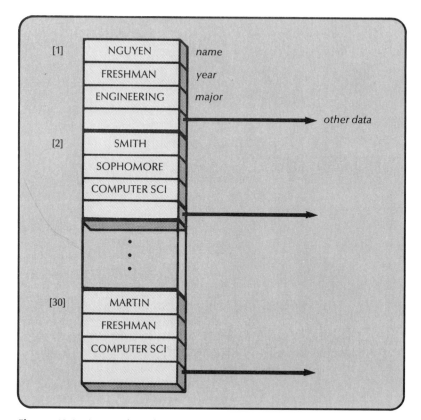

Figure 12.6. Array of student records indexed by ID number (1–30).

and their properties are well understood. The most important property of a good function (other than that it must yield a value in the range of 0 to $m-1$) is that it do a reasonably good job of "randomizing" the keys, for reasons that we will see shortly. That is, a desirable property of the hash function $H(k)$ is that it take two keys that are close and map them into two well-separated values.

We can get quite elaborate in the selection of a hash function, but some simple ones turn out to be surprisingly good. Since we would also like our hash function to be fast, simple ones have an added advantage. One form of a hash function that has been shown to be quite good is the simple **mod** function:

$$H(k) = k \bmod M$$

where m is the size of the table, indexed from 0 to $m-1$. Such a function

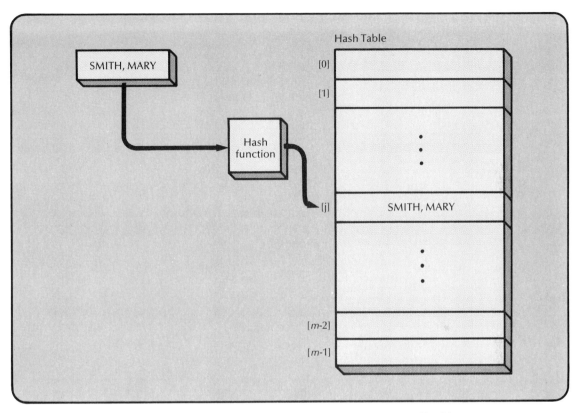

Figure 12.7. Diagram of hashing a large key into a small table.

has been shown to be particularly effective when *m* is a prime number. In the example in Fig. 12.7, we used a character string as the key. In such a case, an intermediate key $k1$ can be generated. This key is the sum of the *ord* function applied to each character in the string:

for $i := 1$ *to* MAXSTRING **do**
$k1 := k1 + ord(word\ [i])$;

This intermediate key is then used as the key for the hash function. As an example, suppose the keys are 10-character upper-case strings, and the *ord* function returns the character's position in the alphabet ($A = 1$, $B = 2$, and so on). Figure 12.8 shows the use of this simple hash function for some sample strings.

If we are using a search table of size $m = 13$ (a prime number), the sample strings in Fig. 12.8 hash into table addresses as shown in Fig. 12.9.

ADA LOVELACE=

A + D + A + bl + L + O + V + E + L + A + C + E =

1 + 4 + 1 + 0 + 12 + 15 + 22 + 5 + 12 + 1 + 3 + 5 = 8 0

BLAISE PASCAL=

B + L + A + I + S + E + bl + P + A + S + C + A + L =

2 + 12 + 1 + 9 + 19 + 5 + 0 + 16 + 1 + 19 + 3 + 1 + 12 = 1 0 0

FREDDY FORTRAN=

F + R + E + D + D + Y + bl + F + O + R + T + R + A + N =

6 + 18 + 5 + 4 + 4 + 25 + 0 + 6 + 15 + 18 + 20 + 18 + 1 + 1 4 = 1 5 4

JOE PROGRAMMER=

J + O + E + bl + P + R + O + G + R + A + M + M + E + R =

1 0 + 1 5 + 5 + 0 + 16 + 18 + 15 + 7 + 18 + 1 + 13 + 13 + 5 + 18 = 1 5 4

Figure 12.8. Calculation of intermediate hash keys for four sample strings.

Figure 12.9. Hash function applied to three sample strings.

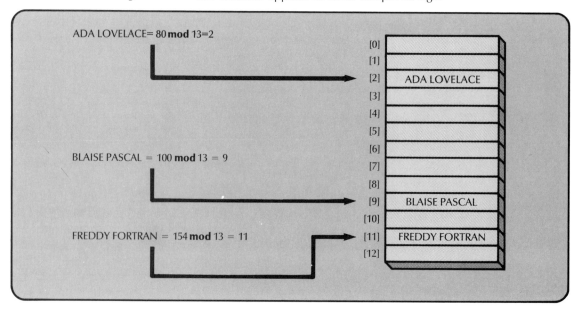

```
const
    MAXTABLE          = 499;                        {size of table: reasonable prime}
    MAXSTRING         = 30;                         {no. of chars in a string}
type
    STRING            = array [1..MAXSTRING] of char;
    WHATEVER          = STRING;
    EntryPtr          = ↑ TableEntry;
    TableEntry        =
      record
        key               : WHATEVER;
        next              : EntryPtr
      end;
    HASHTABLE         = array [0..MAXTABLE] of EntryPtr;
    SEARCHTABLE       = HASHTABLE;
```

Figure 12.10. Data declarations for an open (chained) hash table.

12.5.2 Collision Resolution: Open Addressing

When we hash the fourth string in the example in Fig. 12.8, we see an immediate problem: it hashes to the same location as the third! Such an occurrence is called a *hash clash*, and it represents the other topic to consider in the design and use of hashing techniques: collision resolution. Perhaps you have already thought of a solution: just build a linked list of all records with keys that hash to the same table location! This form of collision resolution is called *chaining* or *open addressing*. If the hash function is well chosen, a key should be equally likely to hash to any one of the m table locations. Consequently the average length of each chain will be about n/m, where n is the number of keys in the table.

The primary search table operations are table initialization, inserting keys, and searching for keys. To perform these operations we define the appropriate underlying Pascal representations for the chained hash table in Fig. 12.10. The major consideration is the table's size, that is, the number of header nodes for the chains. The more we have, the shorter the average chain will be, and the faster the insertion and searching will be. However, this is accomplished at the expense of additional preallocated storage space. Quite often the best choice must be made experimentally: determine the most important characteristics of the particular application (speed or space) and make a choice based on the needs of the job at hand. In the declarations of Fig. 12.10, we have used a table space of 499 header nodes (a prime

```
      procedure InsertTable (var Table : SEARCHTABLE; key : WHATEVER;
                      var duplicate, overflow : boolean);
      {
      DESCRIPTION: Insert key into the open hash table, Table.
      INPUT:        The hash table and the key.
      OUTPUT:       The key is entered into the table, if it is not a duplicate.
                    duplicate — true if key already in Table, false otherwise.
                    overflow — Always false: overflow cannot occur.
      Defined under InsertTable:
          H             The hash function.
      }
      var
        current                 : EntryPtr;
        HFunction               : integer;
        temp                    : EntryPtr;

        function H (key : WHATEVER) : integer;
        {The hash function.}
        var
          i                     : integer;
          sum                   : integer;
        begin
          sum := 0;
          for i := 1 to MAXSTRING do
            sum := sum + ord (key [i]);
          H := sum mod MAXTABLE
        end; {H}

      begin {InsertTable}
        overflow := false;                  {overflow never occurs in chained table}
        new (temp);                         {get a new node}
        temp ↑ .key := key;
        temp ↑ .next := nil;
        HFunction := H (key);               {calculate the hash function}
        current := Table [HFunction];
        if current = nil then               {insert at start of chain}
          Table [HFunction] := temp
        else begin
          duplicate := current ↑ .key = key;
          while (current ↑ .next <> nil) and not duplicate do begin
            current := current ↑ .next;
            duplicate := current ↑ .key = key
          end;
          if not duplicate then
            current ↑ .next := temp
        end
      end; {InsertTable}
```

Figure 12.11. Insertion into an open (chained) hash table.

number). The table itself is an array of pointers (*EntryPtr*). Initializing the table just involves setting each element of the table to **nil**.

```
procedure InitTable (var Table : SEARCHTABLE);
{Initialize the chained hash table, Table.}
var
  i : integer;
begin
  for i := 0 to MAXTABLE − 1 do
    Table [i] := nil
end; {InitTable}
```

Inserting a key into the hash table is a two-step process: first, calculate the hash function of the key; then, using this as the address into the array of header nodes, search the chain of records for the key. If the key is already in the list, a boolean, *duplicate* is set to *true*. Otherwise, insert the new record with the key at the end of the list. If the hash function performs reasonably, the average length of a chain should be about n/m, where m is the number of header nodes in the table and n is the number of records already in the table. The procedure in Fig. 12.11 defines the hash function H within it. This function sums the *ord* of the individual characters, and then performs the **mod** operation to produce the hash function.

Finally, searching for a record with a given key in the table is similar to hash insert. We generate the hash function of the key, then search its chain for the existence of the key. Since duplicate keys were not allowed during insertion, we stop the search when the key is found. We do not show the procedure here because it is quite similar to hash table insert.

Deleting a record with a given key from the hash table is similarly straightforward. We apply the hash function to the key, and then search the chain. If the key is found, we remove the node in the same way that we remove nodes from linked lists.

12.5.3 Collision Resolution: Closed Addressing

The second technique for handling hash clashes is to use another available location in a fixed size table. When a key hashes to a location that is already occupied, we try to find another empty slot in the table. Usually we just examine the next location in the array (modulo the table size) and continue this process until an empty cell is found. This process and the one used for chained tables are illustrated in Fig. 12.12.

Since we must differentiate between an empty and an occupied table cell, it is necessary to add an additional field to a cell, a *tag* field. The data definitions for a closed hash table are shown in Fig. 12.13.

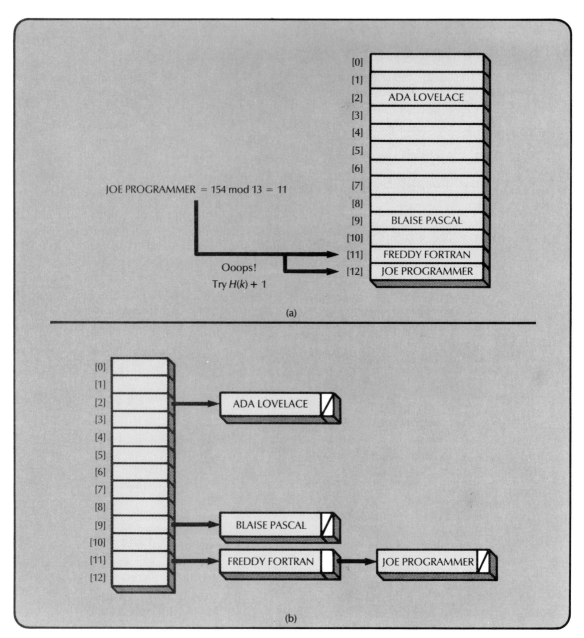

Figure 12.12. Diagrams showing collision resolution. (a) Closed addressing. (b) Open addressing (chaining).

```
const
   MAXTABLE          = 499;                    {size of table: reasonable prime}
   MAXSTRING         = 30;                     {no. of chars in a string}
type
   STRING            = array [1..MAXSTRING] of char;
   WHATEVER          = STRING;
   TableEntry        =
      record
         tag             : (empty, occupied);
         key             : WHATEVER
      end;
   HASHTABLE         =
      record
         Number          : integer;           {number of occupied cells}
         data            : array [0..MAXTABLE] of TableEntry
      end;
   SEARCHTABLE       = HASHTABLE;
```

Figure 12.13. Data definitions for a closed hash table.

Initialization requires that we set the number of occupied cells to zero and that we set the *tag* field of each location to *empty*. In contrast to the previous chained table, we include the number of occupied cells as a field in the table record.

```
procedure InitTable (var Table : SEARCHTABLE);
{Initialize closed hash table.}
var
   i : integer;
begin
   for i := 0 to MAXTABLE − 1 do
      Table.data [i].tag := empty;
   Table.Number := 0
end; {InitTable}
```

Inserting a new key into the table is again a two-step process: first, calculate the hash function for the key; then, using this as the index into the table, place the new key into the table. If that location is occupied, go to the next location and repeat the process. A simple scheme for the "next" location is to go to the current location plus 1, modulo *m*. We first test if the table is full so that we will not loop endlessly. When we finally insert the key into the table, we also set the current location's *tag* field to *occupied*. The procedure is shown in Fig. 12.14.

```
procedure InsertTable (var Table : SEARCHTABLE; key : WHATEVER;
                          var duplicate, overflow : boolean);
{
DESCRIPTION:           Finds an available empty slot in Table. Calls H to calculate the hash
                       function.
INPUT:                 The hash table and the key.
OUTPUT:                The key is entered into the table, if there is room.
                       duplicate — true if key already in table, false otherwise.
                       overflow — true if the table is full, false otherwise.
}
var
  location : integer;

#include "Hash.i";                                                  {hash function}

begin
  overflow := false;
  duplicate := false;
  with Table do
    if Number = MAXTABLE then
      overflow := true
    else begin
      location := H (key);
      while (data [location].tag = occupied) and not duplicate do
        if data [location].key = key then
          duplicate := true
        else
          location := (location + 1) mod MAXTABLE;                  {try next location}
      if not duplicate then begin
        Number := Number + 1;
        data [location ].key := key;
        data [location ].tag := occupied
      end
    end
end; {InsertTable}
```

Figure 12.14. Insertion into a closed hash table.

Searching for a key in a closed hash table is similar to inserting. We can't simply examine the *tag* field of the hashed address; rather, we must continue to examine the cycle of all occupied locations after the initial ones, since more than one key may hash to the same address. We continue probing until we either find the key or find an empty cell. We must obviously use the same hash function as when inserting into the table, and we must use the same cycle of secondary probes (in this case, just (*location* + 1) **mod** *MAXTABLE*). We use the compiler's file inclusion mechanism to ensure that the same hash function will be used in both insertion and searching. The search procedure is shown in Fig. 12.15.

Figure 12.15. Searching a closed hash table.

```
procedure TableSearch (var Table: SEARCHTABLE; key : WHATEVER;
                       var found : boolean; var location : integer);
{
Find key in Table.

INPUT:                 Table and key.
OUTPUT:                found — true if key in Table; false otherwise;
                       location — index into Table where key is found.
}
var
   RoundTrip           : boolean;              {used in full table}
   start               : integer;              {starting location in table}

#include "Hash.i";                             {the hash function}

begin
   with Table do begin
      location := H (key);
      start := location;
      found := false;
      RoundTrip := false;
      while (data [location].tag = occupied) and not found and not RoundTrip do
         if data [location].key = key then
            found := true
         else begin
            location := (location + 1) mod M;
            RoundTrip := location = start
         end
   end
end; {TableSearch}
```

Programming Notes

Comparison of Searching Techniques

In this chapter we examined five search table strategies:

- Sequential search
- Binary search
- Binary tree search
- Chained (open) hashing
- Closed hashing

The choice of an appropriate technique is often heavily application dependent. The best choice depends on the relative frequency of insertions, searches, and deletions. It also depends on the nature of searches: if unsuccessful searches are very likely, the best technique may be different than if successful searches are the norm. In addition, environment constraints may preclude the use of various dynamic list techniques. As chefs in the creation of program delights, we must be familiar with many techniques in order to select an appropriate one for a particular application and environment. A reasonable strategy is to pick one that works, and then worry about the best only after the use characteristics of the table are well known. It is tempting, even in single-use programs, to spend a considerable amount of time finding the "optimal" technique; such effort is usually not justified until the program can be tested for critical timing information in real use. In the exercises, you are given typical application scenarios and are asked to suggest a reasonable search table technique for that application. To do this, keep in mind the basic (or abstract) table operations, and their important parameters.

InsertTable	Relative frequency of insertions versus searches. Are duplicate keys allowed? Space versus time requirements. Are dynamic structures available? Can we estimate in advance the maximum size of the table (so that closed hashing can be used)? Is it necessary to sort the table at some point?
TableSearch	Relative frequency of successful versus unsuccessful searches. Are duplicate keys allowed? Do we need to search for all duplicates, or just the first occurrence? Relative frequency of searches versus insertions.

DeleteTable	Are deletions necessary? Do we need to delete a single record, or all records with a given key? Other concerns are similar to *InsertTable*.
SortTable	Is it necessary to provide the keys in order?

Using these questions as a checklist should make it simpler to select an appropriate search table strategy for any application. Remember, if the size of the table is fairly small (less than 50 items or so), and the application is not time critical, there is little value in using a technique more sophisticated than simple linear search of an unordered table. The table can be represented as an array or as a linked list, using the basic list insert, search, and delete procedures. If the list is completely known in advance (that is, no insertions or deletions, only searches, as would be the case in a table of Pascal reserved words, for example), binary search can provide significant performance improvements.

If time becomes critical, hashing into a relatively large table will produce the fastest table insert and search times (though deletions are troublesome). Analytical results on hashing performance indicate that only about two probes per insertion are required (on average) for a table that is about half full (whether open or closed hashing is used). With Pascal's dynamic data structures, open (chained) hashing is built on the primitive linked list operations of Chapter 8. In addition, we do not need to worry about guessing a maximum table size when chained hashing is used. Unless there are important additional considerations (including the need for frequent sorting and the lack of dynamic storage allocation), hashing will be the search table technique of choice, except as just noted for very small tables. All the routines of this chapter can easily be extended to represent keys of whatever type is needed, just by redefining *WHATEVER*. When the table is needed to keep records, of which the key is just one field, the data definitions are extended in the obvious way.

Exercises

1. Implement binary search without using recursion. Does this result in a significant performance improvement?
2. Binary search can involve relatively expensive arithmetic (division by two, unless the compiler optimizes this to a shift operation). In a segmented search, the table is considered to be divided into k-element segments. The

search key is compared against the first element of every segment (that is, against element 1, then element k, then element $2k$, and so on). When an appropriate segment is found, each element in the segment is compared to the key. Implement a segmented search algorithm and test it with various values of k.

What is the time complexity of segmented search as a function of the size of the table?

3. When searching a phone book, we don't open the book to the middle every time, as a binary search algorithm would. Instead, we guess where the name is likely to be, and start our search there. If we are searching for a name beginning with a "T", we start our search about two-thirds of the way through the phone book, rather than at the middle. If our guess is wrong, we use the names actually appearing on that page of the phone book to make another guess. We repeat this process until we find the name we are looking for. This type of search is called an "interpolation" search. Implement an interpolation search assuming even numbers of names beginning with each letter.

4. A self-organizing table can change the order of its elements as they are accessed. One way to order a table is by frequency of access. Each element has an additional entry counting the number of accesses; the elements accessed most frequently appear at the front of the table. Implement such a search table. When is this organization good? When is it bad?

5. Implement *DeleteTable* using a hash table with open (chained) addressing.

6. Implement *DeleteTable* using a hash table with closed addressing. (*Hint:* Consider adding a new value to the enumerated type of cell occupancy: *empty, occupied* and now *deleted.*)

7. Prove binary search will make $\log_2 n$ comparisons in the worst case.

8. Assuming a pointer requires 1 word, a key requires 2 words, a record requires 10 words, and we have 100 records, and each entry in the table contains a key and a pointer to the corresponding record, how much storage would each of the following search table organizations require?

a) A sorted array.
b) A sorted linked list.
c) A binary search tree.
d) Hash table of 25 elements using open (chained) addressing.
e) Hash table of 100 elements using open addressing.
f) Hash table of 150 elements using open addressing.
g) Hash table of 200 elements using closed addressing.

Which of the preceding methods is the most space efficient? The least efficient?

9. Repeat Exercise 8, assuming there are 50 elements and the records are of size 0 (that is, the records consist of a key field only).

10. Suppose you have to write a program to manage student grading records. Each record contains a student number, a name, and a list of grades received from various classes. For each of the following conditions, design an appropriate data structure, and discuss the time complexity of the insert, search, delete, and sort operations.
    a) There are 30 students, each with a unique student number, and each student has no more than 10 grades. Printing all students sorted by student number is a common operation.
    b) Same as part (a), but student names are unique instead of the student number (that is, the name is used as the key).
    c) There are a large number of students, the combination of student number and name is unique, and there is no need to print student names in order. Searching by student name is a common operation.
    d) Same as part (c), but printing all student names in sorted order is a common operation.

11. [PROGRAMMING PROJECT] Write a program to print a frequency table of the words in a text file.

    Input: A text file.
    Output: Each word in the file, and its frequency of occurrence, is printed, one word per line, sorted alphabetically by word.

    For this program, words are case independent (for example, "Now" = "NOW"). A word is defined as a maximal string of alphabetic characters ('a'..'z', 'A'..'Z'). Words are unique in the first n characters. n should be a program constant, initially set to 10.

    The output consists of the word followed by its frequency; the words are left-justified; the frequencies begin in column $n + 5$. The words are printed in alphabetical order.

    Before you begin this program, write a simple design, showing the stages in input, searching the word table, and sorting and printing the table. Implement the program using two different search table representations from this chapter, and compare the execution time on the same input. What are the abstract "search table" operations that need to be performed in this problem (inserting, counting, and so on)? Write the program in such a way that the definitions of the table and the implementation of the abstract table operations are hidden from the rest of the program.

12. Exercise 11 does not require that the frequency table be kept sorted by word. If you must keep the table sorted, what representation for the search table will you use?

If you must produce two outputs for the previous exercise—one sorted alphabetically (as in the original) and the other sorted by frequency—what search table representation will you use? What sorting techniques are most appropriate?

13. Extend the programming project of Exercise 11 so that two output tables are produced. The first is the table of words and frequencies sorted alphabetically; the second is the table sorted by frequency.

14. Extend Exercise 11 so that *after* all words and frequencies, you print an additional table of frequencies. This consists of a table with the frequency of occurrence, and the number of words with that frequency, such as the following table.

Frequency	Number of Words
8	4
7	1
6	3
.	.
.	.
1	38

This is interpreted to mean that four words occurred eight times, one word occurred seven times, and so on.

15. [PROGRAMMING PROJECT] Write a cross-referencer for Pascal. A cross-referencer is a program that takes each identifier and each routine in the Pascal program and produces a listing showing the line number where the identifier is used (or the routine called). The cross-referencer should not print reserved words in the language, only user- and system-defined constants, variables, and routines. When finished with the input, print out the table sorted alphabetically by identifier.

For example, the Pascal program in Fig. 12.16. produced the cross-reference listing shown in Fig. 12.17.

Note that if an identifier appears more than one time on the same line, the line number appears more than once.

This is an exercise in both reuseable code, and decision making. The code you will reuse is *GetToken*. The decision making comes in because you must select a reasonable search table to represent the words in the program, and because you also must select a reasonable representation and search

```
program PRIME (input, output);
{Determines if input integer is a prime. Not too efficient.}
var
   factor            : integer;
   number            : integer;
begin
   writeln ('This program helps determine if a number is prime');
   writeln ('Enter an ODD integer. The program will print all values <= sqrt (n)');
   writeln ('A number is prime if the quotient is an integer. GOOD LUCK');
   write ('> ');
   while not eof do begin
      readln (number);
      factor := trunc (sqrt(number));
      if not odd (factor ) then
         factor := factor + 1;
      writeln ('initial factor := ', factor : 1);
      while factor > 0 do begin
         writeln ('Dividing by :', factor : 4, '      ', number / factor : 8 : 3);
         factor := factor - 2
      end
      writeln;
      write ('> ')
   end
end.
```

Figure 12.16. Program to print out prime numbers.

PRIME	1								
eof	11								
factor	4	13	14	15	15	16	17	18	18	19
input	1								
integer	4	5							
number	5	12	13	18					
odd	14								
output	1								
readln	12								
sqrt	13								
trunc	13								
write	10	22							
writeln	7	8	9	16	18	21			

Figure 12.17. Output from cross-referencer run on program of Figure 12.16.

strategy for the Pascal reserved words. One more point, the cross-referencer should not include words that are in comments or in quoted strings.

16. After implementing the program in Exercise 15, instrument your code, either by adding counters for each routine, or by using an available execution monitor on your own machine, and determine where the program is spending its time.

    a) If you have not already done so, implement the reserved word table as a closed hash table. How does the program's time compare with your original implementation?

    b) Now implement the reserved word table as a sorted array, and use binary search. How does the program's time compare now? Was hashing substantially faster? Remember, a search of the reserved word table will have to be done for each word in the program, so this might be an area where we would predict the need for performance tuning.

17. [PROGRAMMING PROJECT] Write a program that takes a table of words, and a cost associated with each, and compiles a list of all of the words found in the table that occur in a given input file. Then calculate the total cost for the entire file.

    This program is intended to be used on another program that invokes a large number of system subroutines, such as an interactive computer graphics program. For example, assume the list of words and costs contains the following:

Word	Size (in bytes)	Function
arc	486	Draw an arc of a circle
circle	446	Draw a circle
circlef	446	Draw a solid circle
draw	16	Draw a straight line segment
move	16	Move to a given location
perspective	90	Perspective projection of a 3-D object
⋮		

Each of these words is an individual token, separated by either punctuation (period, comma, etc.), space, or a left parenthesis, from other tokens. A typical piece of a program that calls on some of these graphics primitives looks like:

```
procedure polygon (x,y : REALARRAY; n : integer);
{Draw a polygon using arrays x and y of n points.}
var
  i : integer;
begin
  if n > 1 then begin
    move (x [1] , y [1]);                          {move to first point}
    for i := 2 to n do
      draw (x [i] , y [i]);
    draw (x [1] , y [1])                           {close the polygon}
  end
end; {polygon}
```

PART IV

**APPLICATIONS
CASE STUDIES**

PARSING EXPRESSIONS:
THE FINAL LAYER OF
THE FUNCTION PLOTTER

13.1 Introduction

In this chapter we finish the implementation of the function plotter. We've been implementing the plotter in layers for at least two reasons. First, it has been an effective way of successfully building small pieces that could be incorporated into the overall structure incrementally. By doing this, we are able to more easily test the program, and we have a useful program, even at early stages of implementation. Second, we needed to understand the appropriate data structures and algorithms to be able to do it correctly and efficiently! So now let's bite the bullet and build the last layer: allowing the user to enter an arbitrary in-fix (parenthesized) expression.

In Fig. 13.1, we repeat the top-level design hierarchy from Chapter 3. Remember in Chapter 9 we implemented the module "get function from user," but we insisted that the function had to be entered in post-fix form. So the submodule "parse input" required that the user's input be a legal post-fix expression. "Convert to internal form" built a linked list of tokens representing the function, and "generate table of values" used the ADT stack to repeatedly evaluate the internal representation of the expression.

To the external world, "get function from user" is called *Convert-Expression*, a function that takes a single parameter, the input string from

Figure 13.1 Top-level design of the function plotter, repeated from Chapter 3.

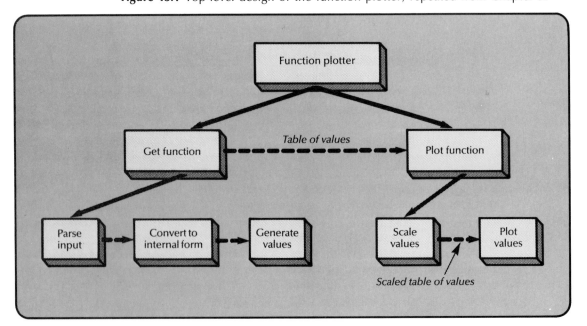

the user, and returns a pointer to the internal expression structure. We generate the table of values by repeatedly evaluating the internal representation. In the new version, no matter what we have to do to handle in-fix expressions, we know that it will be limited to just these routines: *ConvertExpression* (which parses the input and builds the internal representation) and *GetPoints* (which takes the internal expression and builds the table of values), and the data types that define the internal form of the expression.

How we go about parsing the in-fix expression, and how we represent the expression internally, make up the bulk of this chapter.

13.2 Design Review

In Chapter 3 we presented an overall design structure for the program, and this is reviewed here. The routines follow the guidelines of Chapter 4: coherence and low coupling. Each routine performs a single or small set of related tasks; the communication between routines consists of well-defined packages of data. For the most part, each routine could as easily have been written as a separate program, writing its outputs to a file. The next routine, in turn, reads the file produced by the previous routine. Consequently the coupling between modules consists only of temporal sequencing and knowledge of (global) data structure definitions.

It should come as no surprise that the design holds no surprises! We have followed a methodical process from specification to design to code in such a way that the overall structure remained clear and well defined throughout. Note that the top-level structure clearly retains the breakdown into discrete steps first stated in Chapter 3 and fully elaborated in Chapter 9:

1. Get the function from the user (*GetInput*).
2. Build the table of values for the function (*ConvertExpression* and *GetPoints*).
3. Plot the table of values (*plot* and *WriteScreen*).

13.3 New Algorithms: Parsing and Expression Trees

The only new data structures and algorithms in this program are those related to expression evaluation. Earlier we allowed the user to enter a post-fix expression. Now we must handle in-fix expressions. We must take the input string, representing a function of x, and evaluate the function for various values of x. First we'll describe the problem in an informal way, indicating the overall solution (avoiding decisions, as we suggested in Chapter 3). Finally, we'll look at the specific solution.

The technique for generating a table of values for $f(x)$ remains the same. We begin at x_{min} and repeatedly evaluate $f(x)$ at increasing values of x until x_{max}. We increment x by a variable given by $x_{max} - x_{min}$ divided by the number of points to plot.

We clearly see that the problem is to take a string of characters (which we hope represents a function of a single real variable x), and repeatedly evaluate it to build the table of values. In Chapter 9 we first solved this problem via two algorithms. First, we converted the function (as a string of characters) into a form compatible with expression evaluation (*ConvertExpression*). Then we repeatedly evaluated the expression for increasing values of x (*GetPoints*).

The next sections of the chapter develop the techniques for parsing an in-fix expression and converting it into the program's internal form. We'll do this back to front. First we describe the representation; then we develop the technique for building it from the input.

13.4   Expression Trees

For this version of the function plotter, we're going to use an alternative internal representation of the expression — an expression tree. An expression tree is a binary tree where each node contains either an operator or an operand. Figure 13.2 shows expression trees for $sin(x)/x$ and $3 * x * x - 5 * x + 17$ (or $3x^2 - 5x + 17$).

We're using a different internal form for the function than we used in Chapter 9 for the post-fix evaluator because evaluating an expression tree is trivial: the post-order traversal yields the post-fix expression. Code for evaluating the tree involves a post-order traversal.

13.4.1 Evaluating the Expression Tree

To evaluate the tree correctly, we need to establish a suitable data structure for the nodes in the tree. Here we strike a blow in favor of incremental implementation. We'll use the same data definitions as in Chapter 9, just add one new pointer field to the type definition of a node, and change the name of the *next* field. In Fig. 13.3, we've repeated the old type definition (from Chapter 9 when we were representing the expression as a one-way post-fix linked list) and shown the new type definition for an expression tree.

An expression tree is a convenient intermediate form for representing the expression. All the tokens in the original have been replaced with enumerated type token identifiers. The tree (and thus the expression it

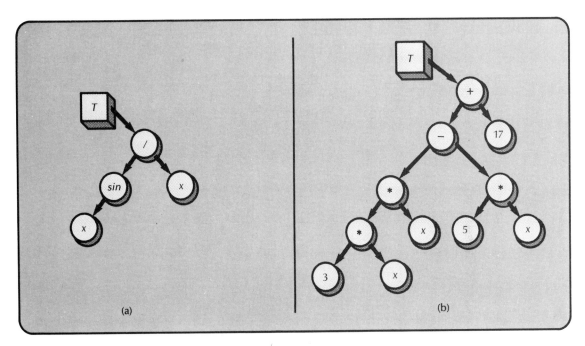

Figure 13.2. Examples of expression trees. (a) $sin(x)/x$. (b) $3 * x * x - 5 * x + 17$.

Figure 13.3. Comparison of one-way post-fix expression data types and expression tree data types. (a) Data type definitions for one-way post-fix expression. (b) Data type definitions for expression tree.

```
type
  NODEPTR          = ↑ NODE;
  NODE             =
    record
      op             : TOKEN;
      value          : integer;
      link           : NODEPTR
    end;

              (a)


type
  NODEPTR          = ↑ NODE;
  NODE             =
    record
      op             : TOKEN;
      value          : integer;
      left, right    : NODEPTR        ⟵— Only change to data structure
    end;

              (b)
```

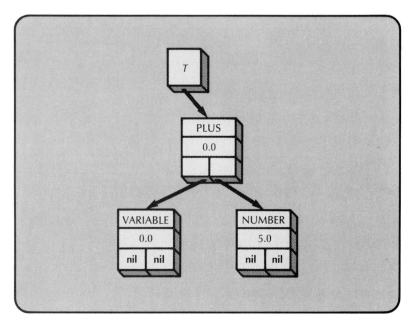

Figure 13.4. Expression tree for $x + 5$.

Figure 13.5. Expression tree evaluation function. The function is a recursive postfix traversal of the tree pointed to by *expr*.

```
function Evaluate (expr : NODEPTR) : real;
{Evaluate the expression tree pointed to by expr, producing a single value for the tree.}
var
    leftresult    : real;              {value returned from evaluating the left
                                        subtree}
    rightresult   : real;              {value returned from evaluating the right
                                        subtree}
begin
    Evaluate := 0;
    if expr <> nil then begin          {tree empty? just exit}
        leftresult := Evaluate (expr ↑ .left);    {evaluate left subtree}
        rightresult := Evaluate (expr ↑ .right);  {evaluate right subtree}
        case expr ↑ .op of             {'visit' the root}
            PLUS : Evaluate := leftresult + rightresult;
            MINUS : Evaluate := leftresult − rightresult;
                         . . .

        end
    end
end; {Evaluate}
```

represents) is evaluated by traversing the tree in a certain order. We'll see this by looking at a simple example, and then applying the technique to a more complex expression tree.

The tree for the expression x + 5 looks like Fig. 13.4. To evaluate the tree in Fig. 13.4, we note that the root of the tree is the enumerated value *PLUS*, representing the addition operation. For addition we take the sum of the two operands, and in an expression tree, the operands are the values obtained from evaluating the left and right subtrees. When we see a node that contains an operator, we perform the indicated operation on the values of its left and right subtrees.

To evaluate the tree, we evaluate the left subtree, returning a real (which we'll call *leftresult*); evaluate the right subtree, also returning a real, *rightresult*; and then apply the operation indicated by the *op* field to these two reals. If the node is a variable, we give it the current value of the function variable (something between x_{min} and x_{max}). This is succinctly represented in the partial version of *Evaluate* in Fig. 13.5.

We pass a pointer to the expression tree to *Evaluate*. We initialize the value of the expression to 0. If the expression tree is empty (*expr* = **nil**), we return with the value of 0. Otherwise, we perform the appropriate operation on the appropriate number of operands. Note that all the interesting work is done within the **case** statement. But also note that some arithmetic operations need special care before they can be evaluated. Some of the operations must be guarded to prevent run-time arithmetic errors (these are associated with division, log, and square root).

To protect against these run-time errors, we guard division, *ln*, and *sqrt*, so that the operation is not performed for out-of-range parameters, just as we needed to protect these operations in the original post-fix evaluator. Again, we'll use a global flag *def*, indicating whether the function we're trying to evaluate is defined for the current operation and current value. So in *Evaluate*, we initialize *def* to *true*, and set it to *false* for any out-of-range operation. Figure 13.6 shows what we'd do in the **case** statement in Fig. 13.5 to handle division. (The complete *Evaluate* code is shown later with the completed plotter program in Fig. 13.19.)

```
         . . .
DIVIDE:
   if rightresult <> 0 then          {test for division by 0}
      evaluate := leftresult / rightresult
   else
      def := false;
         . . .
```

Figure 13.6. Divide operation in Evaluate, showing testing for division by 0. Similar tests are needed before performing the *ln* and *sqrt* operations.

13.5   Building the Expression Tree

Now our goal is to build the expression tree. To do this, we're going to explore some issues in the process of translating an input string into an internal representation. This process, as we've come to know, is called parsing, and it is an important and widely studied topic in computer science. We'll look at some of the simpler, but also some of the most useful techniques, and apply them to the task of converting the user's typed expression into the expression tree.

First, we must define just what a legal expression is. Informally, an expression involves the usual in-fix notation of mathematical operations (addition, subtraction, multiplication, and division) and certain allowable functions (sine, cosine, natural log, exponentiation, and square root). We may compose operations and indicate the order of evaluation using parentheses. We're familiar with mathematical expression syntax from earlier experience. We'll specify a simpler expression syntax to illustrate the process of recognizing a legal expression (and similarly, recognizing an illegal one), and for the case of a legal one, building the expression tree.

13.5.1 Simplified Expression Syntax

Our simplified expressions allow only addition and subtraction (the lowest priority), and multiplication and division (next highest priority), and parenthesized expressions (highest priority). For simplicity, we won't allow function operators such as sine, cosine, and so on, nor will we allow unary plus or minus. And operands are restricted to single character lower-case letters. Table 13.1 lists examples of legal and illegal expressions of this simple form, and Fig. 13.7 shows the syntax diagrams.

The parser for these simple expressions has the task of "recognizing" a legal expression. That is, we'll build a parser that notifies us if the expression is legal or illegal. So one job of the parser is to indicate whether a given string of characters is, or is not, an expression. For simplicity, we'll assume

Table 13.1. Examples of legal and illegal expressions.

Legal	Illegal	Reason
$a+b$	$-a$	Unary minus
$a-b$	$a+12$	Illegal characters (12)
$a*b+c$	$ab+c$	Operator missing
$((a-b)*(c-d))$	$((a+b)$	Missing right parenthesis
	$(a+b))$	Extra right parenthesis

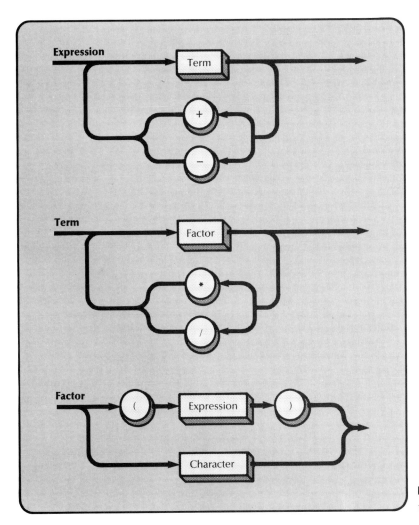

Figure 13.7. Syntax diagrams for simple expressions.

that the input comes from the terminal and no blanks are allowed. We get the next character via a call to *read(NextChar)*.

Let's trace through the process of recognizing the expression $a+b$. We start the process by getting the first character, the a. But the syntax for an expression (Fig. 13.7) indicates that an expression is a term, or zero or more occurrences of a term plus or minus a term.

So perhaps the a is a term. A term is either a factor, or zero or more occurrences of a factor times or divided by a factor.

So perhaps the a is a factor. A factor is either one of the alphabetic characters ('a' ... 'z'), or a left parenthesis, followed by an expression

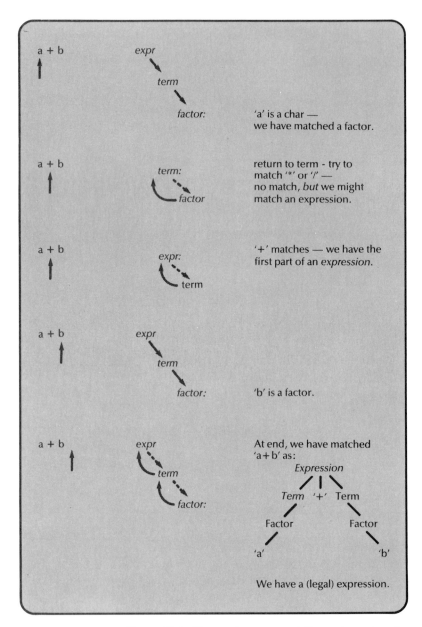

a + b   expr
         ↓
         term
         ↓
         factor: 'a' is a char —
                    we have matched a factor.

a + b   term: return to term - try to
                     match '*' or '/' —
         factor   no match, *but* we might
                     match an expression.

a + b   expr: '+' matches — we have the
                     first part of an *expression*.
         term

a + b   expr
         ↓
         term
         ↓
         factor: 'b' is a factor.

a + b   expr   At end, we have matched
                     'a+b' as:
         term   *Expression*
                               / | \
         factor: *Term* '+' Term
                            | |
                          Factor   Factor
                            | |
                           'a'   'b'

                     We have a (legal) expression.

Figure 13.8. Trace of movement through syntax diagrams for *a* + *b*.

followed by a right parenthesis. So the first character, the a, is a factor! We're making progress.

After we've recognized the a as a factor, we read the next character, the $+$. Now, since a term could be a factor followed by a $*$ or $/$, we compare the current character ($+$) with $*$ and $/$. Neither matches, so we know that we don't have a factor times or divided by another factor.

Well, perhaps we have a term plus or minus a term. We compare the $+$ with $+$ and $-$, and indeed we have a match. Our string is *potentially* an expression, which, as Fig. 13.7 shows, is a term plus another term. Now that we've matched the $+$, we read the next character from the input, the b, and try to match that as a term.

Again, a term could be a factor, and a factor is one of the alphabetic characters. So, indeed, $a + b$ is an expression, since it is a term plus a term! In Fig. 13.8, we've traced out the movement through the syntax diagrams in recognizing $a + b$ as an expression.

13.5.2 Coding the Parser

The description in Section 13.5.1 makes recognizing a string as an expression sound like a pretty formidable task, but, in fact, the process is simpler to code than it might seem at first. When we examine the syntax diagrams representing an expression in Fig. 13.7 closely, we note that they have quite a simple structure to them. One way to write code to implement the parser is to simply follow a systematic way of writing Pascal statements that correspond to each box in the syntax charts.

For example, in the chart for an expression (Fig. 13.9), we see that the first "piece" must be a term. Since there is another diagram for a term, we call such a box a *nonterminal*. Our coding rule will be to code a nonterminal as a procedure call with that name:

```
procedure expression;
begin
   term;
   . . .
end; {expression}
```

The next component of the expression syntax indicates that the next "piece" of an expression is zero or more occurrences of a plus sign ($+$) or a minus sign ($-$), followed by another term. We translate this cycle or loop via a **while** statement:

```
while NextChar in ['+', '-'] do begin
   read (NextChar);
   term
end
```

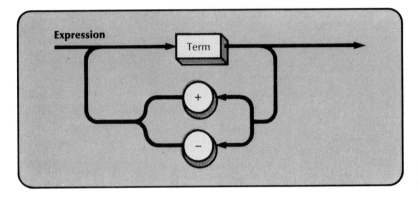

Figure 13.9. Syntax for an expression, from Fig. 13.7.

```
procedure expression;
begin
  term;
  while NextChar in ['+', '−'] do begin
    read (NextChar);
    term
  end
end; {expression}
```

Figure 13.10. Procedure *expression*.

As in the syntax diagram, we just cycle, reading characters and calling *term*, as long as the next character is a + or −. Figure 13.10 shows the entire *expression* procedure.

The syntax diagram for a term is virtually identical to that for an expression, except that we cycle over ∗ and /. Figure 13.11 shows the entire *term* procedure.

Figure 13.11. Procedure *term*.

```
procedure term;
begin
  factor;
  while NextChar in ['*', '/'] do begin
    read (NextChar);
    factor
  end
end; {term}
```

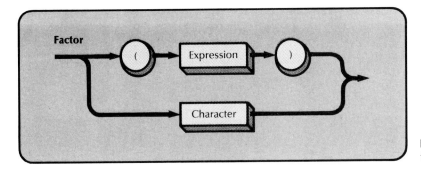

Figure 13.12. Syntax for a factor, from Fig. 13.7.

Now in *factor*, we do the interesting work of determining whether the next character is really part of a legal factor or not. Let's look at the syntax diagram of a factor again (see Fig. 13.12). Here we have a choice: a factor is *either* an alphabetic character [a..z] or it's a left parenthesis followed by an expression, followed by a right parenthesis.

We can easily write code for each of these cases separately. If *NextChar* is an alphabetic, we read the next character in the input, and exit the procedure. Otherwise, *NextChar* must be a left parenthesis. If it is not, we call an error handling routine to write an error message (such as "Expected left parenthesis"), and exit.

If the character is a left parenthesis, we call *expression*. Upon returning from *expression*, the next character must be a *right* parenthesis. If it is, we just exit; if not, we call the error handler with the message "Expected right parenthesis." Figure 13.13 is the entire *factor* procedure. In *factor*, we call

Figure 13.13. Procedure *factor*.

```
procedure factor;
begin
    if NextChar in ['a'..'z'] then
        read (NextChar)
    else if NextChar = '(' then begin
        read (NextChar);
        expression;
        if NextChar = ')' then
            read (NextChar)
        else
            ErrorHandler (NORPAREN)
    end else
        ErrorHandler (BADFACTOR)
end; {factor}
```

another routine, *ErrorHandler*, a procedure that takes an enumerated type representing the type of error, prints an appropriate error message, and sets a global flag indicating that an error in parsing has occurred.

We start the whole process going in the main program by reading the first character, and then calling *expression*. If we return without having called the error handler (that is, the global flag *ok* is still *true*), we have a legal expression; otherwise, the string is not an expression and the error handler will have written an error message. Figure 13.14 is a complete program that reads input from the standard input and attempts to recognize the input as an expression. The main program begins by reading the first character, and then calling *expression*. The work of recognition is done in the three routines *expression*, *term*, and *factor*. The routines *term* and *factor* are defined underneath *expression*, because *term* is called only by *expression* and *factor* is called by *term*.

```
program PARSE (input, output);
{
DESCRIPTION:        Parses a simple syntax expression, producing an appropriate error message
                    if the expression is not legal.
INPUT:              An expression, consisting of single letter operands and the operators '+',
                    '−', '*' and '/'. No blanks are allowed in the input.
OUTPUT:             If the expression is legal, 'Legal expression' is written. If not legal, an
                    appropriate error message is written.
}
type
  ERRORTYPE         = (BADFACTOR, BADOP, BADTERM, EXCESS, NORPAREN);
                                       {error types}

var
  NextChar          : char;                 {next character from input line}
  next              : 0..maxint;            {where char came from − used in ErrorHandler}
  ok                : boolean;              {error in input?}

  procedure ErrorHandler (Error : ERRORTYPE);
  {Prints an appropriate error message based on Error.}
  begin
  write (' ' : next, '↑');                  {write appropriate number of blanks}
    case Error of
      BADFACTOR   : writeln ('Not a legal FACTOR');
      BADOP       : writeln ('Not a legal OPERATOR');
```

Figure 13.14. Program that recognizes expressions according to the syntax of Fig. 13.7.

```
    BADTERM      : writeln ('Not a legal TERM');
    EXCESS       : writeln ('Expected OPERATOR after EXPRESSION');
    NORPAREN     : writeln ('Expected right parenthesis')
  end;
  ok := false
end; {ErrorHandler}

procedure expression;

  procedure term;

    procedure factor;
    begin
      if NextChar in ['a'..'z'] then begin
        read (NextChar);
        next := next + 1
      end else if NextChar = '(' then begin
        read (NextChar);
        next := next + 1;
        expression;
        if NextChar = ')' then begin
          read (NextChar);
          next := next + 1
        end else
          ErrorHandler (NORPAREN)
      end else
        ErrorHandler (BADFACTOR)
    end; {factor}

  begin {term}
    factor;
    while NextChar in ['*', '/'] do begin
      read (NextChar);
      next := next + 1;
      factor
    end
  end; {term}

begin {expression}
  term;
  while NextChar in ['+', '-'] do begin
    read (NextChar);
    next := next + 1;
    term
  end
end; {expression}
```

(continued)

Figure 13.14. (continued)

```
begin {main}
  next := 1;                              {get next character from this index}
  ok := true;
  read (NextChar);
  next := next + 1;
  expression;
  if ok and eoln then
    writeln ('Legal Expression')
  else if ok then
    ErrorHandler (EXCESS)
end.
```

13.5.3 Letting the Parser Build the Expression Tree

As we descend in the multiple layers of procedure calls, we can build the expression tree at the same time. We can do this because the expression tree closely resembles the layers of procedure calls and recursion required to recognize a string as an expression. Note that an expression tree's nodes are made up only of terminal symbols from the syntax diagram; that is, a node in the expression tree must be either an operator $(+, -, *, /)$ or an operand $(a..z)$.

Looking at the syntax diagrams, we see that an expression is defined as a term, plus or minus another term. So, for a simple string without parentheses such as $a*b+c$, the parser will recognize this expression as a term plus a term. The term on the left is, of course, $a*b$, and on the right, c. The expression tree that corresponds to this parse is shown in Fig. 13.15.

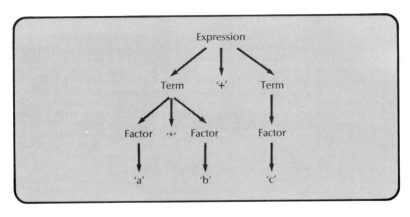

Figure 13.15. Parse tree for term '+' term.

So, within the procedure that recognizes an expression, we should build a node consisting of the three fields: the operator (either + or −), a pointer to the left term, and a pointer to the right term. Since this is a tree, we'll change *expression* in Fig. 13.10 to be a function that returns a pointer to this node. If we define the data types for a node in an expression tree as:

```
type
   NODEPTR        =  ↑ NODE;
   NODE           =
      record
         op           : char;
         left, right  : NODEPTR
      end;
```

then all we need to do is add a line or two to each of the procedures *expression, term,* and *factor.* Since a term is a factor times or divided by another factor, the routine for recognizing a term needs to build a node consisting of the appropriate operator (∗ or /), a pointer to the left factor, and a pointer to the right factor. Since we're rewriting the routines to be functions that return a pointer to the created node (type *NODEPTR*), we'll call the next lower function in the context of building the node's contents.

Figure 13.16 is the modified version of *expression; term* is virtually identical, as we saw in Fig. 13.11. *factor* is modified similarly and can be seen in the completed function plotter in Section 13.6.

Figure 13.16. Modified *expression* routine that also builds an appropriate node in the expression tree.

```
function expression  : NODEPTR;
var
   op                 : char;
   temp               : NODEPTR;
begin
   temp := term;                              {term returns a NODEPTR}
   while NextChar in ['+', '−'] do begin
      op := NextChar;
      read (NextChar);
      next := next + 1;                       {increment index for ErrorHandler}
      temp := MakeNode (op, temp, term)       {call term again, returning ptr. to right subtree}
   end;
   expression := temp
end; {expression}
```

```
function MakeNode (opchar : char; ls, rs : NODEPTR) : NODEPTR;
{Makes a new node with the given fields, returning a pointer to it.}
var
  temp : NODEPTR;
begin
  new (temp);
  with temp ↑ do begin
    op := opchar;
    left := ls;
    right := rs
  end;
  MakeNode := temp
end; {MakeNode}
```

Figure 13.17. Function *MakeNode* for building the individual node in an expression tree.

To keep the function simple in structure, we do the node building in a separate function *MakeNode*, as shown in Fig. 13.17. This function is then called from each of the three routines (*expression*, *term*, and *factor*) that adds nodes to the tree.

As we first suggested in tracing the actions of the parser on various input strings, it is quite useful to trace the enhanced parser/tree builder on similar strings, and to observe its activities in building the expression tree. When you do this, you should pay particular attention to the way in which the parser handles parentheses, since the expression $a+b*c$ yields the tree in Fig. 13.18(a) and the expression $(a+b)*c$ yields the different tree in Fig. 13.18(b).

Figure 13.18. (a) Expression tree for $a+b*c$. (b) Expression tree for $(a+b)*c$.

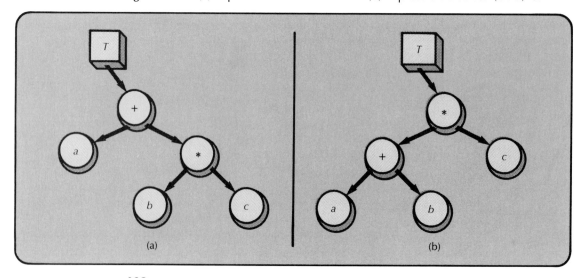

(a)   (b)

13.6 The Program

In the code that follows (Fig. 13.19) we have not included the complete bodies of routines that are reused from previous layers of the plotter. Rather, we show the routine's header and comment block, along with the chapter where the routine was originally defined. For this program to properly compile and run, it is necessary to replace the header with the entire procedure or function body, or these reusable routines can be kept in *include* files, as we have done with Chapter 1's *NEWREADLN* and the direct cursor movement routines in the *include* file *cursor.i*.

By not reprinting the body of the reused routines we emphasize even more the expanding nature of the program, and the new routines added for this layer. In Chapter 14 we'll again use some of the earlier routines for parsing, and the routines from this chapter for expression evaluation, along with new algorithms on data structures.

```
program PLOTTER (input, output);
{
DESCRIPTION:        Simple function plotter. This is the third and final implementation layer
                    of the interactive function plotter. In this version, fully parenthesized, in-
                    fix expressions are allowed. Functions are represented internally as
                    expression trees.
INPUT:              The function of a single real variable is entered by the user. The user is
                    prompted for minimum and maximum x values. The program does
                    automatic scaling in y. After the user enters a function, the program
                    prompts for minimum and maximum x values. After a table of values
                    has been computed internally, the minimum and maximum y values are
                    displayed. The user is asked whether he or she wishes to change these
                    values.
OUTPUT:             The function is plotted to the standard output (the display screen).
}
const
  FUNCCOL          = 0;                        {first column for various messages –
                                                term specific}
  FUNCLINE         = 0;                        {first line for various messages –
                                                term specific}
  MAXCOL           = 78;                       {columns of screen – term specific}
  MAXFUNC          = 5;                        {number of predefined functions}
  MAXIDLEN         = 10;                       {longest identifier}
  MAXLINE          = 79;                       {longest input line}
  MAXPOINTS        = 500;                      {max number of points to plot}
  MAXROW           = 22;                       {rows on screen – term specific}
```

(continued)

Figure 13.19. Final version of the interactive function plotter.

Figure 13.19. (continued)

```
type
  COLS             = 0..MAXCOL;
  ROWS             = 0..MAXROW;
  POINTCNT         = 0..MAXPOINTS;
  POINT            =
    record
      x, y           : real
    end;
  POINTARRAY       = array [POINTCNT] of POINT;
  SCREENARRAY      = array [ROWS, COLS] of char;
  COUNTER          = 0..maxint;
  PLOTINFO         =
    record
      count          : POINTCNT;                        {number of elements}
      minx, maxx     : real;                            {minimum, maximum values of x}
      miny, maxy     : real;                            {minimum, maximum values of y}
      table          : POINTARRAY                       {table of points to plot}
    end;
  INPUTTYPE        =                                    {input line from user}
    record
      line           : array [1..MAXLINE] of char;      {chars from user}
      length         : COUNTER;                         {number of chars entered}
      last           : COUNTER                          {last char examined by GetToken}
    end;
  TOKEN            = (LEFTPAREN, RIGHTPAREN, PLUS, MINUS, TIMES, DIVIDE,
                      EQUALS, SINFUNC, COSFUNC, EXPFUNC, LNFUNC, SQRTFUNC,
                      VARIABLE, NUMBER, NOMORE, UNKNOWN);
  ERRORTYPE        = (NORPAREN, NOLPAREN, NOFACTOR, EXCESS);
  ID               = array [1..MAXIDLEN] of char;
  NODEPTR          = ↑ NODE;
  NODE             =
    record
      op             : TOKEN;                           {the type of this node}
      value          : integer;                         {value if TOKEN is NUMBER}
      left, right    : NODEPTR                          {pointers to left and right subtrees}
    end;
var
  def              : boolean;                           {expression defined for current
                                                         value}
  experror         : boolean;                           {error in current expression}
```

FUNCDESC	: **array** [1..MAXFUNC] **of** ID;	{table of functions}
FUNCTOKEN	: **array** [1..MAXFUNC] **of** TOKEN;	{table of function tokens}
NextExpression	: NODEPTR;	{pointer to internal expression}
nexttoken	: TOKEN;	{next token in input}
nextval	: real;	{current value of expression variable}
num	: real;	{global if next token is a number}
points	: PLOTINFO;	{table of points to plot}
screen	: SCREENARRAY;	{screen representation}
tokenval	: ID;	{global if next token is a character string}
userinput	: INPUTTYPE;	{line of input from the user}
ZeroRow	: integer;	{the row where 0.0 is labeled}

```
#include "cursor.i";                            {direct cursor movement}
#include "NEWREADLN.i";                          {from Chapter 1}
```

function GetInput (**var** userinput : INPUTTYPE) : boolean;
{
Get a line of input from the user, storing it in userinput. We return true if we got any input,
false otherwise. The actual number of characters read is placed in the length field.
FROM CHAPTER 9
}

procedure getchar (**var** userinput : INPUTTYPE; **var** ch : char);
{
Places the next character in the input array into ch. If no more characters are there, a blank.
FROM CHAPTER 9
}

procedure ungetchar (**var** userinput : INPUTTYPE; **var** ch : char);
{
Undoes the last getchar so we can get the character over again later. If the character is a
blank, then there is no need to put it back, we would only skip it later.
FROM CHAPTER 9
}

(continued)

Figure 13.19. (continued)

```
function skipblanks (var userinput : INPUTTYPE) : boolean;
{
Skips blanks, and returns true if eoln is hit, and false otherwise. The last pointer is set to
the first nonblank character.
FROM CHAPTER 9
}

function ConvertExpression (userinput : INPUTTYPE) : NODEPTR;
{
Build the expression tree for the function.
The following routines are defined under ConvertExpression :
  GetToken
  expression
    makenode
    term
      factor
        subexpression
  ErrorHandler
}

  procedure GetToken (var userinput : INPUTTYPE);
  {
  Get the next token, returning the appropriate type, skipping any blanks.
  Defined under GetToken :
    Alphabetic
    Numeric
    SimpleToken
  FROM CHAPTER 9
  }

  procedure ErrorHandler (Error : ERRORTYPE);
  {Writes an error message and sets the global variable experror to true.}
  begin
    if not experror then begin
      experror := true;                                        {error in current expression}
      case Error of
        NOLPAREN : write ('Expected left parenthesis.');
        NORPAREN : write ('Expected right parenthesis.');
        NOFACTOR : write ('Expected factor.');
        EXCESS : write ('Expected OPERATOR after EXPRESSION.')
      end;
      ClearEOL
    end
  end; {ErrorHandler}
```

```
function MakeNode (op : TOKEN; value : real; left, right : NODEPTR) : NODEPTR;
var
  next : NODEPTR;
begin
  new (next);
  next ↑ .op := op;
  next ↑ .value := value;
  next ↑ .left := left;
  next ↑ .right := right;
  MakeNode := next
end; {MakeNode}


  function expression : NODEPTR;
  var
    op    : TOKEN;
    temp : NODEPTR;


    function term : NODEPTR;
    var
      op    : TOKEN;
      temp : NODEPTR;


      function factor : NODEPTR;
      var
        temp : NODEPTR;


        function subexpr : NODEPTR;
        var
          temp : NODEPTR;
        begin
          temp := nil;
          if nexttoken = LEFTPAREN then begin
            GetToken (userinput);
            temp := expression;
            if nexttoken <> RIGHTPAREN then
              ErrorHandler (NORPAREN)
            else
              GetToken (userinput)
          end;
          subexpr := temp
        end; {subexpr}
```

(continued)

Figure 13.19. (continued)

```
begin {factor}
   temp := nil;
   if nexttoken in [NUMBER, VARIABLE] then begin
      temp := MakeNode (nexttoken, num, nil, nil);
      GetToken (userinput)
   end else if nexttoken in [SINFUNC, COSFUNC, EXPFUNC,
                             LNFUNC, SQRTFUNC] then begin
      op := nexttoken;
      GetToken (userinput);
      temp := subexpr;
      if temp = nil then
         ErrorHandler (NOLPAREN)
      else
         temp := MakeNode (op, 0, temp, nil)
   end else
      temp := subexpr;
   factor := temp
end; {factor}


begin {term}
   temp := factor;                                    {get the factor}
   while nexttoken in [TIMES, DIVIDE] do begin
      op := nexttoken;
      GetToken (userinput);
      temp := MakeNode (op, 0, temp, factor)          {get possible other factor}
   end;
   term := temp
end; {term}


begin {expression}
   temp := term;
   while nexttoken in [PLUS, MINUS] do begin
      op := nexttoken;
      GetToken (userinput);
      temp := makenode (op, 0, temp, term)            {get possible other term}
   end;
   expression := temp
end; {expression}


begin {ConvertExpression}
   GetToken (userinput);
   ConvertExpression := expression;
```

```
      if nexttoken <> NOMORE then
        ErrorHandler (EXCESS)
    end; {ConvertExpression}

    function Evaluate (expr : NODEPTR) : real;
    {
    Evaluate the expression tree pointed to by expr, producing a single value for the tree. If a node
    represents a variable, the locally global value nextval is used. The locally global def is set to
    false if the result is undefined. If is assumed to have been set to true at the start.
    }
    var
      leftresult      : real;              {value returned from evaluating the left subtree}
      rightresult     : real;              {value returned from evaluating the right subtree}
    begin
      Evaluate := 0;
      if expr <> nil then begin            {tree empty? just exit}
        leftresult := Evaluate (expr ↑ .left);
        rightresult := Evaluate (expr ↑ .right);
        case expr ↑ .op of
          PLUS : Evaluate := leftresult + rightresult;
          MINUS : Evaluate := leftresult − rightresult;
          TIMES : Evaluate := leftresult ∗ rightresult;
          DIVIDE :
            if rightresult <> 0 then       {test for division by 0}
              Evaluate := leftresult/rightresult
            else
              def := false;
          NUMBER : Evaluate := expr ↑ .value;
          SQRTFUNC :
            if leftresult >= 0 then         {test for sqrt of negative number}
              Evaluate := sqrt (leftresult)
            else
              def := false;
          SINFUNC : Evaluate := sin (leftresult);
          COSFUNC : Evaluate := cos (leftresult);
          EXPFUNC : Evaluate := exp (leftresult);
          LNFUNC :
            if leftresult > 0 then          {ln defined only for positive number}
              Evaluate := ln (leftresult)
            else
              def := false;
          VARIABLE : Evaluate := nextval    {nextval is locally global}
        end
      end
    end; {Evaluate}
```

(continued)

Figure 13.19. (continued)

function *GetPoints* (**var** *points* : PLOTINFO; *expr* : NODEPTR) : *integer*;
{
Reads in points, saving them in an array so they can be printed out later. Also gathers some information about the points, including the maximum and minimum values for x and y, as well as the number of each value greater and less than zero. The number of points actually read in is returned as well as being placed into the *points* data structure.
FROM CHAPTER 9
}

procedure *updaterange* (**var** *minval, maxval* : *real; nxtval* : *real*);
{
Update the values of *minval* and *maxval* appropriately, depending on whether or not *nxtval* is the smallest or largest value so far.
FROM CHAPTER 9
}

procedure *plot* (**var** *screen* : SCREENARRAY; **var** *points* : PLOTINFO);
{
Places the axis and points into the screen array for later printing.
Defined under *plot*:
    plotaxis
    plotpoints
    computescale
FROM CHAPTER 7
}

procedure *WriteScreen* (**var** *screen* : SCREENARRAY);
{
Writes out the screen array. Uses a carriage return (CR) (via *writeln*) to go to the next line on the display.
FROM CHAPTER 7
}

procedure *LabelScreen* (*points* : PLOTINFO; *ZeroRow* : *integer*);
{
Places the min and max y values on the y axis and also labels the 0.0 point.
FROM CHAPTER 7
}

procedure *Initialize*;
{
Initializes various globals; opens plotting file for writing; gets terminal-specific information from the user.
FROM CHAPTER 9
}

```
begin {main}
  Initialize;
  while GetInput (userinput) do begin
    experror := false;                                      {no error yet}
    if userinput.length > MAXLINE then
      writeln ('Function is too long.')
    else begin
      NextExpression := ConvertExpression (userinput);      {convert to internal format}
      if experror then begin
        write ('Type CR to continue.');
        readln
      end;
      MoveCursor (FUNCLINE + 1, FUNCCOL);
      ClearEOL;
      if (NextExpression <> nil) and not experror then begin
        if GetPoints (points, NextExpression) > MAXPOINTS then
          writeln ('Too many points given.')
        else if points.count = 0 then
          writeln ('No points given.')
        else begin
          plot (screen, points);
          WriteScreen (screen);
          LabelScreen (points, ZeroRow)
        end
      end
    end
  end
end.
```

13.7 Efficiency

The program has been written to emphasize modularity, clarity of design and structure, and to conform to suggestions for module design of Chapter 4. To maintain module independence there has been some sacrifice in running time efficiency, and we identify those places here. However, countering this, we have written the program using top-down design and hierarchical refinement. Consequently, the program has been designed, coded, debugged, and tested more quickly than it would have had the emphasis been entirely on run-time efficiency.

We first encounter potentially detrimental effects on efficiency in *ConvertExpression*. This routine recursively builds the expression tree. Since the routines are recursively defined, there is a relatively large system overhead in control passage. More importantly, there are nonrecursive expression evaluation algorithms (using a stack, suggested in the exercises), that are generally faster. The length of the typical expression that is likely to be used with the function plotter, however, would tend to indicate that the amount of time actually spent in building the tree is quite small. Typical execution times for *ConvertExpression* amount to only about 0.5 percent of the total CPU time for the program. Whatever our thoughts might be about the efficiency of the recursive calls throughout *ConvertExpression* (actually, throughout *expression*), the actual running of the program with a number of sample functions shows that very little time is being spent in building the expression tree.

The expression tree must be repeatedly evaluated (*MAXPOINTS* number of times) for increasing values of *x*. Whether the expression is represented as a tree, or in some other form not requiring recursive procedure calls, we would expect *Evaluate* to be a potential bottleneck. The routine is recursively defined, and we note that it is called twice for each node, or token, in the tree. It is first called externally from *GetPoints*, once for each value of *x* (that is, *MAXPOINTS* times). For a typical small function with 10 tokens, the tree is evaluated about 20 times for each of 500 points, about 10,000 total calls to *Evaluate*!

We can predict that the plotting routines, *plot* and *WriteScreen*, will take time proportional to the number of points in the table of points. We note that *plot* takes each point in the table, multiplies it by an appropriate scaling factor to yield an index into the two-dimensional screen array, and writes the appropriate plotting symbol into the array. Then *WriteScreen* takes the screen array and loops through, writing points to the standard output. It should take time proportional to the size of the screen array.

If our main concern were running time efficiency, building the table of values (via *GetPoints*) and writing the screen array (via *plot*), could be performed simultaneously. In this case, the evaluation of the expression tree would include multiplying the values by an appropriate scale factor for *x* and for *y*. Unfortunately this requires the user to give not only the range of *x* values, but also the range of *y* values. Our specification indicated that the program should automatically scale the function's graph to fit onto the screen, and also allow the user to change the scale factor if he or she desires. In any event, given the substantial number of calls to *Evaluate*, we would not expect much time improvement by merging *GetPoints*, *plot*, and *WriteScreen*.

The program was run separately on a number of functions. Table 13.2 is the execution time profile for the program, run separately on two different functions. The first is for a plot of *cos(x)*, for *x* from 0 to 8 radians. The

Table 13.2. Execution time profiles for two functions.

Routine	% time	# calls	ms/call	Source
Evaluate	36.8	11,477	0.1	program
cos	27.2			system
GetPoints	4.7	1	150.0	program
WriteScreen	4.2	1	133.4	program
flsbuf	3.8			system
mcount	3.7			monitoring code
GetPoints_updaterange	3.7	996	0.1	program
plot_plotpoints	3.7	1	116.7	program

(a) Execution profile for $f(x) = \cos(x)$

Routine	% time	# calls	ms/call	Source
Evaluate	54.3	11,477	0.1	program
flsbuf	10.5			system
plot_plotpoints	6.0	1	116.7	program
GetPoints	4.3	1	83.3	program
WriteScreen	4.3	1	83.3	program

(b) Execution profile for $f(x) = x^3 - 14x^2$

second is a polynomial, x*x*x − 14*x*x ($x^3 - 14x^2$, 11 tokens). The tables are abbreviated to show only those routines that accounted for more than about 3 percent of the total CPU time. The tables give the percentage of the total running time spent in each routine, the number of times the routine was called, the time (in msecs) per call, and the source of the routine (that is, whether it is defined in the program or is a system call). Generally we have control over those routines we write ourselves, but little control over system routines.

All of the programs were run on a DEC VAX 11/750, running the Berkeley version of the UNIX operating system. The programs were compiled with the Berkeley UNIX Pascal compiler, which is able to include the additional code to generate the program profiles. The running times of the program are degraded by only a very small percentage by the inclusion of monitoring.

The first thing to note is that the program is spending anywhere from about 37 percent to as much as 54 percent of its time in *Evaluate*. In addition, note that some routines require a relatively large amount of time per call, but since they are called only once, their contribution to the total running time is very small. A substantial percentage of program time is being spent in the system-defined routines *cos, exp, ln,* and so on. In the first function, over 27 percent is in *cos.* Our conclusion for efficiency: focus attention on *Evaluate.*

(We might consider coding efficient in-line algorithms for the plotter's allowable functions *sin, cos, exp, ln,* and *sqrt.* However, these are often provided as particularly efficient assembly language routines, and it is difficult to improve on their efficiency.)

On examining the execution profiles of Table 13.2, we looked at *Evaluate* carefully to see if we could either improve its efficiency (time per call), or

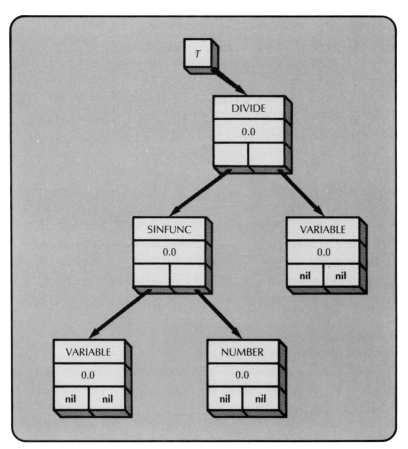

Figure 13.20. Expression tree of *sin(x)/x.*

reduce the number of recursive calls. Remember, we are making an external call to *Evaluate* once for each point in the plot, and recursively, twice for each node. It is in the internal calls that we find a source of inefficiency. We are calling *Evaluate* on the node's left and right subtrees, even if those subtrees are nonexistent (**nil**). In addition, we are calling *Evaluate* on both the left and right subtrees, even though some functions are unary (they require only a single operand: these are *sin*, *cos*, *ln*, *exp*, and *sqrt*). We see this in the expression tree for *sin(x)/x*. Note that the right subtree of *SINFUNC* is (always) 0. Also, any number or variable always has empty (**nil**) left and right subtrees (see Fig. 13.20).

We then made a change to *Evaluate*, so that the subtrees are evaluated (that is, the function is called) only when needed. The new function is shown in Fig. 13.21.

```
function Evaluate (expr : NODEPTR) : real;
{
Evaluate the expression tree, producing a single value for the tree. def is set to false if the
result is undefined. It is assumed to have been set to true at the start.
THIS IS THE MODIFIED, FASTER VERSION OF EVALUATE.
}
var
   leftresult            : real;
   rightresult           : real;
begin
   Evaluate := 0;
   if expr <> nil then begin
      case expr ↑ .op of
         PLUS: Evaluate := Evaluate(expr ↑ .left) + Evaluate(expr ↑ .right);
         MINUS: Evaluate := Evaluate(expr ↑ .left) − Evaluate(expr ↑ .right);
         TIMES: Evaluate := Evaluate(expr ↑ .left) * Evaluate(expr ↑ .right);
         DIVIDE:
            begin
               rightresult := Evaluate(expr ↑ .right);
               if rightresult <> 0 then
                  Evaluate := Evaluate(expr ↑ .left) / rightresult
               else
                  def := false
            end;
```

(continued)

Figure 13.21. Expression tree evaluation routine, modified for greater efficiency.

Figure 13.21. (continued)

```
NUMBER: Evaluate := expr ↑ .value;
SQRTFUNC:
  begin
    leftresult := Evaluate(expr ↑ .left);
    if leftresult >= 0 then
      Evaluate := sqrt(leftresult)
    else
      def := false
  end;
SINFUNC: Evaluate := sin (Evaluate (expr ↑ .left));
COSFUNC: Evaluate := cos(Evaluate (expr ↑ .left));
EXPFUNC: Evaluate := exp(Evaluate (expr ↑ .left));
LNFUNC:
  begin
    leftresult := Evaluate(expr ↑ .left);
    if leftresult <> 0 then
      Evaluate := ln(leftresult)
    else
      def := false
  end;
VARIABLE: Evaluate := nextval
  end
end; {Evaluate}
```

Running the same functions as with the previous examples, we obtained execution time percentages and routine calls that were substantially improved, shown in Table 13.3.

The time the program spends in *Evaluate* has been reduced from about 37 percent (with over 11,400 calls) to about 8 percent (and about 1000 calls) for the cosine function, and from about 54 percent (also with about 11,400 calls) to 29 percent for the polynomial (with about 5500 calls). Since this is time that the user is waiting for response from the program, this is an important and substantial improvement in program efficiency.

This example was not artificially constructed to be inefficient. Rather, it was designed for simplicity of design and structures, and for ease of implementation. We did not know in advance where the program would be spending its time, though we were able to predict that *Evaluate* might be a likely trouble spot. After the code was written, tested, and debugged to our satisfaction, we used execution monitors to let us know where the program was really spending its time. Based on this, we felt justified in

Table 13.3. Execution time profiles for two functions with efficient *evaluate.*				
Routine	**% time**	**# calls**	**ms/call**	**Source**
cos	13.7			system
WriteScreen	12.4	1	316.7	program
Evaluate	7.8	998	0.2	*program*
SUBSC	7.8			system
plot_plotpoints	7.2	1	183.4	program
GetPoints	5.2	1	133.4	program

(a) New execution profile for $f(x) = cos(x)$

Routine	**% time**	**# calls**	**ms/call**	**Source**
Evaluate	29.3	5,489	0.2	program
NIL	9.0			system
WriteScreen	9.0	1	316.7	program
SUBSC	6.1			system
plot_plotpoints	5.7	1	200.1	program
flsbuf	5.4			system
plot_plotaxis	5.2	1	183.4	program

(b) New execution profile for $f(x) = x^3 - 14x^2$

spending time in close examination of the code, specifically seeking running time improvements. That we were successful with very little effort is testimony to the advantages of this technique for program writing, monitoring, and refining.

Exercises

1. A number of additional commands would make the function plotter more useful. This exercise involves adding these commands. Most of these exercises involve modifying only a small portion of the function plotter.
   a) Modify the function plotter to require the user to type in all the letters in the command the user wants, rather than single-letter commands. (*Hint*: To do this requires only a minor modification to a table, and a few changes to *getcommand* from Chapter 9.) Does this make the function plotter easier or harder to use?

b) Add the commands "size", "xrange", and "yrange" to the function plotter. The size command sets the size of the graph the function plotter plots. It has two arguments: the number of columns and the number of rows. For example, "size 10 40" sets the size of the graph to 10 columns by 40 rows. The "xrange" and "yrange" commands set the range over which the x and y values of the function will be plotted. For example, "xrange − 3.0 + 5.0" means that x will be evaluated from − 3.0 to 5.0 when the y values of the function are computed. Any y values outside the "yrange" are ignored when the function is plotted. Set up some reasonable defaults for the size and range that should be printed when the program starts up. Of course, the size the user sets should not be greater than the maximum size graph the program can plot, or too small for a reasonable plot.

c) Modify the "plot" command to take the function the user wishes to plot as an argument. An example use of the "plot" command would be "plot $sin(x)/cos(x)$" to plot the tangent function. Note that the user no longer has to be prompted for the function to be plotted.

d) Add the command "overlay" to the function plotter. This command takes a function as an argument, and then plots this function on the same graph of the function last printed by the plot command. For example, "plot $sin(x)$" followed by "overlay $cos(x)$" results in a graph with the cosine function plotted on the same graph as the sine function.

e) Add the command "points" to the function plotter. This command sets the percentage of points plotted to the number of possible points on the graph. For example, the command sequence "size 20 20", "range 0 10", "points 25", "plot $sin(x)$" results in the sine function being evaluated at 100 (20*20 *.25) different x values ranging from 0.0 through 10.0.

f) Add the command "show" to the function plotter. This command prints the current size of the graph, ranges of x and y, and value of points.

g) Modify the function plotter so that the user needs to type only the minimum part of any command that disambiguates it from any other command. For example, rather than typing "plot", the user should be able to type "pl", since this disambiguates "plot" from "points." Of course, if the user types "plo" or "plot", that should still be recognized as the "plot" command. Inputs such as "plotthis" or "pluto" should be unrecognized commands and cause an error.

2. The function plotter currently accepts expressions such as "$sin(x)/cos(z)$". Modify the function plotter to require a single variable in the expression to be plotted instead of allowing many variables and assuming the user meant to use only one variable.

3. Add the functions *tan* (tangent), *asin* (arcsin), *acos* (arccos), *atan* (arctan), *trunc* (truncation), *round* (rounding), *sqr* (square: $sqr(x) = x*x$), *cube* (cube: $cube(x) = x*x*x$), *log* (log base 10), *abs* (absolute value), and *recip* (reciprocal: $recip(x) = 1/x$) to the function plotter. Make sure the values of these functions are defined for any x the function is evaluated with.

4. Add the "define" command to the function plotter. This allows the user to define new functions. For example, "define $quad(x) = x*x*x*x$" should define a new function *quad* which is x to the fourth power. Once a function has been defined, it can then be used like any built-in function. The user should be allowed to redefine any defined function. The user should not be allowed to recursively define functions. For example, the sequence "define $a(x) = sin(x)$", "define $b(x) = a(x)$", "define $c(x) = b(x)$", "define $a(x) = c(x)$" would result in the function $a(x)$ being defined in terms of itself and should be disallowed. Should the user be allowed to redefine the built-in functions *sqrt, sin, cos,* and so on?

5. Currently if a syntax error is discovered while the function plotter is building the expression tree, the tree is simply ignored. Since the tree is dynamically allocated, this means that whatever memory the tree used is no longer available to the program. To correct this, add the procedures *AllocateNodes*, *ResetUsed*, and *FakeNew* to the function plotter. The procedure *AllocateNodes* should allocate a group of empty expression tree nodes, keeping pointers to them in an array. The procedure *ResetUsed* sets the counter of currently used nodes to zero. The procedure *FakeNew* gets the next available node from the array that *AllocateNodes* created, adding one to the counter of currently used nodes. *AllocateNodes* should be called when the program starts, *FakeNew* whenever the program needs a new expression tree node, and *ResetUsed* before any expression tree is built.

6. [PROGRAMMING PROJECT] There are several techniques for approximating the *integral* of a function of a real variable x between a lower and an upper bound. One of the more common and intuitive techniques (though not the most accurate) is the trapezoidal rule. In this technique, the interval between x_{min} and x_{max} is divided into small pieces of size Δx, and the function $f(x)$ is approximated by the trapezoid defined at $(x_i, f(x_i))$ and $(x_i + \Delta x, f(x_i + \Delta x))$ (see Fig. 13.22). The integral is approximated by summing up the areas of all the trapezoids from x_{min} to x_{max}. The accuracy of the approximation depends on how small the interval Δx is: the smaller the interval, the more accurate the approximation. However, as the approximation becomes too small, the accuracy is reduced because of roundoff errors in the calculations of $x + \Delta x$ and $f(x)$.

Write a program that allows the user to interactively enter a function of a single real variable x and the minimum and maximum x values over which

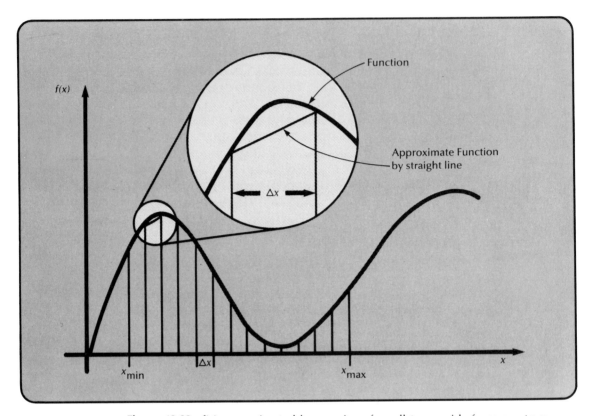

Figure 13.22. $f(x)$ approximated by a series of small trapezoids from x_{min} to x_{max}.

the integral will be approximated. Obtaining the function from the user should reuse the code already contained in this chapter for obtaining a function for the plotter. The new code involves interfacing the existing routines with your program and writing the code to approximate the integral. [*Hint*: This is an exercise in "reusable code," and should be thought of as such. You should be able to reuse the routines *GetExpression* (and all of the routines defined under it) and *Evaluate*. Your effort will be in adding the new routines to evaluate the expression at the appropriate values of x in order to calculate the areas, adding new routines for functions with singularities (points at which the function is undefined, and so on) and whatever additional error handling routines you feel are necessary.]

7. Modify the first parsing program (Fig. 13.14, program *PARSE*), so that it prints out the name of the parsing procedure as it's about to enter it. The

name of the procedure should be indented by the number of spaces of the depth of the level of calls. That is, since *expression* is called at the first level, its name should be indented one space. Then *expression* calls *term*, so its name should be indented two spaces and so on. Use a global variable *depth* that is incremented by one before each procedure call, and decremented by one after each call. *depth* is then used as a field width indicator in a *writeln* statement, such as *writeln(' ' : depth, 'Entering TERM')*.

8. Trace the action of the parser/tree builder described in Section 13.5.3 on the following strings. For each, indicate whether the string is a legal *expression*, and if so, draw the expression tree. If the string is not an *expression*, explain why.
   a) $a + b*c$
   b) $a\&b*c$
   c) $ab*c$
   d) $(a + b)*c$
   e) $a + b + c + d + e + f$
   f) $(a + (b + (c + (d + (e + f)))))$
   g) $a*b/c + d/e$

9. [PROGRAMMING PROJECT] An alternative parsing scheme to building expression trees directly converts the in-fix expression to the same post-fix form used in Chapter 9. The algorithm to do this explicitly specifies the precedence of each operator, rather than implying the operator precedence in the syntax diagrams. The following table gives the relative precedence of the usual operators (the larger the value, the higher the precedence).

Operator	Precedence
(	7
Unary $+, -$	6
$*, /$	5
$+, -$	4
)	0

The algorithm for converting from in-fix to post-fix is a simple three-step process:

1. Get the next token, No more? — done. Operand? — emit to output. Otherwise, go to 2.
2. Operator is ')'? No — go to 3. Pop the stack and emit to output, until a '(' is popped. Do not emit the '(' to the output. Go to 1.

3. If the operator has greater precedence than the operator at the top of the stack, push the operator onto the stack. Otherwise, pop the stack and emit to the output. Go to 3. (Note that this ensures that '(' always gets pushed.)

The only fly in the ointment deals with left parentheses. Left parentheses are used to imply that the following operations are to have highest precedence. So the expression $(a + b)*c$ should be converted to $a\ b + c\ *$. However, the algorithm implies that the '(' is pushed onto the stack, and then since the '+' has lower precedence than the '(', we should pop and emit the '('. To avoid this, and to ensure that the plus gets stacked properly (that it will have higher precedence than the '('), we change the precedence of the '(' when it is in the stack. That is, when comparing the current operator with the top of stack, we use a precedence of 0 for the '(' (instead of its original precedence of seven).

Write a routine that converts full in-fix expressions to the tokenized post-fix form used in Chapter 9. To test your routine, incorporate it into the function plotter of that chapter. Use the same data structure definitions, incorporating your code in *ConvertExpression*, a function that takes a record representing a line of input (type *INPUTTYPE*) and returns a pointer to a linked list representing the tokenized post-fix expression (of type *NODEPTR*).

MINICALC —
A MINIATURE SPREADSHEET

In Chapter 10 we introduced a number of multilinked data structures and a number of graph algorithms. In this chapter we put together a complete mini-spreadsheet program. This program is interesting for a number of reasons: it combines many of the data structures and algorithms of Parts III and IV (expression evaluation, multilinked representations, and graphs); it requires the program design, development, and testing strategies of Part II; and it offers the very nice prospect of highly modularized design (which means that it can be implemented in pieces); it provides a vehicle for well-designed user interfaces that can be adapted and expanded to higher capability displays; and it's an interesting program that's fun to use.

Even though this program is quite comprehensive, rather efficiently implemented, similar to programs that have proven to be of enormous commercial value, and over 1000 lines long (including comments, however), it is astounding that we are going to assemble it largely from "spare parts" and using algorithms and representations with which we are already familiar. Virtually the entire program involves pieces from other programs and algorithms that we've already developed. Our development of the program follows the overall outline of the entire book. First, we give an abbreviated functional specification for what the program is to do. Next, we look at the design top down. Then we decide on the appropriate data structures and algorithms. Finally, we write, test, and debug the program, and release it for general use.

The program is a miniature version of a spreadsheet program. It is designed to illuminate the coming together and culmination of the program design, development, and implementation concerns of this book. Of course, a number of useful capabilities are missing; it can serve as a vehicle for your own additional ideas and extensions.

14.1 Specification and Design

First, we should describe informally just what a "spreadsheet" is supposed to be. Simply, it is an interactive program that allows the user to create and calculate numerical information in a two-dimensional display and have values in one part of the display depend on values in another part. The fields within a display that depend on other parts are called "calculated fields." A spreadsheet program allows us to enter various kinds of information in each of the fields of the display: numbers, expressions that may depend on values in other fields, and labels. Commercial spreadsheet programs are among the largest selling personal and small business programs, and their capabilities and ease of use have been important in the success of the

personal computer market. They are used for business budgeting and forecasting, personal finances, income tax analysis and preparation, and a whole
range of similar purposes.

A simple example is shown in Table 14.1. Here we've created a sample
display for a small business that is projecting out its income and expenses
for three years. Table 14.1(a) shows the display as it is seen with data
entered. Table 14.1(b) shows the fields of the display with the formulas

Table 14.1. (a) Typical spreadsheet display for income forecasting. (b) Spreadsheet showing formulas for cells that depend on other cells. (c) Spreadsheet recalculated after income estimate has been changed.

	1983	1984	1985
Income	$125,000.00	$146,250.00	$171,112.50
Expenses	$132,000.00	$147,300.00	$165,201.00
Profit	$ (7,000.00)	$ (1,050.00)	$ 5,911.50

(a)

	A	B	C	D
1				
2		1983	1984	1985
3	Income	$ 125,000.00	1.17*B3 = $ 146,250.00	1.17*C3 $ 171,112.50
4	Expenses	42000 + .72*B3 = $ 132,000.00	42000 + .72*C3 = $ 147,300.00	42000 + .72*D3 = $ 165,201.00
5	Profit	B3 − B4 = $ (7,000.00)	C3 − C4 = $ (1,050.00)	D3 − D4 = $ 5,911.50

(b)

	1983	1984	1985
Income	$137,500.00	$160,875.00	$188,223.75
Expenses	$141,000.00	$157,830.00	$177,521.10
Profit	$ (3,500.00)	$ 3,045.00	$ 10,702.65

(c)

entered. Table 14.1(c) shows our modified projection of income for the year 1984 and highlights the changes that occur in the display. What makes a spreadsheet program useful is that these changes occur in real time. When a new value is entered for a cell, all fields that depend on that cell are recalculated, and the display is updated.

The formulas for income and expenses are functions of the (known) 1983 income: 1984 income is 1.17 times 1983 income, and 1985 is 1.17 times 1984. Expenses were considered to be 0.72 times income, plus a fixed expense of $42,000. Changes in either the multipliers, the fixed expense, or the base year income, will lead to changes in other fields.

14.1.1 Functional Specification

Input	The user enters a command indicating that he or she wishes to enter a cell ID and an expression or label for the cell. The system responds accordingly.
Output	The display is divided into cells, labeled A to H vertically, and 1 to 5 horizontally (see Fig. 14.1).

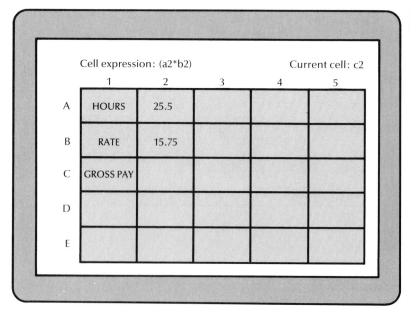

Figure 14.1. MiniCalc screen display.

| | The top line of the screen is used to indicate the new expression or value being entered for the cell, and the current expression or value for a given cell. The bottom two lines are command and system feedback lines. |

Commands
Each command is a single letter.
C — enter a cell ID. This becomes the current cell.
E — enter an expression or value for the current cell. If the expression is invalid, then the old value, expression, or label for the cell is retained.
L — enter a label for the current cell. If the label is invalid, then the old value, expression, or label for the cell is retained.

Expressions
The value in a cell may be a label or an expression, or the cell may be empty. An expression is a numerical constant, or an in-fix formula involving constant values and the contents of other cells. The operations allowed are the usual four functions (+, −, /, and ∗), unary minus, and the mathematical functions *sin*, *cos*, *ln*, *exp*, and *sqrt*. Parentheses are allowed in expressions, and may be nested to an arbitrary depth. It is an error for a cell to depend on another cell that contains a label. The value of an empty cell is assumed to be 0.0 for evaluation purposes. Since expressions for cells are entered interactively, a call can contain a legal expression that involves illegal values. For example, if *A1* = *sqrt(B1)*, and *B1* contains a negative number, the evaluation returns an "undefined" result. In such a case, the user is notified, an appropriate message is posted, and the value for the offending cell is set to 0.0. The expression, however, is valid. When the contents of *B1* are changed to a positive value, the expression is evaluated correctly.

User Interface
This is an interactive program. The user enters commands when the system is in command entry mode (which is at all times other than when it is calculating or updating the screen). Commands are single letters, as described.

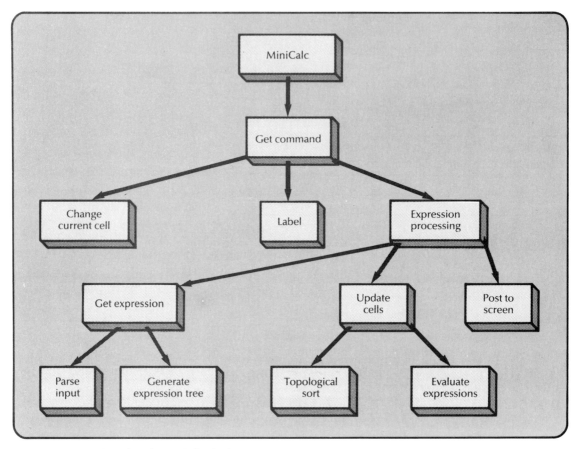

Figure 14.2. Highest level MiniCalc design.

Figure 14.3. Main program structure of MiniCalc.

```
begin {MiniCalc}
  {Initialization}
  ClearScreen;
  InitCells;
  WriteCells;
  {Main command loop}
  while GetCommand (nextcommand) do begin
    case nextcommand of
      HELP : DoHelp;
      CHANGECELL : DoCellChange (currcell);
      ENTEREXPR : DoCellExpr (currcell);
      ENTERLABEL : DoCellLabel (currcell);
      BAD : WriteUser (CMDLIST, CMDERRLINE)
    end;
    WriteUser (CMDPROMPT, CMDLINE)
  end
end.
```

Errors   Errors are flagged via simple error messages. The major classes of errors are incorrect command/ parameter entry, illegal expression entry, and mutual dependencies in the order of calculations. In the case of illegal expressions or mutual or recursive dependencies, an appropriate error message is displayed and the contents of all cells remain as they were before the incorrect or problem expression.

14.2 Program Design

The structure for MiniCalc naturally breaks into two distinct phases: getting an expression from the user and evaluating/updating the cells (Fig. 14.2). In fact, the overall structure is a bit more comprehensive, but we don't want to neglect these two essential functions.

The main program is quite simple: data structure and display initialization, followed by the main command loop. The program's structure is shown in Fig. 14.3. The highest level procedure calls are clearly seen in the command loop of that figure.

14.3 Data Structures and Algorithms

The data structures have already been seen for most of this program, in Chapter 13 (expression representation for the function plotter) and Chapter 10 (graphs). In those chapters we also investigated the appropriate algorithms, and developed an understanding of the concerns for efficiency (time) and memory use (space).

Our usual implementation scheme calls for us to do the best we can in selecting initial data structures and algorithms, but not to be overly worried about the last little bits of efficiency. We will use the algorithms and representations that we already know about. Only when our program is finished and in use will we run an instrumented version to see where, in fact, our program is spending its time.

Of equal concern with run-time efficiency, we wish to maximize our efficiency as program designers and implementors. We will design and begin coding under the assumption that errors will occur, and that a (somewhat) systematic test plan, with a representative group of users, will be performed.

14.3.1 Algorithms

The only new algorithm is concerned with the order of evaluating the cells in the display. As a simple example, suppose cell C1 is defined as:

$$C1 = B1*B2$$

Then we say that C1 depends on B1 and B2. Now suppose B1 and B2 are further defined in terms of other cells:

$$B1 = A1 + 15.5$$

$$B2 = B1 - A1$$

Here we see that B1 depends on the value in A1, and B2 depends on the values in both B1 and A1. A natural way to represent these dependencies is to use a directed graph. For each cell on which another depends (for example, we see that C1 depends on B1 and B2), we construct an edge from the vertex to the cell on the left of the equal sign. So, using the three sample equations just given, we have the graph of Fig. 14.4.

The order of evaluating the cells is easily determined when we look at the graph of Fig. 14.4. We obviously should first evaluate those cells that do not depend on any others. From Fig. 14.4, the only cell that does not need any other cell's value is A1.

Once the value in A1 is known, we are free then to evaluate B1 and B2. In a sense we "remove" A1 from the graph, producing a reduced graph

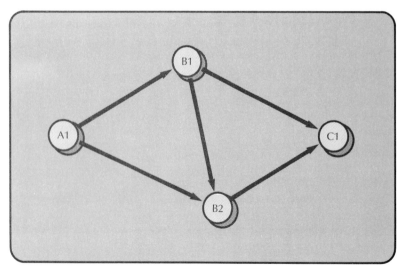

Figure 14.4. Graph of dependencies of sample equations for MiniCalc.

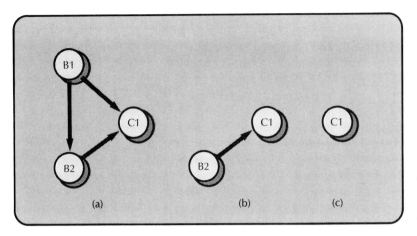

Figure 14.5. Stages in the removal of nodes from a graph during topological sort. (a) Graph of Fig. 14.4 with cell $A1$ removed. (b) Previous graph with $B1$ removed. (c) Previous graph with $B2$ removed.

as in Fig. 14.5(a). We continue like this, next evaluating $B1$, then $B2$, and finally $C1$. This process of examining the graph, looking for vertices with no dependencies, removing them and their edges, and continuing until the entire graph has been evaluated is called *topological sort*. It is the equivalent of taking the vertices of the graph and placing them on a straight line in such a way that, if we then evaluate the vertices left to right, no vertex is evaluated before all the vertices on which it depends have been evaluated. The topological sort of Fig. 14.4 produces the following list or ordering of the cells.

$$A1 \qquad B1 \qquad B2 \qquad C1$$

Note that if we attach the edges to this listing, all the edges point to the right:

$$A1 \qquad B1 \qquad B2 \qquad C1$$

In Section 14.4 we'll look in detail at the topological sort algorithm and how we incorporate it into the overall program design.

14.3.2 Data Structures

Clearly the two major operations to be performed on the display are expression evaluation and topological sort. All the information about the display is contained within the cells. Since the display is so obviously a two-dimensional structure, our representation of the display should be a two-dimensional array of cells. Within each cell we must keep the information necessary to

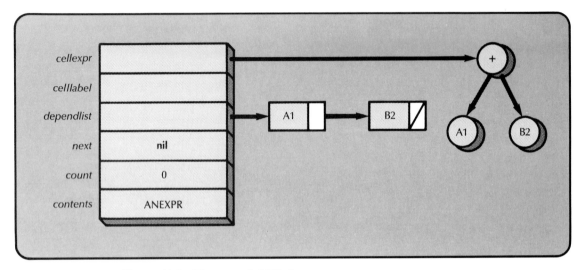

Figure 14.6. Diagram of *CELL* data type.

determine the value of the cell and to be able to perform the topological sort.

From the functional specification, each cell may contain a *label*, an *expression* (and its associated value), or a *value*, or it may be *empty*. In addition, we want to be able to implement an efficient topological sort, so we must know the identities of all cells on which the current one depends. That is, if the expression for cell *A*1 is *B*1 + *C*1, then *A*1 depends on *B*1 and *C*1. We define a data type, *CELL*, to look as shown in Fig. 14.6. We define its type with the declarations in Fig. 14.7. We show all of the constant and type declarations for the entire program, since they are rather hierarchically defined. Note in particular the definition of the *CELL* type. It contains the fields shown in Fig. 14.6, plus two additional ones, *next* and *count*, which are used during topological sorting.

The data type *CELL* contains six fields, with self-explanatory contents: *cellexpr* is a pointer to the expression tree for the cell; *celllabel* is the string label for this cell; *dependlist* is a pointer to a linked list of cell IDs on which the current cell depends; *next* and *count* are used during topological sort; and *contents* is an enumerated type indicating whether the cell contains a *value*, a *label*, or an *expression*, or whether it is *empty*. We distinguish between a *value* and an *expression* for efficiency in updating the screen. A cell with an expression must depend on other cells. A cell with a value only does not depend on others, and so its value cannot change during cell evaluation.

```
const
    BASECOL         = 5;                    {column cells start on}
    BASEROW         = 4;                    {row cells start on}
    CELLLINE        = 1;                    {line to get cells from}
    CMDERRLINE      = 23;                   {line for error messages}
    CMDLINE         = 22;                   {line to get commands}
    COLSPERCELL     = 10;                   {columns allowed inside cell}
    EXPRLINE        = 1;                    {line to get expressions from}
    FAKENIL         = 0;                    {dummy cell number}
    FIRSTCOL        = 1;                    {first column to write messages}
    MAXCOL          = 6;                    {last column label of cells}
    MAXIDLEN        = 10;                   {longest possible cell label}
    MAXLINE         = 60;                   {longest possible input line}
    MAXROW          = 'h';                  {last row label of cells}
    MINCOL          = 1;                    {first column label of cells}
    MINROW          = 'a';                  {first row label of cells}
    ROWSPERCELL     = 1;                    {rows allowed inside cell}
    SHOWCELLLINE    = 3;                    {line to show current cell}
type
    COUNTER         = 0..maxint;
    ROWINDEX        = MINROW..MAXROW;
    COLINDEX        = FAKENIL..MAXCOL;
    LINETYPE        = array [1..MAXLINE] of char;
    INPUTTYPE       =
      record
        line        : LINETYPE;            {user input line}
        length      : COUNTER;             {number of characters}
        last        : COUNTER              {last character looked at}
      end;
    TOKEN           = (SINFUNC, COSFUNC, EXPFUNC, LNFUNC, SQRTFUNC,
                       UMINUS, PLUS, MINUS, TIMES, DIVIDE, CELLLABEL,
                       LEFTPAREN, RIGHTPAREN, NUMBER, NOMORE, UNKNOWN,
                       ACELLNAME, BADCELL);             {various input tokens}
    USERMSGS        = (CMDPROMPT, CMDLIST, EXPRPROMPT, NORPAREN,
                       NOLPAREN, NOFACTOR, EXTRA, EXTRAJUNK, NOLABEL,
                       SORTFAILED, NOLINE, TOOLONG, TOOSHORT, CELLPROMPT,
                       LABELPROMPT, LABELDEPENDS, BADACELLNAME,
                       NOCURRCELL, BADCELLLABEL, SHOWCELLMSG);
    CELLCONTENTS    = (EMPTY, ANEXPR, AVALUE, ALABEL);
    COMMANDS        = (HELP, CHANGECELL,
                       ENTEREXPR, ENTERLABEL, BAD);     {MiniCalc commands}
    ID              = array [1..MAXIDLEN ] of char;
    NODEPTR         = ↑ NODE;
```

                                                                  (continued)

Figure 14.7. Data types used in MiniCalc.

Figure 14.7 (continued)

```
CELLID              =                               {identifies a cell}
   record
      name          : ROWINDEX;
      num           : COLINDEX
   end;
NODE                =                               {expression tree node}
   record
      cellname      : CELLID;
      op            : TOKEN;
      value         : real;
      left, right   : NODEPTR
   end;
DEPENDPTR           = ↑ DEPEND;                     {ptr to a dependency list node}
DEPEND              =                               {node in the dependency list of a cell}
   record
      dependee      : CELLID;
      next          : dependptr
   end;
CELL                =                               {individual cell in MiniCalc}
   record
      cellexpr      : NODEPTR;                       {ptr to expression for this cell}
      celllabel     : INPUTTYPE;                     {label for this cell}
      dependlist    : DEPENDPTR;                     {ptr to cells this one depends on}
      next          : CELLID;                        {next cell (used for top. sort)}
      count         : COUNTER;                       {in-degree of this cell (used for top. sort)}
      contents      : CELLCONTENTS                   {type of contents: EMPTY, AVALUE, etc.}
   end;
```

14.3.3 Reusable Code: Expression Evaluation

Expression entry and expression evaluation are "borrowed" from the function plotter of Chapter 13. The only change is that we must extend our notion of operands in an expression to include cell IDs; their essential structure, however, is identical. Remember that obtaining the expression from the user requires a complex set of actions: first, parse the input (and handle errors at that point), and then convert to internal representation (an expression tree). Parsing the input made use of the lower level procedure *GetToken* first described in Chapter 3, and used in two layers of the plotter in Chapters 9 and 13. Converting the in-fix expression to an expression tree requires the highly recursive functions *expression*, *term*, *factor*, and *subexpr* of Chapter 13. The ability to reuse all this code makes the implementation of the MiniCalc program an easier task.

The representation of the display as a graph of dependencies uses the graph structures of Chapter 10. Topological sort is a natural extension of the multilinked structures from that chapter. We take advantage of the fact that all changes are made incrementally. As a typical result, most of the graph will not participate in the topological sort and screen reevaluation on each new expression. Only those cells that are affected by the new expression need participate. As a result, we expect the topological sorting of the cells to be fairly efficient.

We have made many of the decisions on data structures and algorithms for the sake of efficiency, yet we have maintained the highly modular structure of the design. In examining the code, we see that the purpose of each routine and where each routine fits into the design are clear. However, before beginning to examine the code in detail, try to design for yourself the representations and algorithms that will support an efficient implementation. Many of the decisions, as discussed briefly here, are based on the fact that each expression entered usually results in only small changes to the totality of cells.

14.4 Determining the Order of Evaluation

In a spreadsheet, the values of cells are related by expressions to the values of other cells in the display. The screen is considered to be arranged into a grid of cells. For this example, we will use a mini display of size 5 by 5, that is, there are 5 rows, each containing 5 cells, as in Fig. 14.1 in the functional specification.

Each cell contains either an expression, or is considered to be "empty." An expression relates the value of the cell to the values of other cells. Using the cell numbering scheme shown in Fig. 14.1, we might use such a chart for constructing a simple payroll program. In cell $A2$ we enter the number of hours worked. In cell $B2$ we enter a rate of pay. Cell $C2$ is a computed cell; its value depends on the values of $A2$ and $B2$. The formula for cell $C2$ is:

$$C2 = A2*B2$$

The value of an empty cell is considered to be 0.0 by default.

We do not want to evaluate the expression for a cell until the cells it depends on have been evaluated and updated. We could, of course, simply evaluate the display in some fixed order: strictly left to right, top to bottom. However, if early cells (such as $A2$) depend on later cells, which in turn depend on other early cells, the contents of some cells will not correctly represent the functional relationships in the expressions. We'll need to develop a method of deciding on the order of evaluating the cells.

14.4.1 Discussion

We would like the entire screen to be updated whenever the contents of a cell is changed. Changes occur when a new value or formula for a cell is given. To calculate the value of a cell that contains an expression, we must evaluate the expression, supplying the current values of other cells on which the current cell depends. Remember that expression evaluation is a two-step process: first, convert the in-fix representation to an expression tree, and then evaluate the tree.

The problem comes in evaluating all the formulas. This is because, in general, a given cell cannot be evaluated until all cells on which it depends are also evaluated, and so on. Furthermore, there may be (illegal) mutual dependencies that we must detect so that we don't get into some form of infinite loop or other indeterminacy. For example, a simple set of formulas such as:

$$A1 = A3 + 1$$

$$A3 = A1 + 1$$

is mutually recursive. There are no values of $A1$ and $A3$ that will satisfy the relationship that $A1$ be $A3 + 1$ *and* $A3$ be $A1 + 1$. Fortunately, as we briefly discussed in Section 14.3, certain techniques provide an ordering of calculations such that all dependencies are satisfied before a formula is evaluated, and also check for mutual dependencies (mutual recursion).

The only difficulty we have is determining the correct order in which to evaluate the cells. Suppose, for example, that cell $A1$, the top left cell, has a formula such as $(B5 - A3)$. To evaluate $A1$, we must look at the contents of $B5$. But suppose $B5$ has a formula such as $(A3 - C2)$, and $A3$ has a formula such as $(A2*B1)$. Graphically the cells and their formulas look like Fig. 14.8. The final result of the cells depends on the order in which they are evaluated. In this case, however, there is a correct way to evaluate the cells, which we will determine by viewing the cells as vertices of a directed graph and by viewing the expressions as edges relating the vertices.

From Fig. 14.8, we construct a graph of the dependencies between cells. We say a cell i *depends on* cell j if j occurs in the expression for i. Cell $A1$ contains the expression $(B5 - A3)$. Thus $A1$ depends on both $B5$ and $A3$. These dependencies can be represented by the unweighted directed

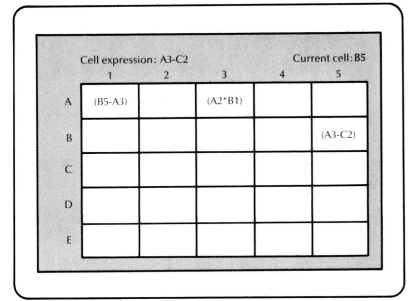

Cell expression: A3-C2   Current cell: B5

	1	2	3	4	5
A	(B5-A3)		(A2*B1)		
B					(A3-C2)
C					
D					
E					

Figure 14.8. MiniCalc display with expressions before evaluation.

graph of Fig. 14.9(a). The nonempty cells in Fig. 14.8 are represented by the graph in Fig. 14.9(b).

The graph of Fig. 14.9 implies an ordering relationship on evaluating the cells: if there is an edge from cell i to cell j, then we must evaluate cell i before cell j, and we say that cell i precedes cell j. Further, if there is an edge from i to j and an edge from j to k, then we have a path from i to k. This implies that cell i must be evaluated before cell k. If we have a series of these precedence relations, we would like to produce an ordering of the cells so that no cell is evaluated until all cells on which it depends have been evaluated, and so on. Such an ordering is called a *topological sort*. A topological sort (the topological sort of a given graph is not unique) of the cells in Fig. 14.8, represented by the graph of Fig. 14.9(b), is:

$$A2 \quad B1 \quad C2 \quad A3 \quad B5 \quad A1$$

That is, we first evaluate $A2$ (which, since it depends on no other cells, must contain a constant), then $B1$ (also a constant), then $C2$ (again a constant), now $A3$ (which depends on $A2$ and $B1$), then $B5$, and finally $A1$. Note that this is equivalent to laying all the cells in a straight line, with all edges pointing to the right, as we have shown earlier.

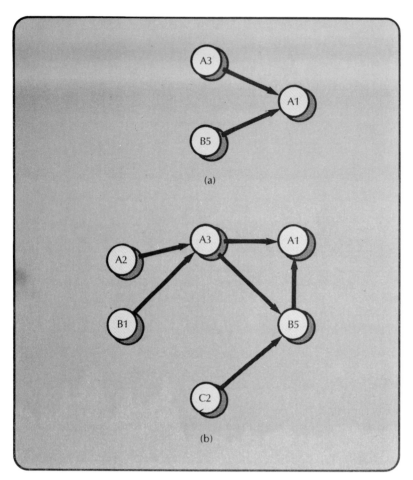

(a)

(b)

Figure 14.9. Directed graph representations of Figure 14.8. (a) Dependencies of cell *A*1. (b) All the dependencies of Fig. 14.8.

Figure 14.10. Modified graph for Figure 14.9. Cycles have been added by adding the edges (*B*1,*C*2) and (*A*1,*C*2).

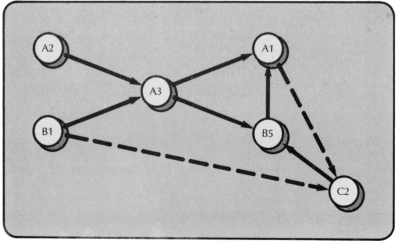

The only fly in this ointment is that the graph may contain a cycle. If we add an expression for $C2$, such as $(A1 - B1)$, we obtain the graph shown in Fig. 14.10. We have created a cycle from $C2$ to $B5$ to $A1$ and back to $C2$. In this case, there is no order of evaluation that will provide that all dependencies are met before a cell is evaluated. This is equivalent to laying all the vertices in a line and finding that one or more edges point back to the left. Such edges are called *back edges*. Fortunately the topological sort algorithm readily detects a cycle; the algorithm has a step that fails if and only if the graph contains a cycle.

If there are no cycles, we continue performing the topological sort, and then evaluate the array of cells in the order given by the sort. When all cells whose values have changed are updated, the new values are posted to the appropriate cells.

14.4.2 Topological Sort Algorithm

The topological sort uses a hybrid representation of the graph — a linked representation involving features of both the adjacency matrix and the adjacency list. To understand its major points, we will construct the algorithm using an adjacency matrix first. We then examine it for efficiency and suggest an alternative representation that will yield substantially faster processing on large cell arrays.

To understand what is required in topological sort, we do not want to lose sight of its purpose, which is to produce an order of evaluation of the cells such that no cell is evaluated before all the cells on which it depends are evaluated. We discover these dependencies by a suitable examination of the adjacency matrix for the graph. In the following adjacency matrix for the graph of Fig. 14.9 (the one without the cycles), only the nonzero entries are shown for clarity.

	A1	A2	A3	B1	B5	C2
A1						
A2			1			
A3	1				1	
B1			1			
B5	1					
C2					1	

From Fig. 14.9(b), it is clear that any of the three cells $A2$, $B1$, or $C2$ could be evaluated first. This is because these cells have no vertices adjacent to them (that is, they do not depend on the values of any other cells). We call the number of vertices adjacent to a given vertex its *in-degree*. In the

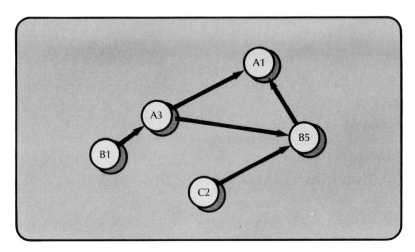

Figure 14.11. Graph of Fig. 14.9 with *A2* removed.

adjacency matrix, a vertex with zero in-degree is equivalent to an all-zero column. The column corresponding to A2 in the adjacency matrix is all 0's because there is no vertex with a directed edge to A2. The first step in the algorithm, then, is to find a column with no 1's. A2 is such a column, and we may put A2 into the topological sorted listing of the vertices. When we do this, we are assuming that A2 will be properly evaluated before any other vertex that needs A2. We simply remove A2 from the graph, and the new graph (with A2 and all edges from it removed) is shown in Fig. 14.11.

The effect of removing A2 from the graph, and all edges from it, is to zero out its *row* in the adjacency matrix. In the following new adjacency matrix, the (A2, A3) entry, which was previously 1, is now specifically shown as 0.

	A1	A2	A3	B1	B5	C2
A1						
A2			0			
A3	1				1	
B1			1			
B5	1					
C2					1	

We continue this process, searching for (new) all-zero columns, and then zeroing out that vertex's corresponding row. The next all-zero column is $B1$: we put $B1$ into the topologically sorted list, and remove it from the graph:

	A1	A2	A3	B1	B5	C2
A1						
A2			0			
A3	1				1	
B1			0			
B5	1				1	
C2						

Now note that there is a new, all-zero column, A3. We select A3 and remove it from the graph, then select B1, and C2, then B5, and finally A1. The topological sort using the preceding adjacency matrix is:

A2   B1   A3   C2   B5   A1

This algorithm has an important additional feature: if the graph has a cycle, the algorithm will reach a stage where *no* column contains all 0's. In fact, the result is even stronger: the algorithm will fail to find an all-zero column if and only if the graph has a cycle.

The algorithm is correct and will work quite well for small displays. But suppose we are dealing with very large spreadsheets; some commercially available ones allow a display of up to 200 by 200, or 40,000 cells. The adjacency matrix for the graph would then be as large as 40,000 by 40,000. Further, most of the operations on the graph involve searching for all-zero columns and removing a vertex by setting a row's entries to 0's. In most cases, the adjacency matrix will be *sparse* (that is, most entries will be 0), so we are spending a lot of time doing nothing. For computational efficiency, for extensibility to large displays, and for storage savings, we will use an adjacency list that allows us to perform the operations of finding all-zero columns and removing a vertex from the graph (or its equivalent, zeroing out a row) efficiently and with minimum storage requirements.

In examining the topological sort algorithm, we clearly see that the purpose of the columns of the matrix is to indicate the in-degree of the vertex. When the in-degree of a vertex is zero, we may add it to the topologically sorted list of vertices. We will use the representation of Fig. 14.12. This is an adjacency list similar to the ones of Chapter 10. The vertices in the graph are in the list pointed to by *Vertex*. In Fig. 14.12, *Vertex* points to cell A2, which points to A3, which points to B1, and so on. The adjacency list should point to each vertex (cell) that is adjacent from the given vertex. So A2 is adjacent to (points to) A3, A3 is adjacent to (points to) B5 and A1, and so on.

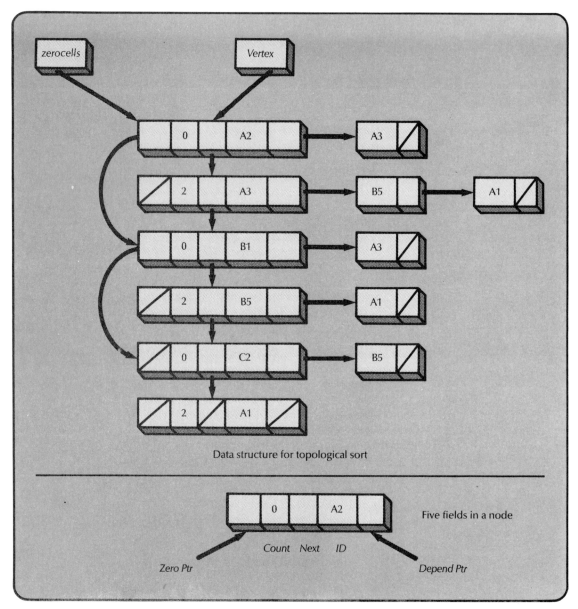

Data structure for topological sort

Five fields in a node

Count Next ID

Zero Ptr   Depend Ptr

Figure 14.12. Adjacency *from* lists with *count* fields and zero-linking fields.

To make it simpler to find the vertices with zero in-degree (nobody points to them), we include two additional fields in each node: *count*, which counts the in-degree of a vertex, and next, the name of the next vertex with zero in-degree. The first vertex with zero in-degree is named by a variable, called *zerocells*.

With the representation of Fig. 14.12, the algorithm becomes a simple three-step process of traversing lists and decrementing counts:

1. Remove the next vertex from the zero list. List empty? Either there is a cycle, or we are finished.
2. Traverse its adjacency list, decrementing the *count* field of each vertex on the list.
3. If any count becomes 0, place it at the head of the zero list. Go to step 1.

This algorithm is efficient in terms of space. It requires space for each cell in the graph, plus a node for each edge (we say that it requires space proportional to $V + E$, where V is the number of vertices and E is the number of edges). Compare this with the space required using the adjacency matrix: V^2. The computing time of the algorithm is equally efficient; it requires about the same time as the matrix representation to build the structure, but the time required to process the vertices is quite fast. The first step requires us to remove the first node from a list. This requires a constant, small amount of time regardless of the size of the list. The second and third steps combined are potentially the most time consuming. They require that we traverse a linked list and perform an action on each node in the list. As we just noted, these adjacency lists are equivalent to the rows of the adjacency matrix, and these can be expected to be sparse. The action performed is to decrement the *count* field of each vertex by one. We must find the vertex (or cell) in the list of active vertices. This step requires that we either search a linked linear list (and so requires time proportional to the size of the list), or that we use the cell ID as an index into an array.

Using an array requires a small fixed amount of time, but there is a price to pay. We must preallocate enough space for all vertices in the graph, and as we've seen, this can be quite large. However, for a display with N cells, this array is of size N, as contrasted with N^2 required in the adjacency matrix algorithm. The choice of best technique for finding the cell in the list involves a space-time tradeoff: faster execution, more space; less space, slower execution. In Fig. 14.13, we present the routine for performing the topological sort on a given representation, using the data definitions of Fig. 14.7. The graph is built in the function *BuildGraph*, seen in the complete program, Fig. 14.14.

```
function SortCells : boolean;
{
Performs the topological sort on the graph representing the functional dependencies in the
MiniCalc display. Returns true if there are no recursive dependencies (i.e., the graph is
acyclic); false, otherwise. The data structures are accessed as globals for efficiency.
}
var
  freecells           : COUNTER;
  nextdep             : DEPENDPTR;
  tempnextcell        : CELLID;
begin
  firstcell.num := FAKENIL;
  lastcell.num := FAKENIL;
  freecells := (ord(MAXROW) − ord (MINROW) + 1) * MAXCOL;
  while zerocells.num <> FAKENIL do begin
    tempnextcell := cells [zerocells.name, zerocells.num].next;
    freecells := freecells − 1;
    if firstcell.num := FAKENIL then begin
      firstcell := zerocells;
      cells [zerocells.name, zerocells.num].next.num := FAKENIL
    end else
      cells [lastcell.name, lastcell.num].next := zerocells;
    lastcell := zerocells;
    nextdep := cells [zerocells.name, zerocells.num].dependlist;
    zerocells := tempnextcell;
    while nextdep <> nil do begin
      with cells [nextdep ↑ .dependee.name, nextdep ↑ .dependee.num] do begin
        count := count − 1;
        if count = 0 then begin
          next := zerocells;
          zerocells := nextdep ↑ .dependee
        end
      end;
      nextdep := nextdep ↑ .next
    end
  end;
  SortCells := freecells = 0
end; {SortCells}
```

Figure 14.13. Topological sort routine used in MiniCalc.

14.5 MiniCalc: The Code

Figure 14.14 is the entire MiniCalc program. We show the entire program, even though there is a good deal of reused code (expression parsing and evaluation, and so on) because we want to impress on you the way we can often build useful programs quickly, by reusing parts (or at least ideas) from previous programs. In addition, this program uses the object packaging of ADTs that we first began using in Part III. At this point, a program such as this should hold no surprises; reading it and noting the routine names should be like visiting old friends. Because we've built the program using ideas from previous programs and using data structures that we've looked at in some detail, we have confidence in the code's correctness, even before we begin the usual code review and testing processes. So review the program with an eye toward seeing how familiar routines have been combined together. We hope you'll get as much satisfaction out of this program — using it, adding to it (maybe even finding bugs in it!) — as we did.

```
program MiniCalc (input, output);
{
DESCRIPTION:        A simple spreadsheet program. The screen is divided into individual
                    cells. Each cell may contain a real value, a label, or an expression.
                    Expressions involve the usual arithmetic operations, simple trigonometric
                    functions, square root, natural log, etc. When an expression is entered for
                    a cell, all other cells with expressions that depend on it are recalculated,
                    and the new values posted to the screen.
INPUT:              This is an interactive, command-based program. Single letter commands
                    are entered from the command line. Commands are help, change the
                    current cell, enter an expression for the current cell, and enter a label for
                    the current cell.
OUTPUT:             The array of cells is drawn on the screen, with vertical and horizontal
                    lines separating the cells. Labels are written truncated to the constant
                    COLSPERCELL (currently 10). Reals are written also using COLSPERCELL
                    space, with two spaces to the right of the decimal point.
}
const
  BASECOL       = 5;               {column cells start on}
  BASEROW       = 4;               {row cells start on}
  CELLLINE      = 1;               {line to get cells from}
  CMDERRLINE    = 23;              {line for error messages}
```

(continued)

Figure 14.14. The complete MiniCalc program.

Figure 14.14. (continued)

```
CMDLINE            = 22;                    {line to get commands on}
COLSPERCELL        = 10;                    {columns allowed inside cell}
EXPRLINE           = 1;                     {line to get expressions from}
FAKENIL            = 0;                     {dummy cell number}
FIRSTCOL           = 1;                     {first column to write messages to}
MAXCOL             = 6;                     {last column label of cells}
MAXIDLEN           = 10;                    {longest possible cell label}
MAXLINE            = 60;                    {longest possible input line}
MAXROW             = 'h';                   {last row label of cells}
MINCOL             = 1;                     {first column label of cells}
MINROW             = 'a';                   {first row label of cells}
ROWSPERCELL        = 1;                     {rows allowed inside cell}
SHOWCELLLINE       = 3;                     {line to show current cell on}
type
  COUNTER          = 0..maxint;
  ROWINDEX         = MINROW..MAXROW;
  COLINDEX         = FAKENIL..MAXCOL;
  LINETYPE         = array [1..MAXLINE] of char;
  INPUTTYPE        =
    record
      line         : LINETYPE;             {user input line}
      length       : COUNTER;              {number of characters}
      last         : COUNTER               {last character looked at}
    end;
  TOKEN            = (SINFUNC, COSFUNC, EXPFUNC, LNFUNC, SQRTFUNC,
                     UMINUS, PLUS, MINUS, TIMES, DIVIDE, CELLLABEL,
                     LEFTPAREN, RIGHTPAREN, NUMBER, NOMORE, UNKNOWN,
                     ACELLNAME, BADCELL);              {various input tokens}
  USERMSGS         = (CMDPROMPT, CMDLIST, EXPRPROMPT, NORPAREN,
                     NOLPAREN, NOFACTOR, EXTRA, EXTRAJUNK, NOLABEL,
                     SORTFAILED, NOLINE, TOOLONG, TOOSHORT, CELLPROMPT,
                     LABELPROMPT, LABELDEPENDS, BADACELLNAME, NOCURRCELL,
                     BADCELLLABEL, SHOWCELLMSG);
  CELLCONTENTS     = (EMPTY, ANEXPR, AVALUE, ALABEL);
  COMMANDS         = (HELP, CHANGECELL,
                     ENTEREXPR, ENTERLABEL, BAD);      {MiniCalc commands}
  ID               = array [1..MAXIDLEN] of char;
  NODEPTR          = ↑ NODE;
  CELLID           =                                   {identifies a cell}
    record
      name         : ROWINDEX;
      num          : COLINDEX
    end;
```

```
NODE                =                          {expression tree node}
   record
      cellname      : CELLID;
      op            : TOKEN;
      value         : real;
      left, right   : NODEPTR
   end;
DEPENDPTR           = ↑ DEPEND;               {ptr to a dependency list node}
DEPEND              =                          {node in the dependency list of a cell}
   record
      dependee      : CELLID;
      next          : DEPENDPTR
   end;
CELL                =                          {individual cell in MiniCalc}
   record
      cellexpr      : NODEPTR;                 {ptr to expression for this cell}
      celllabel     : INPUTTYPE;               {label for this cell}
      dependlist    : DEPENDPTR;               {ptr to cells this one depends on}
      next          : CELLID;                  {next cell (used for top. sort)}
      count         : COUNTER;                 {in-degree of this cell (used for top. sort)}
      contents      : CELLCONTENTS             {type of contents: EMPTY, AVALUE, etc.}
   end;
var
   funcdesc         : array [SINFUNC..SQRTFUNC] of ID;        {function name table}
   cells            : array [ROWINDEX, COLINDEX] of CELL;     {calculator cells}
   nextcommand      : COMMANDS;
   currcell         : CELLID;

#include "cursor.i";                          {direct cursor positioning}

   procedure WriteCells;
   {Writes the empty cell display on the screen with labeled cells.}
   const
      BOTTOM        = '=';                      {bottom border of last cells}
      EMPTYCELL     = ' ';                      {contents of an empty cell}
      INTERSECT     = '+';                      {where cells intersect}
      NOLABEL       = ' ';                      {used if row has no label}
      SIDEBORDER    = '|';                      {separates cells on side}
      TOPBORDER     = '-';                      {separates cells on top}
   var
      nextcol       : integer;
      nextrow       : char;
```

(continued)

Figure 14.14. (continued)

```
procedure WriteCellRow (border, filler, celllabel : char);
{
Writes one row of a cell in a nice format, with an optional label. This is used to write the
outsides of the cell on the screen.
}
var
  nextcell        : integer;
  nextcol         : integer;
begin
  write (celllabel , ' ');
  for nextcell := MINCOL to MAXCOL do begin
    write (border);
    for nextcol := 1 to COLSPERCELL do
      write (filler)
  end;
  writeln (border)
end; {WriteCellRow}

begin {WriteCells}
  MoveCursor (BASEROW, FIRSTCOL);
  for nextcol := MINCOL to MAXCOL do
    write (' ' : COLLSPERCELL, nextcol : 1);
  writeln;
  for nextrow := MINROW to MAXROW do begin
    WriteCellRow (INTERSECT, TOPBORDER, NOLABEL);
    WriteCellRow (SIDEBORDER, EMPTYCELL, nextrow)
  end;
  WriteCellRow (INTERSECT, BOTTOM, NOLABEL)
end; {WriteCells}

procedure WriteUser (msg : USERMSGS; line : integer);
{Goes to particular line on the screen, blanks it out, and then writes a message there.}
begin
  MoveCursor (line, FIRSTCOL);
  ClearEOL;
  case msg of
    CMDPROMPT      : write ('Command : ');
    CMDLIST        : write ('Commands : c(ell), h(elp), e(xpression), l(abel), q(uit)');
    NOLPAREN       : write ('Expected left parenthesis');
    NORPAREN       : write ('Expected right parenthesis');
```

```
        NOFACTOR        : write ('Unrecognized token in expression');
        EXTRA           : write ('Operator missing after an expression');
        EXTRAJUNK       : write ('Extra characters in an expression or cell name');
        EXPRPROMPT      : write ('Cell Expression : ');
        CELLPROMPT      : write ('Change to Cell : ');
        LABELPROMPT     : write ('Label of Cell : ');
        TOOLONG         : write ('Input line was too long');
        TOOSHORT        : write ('Empty input line ');
        BADACELLNAME    : write ('Bad cell name given');
        LABELDEPENDS    : write ('Cells may not depend on labels');
        BADCELLLABEL    : write ('Expected a cell name, function or operator');
        NOLABEL         : write ('Can't place a label : other cells depend on this cell');
        NOCURRCELL      : write ('No current cell yet');
        SORTFAILED      : write ('Attempt to create a recursive dependency');
        SHOWCELLMSG     : write ('Current cell is : ')
    end
end; {WriteUser}


function GetInp (var userinp : INPUTTYPE) : boolean;
{
Get a line of input from the user, storing it in userinp. Return true if we got any input, false
otherwise. The actual number of characters read in is placed in the length field.
}
var
    ch : char;
begin
    userinp.length := 0;
    userinp.last := 0;
    if eof then
        GetInp := false
    else begin
        while not eoln do begin
            read (ch);
            userinp.length := userinp.length + 1;
            if userinp.length <= MAXLINE then
                userinp.line [userinp.length] := ch
        end;
        readln;                                      {read the eoln char}
        GetInp := true
    end
end; {GetInp}
```

(continued)

Figure 14.14. (continued)

```
function GetUserInput (var userinp : INPUTTYPE) : boolean;
{
Gets the input from the user, and makes sure it is the appropriate length (informing the user
if it isn't).
}
begin
  GerUserInput := false;
  if not GetInp (userinp) then
    WriteUser (NOLINE, CMDERRLINE)
  else if userinp.length > MAXLINE then begin
    GetUserInput := true;
    userinp.length := MAXLINE
  end else if userinp.length = 0 then
    WriteUser (TOOSHORT, CMDERRLINE)
  else
    GetUserInput := true
end; {GetUserInput}

procedure WriteUserInput (userinp : INPUTTYPE; maxlen : COUNTER);
{
Writes the first maxlen characters of userinp to the current location on the screen. Pads with
blanks so that maxlen chars are always written.
}
var
  next : COUNTER;
begin
  next := 1;
  while (next <= maxlen) and (next <= userinp.length) do begin
    write (userinp.line [next]);
    next := next + 1
  end;
  if next <= maxlen then                          {pad with blanks}
    write (' ' : maxlen - next + 1)
end; {WriteUserInput}

procedure GetChar (var userinp : INPUTTYPE; var ch : char);
{
Places the next character in the input array into ch, or if at the end of the array, a blank.
Called by GetToken to get the next character in the input token.
}
begin
  if userinp.last < userinp.length then begin
    userinp.last := userinp.last + 1;
    ch := userinp.line [userinp.last]
  end else
    ch := ' '
end; {GetChar}
```

```
procedure UnGetChar (var userinp : INPUTTYPE; var ch : char);
{
Undoes the last GetChar so we can get the character again later. If the character is a blank,
then there is no need to put it back, we would only skip it later. Called by GetToken.
}
begin
  if ch <> ' ' then
    userinp.last := userinp.last − 1
end; {UnGetChar}
function SkipBlanks (var userinp : INPUTTYPE) : boolean;
{
Skips blanks, and returns true if eoln is hit, false otherwise. The last field is set to the first
nonblank character.
}
var
  blank : boolean;
begin
  blank := true;
  while (userinp.last < userinp.length) and blank do begin
    userinp.last := userinp.last + 1;
    if userinp.line [userinp.last] <> ' ' then
      blank := false
  end;
  if not blank then
    userinp.last := userinp.last − 1;
  SkipBlanks := blank
end; {SkipBlanks}
procedure GetToken (var userinp : INPUTTYPE; var nexttoken : TOKEN;
                    var num : real; var field : CELLID);
{
Places the type of the next token in the user input line into nexttoken, and if that token is a
number, its value into num. Uses GetChar to get characters as it builds up tokens. Since we
don't know if we are done with a token until we have read one character past the end of it,
we use UnGetChar to put that character back. SkipBlanks is used to skip any blanks before
the current token. If there are no more characters in the line, the token NOMORE is
returned, and if we can't figure out what token this is, the token UNKNOWN is returned.
}
type
  CHARSET       = set of CHAR;
var
  ch            : char;           {next character to build token with}
  DIGITS        : CHARSET;        {numeric digits}
  IDCHARS       : CHARSET;        {legal chars in function/ID name}
  LOWER         : CHARSET;        {lower case letters}
  OPERATORS     : CHARSET;        {legal operators}
  UPPER         : CHARSET;        {upper case letters}          (continued)
```

Figure 14.14. (continued)

function *Alphabetic* (**var** *ch* : *char*; **var** *userinp* : *INPUTTYPE*; **var** *field* : *CELLID*) : *TOKEN*;
{Figures out whether the next token is a variable or a function, and returns the correct token.}
var

next	: *integer*;	{pointer to next saved token}
nextfunc	: *TOKEN*;	{next function in table}
tempch	: *char*;	{for extra character lookahead}
tokenval	: *ID*;	{current token}

function *GetCell* (**var** *ch* : *char*; **var** *userinp* : *INPUTTYPE*; **var** *field* : *CELLID*) : *boolean*;
{
Figures out if the next token is a cell name and returns the cell name and cell value, return *true* if this token is a cell name, and *false* otherwise. There is a side effect that the first character read in is placed as the cell name, whether or not this really is a cell name.
}
var
  number : *integer*;
begin
  GetCell := *false*;
  tempch := *ch*;   {save us from letters out of cell range}
  GetChar (*userinp*, *ch*);
  if *ch* **in** *DIGITS* **then begin**
    number := 0;
    while *ch* **in** *DIGITS* **do begin**
      number := *number* * 10 + (ord (*ch*) − ord ('0'));
      GetChar (*userinp*, *ch*)
    end;
    UnGetChar (*userinp*, *ch*);
    GetCell := *true*;
    if (*number* < *MINCOL*) **or** (*number* > *MAXCOL*) **or**
        (*tempch* < *MINROW*) **or** (*tempch* > *MAXROW*) **then**
      Alphabetic := *BADCELL*
    else begin
      Alphabetic := *ACELLNAME*;
      field.name := *tempch*;
      field.num := *number*
    end
  end else
    UnGetChar (*userinp*, *ch*)
end; {GetCell}

```
begin {Alphabetic}
  if not GetCell (ch, userinp, field) then begin
    ch := tempch;
    next := 0;
    tokenval := '     ';                    {initialize to blanks}
    while ch in IDCHARS do begin
      next := next + 1;
      if next <= MAXIDLEN then begin
        tokenval [next] := ch;
        GetChar (userinp, ch)
      end
    end;
    UnGetChar (userinp, ch);
    Alphabetic := CELLLABEL;
    for nextfunc := SINFUNC to SQRTFUNC do
      if funcdesc [nextfunc] = tokenval then
        Alphabetic := nextfunc
  end
end; {Alphabetic}
function Numeric (var ch : char; var userinp : INPUTTYPE) : real;
{
Called when the first character of the current token is known to be a digit, Numeric
returns the actual real value of that token.
}
var
  factor           : real;
  frac             : real;
  num              : real;
begin
  num := 0.0;
  frac := 0.0;
  factor := 0.1;
  nexttoken := NUMBER;
  while ch in DIGITS do begin
    num := num * 10 + (ord (ch) − ord ('0'));
    GetChar (userinp, ch)
  end;
  if ch = '.' then begin
    GetChar (userinp, ch);
    while ch in DIGITS do begin
      frac := frac + (ord (ch) − ord ('0')) * factor;
      factor := factor * 0.1;
      GetChar (userinp, ch)
    end
  end;
  UnGetChar (userinp, ch);
  Numeric := num + frac
end; {Numeric}
```

(continued)

Figure 14.14. (continued)

```
procedure SimpleToken (ch : char);
{Token is one of the one-symbol tokens.}
begin
  case ch of
    '+' : nexttoken := PLUS;
    '−' : nexttoken := MINUS;
    '*' : nexttoken := TIMES;
    '/' : nexttoken := DIVIDE;
    '(' : nexttoken := LEFTPAREN;
    ')' : nexttoken := RIGHTPAREN
  end
end; {SimpleToken}


begin {GetToken}
  DIGITS := ['0'..'9'];
  LOWER := ['a'..'z'];
  UPPER := ['A'..'Z'];
  IDCHARS := LOWER + UPPER;
  OPERATORS := ['+', '−', '*', '/', '(', ')'];
  nexttoken := UNKNOWN;
  if SkipBlanks (userinp) then
    nexttoken := NOMORE
  else begin
    GetChar (userinp, ch);
    if ch in OPERATORS then
      SimpleToken (ch)
    else if ch in IDCHARS then begin
      if ch in UPPER then                    {convert to lower case}
        ch := chr (ord (ch) − ord ('A') + ord ('a'));
      nexttoken := Alphabetic (ch, userinp, field)
    end else if ch in DIGITS then
      num := Numeric (ch, userinp)
  end
end; {GetToken}


procedure WriteExpression (expr : NODEPTR; level : COUNTER);
{Writes out the expression tree pointed to by expr.}
begin
  if expr <> nil then begin
    if expr↑.op = NUMBER then
      write (expr↑.value : 1 : 2)
    else if expr↑.op = ACELLNAME then
      write (expr↑.cellname.name, expr↑.cellname.num : 1)
```

```
    else if expr↑.op in [MINUS, PLUS, TIMES, DIVIDE] then begin
      if level <> 0 then
        write ('(');
      WriteExpression (expr↑.left, level + 1);
      case expr↑.op of
        MINUS   : write ('−');
        PLUS    : write ('+');
        TIMES   : write ('*');
        DIVIDE  : write ('/')
      end;
      WriteExpression (expr↑.right, level + 1);
      if level <> 0 then
        write (')')
    end else begin
      case expr↑.op of
        COSFUNC  : write ('cos');
        EXPFUNC  : write ('exp');
        LNFUNC   : write ('ln');
        SINFUNC  : write ('sin');
        SQRTFUNC : write ('sqr');
        UMINUS   : write ('−')
      end;
      write ('(');
      WriteExpression (expr↑.left, 0);
      write (')')
    end
  end
end; {WriteExpression}

procedure MoveToCell (cellrow : ROWINDEX; cellcol : COLINDEX);
{Move to the appropriate place on the screen so that values can be posted to this cell.}
var
  coloffset           : integer;
  rowoffset           : integer;
begin
  rowoffset := (ord (cellrow) − ord (MINROW) + 1) * (ROWSPERCELL + 1);
  coloffset := (cellcol − MINCOL) * (COLSPERCELL + 1);
  MoveCursor (BASEROW + rowoffset, BASECOL + coloffset)
end; {MoveToCell}

procedure PostLabel (cellrow : ROWINDEX; cellcol : COLINDEX; value : INPUTTYPE);
{Post the nonnumeric value to the correct cell. We truncate extra characters.}
begin
  MoveToCell (cellrow, cellcol);
  WriteUserInput (value, COLSPERCELL)
end; {PostLabel}
```

(continued)

Figure 14.14. (continued)

function *Evaluate* (*expr* : NODEPTR; **var** *defined* : *boolean*) : *real*;
{
Evaluate the expression tree, producing a single value for each point in the tree. It is noted if
the point is undefined. Modified from the function plotter to handle cell IDs.
}

var
  leftresult   : *real*;
  rightresult   : *real*;
begin
  Evaluate := 0;
  if *expr* <> **nil then begin**
    if not (*expr* ↑ .*op* **in** [*ACELLNAME, NUMBER*]) **then begin**
      leftresult := *Evaluate* (*expr* ↑ .*left, defined*);
      if *expr* ↑ .*op* **in** [*PLUS, MINUS, TIMES, DIVIDE*] **then**
        rightresult := *Evaluate* (*expr* ↑ .*right, defined*)
    end;
    case *expr* ↑ .*op* **of**
      UMINUS : *Evaluate* := − *leftresult*;
      PLUS   : *Evaluate* := *leftresult* + *rightresult*;
      MINUS   : *Evaluate* := *leftresult* − *rightresult*;
      TIMES   : *Evaluate* := *leftresult* * *rightresult*;
      DIVIDE   :
        if *rightresult* <> 0 **then**
          Evaluate := *leftresult* / *rightresult*
        else
          defined := *false*;
      NUMBER : *Evaluate* := *expr* ↑ .*value*;
      SQRTFUNC :
        if *leftresult* >= 0 **then**
          Evaluate := *sqrt* (*leftresult*)
        else
          defined := *false*;
      SINFUNC : *Evaluate* := *sin* (*leftresult*);
      COSFUNC : *Evaluate* := *cos* (*leftresult*);
      EXPFUNC : *Evaluate* := *exp* (*leftresult*);
      LNFUNC   :
        if *leftresult* > 0 **then**
          Evaluate := *ln* (*leftresult*)
        else
          defined := *false*;

```
    ACELLNAME :
      with expr ↑ .cellname do
        Evaluate := Evaluate (cells [name, num].cellexpr, defined);
      CELLLABEL : defined := false
    end
  end
end; {Evaluate}




function GetCommand (var command : COMMANDS) : boolean;
{
Get a single letter command from the user, making sure it is in the set of valid commands.
Returns true if command is legal, false otherwise. If command is not legal, it is set to BAD.
}
var
  ch              : char;
  userinp         : INPUTTYPE;
begin
  GetCommand := false;
  command := BAD;
  if not GetInp (userinp) then
    WriteUser (NOLINE, CMDERRLINE)
  else begin
    GetCommand := true;
    if not SkipBlanks (userinp) then begin
      GetChar (userinp, ch);
      if SkipBlanks (userinp) then
        if ch in ['c', 'C', 'e', 'E', 'h', 'H', 'l', 'L'] then
          case ch of
            'c', 'C'  : command := CHANGECELL;
            'e', 'E'  : command := ENTEREXPR;
            'h', 'H'  : command := HELP;
            'l', 'L'  : command := ENTERLABEL
          end
        else if ch in ['q', 'Q'] then
          GetCommand := false
    end
  end
end; {GetCommand}
```

(continued)

Figure 14.14. (continued)

```
procedure DoCellChange (var currcell : CELLID);
{
Changes the current cell to a new cell. This is useful because all expression and label
changes affect the current cell. Checks for errors before the current cell is changed.
}
var
  field           : CELLID;
  nexttoken       : TOKEN;
  num             : real;
  userinp         : INPUTTYPE;
begin
  WriteUser (CELLPROMPT, CELLLINE);
  if GetUserInput (userinp) then begin
    GetToken (userinp, nexttoken, num, field);
    if nexttoken <> ACELLNAME then
      WriteUser (BADACELLNAME , CMDERRLINE)
    else begin
      currcell := field;
      WriteUser (SHOWCELLMSG, SHOWCELLLINE);
      write (currcell.name, currcell.num : 1, ' ');
      with cells [currcell.name, currcell.num] do
        if contents = ANEXPR then
          WriteExpression (cellexpr, 0)
        else if contents = ALABEL then
          WriteUserInput (celllabel, COLSPERCELL)
    end;
    GetToken (userinp, nexttoken, num, field);
    if nexttoken <> NOMORE then
      WriteUser (EXTRAJUNK, CMDERRLINE)
  end
end; {DoCellChange}




procedure DoCellExpr (nextcell : CELLID);
{Places a new expression in the current cell.}
var
  firstcell       : CELLID;
  lastcell        : CELLID;
  nextexpr        : NODEPTR;
  zerocells       : CELLID;
```

function GetExpression : NODEPTR;

{

Gets an expression from the user, returning a pointer to the parse tree representing that expression if there are no errors.

}

var

　　userinp : INPUTTYPE;

function ParseExpression (userinp : INPUTTYPE) : NODEPTR;

{

Parse the input expression, building an expression tree as we parse. Uses GetToken to get the next token in the input. The internal procedures expression, factor, term and subexpression are based on the syntax diagrams in Chapter 13. This is the same as ParseFunction in the function plotter, with the changes necessary to handle cell tokens.

}

var

error	: boolean;	{syntax error flag}
field	: CELLID;	{current cell name/number}
FUNCTIONS	: **set of** TOKENS;	{legal functions}
nexttoken	: TOKENS;	{current token}
realnum	: real;	{current real number}

　　procedure ErrorHandler (errormsg : USERMSGS);
　　{Writes appropriate error message and sets the global variable error to true.}
　　begin
　　　if not error **then**
　　　　WriteUser (errormsg , CMDERRLINE);
　　　error := true
　　end; {ErrorHandler}

　　function MakeNode (op : TOKEN; value : real; field : CELLID;
　　　　　　left, right : NODEPTR) : NODEPTR;
　　var
　　　next : NODEPTR;
　　begin
　　　new (next);
　　　next ↑ .op := op;
　　　next ↑ .cellname := field;
　　　next ↑ .value := value;
　　　next ↑ .left := left;
　　　next ↑ .right := right;
　　　MakeNode := next
　　end; {MakeNode}

(continued)

Figure 14.14. (continued)

```
function expression : NODEPTR;
var
  op          : TOKEN;
  temp        : NODEPTR;

  function term : NODEPTR;
  var
    op          : TOKEN;
    temp        : NODEPTR;

    function factor : NODEPTR;
    var
      temp : NODEPTR;

      function subexpr : NODEPTR;
      var
        temp : NODEPTR;
      begin
        temp := nil;
        if nexttoken = LEFTPAREN then begin
          GetToken (userinp, nexttoken, realnum, field);
          temp := expression;
          if nexttoken <> RIGHTPAREN then
            ErrorHandler (NORPAREN)
          else
            GetToken (userinp, nexttoken, realnum, field)
        end;
        subexpr := temp
      end; {subexpr}


    begin {factor}
      temp := nil;
      if nexttoken = MINUS then begin                    {unary minus}
        GetToken (userinp, nexttoken, realnum, field);
        temp := MakeNode (UMINUS, 0.0, field, Expression, nil)
      end else if nexttoken in [NUMBER, ACELLNAME] then begin
        temp := MakeNode (nexttoken, realnum, field, nil, nil);
        GetToken (userinp, nexttoken, realnum, field)
      end else if nexttoken = BADCELL then
        ErrorHandler (BADACELLNAME)
      else if nexttoken = CELLLABEL then
        ErrorHandler (BADCELLLABEL)
```

```
        else if nexttoken in FUNCTIONS then begin
          op := nexttoken;
          GetToken (userinp, nexttoken, realnum, field);
          temp := subexpr;
          if temp = nil then
            ErrorHandler (NOLPAREN)
          else
            temp := MakeNode (op, 0.0, field, temp, nil)
        end else if nexttoken = LEFTPAREN then
          temp := subexpr
        else
          ErrorHandler (NOFACTOR);
        factor := temp
      end; {factor}

  begin {term}
    temp := factor;
    while nexttoken in [TIMES, DIVIDE] do begin
      op := nexttoken;
      GetToken (userinp, nexttoken, realnum, field);
      temp := MakeNode (op, 0, field, temp, factor)
    end;
    term := temp
  end; {term}

begin {expression}
  temp := term;
  while nexttoken in [PLUS, MINUS] do begin
    op := nexttoken;
    GetToken (userinp, nexttoken, realnum, field);
    temp := MakeNode (op, 0.0, field, temp, term)
  end;
  expression := temp
end; {expression}

begin {ParseExpression}
  FUNCTIONS := [SINFUNC, COSFUNC, SQRTFUNC, LNFUNC, EXPFUNC];
  error := false;
  GetToken (userinp, nexttoken, realnum, field);
  ParseExpression := expression;
  if nexttoken <> NOMORE then
    ErrorHandler (EXTRA);
  if error then
    ParseExpression := nil
end; {ParseExpression}
```

(continued)

Figure 14.14. (continued)

```
begin {GetExpression}
  WriteUser (EXPRPROMPT, EXPRLINE);
  GetExpression := nil;
  if GetUserInput (userinp) then
    GetExpression := ParseExpression (userinp)
end; {Get Expression}



procedure AddToDependList (dependon : CELLID; currcell : CELLID;
                               var count : COUNTER);
{
Adds a new field to the dependon list for the next cell, noting that dependon has one
more cell which depends on it.
}
var
  current          : DEPENDPTR;
  found            : boolean;
begin
  current := cells [dependon.name, dependon.num].dependlist;
  found := false;
  while not found and (current <> nil) do
    if (current ↑ .dependee.name = dependon.name) and
       (current ↑ .dependee.num = dependon.num) then
      found := true
    else
      current := current ↑ .next;
  if not found then begin
    new (current);
    current ↑ .dependee := currcell;
    with cells [dependon.name, dependon.num] do begin
      current ↑ .next := dependlist;
      dependlist := current
    end;
    count := count + 1
  end
end; {AddToDependList}



function CheckExprTree (exprtree : NODEPTR; currcell : CELLID;
                            var count : COUNTER) : boolean;
{
Goes through the expression tree for a given cell, adding each name found to the data
structure representing the dependency graph, noting that currcell depends on each of the
cells in its expression tree.
```

It is considered an error if a cell depends on another cell containing a label, so the function returns *true* if no element in the expression tree is a label, and *false* otherwise.
}

```
var
  nolabels : boolean;
begin
  nolabels := true;
  if exprtree <> nil then
    with exprtree ↑ do begin
      if op = ACELLNAME then
        if cells [cellname.name, cellname.num].contents = ALABEL then
          nolabels := false
        else
          AddToDependList (cellname, currcell, count);
      if nolabels then
        nolabels := CheckExprTree (left, currcell, count) and
                CheckExprTree (right, currcell, count)
    end;
  CheckExprTree := nolabels
end; {CheckExprTree}
function BuildGraph : boolean;
```
{
Builds the dependency graph by traversing each cell in the graph and adding those cells to the graph. Returns *false* if the dependency graph would include cells with labels, and *true* otherwise.
}

```
var
  nextcell          : CELLID;
  nextcol           : COLINDEX;
  nextrow           : ROWINDEX;
begin
  for nextrow := MINROW to MAXROW do          {initialize dependencies}
    for nextcol := MINCOL to MAXCOL do
      with cells [nextrow, nextcol] do begin
        dependlist := nil;
        next.num := FAKENIL;
        count := 0
      end;
  BuildGraph := true;
  for nextrow := MINROW to MAXROW do          {build new list}
    for nextcol := MINCOL to MAXCOL do
      with cells [nextrow, nextcol] do begin
        nextcell.name := nextrow;
        nextcel.num := nextcol;
        if not CheckExprTree (cellexpr, nextcell, count) then
          BuildGraph := false
      end
end; {BuildGraph}
```
(continued)

Figure 14.14. (continued)

procedure *FindZeroes*;
{
Create a list of all of the cells that have no dependencies on any other cells. (There is no need for a list of the cells that do depend on other nodes — it can be derived from this list.)
}
var
   nextname   : *ROWINDEX*;
   nextnum   : *COLINDEX*;
begin
  zerocells.num := *FAKENIL*;
  for *nextname* := *MINROW* **to** *MAXROW* **do**
    for *nextnum* := *MINCOL* **to** *MAXCOL* **do**
      with *cells* [*nextname, nextnum*] **do**
        if *count* = 0 **then begin**
          next := *zerocells*;
          zerocells.name := *nextname*;
          zerocells.num := *nextnum*
        end
end; {FindZeros}

function *SortCells* : boolean;
{
Performs the topological sort on the graph representing the functional dependencies in the MiniCalc display. Returns *true* if there are no recursive dependencies (i.e., the graph is acyclic), *false* otherwise. The data structures are accessed as globals for efficiency.
}
var
   freecells   : *COUNTER*;
   nextdep   : *DEPENDPTR*;
   tempnextcell   : *CELLID*;
begin
  firstcell.num := *FAKENIL*;
  lastcell.num := *FAKENIL*;
  freecells := (ord (*MAXROW*) − ord (*MINROW*) + 1) * *MAXCOL*;
  while *zerocells.num* <> *FAKENIL* **do begin**
    tempnextcell := *cells* [*zerocells.name, zerocells.num*].*next*;
    freecells := *freecells* − 1;
    if *firstcell.num* = *FAKENIL* **then begin**
      firstcell := *zerocells*;
      cells [*zerocells.name, zerocells.num*].*next.num* := *FAKENIL*
    end else
      cells [*lastcell.name, lastcell.num*].*next* := *zerocells*;

```
      lastcell := zerocells;
      nextdep := cells [zerocells.name, zerocells.num].dependlist;
      zerocells := tempnextcell;
      while nextdep <> nil do begin
        with cells [nextdep ↑ .dependee.name, nextdep ↑ .dependee.num] do begin
          count := count − 1;
          if count = 0 then begin
            next := zerocells;
            zerocells := nextdep ↑ .dependee
          end
        end;
        nextdep := nextdep ↑ .next
      end
    end;
  SortCells := freecells = 0
end; {SortCells}


procedure PostValue (cellrow : ROWINDEX; cellcol : COLINDEX; value : real);
{
Posts the value given to the correct cell. For now we are not worried about really large
values or other values which would cause overflow/underflow or produce a messy display.
}
begin
  MoveToCell (cellrow, cellcol);
  write (value : COLSPERCEL : 2)
end; {PostValue}


procedure EvaluateCells;
{
Evaluates the cells in sorted order, posting the results to the screen. Only expressions are
evaluated — values are already on the screen and don't have to be evaluated again.
}
var
  defined          : boolean;
  result           : real;
begin
  while firstcell.num <> FAKENIL do begin
    with cells [firstcell.name, firstcell.num] do
      if contents = ANEXPR then begin
        defined := false;
        result := Evaluate (cellexpr, defined);
        PostValue (firstcell.name, firstcell.num , result)
      end;
    firstcell := cells [firstcell.name, firstcell.num].next
  end
end; {EvaluateCells}
```

(continued)

Figure 14.14. (continued)

```
begin {DoCellExpr}
  if nextcell.num = 0 then
    WriteUser (NOCURRCELL, CMDERRLINE)
  else begin
    nextexpr := GetExpression;
    if nextexpr <> nil then begin
      with cells [nextcell.name, nextcell.num] do begin
        if nextexpr↑.op = NUMBER then begin
          contents := AVALUE;
          PostValue (nextcell.name, nextcell.num, nextexpr↑.value)
        end else
          contents := ANEXPR;
        cellexpr := nextexpr
      end;
      if BuildGraph then begin
        FindZeroes;
        if SortCells then begin                {SortCells returns true if the graph is acyclic}
          EvaluateCells;
          WriteUser (SHOWCELLMSG, SHOWCELLLINE);
          write (currcell.name, currcell.num : 1, ' ');
          WriteExpression (cells [nextcell.name, nextcell.num].cellexpr, 0)
        end else begin
          cells [nextcell.name, nextcell.num].cellexpr := nil;
          WriteUser (SORTFAILED, CMDERRLINE)
        end
      end else begin
        cells [nextcell.name, nextcell.num].cellexpr := nil;
        WriteUser (LABELDEPENDS, CMDERRLINE)
      end
    end
  end
end; {DoCellExpr}
```

```
procedure DoCellLabel (nextcell : CELLID);
{
Places a label into the current cell. The entire input line is placed into the label for that cell.
Labels may not be placed into a cell that other cells depend on.
}
var
  userinp : INPUTTYPE;
begin
  with cells [nextcell.name, nextcell.num] do
    if dependlist <> nil then
      WriteUser (NOLABEL, CMDERRLINE)
    else begin
      WriteUser (LABELPROMPT, EXPRLINE);
      if GetUserInput (userinp) then begin
        celllabel := userinp;
        cellexpr := nil;
        contents := ALABEL;
        PostLabel (nextcell.name, nextcell.num, celllabel)
      end
    end
end; {DoCellLabel}


procedure InitCells;
{Initializes all cells to empty with nil expression trees.}
var
  nextcol              : COLINDEX;
  nextrow              : ROWINDEX;
begin
  for nextrow := MINROW to MAXROW do
    for nextcol := MINCOL to MAXCOL do begin
      cells [nextrow, nextcol].cellexpr := nil;
      cells [nextrow, nextcol].contents := EMPTY
    end;
  currcell.name := MINROW;                              {initialize current cell}
  currcell.num := MINCOL;
  WriteUser (SHOWCELLMSG, SHOWCELLLINE);
  write (currcell.name, currcell.num : 1, ' ')
end; {InitCells}
```

(continued)

Figure 14.14. (continued)

```
begin {main}
  {Initialization}
  funcdesc [SINFUNC] := 'sin    ';
  funcdesc [COSFUNC] := 'cos    ';
  funcdesc [EXPFUNC] := 'exp    ';
  funcdesc [LNFUNC] := 'ln     ';
  funcdesc [SQRTFUNC] := 'sqrt   ';
  ClearScreen;
  WriteCells;
  InitCells;

  {Main command loop.}

  WriteUser (CMDPROMPT, CMDLINE);
  while GetCommand (nextcommand) do begin
    MoveCursor (CMDERRLINE, FIRSTCOL);        {blank out previous messages}
    ClearEOL;
    case nextcommand of
      HELP : WriteUser (CMDLIST, CMDERRLINE);
      CHANGECELL : DoCellChange (currcell);
      ENTEREXPR : DoCellExpr (currcell);
      ENTERLABEL : DoCellLabel (currcell);
      BAD : WriteUser (CMDLIST, CMDERRLINE)
    end;
    WriteUser (CMDPROMPT, CMDLINE)
  end
end.
```

Exercises

1. Modify MiniCalc to handle large numbers and lengthy expressions appropriately. Before large numbers or lengthy expressions are written out, a check should be made that they won't overflow the allowed space for cell output. When there isn't enough space, a number of stars should be printed rather than the number or expression.

   One way to do this is to write a formatted output procedure, similar to Pascal's formatted *write*, that specifies a maximum field width and the maximum number of places to the right of the decimal point. Unlike the standard Pascal version, the formatted write will only fill the number of columns given. If the number is too large, asterisks (*) are printed.

2. Since it can take a long time to enter all of the expressions into the cells, and once expressions are entered they can be used for numerous sets of values, there should be a way for the user to save a set of expressions into a file and then to read in these expressions during other runs of the program. Add the command *save*, which writes out the MiniCalc commands necessary to enter all of the expressions currently in the cells, and the command *read*, which reads in MiniCalc commands from a file.

3. Write a stand-alone topological sort program that reads in a list of vertices and their dependencies and outputs the order in which the vertices should be evaluated. Each line of input should contain the name of a vertex, followed by a list of the names of vertices that depend on it.

4. Extend MiniCalc to handle a number of cells greater than can be displayed at one time on the screen. The terminal screen should be thought of as a window through which part of the array of cells can be viewed. The user should be able to move this window around to view different parts of the array. Write the commands *up*, *down*, *left*, and *right* which move this window around the array in the direction of the command.

5. Extend MiniCalc to handle variable sized cells. Add the command *cellsize* which sets the default number of columns used to write out the value of a cell. The width will hold for all cells in the given column.

6. Extend MiniCalc to allow functions with more than one argument and add a number of useful multiple argument functions to the list of built-in functions that MiniCalc can handle. For example, *power(x,y)* should raise x to the y power, where x and y are cell IDs.

7. Extend MiniCalc to allow the colon (:) operator to stand for the cells in the range from the first through the last. For example, A1:A6 would stand for the cells A1, A2, A3, A4, A5, and A6. If the first and last cells are not in the same row or column, the entire rectangle defined by the two cells is indicated.

   Write the function *sum* which given an argument in this notation will produce the sum of the expanded cells. For example, *sum(A1:B3)* produces the sum of the values in the cells A1, A2, A3, B1, B2, and B3. Can you think of other functions that should handle arguments in this notation?

8. Sometimes it is nice to be able to assign a value to a cell conditionally. For example, assign the value zero to A1 if cell B1 is not zero and the value of cell C1, otherwise. Add this capability to MiniCalc. To do this you will need to add relational operators as well as an appropriate conditional operator. One way to do this is to define the "ternary" (three operand) operator *if*.

The syntax of the *if* operator requires that three operands be specified, separating them by colons: *if*(<*relation*> : <*then part*> : <*else part*>). *relation* is a boolean expression involving the tests of equality (=), less than (<) and (>). If the expression evaluates to *true*, the *then part* is performed; if *false*, the *else part* is evaluated. As an example, in the simple payroll example, we might have the calculation of the gross pay be something like: *if*(A2>40 : ((A2−40)∗1.5+40)∗A3 : A2∗A3). This is interpreted to mean that if the contents of cell A2 is greater than 40, we calculate ((A2−40)∗1.5+40)∗A3; otherwise, we calculate A2∗A3.

Appendixes

APPENDIX 1
MACHINE REPRESENTATION

A1.1 Introduction

Pascal defines four standard data types, integer, real, character, and boolean. In addition, Pascal lets us define or construct data types that are made up of the four fundamental types (such as arrays, sets, and records) and to construct, to some extent, our own types (such as enumerated types). In addition Pascal provides pointers that allow structures of almost unlimited size and complexity, through dynamic storage allocation. In this appendix we briefly explore the manner in which these data types are represented internally in a typical machine. To clarify the representations, we'll use a hypothetical computer, called the "C0," representative of typical 32-bit machines.

A1.2 The C0 Computer

The C0 computer (Fig. A1.1) is a basic machine that follows the usual architecture of sequential computers: an information store, the memory, and a CPU for performing the necessary logical, arithmetic, and control operations.

Of interest to us is the representation of data in main memory. The instructions that the computer carries out and the extent of the arithmetic and other operations are not necessary to understand the way that information is represented. The C0 is a 32-bit machine. The memory is divided into at least 64,000 *words*, each consisting of four 8-bit *bytes*. As a binary machine, each byte consists of 8 bits, and so each byte may represent in integer in the range 00000000_2 to 11111111_2 (or 0 to 255_{10}). As we will see, the individual words may be used to represent integers, characters, reals, booleans, and any of the predefined or user-defined data types.

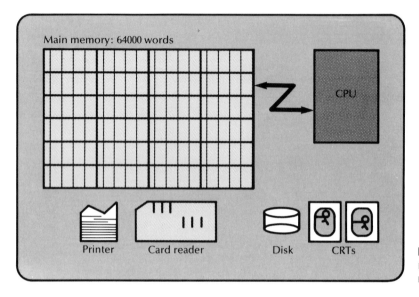

Figure A1.1. Diagram representation of the mythical C0 machine.

A1.3 Representation

Each Pascal predefined type (integer, real, character, and boolean) has a different C0 representation. Similarly, the user-defined types (including arrays, enumerated types, sets, and records) must be converted to an appropriate machine representation. Each is briefly discussed in the following sections.

A1.3.1 Integers

C0 is an integer machine, using four 8-bit bytes per machine word. The Pascal integer type is represented as a single C0 word. Consequently the machine-dependent, predefined constant *maxint* has the value $2^{31} - 1$, or 2,147,483,647. Any integer in the range $-maxint$ to $+maxint$ is uniquely represented in a single C0 word. For integers, only 31 bits are used to represent the magnitude of the number; the 32nd bit is the sign bit that indicates the sign of the number. On a byte-by-byte basis, one byte represents any value in the range -255 to $+255$; two bytes, $-65,535$ to $+65,535$, and so on up to all four bytes, $-2,147,483,647$ to $+2,147,483,647$ (which defines *maxint* for C0).

Negative Integers

Negative numbers are stored using a two's complement representation. Two's complement represents negative numbers in a manner analogous to a car's mileage indicator if it were wound backwards. As an example, suppose we use four bits for each integer. The left-most bit is the sign, and the remaining three are the magnitude. Here is how we would represent all values in the range of $+7$ to -8 (not, surprisingly, -7). The positive numbers are stored in the usual way:

Bit string	Value
0 1 1 1	7
0 1 1 0	6
0 1 0 1	5
0 1 0 0	4
0 0 1 1	3
0 0 1 0	2
0 0 0 1	1
0 0 0 0	0

As we continue to "roll" back the four bit odometer, the first value we'd see is all 1's — this represents -1. If we continue this way, here is how the negative values are represented:

Bit string	Value
1 1 1 1	-1
1 1 1 0	-2
1 1 0 1	-3
1 1 0 0	-4
1 0 1 1	-5
1 0 1 0	-6
1 0 0 1	-7
1 0 0 0	-8

There is a simple way of mapping a negative number into its two's complement form — take a word of all 1's and subtract the binary representation of the absolute value of the number. Then add 1. For example, the representation for -5 is determined by:

$$
\begin{array}{ll}
\begin{array}{r} 1\ 1\ 1\ 1 \\ -0\ 1\ 0\ 1 \\ \hline 1\ 0\ 1\ 0 \\ 0\ 0\ 0\ 1 \\ \hline 1\ 0\ 1\ 1 \end{array}
& \begin{array}{l} \text{Word of all 1's} \\ \text{Binary representation of 5} \\ \\ \text{Result} \\ \text{Add 1} \\ \\ \text{Two's complement representation of } -5 \end{array}
\end{array}
$$

The reverse mapping is accomplished in the same way. Take the two's complement negative number, subtract from a word of all 1's, then add 1. This gives the magnitude of the negative number:

$$
\begin{array}{ll}
\begin{array}{r} 1\ 1\ 1\ 1 \\ -1\ 0\ 1\ 1 \\ \hline 0\ 1\ 0\ 0 \\ 0\ 0\ 0\ 1 \\ \hline 0\ 1\ 0\ 1 \end{array}
& \begin{array}{l} \text{Word of all 1's} \\ \text{Binary representation of } -5 \\ \\ \text{Result} \\ \text{Add 1} \\ \\ \text{Result: 5} \end{array}
\end{array}
$$

A1.3.2 Reals

C0 uses a representation for reals typical of most computers. It is basically "scientific" notation, that is, a signed fraction and an exponent. We are used to seeing numbers such as 1.731×10^5 or -151.732×10^{-6}, and so on. Of course, such numbers could be given to any base. An octal fraction such as 12.46×8^4 represents the octal number 124600_8. In engineering and scientific notation we usually assume a base of 10 and write the exponent without the base, but using the letter E instead, for example, 1.731E5 or $-151.732E-6$. To include both the fraction and the exponent, we may either use two words per number, or try to pack both the fraction and the exponent into a single C0 word. In C0, we use the later representation to gain storage space efficiency. Figure A1.2 shows a representation for reals in C0: the

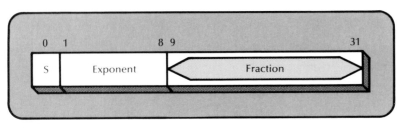

Figure A1.2. Packed floating-point representation. Bit 0 is the sign of the fraction, bits 1–8 are the exponent (excess 128), and bits 9–31 are the fraction.

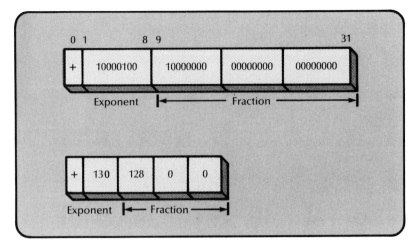

Figure A1.3. Packed floating-point representation. The word is interpreted as $0.1_2 \times 4^2$, or $0.5 \times 16 = 0.0$.

sign field is the sign of the number. The first byte holds the exponent; the next three bytes hold the fraction.

The fraction is assumed to be *normalized*. That is, the decimal point is assumed to be to the left of f_1, and f_1 is assumed to be nonzero. The exponent is assumed to have a base of 2, that is, the entire number represents a base 2 fraction: $0.f_1f_2f_3 \times 2^{exp}$. Since there is only one sign bit in the word, the sign of the exponent must be carried in the exponent itself. This is accomplished by using an "excess" notation. Any exponent, positive or negative, has the "excess" (in this case, 128) added to it. This value is then stored in the exponent field. To convert the stored exponent to the actual value, the "excess" is subtracted. In Fig. A1.3, the actual exponent (to a base of 2) is $130 - 128 = 2$. With this scheme, any exponent in the range -128 to $+127$ (not $+128$) can be stored as a single byte, with a value in the range 0 to 255 (after the excess is added).

In general, however, it is not possible to represent an exact base 10 real number as an exact base 2 real number because of rounding in the division and truncation after the last term. We see why Pascal distinguishes between integers and reals, and why most operations are slower with reals than with integers.

A1.3.3 Characters

Figure A1.4 is the ASCII character set used in the C0. Each Pascal character variable requires one C0 word, with the character right-adjusted in the word. All other bytes are set to 0 and the sign is $+$. Since the character set is the standard ASCII set, which uses only 7 bits per character, there are a total of 128 different characters. Other 8-bit byte machines use the full 8 bits for each character, giving 256 different characters. In ASCII, both upper- and lower-case characters are represented.

Since one character per word is quite wasteful, Pascal provides a more compact data type used for arrays of characters, the packed array. In a packed array of characters, each byte is a single character, so in C0, we can pack four characters per word. Unfortunately C0 contains very few byte-oriented instructions (basically shift instructions), so it is quite tedious to manipulate individual characters in a packed array. Some compilers ignore the packed directive, forcing all character arrays to be unpacked (one character per word). In systems with large amounts of memory, this is not a serious problem; we trade storage efficiency for faster execution.

A1.3.4 Booleans

Pascal boolean variables may take one of two values: *true* or *false*. We need to decide on a reasonable representation. Any choice of two distinct values will work, but for ease of testing through C0's instructions, and in accordance

0	1	2	3	4	5	6	7	8	9	10	11	12	13	14	15
↑@	↑A	↑B	↑C	↑D	↑E	↑F	↑G	↑H	↑I	↑J	↑K	↑L	↑M	↑N	↑O

16	17	18	19	20	21	22	23	24	25	26	27	28	29	30	31
↑P	↑Q	↑R	↑S	↑T	↑U	↑V	↑W	↑X	↑Y	↑Z	esc				

32	33	34	35	36	37	38	39	40	41	42	43	44	45	46	47
sp	!	"	#	$	%	&	'	(	)	*	+	,	−	.	/

48	49	50	51	52	53	54	55	56	57	58	59	60	61	62	63
0	1	2	3	4	5	6	7	8	9	:	;	<	=	>	?

64	65	66	67	68	69	70	71	72	73	74	75	76	77	78	79
@	A	B	C	D	E	F	G	H	I	J	K	L	M	N	O

80	81	82	83	84	85	86	87	88	89	90	91	92	93	94	95
P	Q	R	S	T	U	V	W	X	Y	Z	[	\	]	↑	—

96	97	98	99	100	101	102	103	104	105	106	107	108	109	110	111
`	a	b	c	d	e	f	g	h	i	j	k	l	m	n	o

112	113	114	115	116	117	118	119	120	121	122	123	124	125	126	127
p	q	r	s	t	u	v	w	x	y	z	{	|	}	˜	del

Figure A1.4. C0 character set and internal representation.

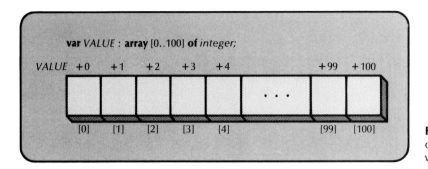

var *VALUE* : **array** [0..100] **of** *integer;*

VALUE +0 +1 +2 +3 +4 +99 +100

· · ·

[0] [1] [2] [3] [4] [99] [100]

Figure A1.5. Representation of an array requiring 101 words of C0 storage.

with the ordering required of booleans, 0 for *false* and 1 for *true* is reasonable. Equally acceptable choices are − 1 for *false* and + 1 for *true*. Some compilers use 0 for *false* and any other value for *true*.

A1.3.5 Arrays

The storage representation of arrays, particularly multidimensional arrays, requires a few rather arbitrary decisions. Once the decisions are made, they must be implemented correctly and consistently. We'll begin with a one-dimensional array of integers:

> **var**
> *value* : **array** [0..100] **of** *integer;*

In C0 such an array requires 101 words of storage, as we see in Fig. A1.5.

With such a representation, indexing (that is, selecting an individual element) from the array is quite simple: *value* [*i*] is found at the first memory location for *value* (the place where *value* [0] is stored) plus *i*, where *i* must be in the range 0..100. When the array has lower bounds other than 0, this simple indexing scheme needs only slight modification. For example, consider:

> **var**
> *value* : **array** [10..100] **of** *integer;*

We require $(100 - 10) + 1$ (or 91) storage locations for *value*, as in Fig. A1.6.

The store for *value* runs from the initial storage location (*value* [10], which in C0 we call location VALUE, using upper-case names to indicate C0 storage locations) to VALUE + $(100 - 10)$. Equating VALUE + 0 with *value* [10], VALUE + 1 with *value* [11], and so on, up to *value* [100] with VALUE + 90, the mapping from Pascal indexing to C0 indexing should be: *value* [*i*] maps to VALUE + $(i - 10)$, *i* in the range 10..100.

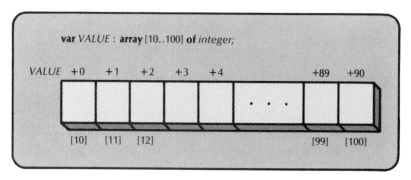

var VALUE : **array** [10..100] **of** *integer;*

VALUE +0   +1   +2   +3   +4   +89   +90

[10]   [11] [12]   [99] [100]

Figure A1.6. Allocation of (100 − 10) + 1, or 91 words, to store array *value.*

Finally, generalizing to:

> **var**
> *value* : **array** [*lower..upper*] **of** *integer;*

we allocate (*upper-lower*) + 1 memory locations, and *value* [*i*] is found at VALUE + (*i* − *lower*), *i* in the range *lower..upper*.

Multidimensional Arrays

Assume V is declared as a two-dimensional array:

> **var**
> V : **array** [1..N, 1..M] **of** *integer;*

We might think of V as being a matrix of N rows, each of M columns:

$$V = \begin{bmatrix} V[1,1] & V[1,2] & . & V[1,M] \\ V[2,1] & V[2,2] & . & V[2,M] \\ . & & . & . \\ . & & . & . \\ V[N,1] & V[N,2] & . & V[N,M] \end{bmatrix}$$

An alternative view is to think of V as a collection of rows, or vectors, or one-dimensional arrays. That is, each row of V is actually an array from 1 to M of integers. There are N of these row arrays. Viewed this way, the mapping from a two-dimensional matrix to the one-dimensional C0 memory is simple: store each row in order, first the M elements of row one, then the M elements of row two, and so on up to the M elements of row N. The memory map looks like Fig. A1.7.

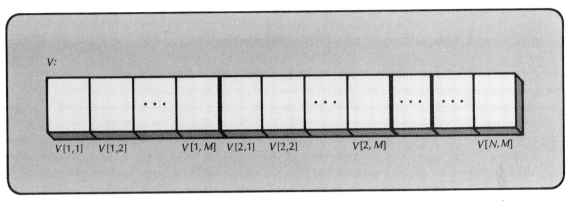

Figure A1.7. Diagram of two-dimensional representation row-major order.

We must allocate $M \times N$ words of C0 storage for the array. Indexing is accomplished by first "finding" the appropriate row, and then the appropriate word within the row. For example, to find $V[3,7]$ (where each row of V has M elements) we first find the third row. The first element of the third row is found at $V + (3 - 1) \times M$ (see Fig. A1.8).

Within the third row, the seventh element is found at the first element plus *six*. Consequently $V[3,7]$ is found at location $V + (3 - 1) \times M + (7 - 1)$. Generalizing, $V[i,j]$ is found at $V + (i - 1) \times M + (j - 1)$. We find the i, jth element of V for the general case:

> **var**
> V : **array** $[L1..U1, L2..U2]$ **of** *integer*;

at $V + [(i - L1)] \times (U2 - L2 + 1)] + (j - L2)$.

Figure A1.8. Selection scheme for $V[3,7]$, an element of a two-dimensional array.

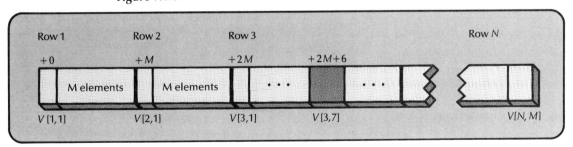

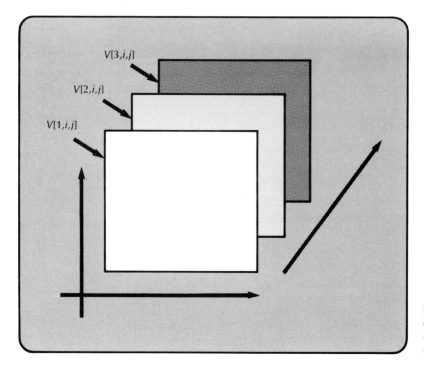

Figure A1.9. Representation of a three-dimensional array as a series of two-dimensional planes.

For three-dimensional arrays, we may view the array as a series of planar arrays (two-dimensional matrices), as in Fig. A1.9.

One indexing scheme is to use the first index to select the plane; the second, the row, and the third, the column.

A1.3.6 Records

Records, like arrays, may require more than one word of storage. The amount of storage for each record depends on the way the record is defined. Each field of the record requires enough storage for its type, and so the number of words per record is the sum of the storage for each of its fields. In the case of variant records, the amount of storage allocated is the amount needed for the largest of the variants. The tag field of the variant record indicates the particular variant for the particular variable. When a variant record is declared, the compiler does not know which variant the variable will be, so it must allocate enough space to allow for the largest variation. In terms of storage allocation, variant records may be treated as if they were ordinary records. Suppose we have the following declarations for a **record** variable:

```
type
    INFO              =
        record
            ID            : integer;
            age           : integer;
            sex           : char
        end;
    . . .
var
    Data              : INFO;
```

When *Data* is declared, the compiler allocates *three* words of storage: one word for the *ID* field, one word for the *age* field, and one word for the (single character) *sex* field. The storage allocation looks like Fig. A1.10.

Selection of the appropriate field within the record is accomplished in a manner analogous to selecting an element of an array. In this case, the

Figure A1.10. Diagram of three words in C0 memory allocated for the record *Data*.

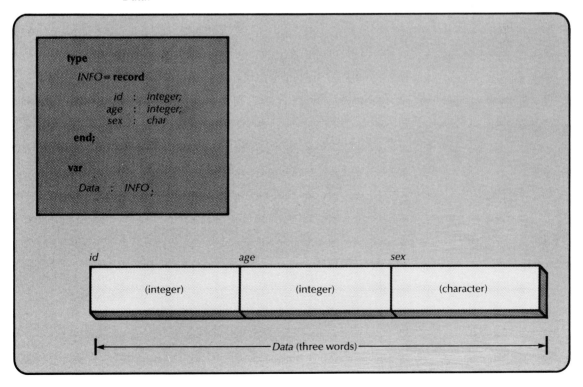

ID field is found at memory location DATA + 0; the *age* field, at DATA + 1; and the *sex* field, at DATA + 2.

A1.3.7 Sets

Sets are usually represented as an array of booleans. The number of values in the array is equal to the size of the base type. In this representation, all possible values that could be in a set are in fact present. For each of those values, we use the boolean *true* to indicate presence and *false* to indicate absence. If *true* is represented as a 1 and *false* as 0, we call such a representation a "bit vector."

If the base type is *char*, each set will need an array of 128 boolean values (in the ASCII character set). If we don't pack the array, 128 words are needed; if we are able to make use of packed arrays, 128/4, or 32 words, are needed. Figure A1.11 shows an example of a set representation for the ASCII character set. The 0th location is used to indicate character 0 (the null character); the 1st location is used for character 1 (Control A) and so on. At the 65th location, we find the bit for A, and at the 97th, the bit for a. Refer back to Fig. A1.4, where we printed the ASCII codes for upper- and lower-case characters.

Figure A1.11. C0 representation of set data type as an array of booleans. For a variable of type **set of** *char*, 128 booleans are required.

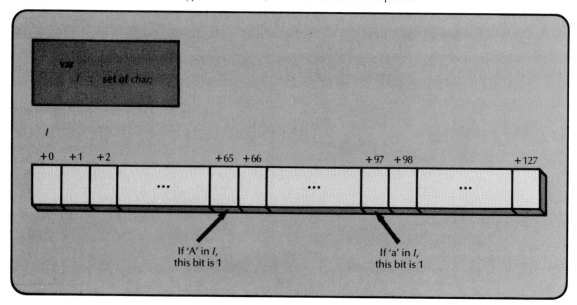

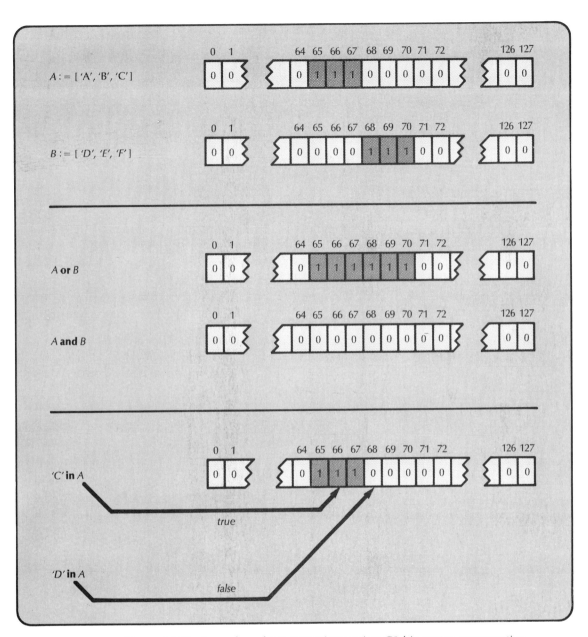

Figure A1.12. Examples of set operations using C0 bit vector represention.

With this representation, the operations that can be performed on sets are implemented using the logical operations **and** and **or**, and inserting or removing items from a set involves setting the appropriate element in the bit array to 1 or 0, respectively. Figure A1.12, shows the operations of union (using logical **or**), intersection (using logical **and**), and testing for membership (the Pascal operation **in**; here we need to test for a 1 at the appropriate array location).

A1.4   Representation of Linked Structures

A linked list consists of a series of nodes. Each node contains at least two fields: a data field and a pointer to the next node in the list. Initially most compilers allocate a large area of memory generally known as the *heap*, or free storage pool, that the run-time environment uses for supplying nodes of the appropriate type whenever the *new* procedure is called. Similarly the run-time environment returns nodes to the heap on a call to *dispose*. The management of this space can become complex in a strongly typed language such as Pascal, because the storage allocation mechanism must provide a node of the required size and field types. We can gain some insight into this mechanism by looking at how nodes and pointer fields are represented in the C0 machine.

If we have declared a one-way linked list in the usual way:

```
type
    NODEPTR    = ↑ NODE;
    NODE       =
    record
        data       : integer;
        link       : NODEPTR
    end;
var
    T              : NODEPTR;
```

space is allocated at the time the **var** statement is processed by the compiler. However, *T* is left uninitialized. We may set it to **nil**; we may assign another variable of type *NODEPTR* to *T*; or we may allocate a new node and have *T* point to it via a call to *new(T)*. Upon making a call to *new*, the storage allocator provides a node with two fields. In addition, it causes *T* to point to the new node. Of course, we don't manipulate arrows inside the machine. Rather, the address of the block of storage is assigned as the value of *T*. Let us assume that the new node begins at memory location 3000; then *T* points to this node, containing two C0 words, as shown in Fig. A1.13.

Now we trace the assignment:

$$T \uparrow .link := \textbf{nil};$$
$$T \uparrow .data := -15;$$

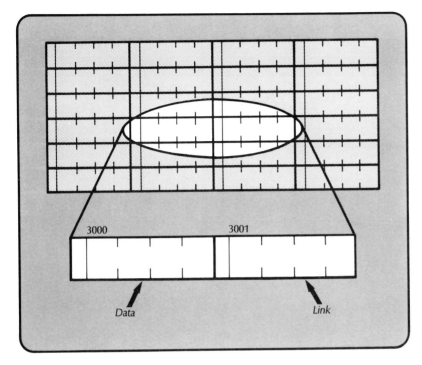

Figure A1.13. Two C0 words representing an *uninitialized* node.

The dereferencing operator (up arrow, $\uparrow$), indicates that T is a pointer variable. We look at its contents and go to the address in T. This is location 3000. At that location we find a record (a node) with two fields. The dot (.) operator selects the *link* field; we assign **nil** to this field. Since the contents of a word is merely a bit string, we need a suitable value for **nil**. Clearly **nil** must be an address guaranteed to be illegal. We may select any negative address or any address greater than 64K. Since we may want to pack two fields of a node together into a single word, we could use an illegal positive value for **nil**, but for ease of testing, we'll use zero. After the preceding assignments, the two words at 3000 and 3001 (that is, the node to which T points) look like Fig. A1.14.

As we build a list by allocating additional nodes and hooking them in, it is the addresses that indicate where to go in the C0 memory. After a series of insertions, the list that T points to might look as shown in Fig. A1.15. Note that nodes in the list are not necessarily contiguous, and that nodes further along in the list are not necessarily at higher memory locations.

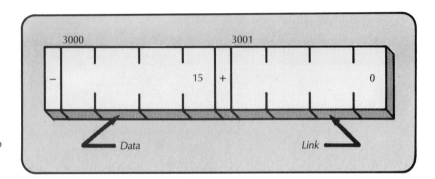

Figure A1.14. Two C0 words with **nil** assigned to the *link* field and −15 to the *data* field.

Figure A1.15. C0 representation of a linked list with four nodes.

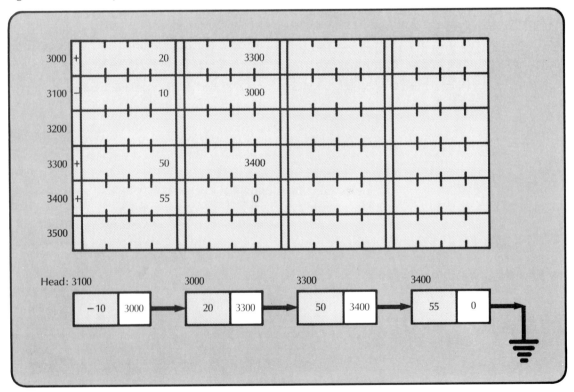

A1.5 Conclusion

Internally Pascal data structures must be represented in ways that are quite different from the way we think about them when writing programs. The process of mechanically translating from a higher level language to machine language has interested programmers and computer scientists since the earliest electronic computers. This "compilation" process, the process of translating a high-level language into machine language, involves a number of complex steps with the typical Pascal compilers (written in Pascal or other high-level languages) requiring upwards of many thousands of lines of codes. In this appendix we have examined only one part of what a compiler must do, that is, allocate storage for the Pascal data structures in the memory architecture of a real machine. This material is presented because understanding the internal representation of data helps us in writing more efficient programs.

PASCAL SYNTAX

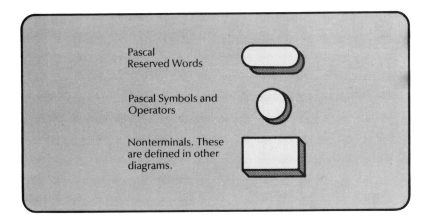

Figure A2.1. Program.

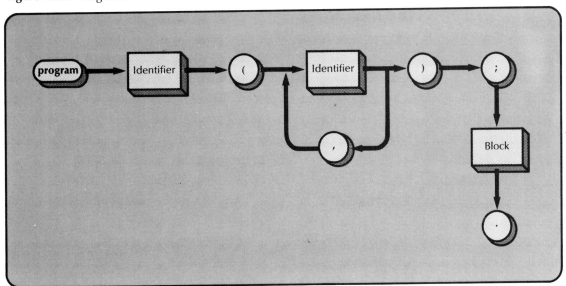

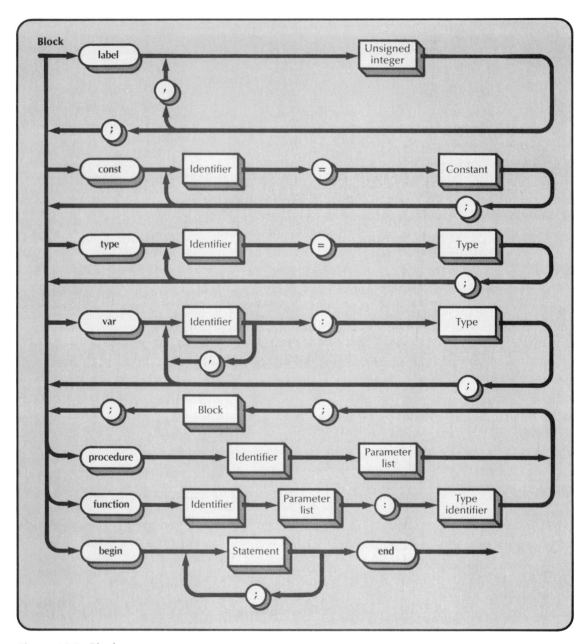

Figure A2.2. Block.

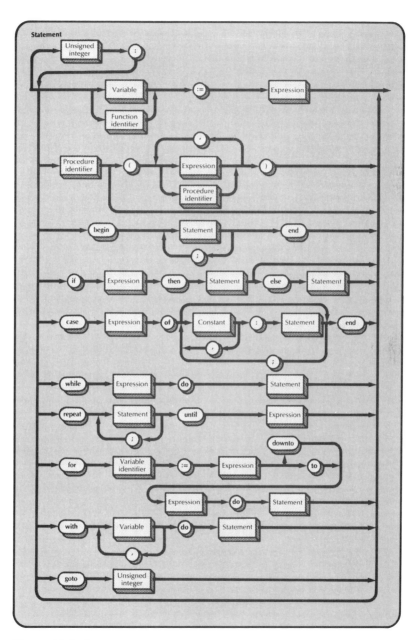

Figure A2.3. Statement.

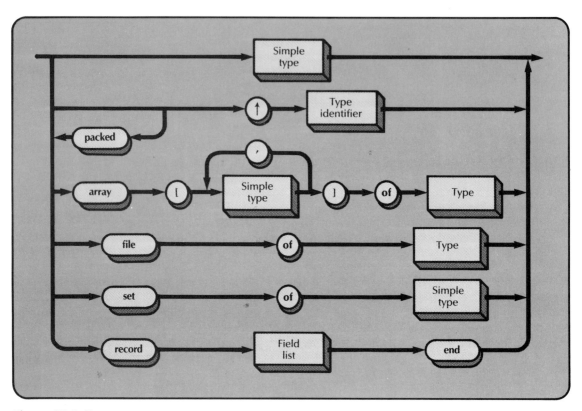

Figure A2.4. Type.

Figure A2.5. Simple type.

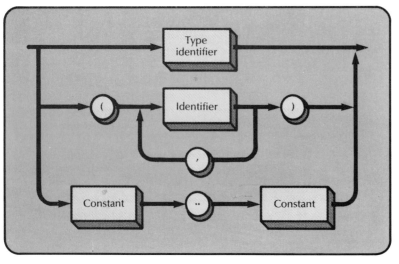

Figure A2.6. Parameter list.

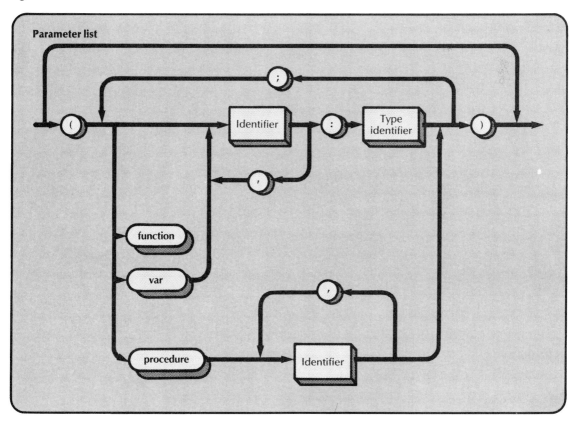

Figure A2.7. Field list.

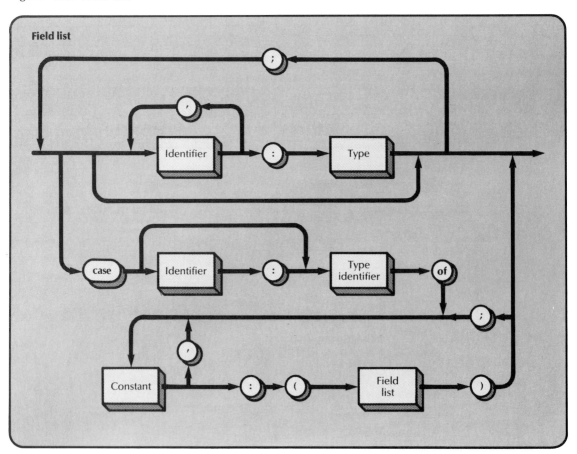

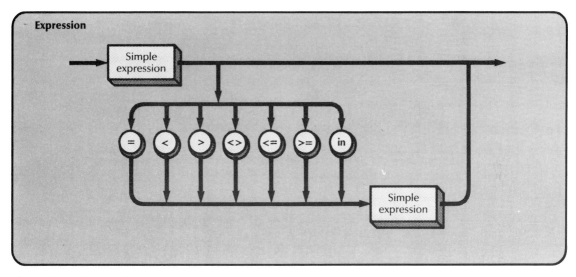

Figure A2.8. Expression.

Figure A2.9. Simple expression.

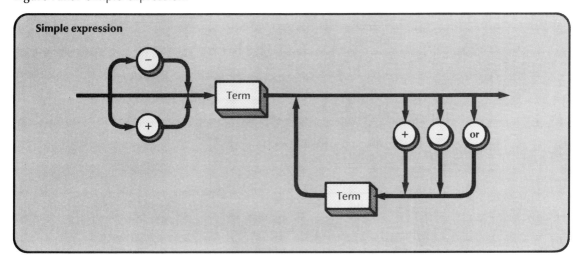

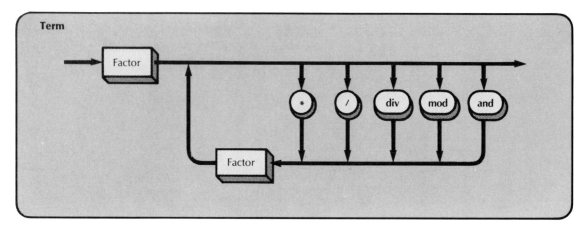

Figure A2.10. Term.

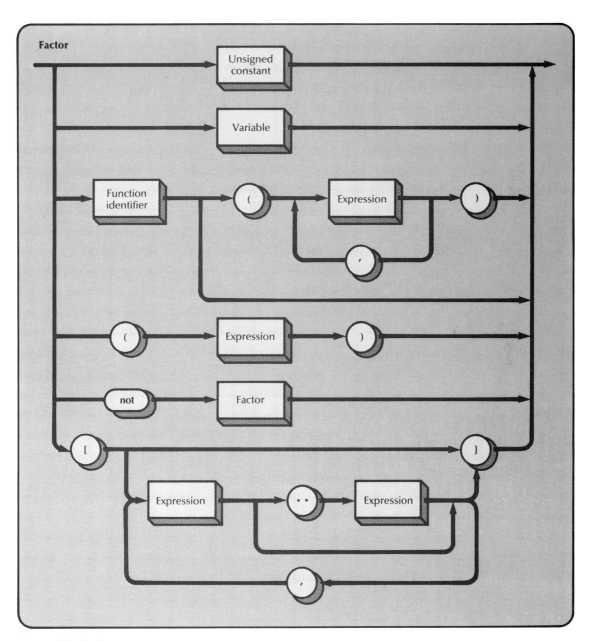

Figure A2.11. Factor.

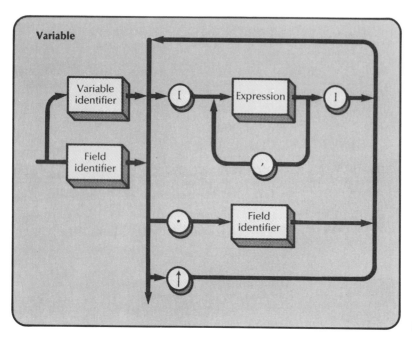

Figure A2.12. Variable.

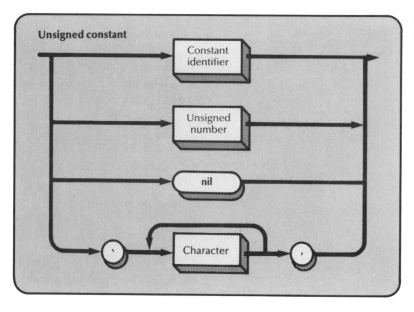

Figure A2.13. Unsigned constant.

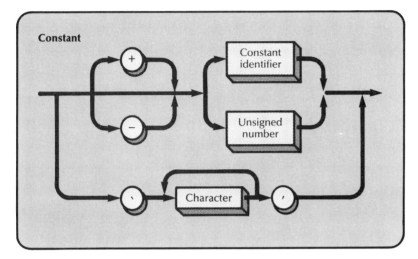

Figure A2.14. Constant.

Figure A2.15. Identifier.

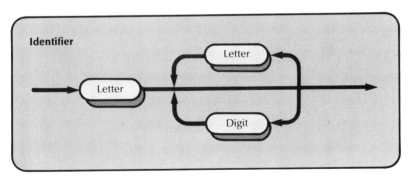

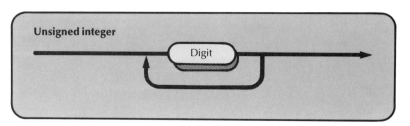

Figure A2.16. Unsigned integer.

Figure A2.17. Unsigned number.

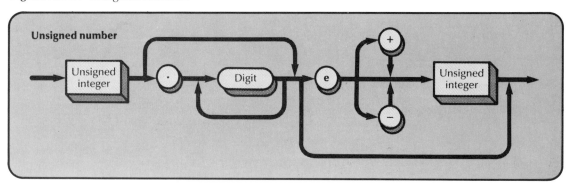

INDEX